Healthy Active Living

HAL 2.0

Information on how to obtain copies of this book is available at
www.thompsonbooks.com
Phone: 416.766.2763
Fax: 416.766.0398

Library and Archives Canada Cataloguing in Publication

Temertzoglou, Ted, 1964–
[Healthy active living]
Healthy active living 2.0 : keep fit, stay healthy, have fun / Ted Temertzoglou.
Includes index.
Previously published under title: Healthy active living.
ISBN 978-1-55077-261-6 (hardcover)
1. Physical education and training—Textbooks. 2. Health—Textbooks.
I. Title. II. Title: Healthy active living.

GV341.T48 2017 613.7 C2017-905867-3

We acknowledge the support of the Government of Canada through the Book Publishing Industry Development Program for our publishing activities.

Canada

Printed in Canada
1 2 3 4 5 6 7 23 22 21 20 19 18 17

Healthy Active Living

HAL 2.0

Ted Temertzoglou

THOMPSON
Toronto

Contents

"Physical education is the most effective means of providing all children and youth with the skills, attitudes, values, knowledge and understanding for lifelong participation in society."

— The Declaration of Berlin 2013, UNESCO's World Conference of Ministers for Sport

"Physical education programs lay the foundation for lifelong active living, enhance health and well-being, and help to prevent and/or reduce future health problems."

— The World Health Organization

About the Author

▶ **Ted Temertzoglou** is a graduate of the University of Toronto and Brock University and is a recognized leader in the physical literacy movement. He is the author of many works in this area and has been welcomed as a keynote speaker across Canada and abroad. He is the 2017 recipient of the R. Tait McKenzie Award, as a Canadian who has made a significant impact on physical education, health education/promotion, recreation, and dance and who has served the profession for more than 20 years.

Introduction

The evidence is all around us. Students who are physically active are healthier...and they have more fun. They perform better academically, they make better decisions, they have an improved quality of life, and they feel better about themselves.

That is exactly why it is a great idea to take Health and Physical Education throughout high school.

Your Health and Physical Education Book

The book you are holding is your Health and Physical Education book, which we affectionately refer to as **HAL2.0**. There is no resource quite like it, anywhere. In reality, it is two books in one:

- The first half of this book (Chapters 1–4) will help you move safely, perform activities competently, and stay fit.
- The second half of this book (Chapters 5–8) will help you stay healthy, develop good decision-making, communication, and coping skills, and strive to be the best version of yourself, each and every day.

Health and Physical Education may be the most important course you will take in high school. You will assess your current fitness level and learn how to design and maintain a personal fitness program that is just right for you. You will learn about responsible sexual decision making, healthy eating, issues related to substance use and addictive behaviours, personal safety, positive mental health, and conflict resolution. You will also learn how to participate in a variety of physical activities and sports of your choice that you can pursue for a lifetime.

HAL2.0 has been shaped by an exciting new vision that seeks to *reimagine* Health and Physical Education by honouring inclusivity and diversity while building on the strengths, goals, and dreams of every student. We hope that you will enjoy **HAL2.0** and that you will refer to it often. We encourage you to share what you learn with family, loved ones, and friends.

Becoming the best version of ourselves will go a long way to helping Canada become the most mentally, spiritually, socially, and physically healthy place on Earth. As you take up your position on "Team Canada," think of **HAL2.0** as a reliable and trustworthy coach.

Meanwhile, keep fit, stay healthy, and have fun along the way.

Acknowledgements

The creation of this book was truly a team effort. I would like first to thank Thompson Educational Publishing, the staff, and their wide-reaching support team for their passion for creating quality resources for our students.

A special thanks to Jane McNulty, who cares so deeply about our teachers and students and the potential they possess. Jane served tirelessly as Managing Editor and Senior Content Manager for HAL2.0 and I am personally indebted to her for her hard work and dedication.

My sincere thanks go out again to the contributors to the first edition back in 2007: Dr. Andy Anderson (in memory, never forgotten), Pauline Auty, Heidi Bates, Alyson Beben, John Griffin, Beau Kent, Justin Maloney, Linda McCarger, and Gary Roberts. Thank you for your support over the years.

Sincere thanks as well to Dr. Dean Dudley, Macquarie University, Sydney, Australia; Dr. David Frost, University of Toronto; and Dr. Dean Kriellaars, University of Manitoba for their invaluable support, advice, and expertise.

I am also grateful to the Institute for Catholic Education for their cooperation and always constructive involvement with us. HAL2.0 is far better as a result of their involvement, and we sincerely hope that it meets their high expectations.

I also extend heartfelt thanks to the following principals and their office staff, teachers, and students for allowing us to take photographs of students in action. From the Toronto District School Board: Wexford C.I., Principal Tom Lazarou, Teachers John Stavropoulos, Paul Savinetti, and Bev Palen. East York C.I., Principal John Bratina, Teachers Scott Driscoll, Stacy Ganogiannis-Reid, Rob Greco, Glenn Edwards, and Tom Drivas. Birchmount Park C.I., Principal Ellen Austrom, Teachers Rob Pacas, Catherine MacInnes, Glenn Duncan, and Bill MacKay. Sir Wilfrid Laurier Collegiate Institute and Native Learning Centre—East, Principal Marios Tenentes, Teachers Louis Foulidis, Heather-Jo Bulloch, Karen Savage, Natasha Gleeson, Lena Recollet, Jennie Town, Alessandro Di Prima, Charlotte Vieth, and Tony Vallejo. Maplewood H.S., Principal Duncan Le Blanc, Teacher Diane Reed. From the Toronto Catholic District School Board: Senator O'Connor College School, Principal Tracey Parish, Teachers Sherwyn Benn, John Macchiocchi, and Tanya Callaghan. From the Durham Catholic District School Board: Monsignor John Pereyma Catholic Secondary School, Principal Sue Laforet, Teacher Lisa Politano. I express deep appreciation as well to Archie Allison, Director of Access and Awareness at Variety Village. Thanks to all of you for allowing us to capture your experiences in Health and Physical Education.

Thanks to the United Nations Educational, Scientific and Cultural Organization (UNESCO) for crafting the Quality Physical Education (QPE) Policy Document. The inspiration it has provided to us has been enormous; here's to helping make its recommendations come to life.

I wish to thank the following specific content reviewers: Barb Lederman, Senior Director, Marketing and Communications, the Dietitians of Canada; Kathy Chau, Director of Specialized Services and April Trewhitt, Concurrent Disorders Coordinator, Canadian Mental Health Association Toronto; Mary Duggan, Manager, the Canadian Society for Exercise Physiology; Jennifer Edwards, Operations Manager, the ACT Foundation; Vicki Harber and Alex Wilson, Sport for Life; Andrew Johnson, Manager, Client and Family Education & CAMH Publications, the Centre for Addiction and Mental Health; Tracee Smith, Founder and Chief Executive Officer, Outside Looking In; Brandy Tanenbaum, Program Coordinator, Sunnybrook Health Sciences Centre, Office for Injury Prevention; and Anne Trueman, Media Coordinator, the Society of Obstetricians and Gynaecologists of Canada.

Thanks to our photography team for taking such wonderful images of the exceptional individuals and students featured throughout this book.

Thanks to France Bertrand, Dietitians of Canada. Lucille, Karin, and Shawn Blainey; Paul Finkelstein, Team Lead, the EatFit Project; Christopher Khokhar; and Derek Perera, Ontario Cricket Academy—all gave generous support.

For the helping hand they gave me: Dr. James Mandigo, Brock University; Amanda Stanec, visionary and President of Move Live Learn; Peter Paputsis (TDSB Principal); Custodian Tom McDonell at East York Collegiate Institute; Bill Mackay at Birchmount Park Collegiate; Randy Ruttan; Enzo Rocca (in memory); Gary Reilly, Don Hibbert, Greg Hughes, Terence Green, Casey Zaph, Ron Whiteside, and former colleagues at East York Collegiate and Birchmount Park Collegiate; and to all my students for trusting me to be their teacher. To all the international, national, and provincial Health and Physical Education associations, thanks for inviting me to share my passion with you over the last several years—and, I hope, into the future.

To all the schools, school boards, and students with whom I continue to learn and work, I extend my deepest gratitude. You make me a better educator!

Last, but not least, I wish to express my gratitude and love to my wife Carolyn and our two inspirational teenagers Rebecca and Zachary. I love you.

Ted Temertzoglou

Organizations and Associations

We are grateful to the following national and provincial associations and organizations. These organizations are champions of healthy active living for all Canadians. Their example and inspiration were critical in the successful completion of this student resource. Responsibility for any errors or omissions rests with the authors and the publisher.

Ontario Association for the Support of Physical and Health Educators (OASPHE)

OASPHE (Ontario Association for the Support of Physical and Health Educators) is a group of Ontario Educators that provides a strong voice to lobby, advocate for, and support the development and delivery of quality curriculum in Health and Physical Education.

Ontario Physical and Health Education Association (Ophea)

As a Provincial Subject Association for Health and Physical Education (H&PE), Ophea has been providing essential resources and professional learning to Ontario's educators and program leaders since 1921. Ophea champions healthy active living in schools and communities and is led by the vision that all children and youth value and enjoy the benefits of healthy active living.

Physical and Health Education Canada (PHE Canada)

PHE Canada is a national leader and vital contributor in fostering achievement and health among Canadian children and youth by supporting physical and health education and active living initiatives where children live, learn, and play. PHE Canada's vision is a future wherein all children and youth in Canada live healthy, physically active lives.

Advanced Coronary Treatment Foundation (ACT Foundation)

The ACT Foundation is the national charitable organization dedicated to establishing free CPR as a mandatory program in every Canadian high school. The program is built on ACT's award-winning community-based model of partnerships and support. ACT raises funds for mannequins and resources for all high schools and guides schools in program set-up. The writing and publishing team would like to thank the management and staff of the ACT Foundation for their support and permission to reproduce the *ACT High School CPR & AED Student Manual* as an appendix to this resource.

The Society of Obstetricians and Gynaecologists of Canada (SOGC)

The SOGC is one of Canada's oldest national specialty organizations. Established in 1944, the Society's mission is to promote excellence in the practice of obstetrics and gynaecology and to advance the health of women through leadership, advocacy, collaboration, and education. The SOGC has over 3,500 members, comprised of obstetricians, gynaecologists, family physicians, nurses, midwives, and allied health professionals working in the field of sexual reproductive health.

Outside Looking In (OLI)

Outside Looking In is a Canada-wide high school credit program centred on dance and leadership development that engages Indigenous youth in regular dance classes and focused life skills. OLI guides youth from Grades 7 and up on a journey to academic achievement, well-being, and prosperous futures. Each spring, OLI's participants invite everyone to celebrate their success with them by attending a culminating dance performance in Toronto.

Canadian Society for Exercise Physiology (CSEP)

The Canadian Society for Exercise Physiology (CSEP) is the principal body for physical activity, health and fitness research, and personal training in Canada. It fosters the generation, growth, synthesis, transfer, and application of the highest quality research, education, and training related to exercise physiology and science. CSEP is the GOLD STANDARD of health and fitness professionals dedicated to getting Canadians active safely by providing the highest quality customized and specialized physical activity and fitness programs, guidance, and advice based on extensive training and evidence-based research.

ParticipACTION

ParticipACTION is a national non-profit organization whose mission is to help Canadians sit less and move more. Originally established in 1971, ParticipACTION works with its partners, which include sport, physical activity, recreation organizations, government, and corporate sponsors, to make physical activity a vital part of everyday life.

Sport for Life (S4L)

Sport for Life (S4L) is a movement to improve the quality of sport and develop physical literacy. Sport for Life works to advance athlete training and ensure better integration within the sport system, including sport organization, education, recreation, and health.

Canadian Mental Health Association Toronto (CMHA)

CMHA Toronto is one of the largest community-based mental health agencies in Toronto. CMHA Toronto supports the mental health of all and supports the resilience and recovery of people experiencing mental health challenges. Their mission is to:

- Provide services for people living with mental health challenges, helping them to live, work, and belong in their communities
- Provide information and education on mental health issues
- Advocate for policies that lead to improved quality of life for individuals with mental health issues

The Canadian Safe School Network (CSSN)

The Canadian Safe School Network is a national charitable organization dedicated to reducing youth violence and making our schools and communities safer. CSSN works with police services, school boards, and the municipal, provincial, and federal governments to find new solutions to safety issues youth face.

Ever Active Schools (EAS, Alberta)

Ever Active Schools is a program to assist schools in addressing and creating healthy school communities. Ever Active Schools seeks to encourage the creation of social and physical environments that improve the health and learning outcomes of students.

Physical Education British Columbia (PE-BC)

Physical Education British Columbia is a provincial specialist association (part of the BC Teachers Federation). The PE-BC executive is a small, dedicated group of full-time physical educators (elementary and secondary). Our role is to assist in curriculum writing, help to support teachers in the implementation of curriculum, provide assistance with professional development opportunities, and help each teacher to the best of our ability. Our goal is to help connect teachers with one another to share their ideas/lessons, successes, and failures and create dialogue across our province.

Physical and Health Educators of Manitoba (PHE Manitoba)

Formerly known as the Manitoba Physical Education Teachers' Association (MPETA), the Physical and Health Educators of Manitoba (PHE Manitoba) is an educational and professional organization which is dedicated to serving physical and health education in Manitoba schools.

New Brunswick Physical Education Society (NBPES)

The New Brunswick Physical Education Society (NBPES) was founded in 1998-99 Its goals are to: (1) act as a voice for professionals of Physical Education and Health; (2) support the profession as an information delivery system; and (3) provide professional development opportunities for its members. In short, its goal is to advocate for Quality Physical Education in the province of New Brunswick.

Physical Education Special Interest Council (PESIC)

The Physical Education Special Interest Council (PESIC) represents, speaks for and provides supports for all physical educators in the Province of Newfoundland and Labrador under the auspices of the Newfoundland and Labrador Teachers' Association (NLTA).

Teachers Association for Physical and Health Education (TAPHE)

The Teachers Association for Physical and Health Education (TAPHE) is a professional organization run through the Nova Scotia Teachers Union. Its mandate is (1) to improve professional practice by increasing member knowledge and understanding; (2) to designate ideas, trends, and new developments; (3) to provide information to the NSTU Professional Associations Coordination Committee and the NSTU Curriculum Committee; and (4) to advise the Provincial Executive on matters affecting NSTU Professional Associations.

Saskatchewan Physical Education Association (SPEA)

The Saskatchewan Physical Education Association (SPEA) is a provincial non-profit incorporated organization that provides quality leadership, advocacy, and resources for professionals in physical and health education to positively influence the lifestyles of Saskatchewan's children and youth. SPEA'S mission is to promote and support active healthy lifestyles through the development of physical education, recreation, and sport at all levels of the educational system.

Sunnybrook Health Sciences Centre

The Office for Injury Prevention was established in 1986 within Sunnybrook's Trauma, Emergency and Critical Care Program and aims to prevent injuries and injury-related death across all ages through education, collaboration, research, and innovation.

Variety Village

As a charitable organization, Variety Village is a unique community that transforms lives through inclusive physical activity and education for every phase of life. Variety Village offers specialized programming and services dedicated to establishing accessible and inclusive opportunities, creating a level playing field devoid of barriers, intimidation, or other obstacles, and making a profound difference in the spirits and lives of people with disabilities and their families.

Reviewers

We are grateful to the following individuals who kindly reviewed all or parts of this resource prior to publication. Responsibility for any errors or omissions rests with the author and the publisher.

Consultant Reviewers

- Julie Anderson, York Region District School Board
- Mary-Lou Andrea, Northside Staff Development Centre, Cape Breton-Victoria Regional School Board
- Karen August, York Region District School Board
- Nicole Beuckelare, Lambton Kent District School Board
- Sean Clancy, Ottawa-Carleton District School Board
- Angela Davis, Durham District School Board
- Nelli Domingues, Toronto Catholic District School Board
- Terri-Lynn Duncan, Horizon School Division 67, Saskatchewan
- Patty Friedrich, London Catholic District School Board
- Erin Gates, Fort McMurray Public School Division No. 2833, Alberta
- Dino Germano, Niagara Catholic District School Board
- Joe Grdisa, Peel District School Board
- Stacey Hannay, Edmonton School District No. 7, Alberta
- Andrea Hansen, Thames Valley District School Board
- Brian Hatherly, River East Transcona School Division, Manitoba
- Graham Hayes, Regina Catholic School District, Saskatchewan
- Sean Juteau, Surrey District School Board, British Columbia
- George Kourtis, Toronto District School Board
- Deb Lawlor, Ottawa Catholic School Board
- Andrea Lewis-Longmuir, Greater Essex County District School Board
- Gail Markin, Langley School District 35, British Columbia
- James MacKinnon, Durham Catholic District School Board
- Grant McManes, Louis Riel School Division, Saskatchewan
- Lynn Montgomery, Stelley's Secondary School, Saanich School District 63, British Columbia
- Monica Moran, Hamilton-Wentworth District School Board
- Lara Paterson, Limestone District School Board
- Sandra Pizuti, Hamilton-Wentworth Catholic District School Board
- Rebecca Richardson, Halton District School Board
- Heather Rootsaert, Edmonton School District No. 7, Alberta
- J.J. Ross, St. James-Assiniboia School Division, Manitoba
- Nicki Roy, Hastings and Prince Edward District School Board
- Marg Schwartz, Apple Schools, Alberta
- Tyler Smith, Dr. K.A. Clark Public School, Fort McMurray Public School Division No. 2833, Alberta
- Amanda Stanec, Move Live Learn
- Jeff Stromgren, School District 43, Coquitlam, British Columbia
- Bob Thomas, Ottawa Catholic School Board
- Karla Tritten, Edmonton School District No. 7, Alberta
- Tammy Woods, Halton District School Board

Provincial Consultants

- Darla Armstrong, Physical and Health Educators of Manitoba (PHE Manitoba)
- Ross Campbell, New Brunswick Physical Education Society (NBPES)
- Graham Hayes, Saskatchewan Physical Education Association (SPEA)
- Jennifer Lloyd-McKenzie, Teachers Association for Physical and Health Education (TAPHE), Nova Scotia
- Lisa Manzini, Physical Education British Columbia (PE-BC)
- Luke Neville, Physical Education Special Interest Council (PESIC), Newfoundland and Labrador
- Jacki Nylen, Physical and Health Educators of Manitoba (PHE Manitoba)

Pedagogy Reviewers

- Wendy Barber, University of Ontario Institute of Technology
- Joe Barrett, Brock University
- Stephen Berg, University of British Columbia
- David Chorney, University of Alberta
- Doug Gleddie, University of Alberta
- Nathan Hall, University of Winnipeg
- M. Louise Humbert, University of Saskatchewan
- Lindsay Lamorre, York University
- James Mandigo, Brock University
- Steve McGinley, University of British Columbia
- Lynn Randell, University of New Brunswick

- Dan Robinson, St. Francis Xavier University
- Dwayne Sheehan, Mount Royal University
- Lauren Sulz, University of Alberta
- Carolyn Temertzoglou, University of Toronto

Teacher Reviewers

- Brent Adam, Martin Collegiate, Regina School Division 4, Saskatchewan
- Margaret Adam, North Park Secondary School, Peel District School Board
- Jennifer Aziz, Peel District School Board
- Tom Beale, St. Thomas of Villanova High School, Windsor Essex Catholic District School Board
- Joel Brough, The Sterling Hall School of Toronto, Canadian Accredited Independent Schools (CAIS)
- Bruce Briard, Sir Winston Churchill Collegiate Institute, Toronto District School Board
- Jennifer Burleigh, Dundas Valley Secondary School, Hamilton-Wentworth District School Board
- Cynthia Campanaro, Westmount Secondary School, Hamilton-Wentworth District School Board
- Troy Casper, Luther College High School, Historic Independent School of Saskatchewan
- Rob Cherepuschak, Martin Collegiate, Regina School Division 4, Saskatchewan
- Jane Clark, Gananoque Secondary School, Upper Canada District School Board
- Patricia Coburn, St. Joseph Morrow Park Catholic School, Toronto Catholic District School Board
- Sue Cotnam, Bishop Smith Catholic High School, Renfrew County Catholic District School Board
- Christopher Deighan, Sacred Heart Catholic High School, York Catholic District School Board
- Nathaniel Dufresne, St. Benedict Catholic Secondary School, Waterloo Catholic District School Board
- Danielle Dutchak, Robert Bateman High School, Halton District School Board
- John Elkins, St. John's, Newfoundland and Labrador
- Anne Facey, Waterloo Catholic District School Board
- Andrew Fair, Earl Haig Secondary School, Toronto District School Board
- Tara Feeney, Trenton High School, Hastings and Prince Edward District School Board
- Sofia Fox, Orchard Park Secondary School, Hamilton-Wentworth District School Board
- Nancy Gould, Lambton Central Collegiate Vocational Institute, Lambton Kent District School Board
- Rob Greco, East York Collegiate Institute, Toronto District School Board
- Laura Gulley, St. Peter's Catholic Secondary School, Simcoe Muskoka Catholic District School Board
- Sandra Haliburton, Richmond Hill High School, York Region District School Board
- Darryl Hancock, Peterborough-Victoria Northumberland and Clarington Catholic District School Board
- Jason Henderson, North Grenville District High School, Upper Canada District School Board
- David Inglis, H.B. Beal Secondary School, Thames Valley District School Board
- Christina Jones, Balwin School, Edmonton Public Schools, Alberta
- Michelle Kasprzak, Monsignor Paul Dwyer Catholic High School, Durham Catholic District School Board
- Pat Lacasse, Colonel By Secondary School, Ottawa-Carleton District School Board
- Angeline Lacasse, Colonel By Secondary School, Ottawa-Carleton District School Board
- Reg Leidl, P.J. Gillen School, Good Spirit School Division, Saskatchewan
- Rebecca MacDonald, Appleby College, Conference of Independent Schools (CAIS)
- Kari Macer, Havergal College, Conference of Independent Schools
- Jeff Masterson, King City Secondary School, York Region District School Board
- Sean McCabe, Dufferin-Peel Catholic District School Board
- Jayne McCullough, Medway High School, Thames Valley District School Board
- Dan McFadden, Earl Haig Secondary School, Toronto District School Board
- John Morelli, Father Michael McGivney Catholic Academy High School, York Catholic District School Board
- Andrew Morgan, Edmonton Public School Board, Alberta
- Carolyn Mossey, St. Jean de Brébeuf Catholic Secondary School, Hamilton-Wentworth Catholic District School Board
- Jamie Nunn, Hamilton-Wentworth District School Board
- Tony Nurse, Leamington District Secondary School, Greater Essex County District School Board
- Barbara O'Connor, Bishop Reding Catholic Secondary School, Halton Catholic District School Board

- Rob Pacas, Birchmount Park Collegiate Institute, Toronto District School Board
- Dave Paddington, Lakehead District School Board
- Tom Pain, Westmount Secondary School, Hamilton-Wentworth District School Board
- Mario Pietrangelo, Father Henry Carr Catholic Secondary School, Toronto Catholic District School Board
- Karin Podlatis-Brown, Chippewa Secondary School, Near North District School Board
- Jennifer Powles, Trinity College School, Conference of Independent Schools
- Nancy Popovich, Trenton High School, Hastings and Prince Edward District School Board
- Tonya Reesor, St. Joseph Catholic Elementary School, Waterloo Catholic District School Board
- Sarah Robertson, Aldershot High School, Halton District School Board
- Dr. Brian Roy, Brock University
- Randy Ruttan, Upper Canada District School Board
- Ivan Saari, Mackenzie Community School, Renfrew County District School Board
- Karl Schroeder, Miles Macdonell Collegiate, River East Transcona School Division, Manitoba
- Mike Sheahan, Brock University
- Sonia Sheehan, Foundation for the Future Charter Academy, Alberta
- Derek Simpson, Murdoch MacKay Collegiate, River East Transcona School Division, Manitoba
- Michael Sinukoff, Tommy Douglas Secondary School, York Region District School Board
- Paul Solarski, Brebeuf College School, Toronto Catholic District School Board
- Daryl Sproule, Collingwood Collegiate Institute, Simcoe County District School Board
- Tracy Streutker, College Avenue Secondary School, Thames Valley District School Board
- Heather Strupat, Ursula Franklin Academy, Toronto District School Board
- Lorna Tremonti, Dryden High School, Keewatin Patricia District School Board
- Michele Van Bargen, Strathroy District Collegiate Institute, Thames Valley District School Board
- Mark Verbeek, Hillfield Strathallan College, Canadian Accredited Independent Schools (CAIS)
- Bill Walters, St. Francis Xavier University
- Brigitte Webster, Waterloo Catholic District School Board
- Karen Whitfield, Havergal College, Conference of Independent Schools
- Linda Whitmarsh, Sinclair Secondary School, Durham District School Board
- Cole Wilson, University of Saskatchewan
- Tammy Wirick, Alpha Secondary School, Burnaby School Division 41, British Columbia
- Glenn Young, Surrey, British Columbia
- Carla Zaroda, Kildonan East Collegiate, River East Transcona School Division, Manitoba

Institute for Catholic Education

- Staff from Thompson Educational Publishing, Inc. requested suggested modifications from the Institute for Catholic Education for use of this text in Ontario Catholic schools.

International Reviewer

- Dr. Dean Dudley, Macquarie University, Australia

Literacy Reviewer

- Joanne Walsh, Ophea (previously with the Halton District School Board)

Specialty Reviewers

- Dr. David Frost, University of Toronto
- Dr. Dean Kriellaars, University of Manitoba
- Dr. Stuart McGill, Professor Emeritus, University of Waterloo

Safety Reviewers

- Dr. Tim Rindlisbacher, Cleveland Clinic, Canada
- Bob Soroko, Ophea

The Benefits of Healthy Active Living

1.1 Health and Physical Literacy

1.2 Why Take Health and Physical Education?

1.3 Play Your Position—We All Fit In!

Major Muscles and Bones of the Human Body

1

Laurier
Blue Devils
ATHLETICS

Brigitte's Story

What are the benefits of leading a healthy active lifestyle for you and your community?

Leading a healthy active lifestyle has many benefits. Regular physical activity strengthens our bodies and builds endurance, and it is also evident that being physically active promotes our mental and social health as well.

Healthy lifestyle practices—including proper nutrition and sleep—enhance our feelings of productivity, boost our self-esteem, and help us maintain a positive body image.

This chapter discusses how increasing our physical activity can help us lead healthier, happier, and more fulfilling lives. It also looks at how developing our physical literacy can contribute to active participation in recreational, sport, and other activities. It highlights the important role of Quality Physical Education in laying the foundation for healthy active living and 21st century learning. Here are the tools and strategies you will need to transform your life and to help others enjoy healthy active lives as well!

Learning Objectives

In this chapter, you will...

- learn about what constitutes healthy active living
- develop an understanding of the many benefits of healthy active living
- demonstrate an understanding of factors that support participation in physical activity throughout our lives
- participate actively and regularly in a wide variety of physical activities
- analyze various factors related to the global inactivity crisis
- develop an understanding of the benefits of Quality Physical Education (QPE)
- learn and practise a model of decision making known as the IDEAL method
- learn how to make your health and physical literacy journey meaningful for you

▶ **Brigitte Neganigwane** loves to dance. A member of the Wikwemikong First Nation from Manitoulin Island, Brigitte is a graduate of the Outside Looking In dance program for Indigenous youth. The program empowers participants all across Canada to succeed academically, build life skills, form lasting friendships, and strengthen ties to their communities.

Key Terms

- health
- health literacy
- physical literacy
- healthy active living
- holistic health
- medicine wheel
- Truth and Reconciliation Commission of Canada
- Calls to Action
- Seven Sacred Teachings
- Long-Term Athlete Development Framework (LTAD)
- Aboriginal Long-Term Participant Development Pathway
- resilience
- Quality Physical Education (QPE)
- IDEAL method (of decision making)
- Sedentary behaviour
- Canadian 24-Hour Movement Guidelines for Children and Youth

1.1 Health and Physical Literacy

Today's concept of what it means to be "healthy" extends well beyond disease reduction and injury prevention. The World Health Organization (WHO) defines **health** as "a state of complete physical, mental and social well-being and not merely the absence of disease or infirmity."

Health is not something that simply happens to us. Instead, it is an ongoing part of our lives for which we are responsible—something we can actively strive for and attain. Promoting and achieving good health—our own and others'—means gaining greater control over the factors that enable us to lead healthy and meaningful lives.

Developing Our Health Literacy

Health literacy refers to how well a person can access, understand, and use the health information needed to make good health decisions. Just like developing literacy skills such as reading and writing, we can develop skills related to health literacy.

Public Health Agency of Canada statistics show that 60 percent of adults and 88 percent of seniors in Canada are not health literate. People who are not health literate have difficulty using the everyday health information that is available in health care facilities, pharmacies, retail outlets, schools, media channels, and community centres.

Clearly, there is a need to increase the health literacy of Canada's population. How health literate are you? This resource will help you determine your own level of health literacy and offer pathways to health and well-being.

Developing Our Physical Literacy

One vitally important way to enhance our overall health is to develop our **physical literacy**. Canada's physical literacy consensus statement (June 2015) has declared that:

> Physical literacy is the motivation and confidence, physical competence, and knowledge and understanding to value and take responsibility for engagement in physical activities for life.

Physical literacy is an inclusive concept accessible to everyone. It represents a unique journey for each individual. It can be enjoyed by means of a wide range of experiences in different environments and contexts. Physical literacy needs to be valued and nurtured throughout life because it contributes to your development as a whole person. The ultimate goal of physical literacy is to enable you to participate in physical activity in safe and meaningful ways.

What Is Healthy Active Living?

Healthy active living embraces both health literacy and physical literacy. It means being active, moving with confidence and competence, eating healthily, getting proper sleep, and feeling good. It involves engaging in physical activity every day in order to be healthy, fit, and happy.

Healthy active living means making as many health-conscious choices as we can. These choices affect not only our daily activity level but also our eating, sleeping, and social habits. They improve our physical and mental health and minimize risks of illnesses, injuries, and emotional harm. Choosing a healthy active lifestyle enhances all aspects of what we generally refer to as "wellness."

The components of healthy active living

The components of healthy active living are good **physical, mental, spiritual,** and **social health**. These four dimensions of healthy active living are interconnected and largely fall under our control. Each of us has the ability to make decisions that can positively influence each one of these dimensions.

Four main factors determine an individual's physical health:

1. physical activity
2. nutrition
3. avoiding harmful substances such as illegal drugs and tobacco
4. heredity (our genetic makeup)

We cannot control our heredity, but we *can* do something about how active we are, what we eat, and what substances to avoid that might do us harm.

We can also learn strategies and adopt daily routines that will benefit our mental, spiritual, and social health so that we can become happier and stronger people.

Canada's Assessment Tools for Physical Literacy

Researchers have developed some excellent evidence-based tools to help assess the movement skills of children and youth. You may encounter some of these tools in your classes. For example:

- Sport for Life has launched a comprehensive suite of tools developed by Dr. Dean Kriellaars at the University of Manitoba called **PLAY—Physical Literacy Assessment for Youth**. Designed primarily for teachers, parents, and coaches, it can also be used by you to assess yourself using "PLAYself."
- Physical and Health Education (PHE) Canada's free online tool **Passport for Life** assesses four curriculum-linked aspects of health and physical literacy: Active Participation, Living Skills, Fitness Skills, and Movement Skills.
- The Healthy Active Living and Obesity Research Group (HALO), led by Dr. Mark Tremblay and his team, has developed the **Canadian Assessment of Physical Literacy (CAPL)** to assess multiple aspects of physical literacy: daily behaviour, motivation and confidence, knowledge and understanding, and physical competence.

To learn more about these tools, ask your Health and Physical Education teacher or visit the associations' websites.

Physical Literacy: Gateway to Active Participation

Physical literacy is the motivation and confidence, the physical competence, and the knowledge and understanding to be physically active for life. It is the most effective strategy for encouraging people of every age to become more active, healthy, successful, and happy throughout their entire lives.

We begin to develop our physical literacy as children by learning fundamental movement skills, largely through unstructured free play in indoor and outdoor settings in each of these **four** environments:

1. **On the ground:** as the basis for most games, sports, dance, and other physical activities
2. **In, on, or under the water:** as the basis for all aquatic activities
3. **On snow and ice:** as the basis for most winter activities
4. **In the air:** as the basis for gymnastics, diving, and other aerial activities

Everyone can improve physical literacy at any age and stage of life, and everyone's physical literacy journey is unique. Physical literacy involves much more than physical competence. At the heart of physical literacy is the motivation and commitment to being active in as many ways as possible and to seek constant opportunities to try new and purposeful activities. An active individual enjoys moving and gains confidence by participating in a wide range of challenging, fun, and meaningful physical pursuits.

Our physical literacy journey leads to physical, mental, spiritual, and social benefits. It encourages us to interact with others in creative and imaginative ways. It helps us form friendships and find our talents.

The Four Elements of Physical Literacy

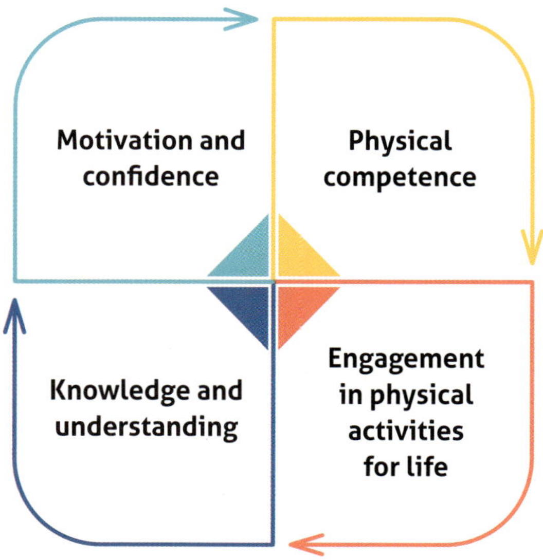

Physical Fitness Comes in All Shapes and Sizes

The first step to healthy active living is to be physically active. For children and teens, this includes participating in Health and Physical Education classes. The goal of these classes is to teach you about healthy living and physical fitness, so that you can design your own fitness plan that suits your needs and interests.

At one time, people tended to view "physical fitness" in narrow terms, such as doing push-ups, jumping jacks, or other repetitive exercises. Today, educators and movement professionals acknowledge that pursuing fitness is not just for athletes working out in a gym or on the track.

- Fitness is for everyone, everywhere. It is up to you to decide what form it takes, with input from your Health and Physical Education teacher.
- Fitness is achieved through regular engagement in specific forms of physical activity, including exercise.

Your fitness level may vary over time, or you may be fit in one respect but not especially fit in another. For example, you may have good muscular strength, but your heart and lungs may not be as strong as you would like.

No matter what your body type, size, or relative ability to play games or sports, you can improve your level of fitness. Improving your fitness level involves assessing your capabilities, devising a plan, and setting goals. Whatever your skill level and whatever the factors that influence your abilities and preferences, you can always improve your fitness in ways that are fun while enjoying a healthy active lifestyle.

Physical literacy is not focused on developing high-performance athletes or promoting a single sport. Instead, it introduces the ABCs of movement skills in a developmentally appropriate way and makes it fun. It helps us develop an awareness of how our bodies work, and it creates opportunities to discover and enjoy the natural environment as well.

The Medicine Wheel

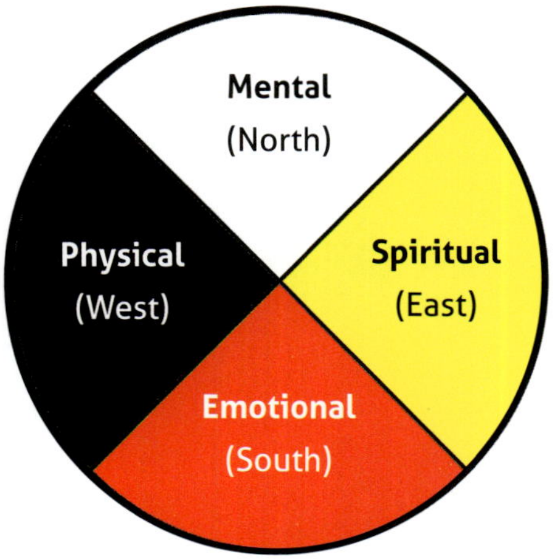

This traditional depiction of the medicine wheel shows the four quadrants with their associated colours and meanings.

Holistic Health—Learning from Indigenous Elders

Traditional Indigenous approaches to medicine and healing embrace the concept of **holistic health**—that is, the idea that the mind, body, and spirit are interconnected and that only when all these elements are healthy will a person experience true wellness.

This is also a concept that is central to quality Health and Physical Education programs today. We need to be attentive to all three dimensions of our health and well-being.

The significance of the Indigenous medicine wheel

The **medicine wheel**, a symbol commonly associated with Indigenous cultures, best symbolizes this interconnectedness. The medicine wheel captures the cycles of nature and represents life as an interconnected, circular journey.

The four points on the wheel represent the four seasons (spring, summer, autumn, winter); the four aspects of a person (physical, mental, emotional, and spiritual); the four kingdoms (animal, mineral, plant, and human); and the four sacred medicines (sweetgrass, tobacco, cedar, and sage).

You may also see the medicine wheel represented as the four points of the compass, marking the spiritual (East), mental (North), physical (West), and emotional (South) aspects of health.

For a traditional Indigenous healer, an imbalance in any one aspect of health will affect a person's overall health and well-being. Holistic health involves bringing all four dimensions into harmony and balance.

Truth and reconciliation through active living

The important role that physical activity can play in promoting wellness was highlighted in the report of the **Truth and Reconciliation Commission of Canada** (2015). The Truth and Reconciliation Commission was set up, under Justice Murray Sinclair, to report on the historical injustices experienced by Indigenous peoples and to find a way forward.

"For over a century," the Commission concluded, "the central goals of Canada's Aboriginal policy were to eliminate Aboriginal governments; ignore Aboriginal rights; terminate the Treaties; and, through a process of assimilation, cause Aboriginal peoples to cease to exist as distinct legal, social, cultural, religious, and racial entities in Canada."

Five of the Commission's 94 **Calls to Action** indicate how, among other things, greater opportunities for young people in Indigenous communities to participate in physical activity and recreation can help redress these historical injustices. The Commission emphasized how active living programs and community sports can play a significant role in the development of Indigenous communities and improve the overall health and well-being of Indigenous peoples.

The Seven Sacred Teachings and healthy active living

The Seven Sacred Teachings—Truth, Humility, Honesty, Wisdom, Respect, Courage, and Love—are lessons that have been passed down from Indigenous Elders and Traditional Knowledge Keepers.

These sacred teachings align well with Health and Physical Education programs in schools across Canada. School-based Health and Physical Education is built on the principles of equity, inclusiveness, and fair play and the idea that personal fitness and active living are essential components of overall health and well-being.

Physical activity and personal fitness are essential steps on the road to overall wellness, lasting friendships, and an optimistic outlook on what the future can bring.

Supporting physical literacy for all of Canada's peoples

Sport for Life's **Long-Term Athlete Development Framework (LTAD)** promotes physical literacy based on seven developmental stages (see the diagram below). This framework describes the developmentally appropriate activities at each stage of life that enable us to pursue the sport or leisure activities of our choosing. LTAD fosters positive active experiences, improved health, and higher goal achievement for everyone.

Recognizing that mainstream models do not necessarily align with Indigenous needs or experiences, Indigenous educators and Sport for Life also developed the **Aboriginal Long-Term Participant Development Pathway**. This pathway builds on a holistic model of health and wellness that takes into account the physical as well as the cultural, mental, and spiritual dimensions of health.

Just like a circle, where there is no end and no beginning, the Aboriginal Long-Term Participant Development Pathway is based on the principle of continuous improvement. The stages of the pathway provide programs for all ages with the aim of increasing participation and optimizing performance in a wide range of culturally appropriate activities.

Section 1.1 Review

1. Distinguish between *health literacy* and *physical literacy*.
2. Briefly explain the significance of the medicine wheel in Indigenous cultures. What connections can you make to health literacy and physical literacy?
3. Create your own infographic depicting the many benefits of healthy active living.

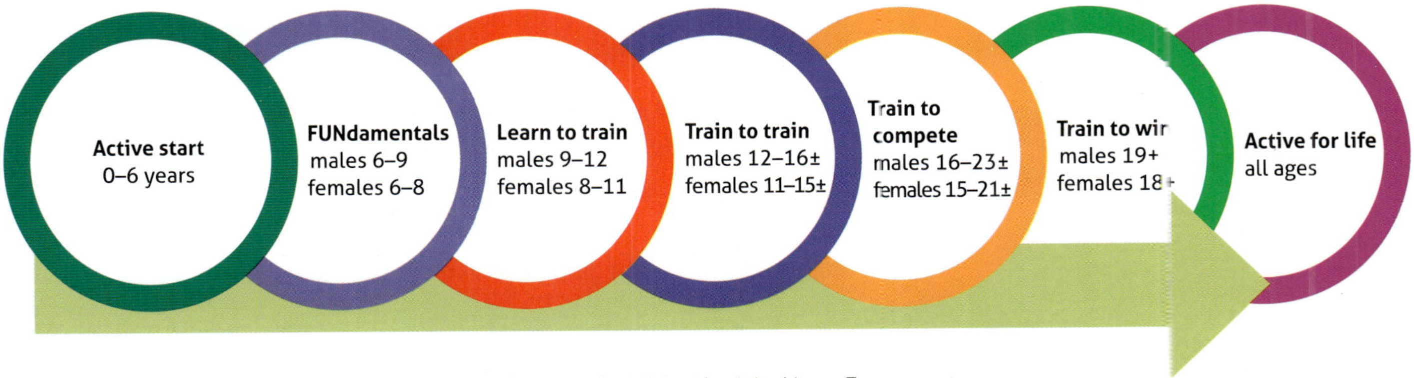

The stages of the Long-Term Athlete Development Framework and the Aboriginal Long-Term Participation Development Pathway. The ages shown for each stage are approximate.

1.2 Why Take Health and Physical Education?

The Health and Physical Education classes you take in school are all about you, your relationships with others, and the choices you make. In these classes, you will learn new concepts and strategies and try out some new, fun, and creative activities.

The ultimate reason for taking Health and Physical Education is to gain knowledge about how to take care of your body, mind, and spirit and how to motivate yourself to engage in physical activities, games, or sports that you enjoy. What is great about Health and Physical Education is that you do not have to be an elite athlete to get a good mark.

Healthy active living *is* athletic—we all qualify as athletes just by knowing how to move! Being athletic is not only for sports, but can help you at work, at play, and even while performing everyday activities.

Tips for Success in Health and Physical Education

All you need to do to succeed in your Health and Physical Education classes is complete your assignments and participate fully. Staying actively involved in class is a good foundation for success. If you participate actively every day, the gains will be evident.

Here are a few tips for enhancing your success as you take part in classes, activities, and discussions:

- **Show up for class on time.** You do not want to miss out on instructions provided by your teacher.
- **Do your best to stay organized.** Bring appropriate clothing, footwear, and other items to class, depending on that day's scheduled activities.
- **Play fair and play safe.** Try as hard as you can, keep moving, and encourage your classmates to do the same. Honour the rules of fair play and the safety guidelines laid out by your teacher.
- **Practise positive social skills.** Always show respect toward others, both in words and in actions. Contribute to social interactions in positive ways. A positive attitude can lead to a stronger sense of well-being and self-worth for both you and your friends.
- **Take (safe) risks and have fun!** Do not be afraid to try new activities and to learn new skills. If you make a "mistake," do not worry about it—it is a vital part of the learning experience. If you are willing to test your limits even just a little, you will discover strengths and capabilities that you didn't even know you had!

It's Time to Get Up and Move!

Countries all around the world are witnessing declining levels of fitness and high levels of inactivity among children and teens. Children and youth are spending an increasing amount of their leisure time sitting in front of a TV, computer screen, tablet, or smartphone, far exceeding the recommended maximum of two hours per day.

Become Active for Life

The decrease in physical activity and increase in sedentary behaviour are associated with a rise in obesity as well as higher risks of diseases such as diabetes, heart disease, and cancer later in life. Physical inactivity also undermines our mental health.

Each of us can take proactive measures to reverse these negative trends. This is where championing physical literacy, Health and Physical Education, and healthy active living can play a vital role.

Creating a lifestyle that includes regular physical activity is the best strategy for improving your long-term health. In addition, an active lifestyle contributes to more than just physical health. It will also help to improve your concentration and self-esteem.

Ultimately, active living is a lifestyle that helps everyone feel more energetic, competent, confident, motivated, and happy!

A Positive Cycle

Calming our mental state allows us to focus on awareness of our physical needs as well as our spiritual needs. Various practices such as mindfulness, meditation, prayer, tai chi, qi gong, yoga, and smudging can have a calming effect.

A calm mental state allows us to concentrate on performing physical movements competently, safely, and accurately. Performing physical movements well helps to settle our mental state, resulting in a positive and beneficial cycle.

The more we move, the better we feel; and the better we feel, the more we move.

The Many Benefits of Being Active

Physical activity delivered through healthy lifestyle habits and physical education offers many **physical, cognitive, academic, social, mental health,** and **spiritual benefits.** The benefits (and the risks of neglecting regular physical activity) apply to people of every age and ability.

- **Physical benefits.** Regular physical activity has many benefits for the heart and lungs. Having healthy cardiovascular and cardiorespiratory systems means less chance of heart disease, high blood pressure, heart attacks, and strokes. Physical activity makes bones stronger, reducing the risk of osteoporosis and joint-related diseases such as arthritis. Regular physical activity also increases the strength, endurance, and flexibility of muscles, ligaments, and tendons.
- **Cognitive/academic benefits.** Many studies have shown that brain health and cognitive performance improve with regular physical activity. These changes boost memory and learning, improve decision making, and allow you to think and communicate more effectively.
- **Social benefits.** Physical activity can improve social health through interactions with other people during recreational activities, games, and sports. Being active with someone else—a friend, family member, teammate, or workout buddy—makes physical activity more enjoyable.
- **Mental health benefits.** Regular physical activity can reduce stress, anxiety, and depression and has been shown to have a positive effect on self-esteem and sleep habits. It also strengthens your **resilience**—your ability to find strength in adapting to difficulty, loss, or anything that causes feelings of distress and uncertainty.
- **Spiritual benefits.** People who are physically active are more likely to make connections with others and with nature, and to be more attuned to their spiritual or religious beliefs. A person's spiritual health—sense of belonging, meaning, and purpose in life—is enhanced by being physically active.

Quality Physical Education (QPE)

UNESCO is the United Nations agency responsible for coordinating international cooperation in education, science, culture, and communication. A part of that task is to promote physical education and sport. UNESCO urges all member states to facilitate the participation in daily **Quality Physical Education (QPE)**: the planned, progressive, inclusive learning experience that forms part of the curriculum for children and youth. Besides promoting healthy active living, QPE also drives inclusion: it empowers girls, breaks down social barriers and stigmas, and encourages dialogue and understanding among different cultures. The following infographic shows some of the many important ways in which QPE contributes to overall quality of life.

THE BENEFITS OF INVESTING

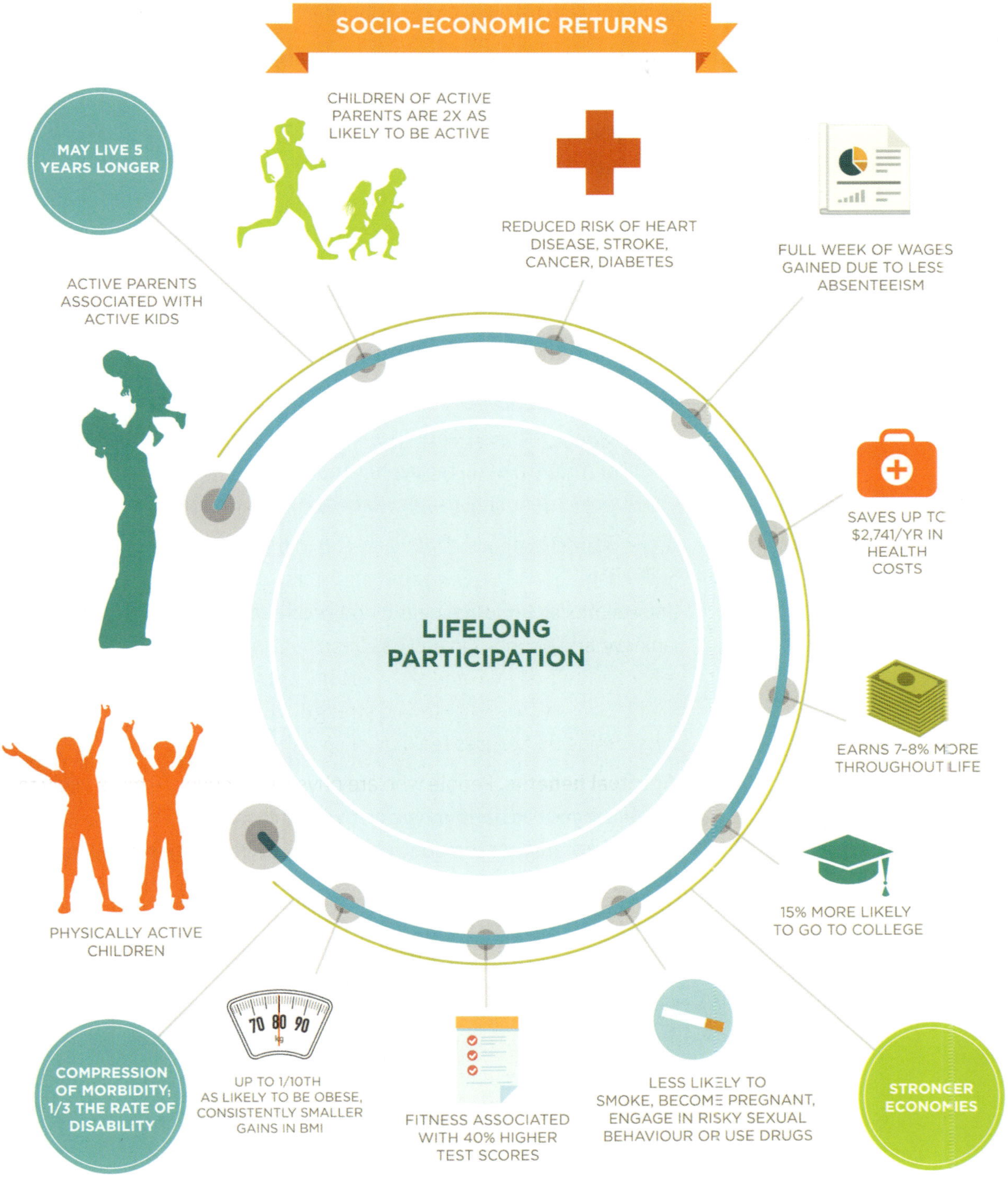

According to UNESCO, Quality Physical Education leads to many significant personal and social gains, including higher academic achievement, better paying jobs, and longer lifespans.

Source: From "Quality Physical Education Policy," courtesy of the United Nations Educational, Scientific and Cultural Organization (UNESCO), 2013

The IDEAL Path to Good Decision Making

The **IDEAL method** is particularly effective if you are faced with a difficult problem or situation. It can help you sort through your options, prioritize them, and then make the best possible decisions.

The key components of the IDEAL method are as follows:

- **I** **Identify** the problem.
- **D** **Discuss** your options.
- **E** **Evaluate** your options and prioritize your concerns.
- **A** **Act** on the best choice.
- **L** **Learn** from the experience.

Decision-making skills in action

Here is how this might play out if, for example, you are trying to decide whether you should go to a late-night party with a group of older friends:

I—Identify the problem.

My friends want me to go, and there will probably be some older kids I like, but I'm sure there will be alcohol and drugs. If my parents ever found out, they would definitely be angry about it and I would get into trouble.

Well, the problem seems to be that going to the party means I will have to lie to my parents, which is wrong. It might also cause other problems, like I might feel pressure to do things I might not be ready for.

D—Discuss your options.

I could go to the party and not tell my parents. I could stay home. I could try to negotiate with my parents. Maybe they will let me go if I promise to act responsibly at the party and if I promise to be home by a certain time.

E—Evaluate your options and prioritize your concerns.

Lying to my parents is not a good thing to do. Staying at home will make my parents happy, but I will end up sitting at home doing nothing.

Do I want to go to this party because I'm hoping to become friends with these people, or is it a way for me to fool myself into thinking I'm cool?

A—Act on the best choice.

It is more important in the long run to have a good relationship with my parents. Lying to them so I can brag to my friends that I went to a party with older kids is not worth it. Knowing that my parents trust me is important.

L—Learn from the experience.

Sometimes decisions are difficult. Making the right decision might feel like I gave something up, but it showed me that I am a strong person who does what is right. Besides, there will always be another party.

Healthy Active Living and Decision Making

Pursuing a healthy active lifestyle involves making thoughtful decisions on a daily basis about how we spend our time, what we eat and drink, how we respond to stress, and how we assess risks and benefits to ourselves. Throughout your Health and Physical Education experiences, you will be introduced to many topics that will require you to make informed decisions based on the choices that are available to you.

During your high school years, you will be confronted with some fairly major decisions. How you deal with them can affect the course of your life. Therefore, it is important to learn how to make decisions that are beneficial to you and that pose minimal risks to you, your family, your friends, or others in your community.

Making decisions does not have to be a random, disorganized process. There are several tried-and-true methods of arriving at decisions that will benefit your health and well-being that you can use whenever you need to determine the best option in a given situation.

The IDEAL method, described on the facing page, is especially effective when you are torn between wanting to impress or please your friends and wanting to remain true to your own deeply held values and beliefs.

Section 1.2 Review

1. List various things you can do to be successful in taking Health and Physical Education classes.
2. Make a table to show the many ways in which Quality Physical Education (QPE) contributes to overall quality of life.
3. Describe one scenario in which you, a friend, or a family member could apply the IDEAL method of decision making.

1.3 Play Your Position—We All Fit In!

Think about all the automated systems and labour-saving devices that people rely on today: elevators, escalators, moving sidewalks, chairlifts, and passive transportation such as cars, trucks, motorcycles, and buses, to name a few. Compared to previous generations, people today also spend far too much time sitting—at their desks, in their cars, and in front of TVs, computer screens, and hand-held devices. Advances in technology have made it increasingly unnecessary to expend physical energy.

Some neurologists believe that, as a result of reduced physical movement, our brain's receptors are being "pruned" away and the neural pathways and connections in our brains may actually be getting smaller.

Prior to 1900, estimated step counts for adults typically exceeded 20,000 per day and up to 40,000 steps per day were possible. Compare this with today's estimate of up to 8,500 steps per day. It takes about 22 steps to use up one calorie of energy. Clearly, we are expending far less energy today compared to pre-automated times. Our overreliance on technology has decreased our physical movement while increasing our sedentary behaviour.

Sedentary behaviour involves postures or activities that require very little movement. Examples include prolonged sitting, watching television, playing passive video or computer games, extended time spent on the computer, and motorized transportation.

CSEP Recommends...

The Canadian Society for Exercise Physiology (CSEP) is a national organization of professionals dedicated to the scientific study of exercise physiology, exercise biochemistry, fitness, and health. They have developed guidelines for every age group that address both physical activity and sedentary behaviour, making recommendations on how to best achieve a healthy active lifestyle.

CSEP's **Canadian 24-Hour Movement Guidelines for Children and Youth** recommend that youth aged 12–17 should

- accumulate at least 60 minutes of moderate- to vigorous-intensity physical activity every day, including vigorous-intensity activities at least three days per week and activities that strengthen muscle and bone at least three days per week
- limit recreational screen time to no more than two hours per day
- limit sedentary (motorized) transport, extended sitting, and time spent indoors throughout the day

Note that moderate-intensity physical activities will cause you to sweat a little and breathe harder. Vigorous-intensity physical activities will cause you to sweat and have some difficulty speaking.

Being Active as a Preferred Way of Life

Today, medical, public health, and educational experts are growing more and more concerned about the serious health risks associated with inactivity, especially among children and youth.

Comparisons across 38 countries from six continents in 2016 confirmed a global childhood inactivity crisis and, most importantly, offered insights for improvement.

The global comparisons were led by Dr. Mark Tremblay, Chair of the Active Healthy Kids Global Alliance and Director of the Healthy Active Living and Obesity Research Group at the Children's Hospital of Eastern Ontario.

Dr. Tremblay identified four global trends that have drastically reduced physical activity levels:

1. automation
2. mechanization
3. urbanization
4. digitization

According to Dr. Tremblay, "Countries with the most active children and youth overall, including Slovenia, New Zealand and Zimbabwe, rely on very different approaches to get kids to move more. But, what is consistent between all of them is that physical activity is driven by pervasive cultural norms—being active is not just a choice, but a way of life."

These photos (from left to right) show young people celebrating a big soccer win in Slovenia, cycling in New Zealand, and walking the Chimanimani mountains of Zimbabwe.

Become an Agent of Change

In response to the global inactivity crisis, organizations such as UNESCO, the World Health Organization (WHO), and the Council of Europe are recommending evidence-based interventions to address physical inactivity and sedentary behaviour at national and school-based levels. As an individual, however, you can choose to make your own long-lasting and far-reaching changes to benefit your brain and your body simply by moving more.

Get up and get active—and invite friends and family to join you. Walk, run, hike, bike, skate, skateboard, swim, toboggan, garden, play games or sports, take the stairs—do anything that puts your brain, muscles, and joints into action. See how much more confident and invigorated you feel!

Go, Team Canada!

As simple as these activities might seem, they are the key to empowering you and your entire generation. Even small changes in your daily routine can make a big difference. Get off the bus one or two stops sooner. Park farther rather than closer to the stores at the mall. Use a phone app or pedometer to record the number of steps you take each day, and encourage your friends and family to do the same.

We can think of ourselves as permanent members of a national activity team called **Team Canada**. We all have a position to play on this team. You do not need to excel at team sports—or even like them, for that matter—to be a star player for Team Canada. The strategies for success are already within your grasp:

- Choose nutritious foods that make you feel energized.
- Get outside more, move more, and explore new and challenging activities in different environments all year round.
- Find just the right level of physical activity for you—not too easy, but not too tough.
- Establish a healthy balance for yourself in terms of your 24-hour movement patterns (stepping, sweating, sitting, and sleeping).
- Get away from screens and socialize more.
- Volunteer in some way to help others.

The topics you will learn about and the activities you will experience in your Health and Physical Education classes will give you all the tools you need to play for Team Canada—and come out a winner!

Section 1.3 Review

1. List five ways that you could add more movement/steps to your daily living.
2. List four global trends that have greatly reduced our physical activity levels.
3. Describe ways in which you could encourage your friends, family, or school community to become more active and health-aware.

Brigitte's Story

"The Outside Looking In program for Indigenous youth is not just about dance. There is a connection between physical activity and positive mental health. Dancing lifts our spirits. It helps us want to do more and to be better in our communities."

— Brigitte Neganigwane

Chapter 1 Review

Knowledge and Understanding

1 What are the four components of healthy active living, and how are they interconnected?

2 Describe what being "healthy" and "fit" looks like and feels like for you.

3 In a small group, collaborate to make a mind map or an infographic showing the many benefits of healthy active living for individuals and for society.

Thinking

4 Compare and contrast the characteristics of a healthy active lifestyle as opposed to a sedentary lifestyle in terms of risks and benefits. Share your thoughts in a table, a drawing, a cartoon, or any other format of your choice.

5 Think about some of the most common obstacles that people describe as barriers to physical activity. What practical steps might they take to overcome those barriers?

Communication

6 Create a blog, a poem, a song, or a short video featuring five benefits of healthy active living.

7 What persuasive arguments could you make to encourage a friend who tends to be inactive to join you in trying a fun new physical activity?

8 If you were in charge of public relations for your community, what catchy campaign slogan would you compose to get everyone up and moving?

Application

9 What criteria could you apply to assess your own level of physical literacy?

10 Research CSEP's Physical Activity Guidelines for adults and discuss them with some older family members.

11 Research CSEP's Sedentary Behaviour Guidelines for adults and devise an action plan to help your whole family combat some sedentary habits.

12 What goals would you like to accomplish in the year ahead as a member of Team Canada?

Major Muscles of the Human Body

Anterior View of the Muscular System

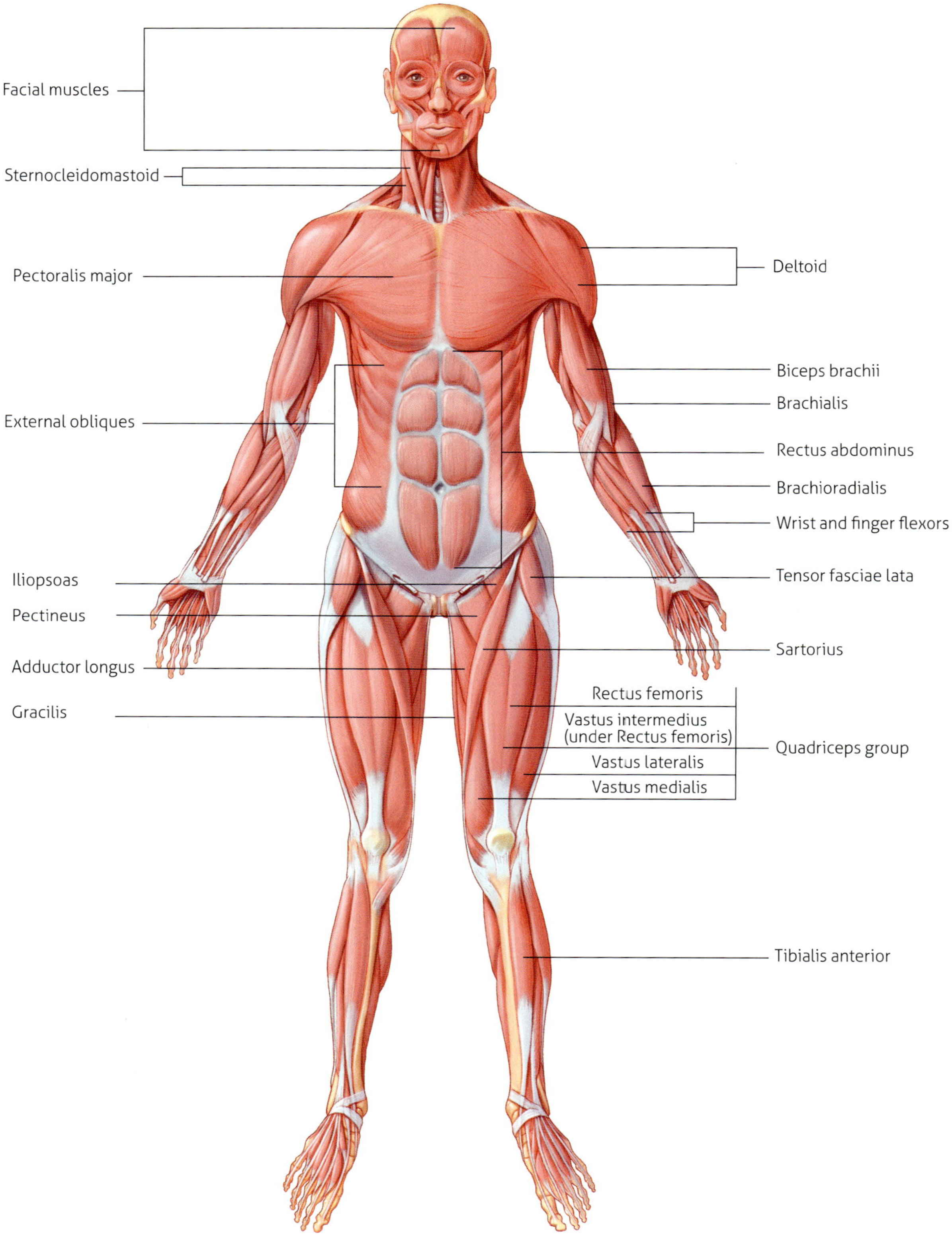

Posterior View of the Muscular System

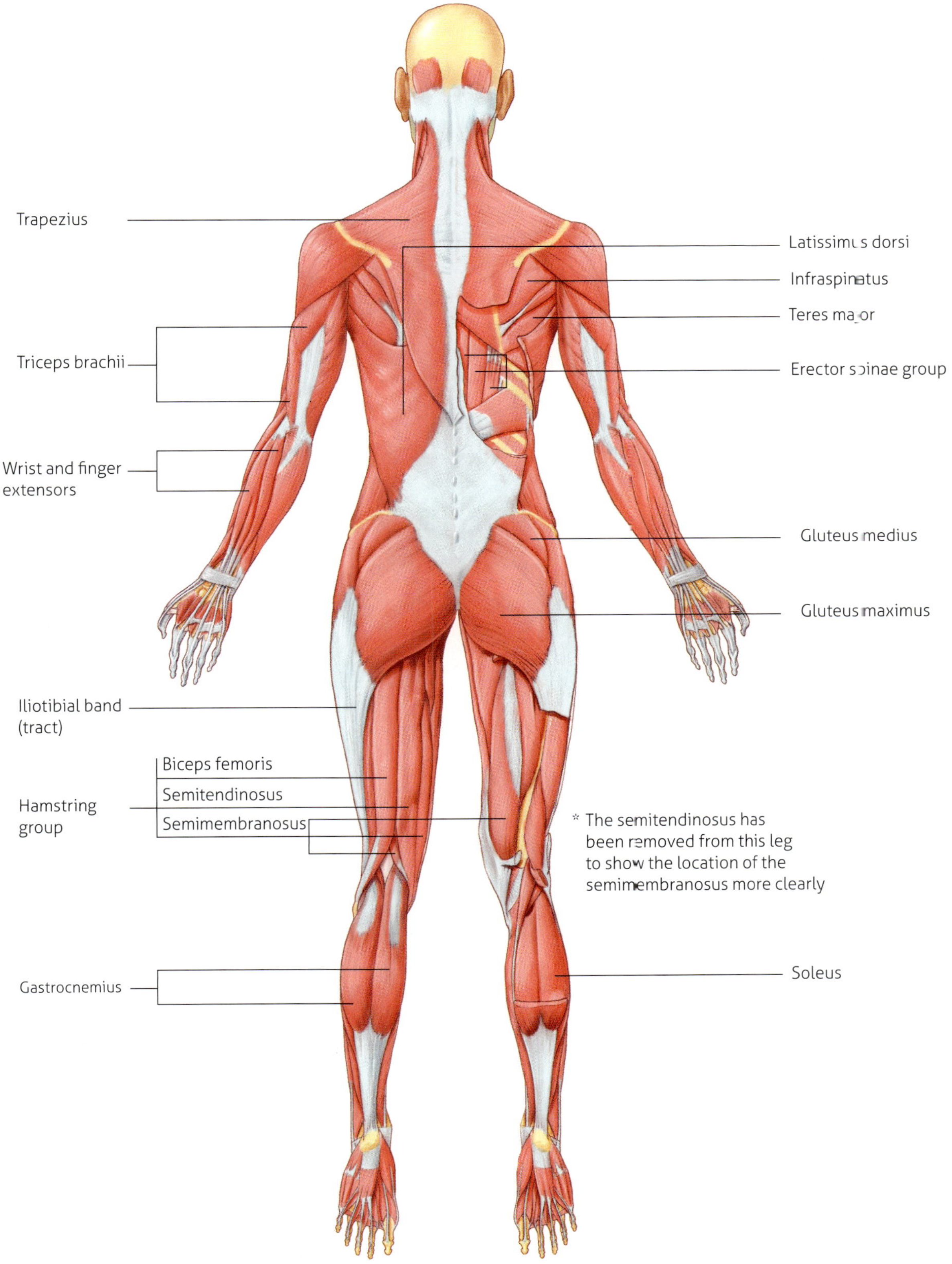

Major Bones of the Human Body

Anterior View of the Human Skeleton

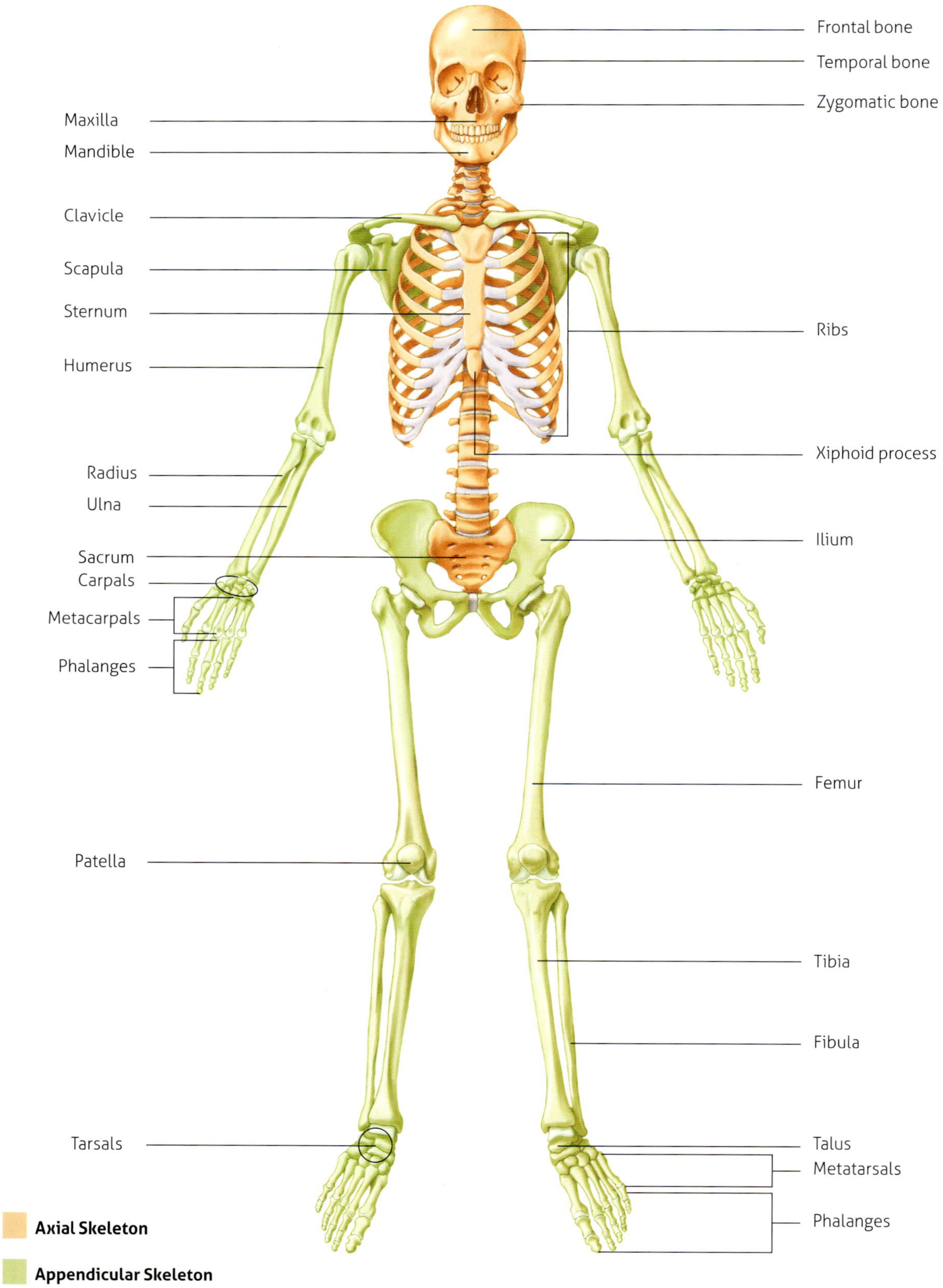

Posterior View of the Human Skeleton

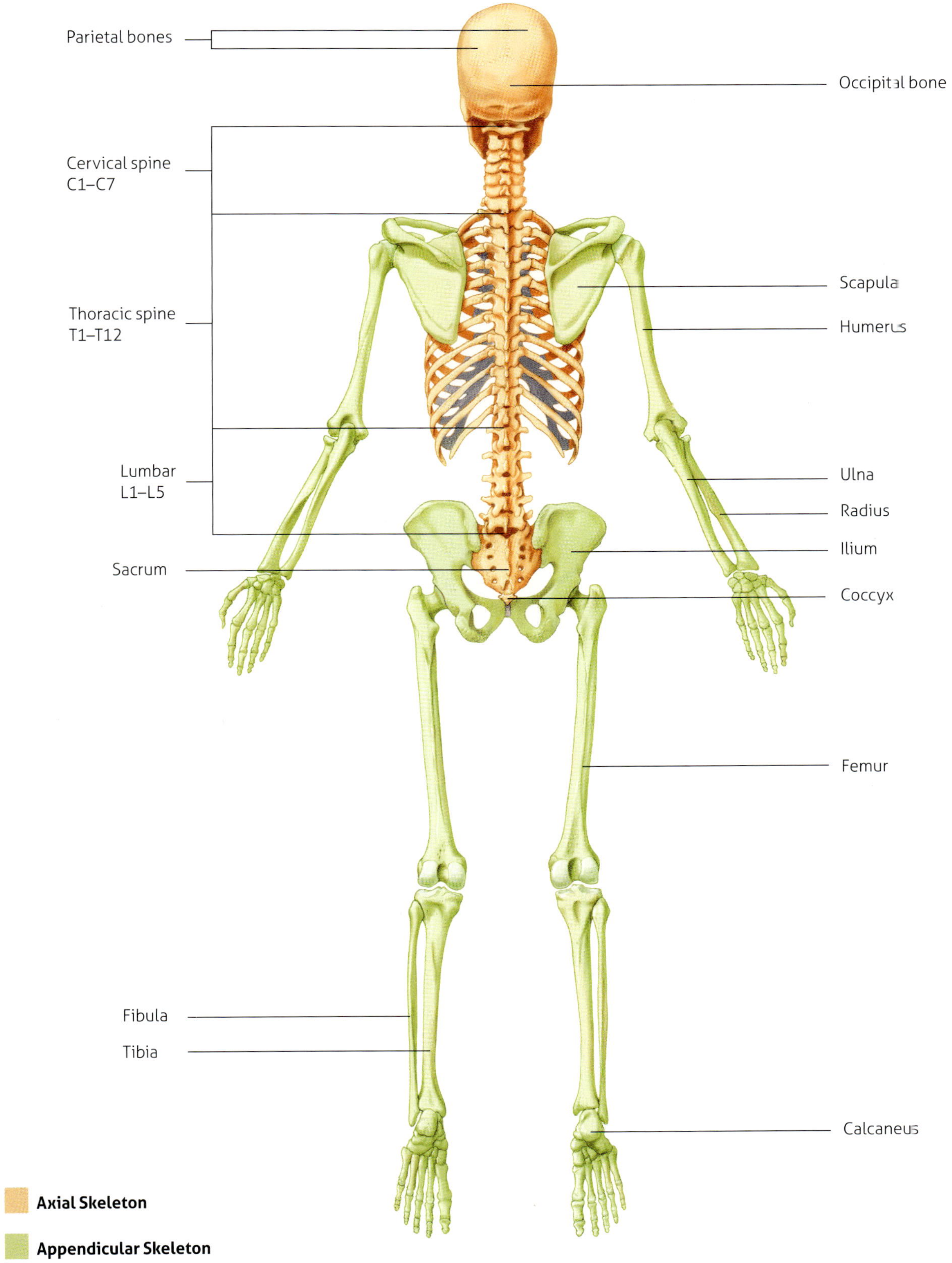

Movement Competence

2

Mike's Story

How can you develop and work toward your own personal level of movement competence?

Each of us has a movement competence journey, no matter what our ability level. Whether we are at work or at play, moving competently can improve our confidence, safety, and overall quality of life. The more movements we can perform competently, the greater the likelihood that we will follow an active lifestyle.

Moving well begins by simply becoming aware of the key features and fundamental patterns that underlie how we move as we perform activities, games, sports, and everyday tasks.

Breaking a movement into its component parts helps us assess and improve how we move. From an early age, we begin to observe that skills learned in one activity can transfer to other activities that involve similar movement patterns. Skills that are not specific to sports can be transferred to a sports context, and vice versa.

This transferability of skills means that you can engage more confidently and competently in a wide range of physical activities, games, and sports in many different environments.

Learning Objectives

In this chapter, you will...

- develop an understanding of how to improve your movement competence
- demonstrate an understanding of skill transferability
- demonstrate an understanding of the phases of movement skills while participating in a variety of physical activities
- apply appropriate movement principles to refine your skills in undertaking a variety of physical activities
- demonstrate and apply an understanding of the components of a range of physical activities
- identify and implement tactical solutions while participating in a variety of physical activities
- demonstrate an understanding of how applying movement concepts, skills, and strategies affects your competence, confidence, and desire to participate in physical activities

▶ **Mike Doherty** was in Grade 9 when he broke his neck in a diving accident. Despite the odds, his determination and the support of his teachers kept him enrolled in his high school physical education program. Today, Mike's movement competence is critical to his career as a firefighter and to his participation in Canada's challenging FireFit Championships.

Key Terms

- movement competence
- demands capacity framework
- the seven key movement features
- fundamental movement patterns
- skill
- deliberate practice
- phases of a movement skill
- skill transferability
- fundamental sports skills
- movement principles
- stability
- maximum effort
- joint range of motion
- Teaching Games for Understanding (TGfU)
- territory activities
- net/wall activities
- striking/fielding activities
- target activities
- individual activities
- outdoor activities

2.1 Why Movement Matters

Stop and ask yourself: "Why does movement matter to me? What physical activities are important to me? What does my typical day look like?"

You may recall from Chapter 1 that movement competence is an important component of physical literacy. **Movement competence** typically refers to *how* someone is moving—when we demonstrate movement competence, we move in a safe or effective manner, or both, in order to achieve the objective of the activity that we are performing.

Regardless of who we are or what activities we are involved in, how we move matters. It matters when we are participating in an activity or a sport, going about our daily routines, or performing a job-related task. Moving competently matters to everyone, everywhere, because we all want to perform well in whatever we do while remaining safe and free of injury.

Ultimately, when we reflect on why movement competence is so important, it comes down to one thing: *being able to do all the things we need or love to do so that we can enjoy life today and well into the future.*

What Influences How We Move?

How we move while performing any physical activity, whether that activity is something we need or want to do, is influenced by many factors—for example, our motivation, our abilities, and the environment. Movement is influenced by our characteristics as individuals and by everything around us. In other words, how we move depends on the context in which we are performing an activity. The factors that influence our movement patterns can be broadly categorized into three types:

Personal factors

Think about how and why you move as an individual while throwing a baseball. How you throw the ball will be influenced by many unique personal characteristics, including your physical attributes, fitness level, coordination, confidence, attitude, emotions, motivation, and awareness of both your body and your surroundings. For instance, factors such as limited shoulder range of motion, feeling exhausted after a late night, or playing baseball every summer for the past six years could all influence how you throw a ball.

Environmental factors

How you throw a baseball is also influenced by the environment you are in. For instance, the surface on which you are standing (e.g., grass versus pavement), the temperature (e.g., hot versus cold), weather conditions (e.g., rainy versus sunny), background sounds or music, verbal instructions from a coach, and the presence of social groups such as friends or peers could all influence how you throw the ball.

The task or activity

Lastly, features of the specific task or activity that you are performing will influence your movement. When you throw a baseball, task-related factors such as the size and weight of the ball or the type of pitch being thrown will influence how you move. Suppose you were throwing a boomerang instead of a baseball. This difference could clearly influence your throwing action.

When someone lifts a bag into an overhead compartment on a plane, various contextual factors affect the person's movement patterns. These factors include the person's size, strength, and fitness; the size, weight, and shape of the bag; and the temperature inside the cabin of the plane. Think of other examples of how your movement patterns are influenced by personal, environmental, or task-specific factors.

Daily Demands Differ

What demands are experienced by a person who enjoys an early morning bike ride, walk, or run before going to school or work each day? The terrain of the biking, walking, or running route imposes physical demands. Paying attention to traffic, pedestrians, and potholes would impose cognitive demands. Anxiety about completing the activity on time would represent an affective, or emotional, demand. Biking, walking, or running with friends and trying to match their pace would constitute a behavioural demand.

Balancing Our Demands and Capacity

How we move is central to balancing our capacity and demands. This perspective is known as the **demands capacity framework**. To perform at our best and maintain good health both today and in the future, we must have the capacity (e.g., the awareness, motivation, and ability) to handle the demands of our lives—the activities we need or want to perform on a daily basis.

For students, teachers, truck drivers, gardeners, athletes, grocery store clerks, and everyone else in our society, physical activity is a part of daily life. We all move differently as a result of the differing contextual factors just described. People working in a grocery store, for example, need to push carts and squat down to stock shelves. People working in a gardening store need to lift heavy bags of soil and carry trays of plants to customers' cars. Farmers need to push and pull equipment and machinery. Table tennis players need to lunge and rotate their shoulders, elbows, and wrists.

Regardless of what activities define your daily life, all the activities you want or need to do reflect your *demands*. *Capacity* is a term used to describe your confidence, motivation, strength, endurance, flexibility, and so on—in performing a physical activity safely and proficiently.

Broadly speaking, the physical activities we participate in each day—playing video games, biking, exercising, walking, carrying a backpack, and so on—all impose demands that will influence our safety and effectiveness. These demands might involve physical, cognitive, affective (emotional), or behavioural components, or a combination of these components.

Demands are the activities you **need** and **want** to perform safely and effectively.

Capacity is your **ability**, **awareness, motivation, etc.** to perform those activities safely and effectively.

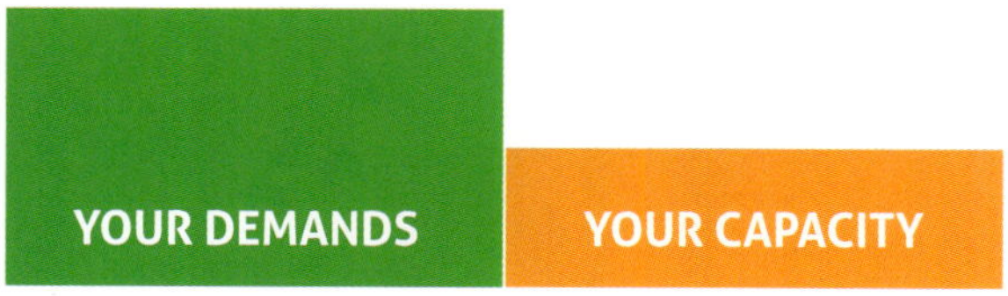

higher risk **lower benefit**

When your demands are greater than your capacity, the risk of musculoskeletal injury, cardiac distress, and respiratory distress **increases**, while your performance and your quality of life **decrease**.

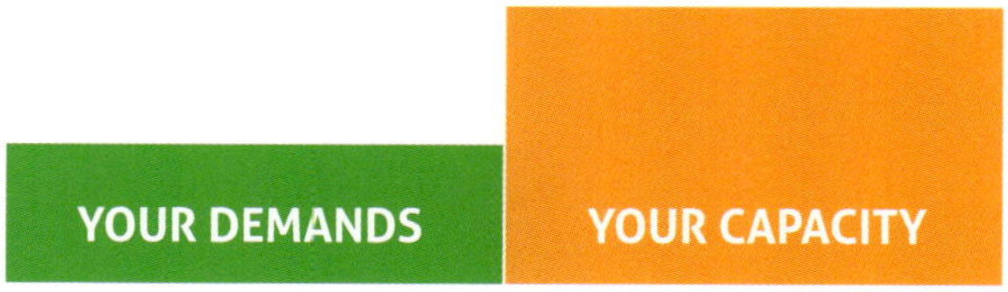

lower risk **higher benefit**

When your capacity is greater than your demands, however, the risk of musculoskeletal injury, cardiac distress, and respiratory distress **decreases**, while your performance and your quality of life **increase**.

Building capacity will improve our movement competence

It is well established that becoming a confident, competent mover will improve not only your performance but also your overall health. Everyone, regardless of age, skill level, ability, or interests, should strive to build the capacity to balance the demands of daily life—all the activities that we need or want to perform with relative proficiency and enjoyment.

This implies that if your capacity exceeds your demands, you will be able to perform anything you want or need to do safely and effectively. But what if your demands exceed your capacity—if you want or need to do more than you can handle—so that you cannot perform all of the activities that appeal to you?

For example, you might want to try paddleboarding but lack the range of motion, strength, or endurance to perform the required movements. Or maybe you have the required physical ability but lack the awareness to move in a safe or effective manner. If you were to attempt paddleboarding, the demands would exceed your capacity, and you would likely fail or hurt yourself.

It is important to remember, however, that failure is a vital part of success. Failure can help to highlight specific areas of our capacity that we need to improve so we can learn to perform all the activities that are important to us. The key is to view failure as a form of valuable feedback and not as a final result.

If your demands exceed your capacity, how can you respond? You might decide to figure out how to increase your capacity so you can move as required in order to paddleboard without falling off the board or injuring yourself. You need to have a level of challenge that *exceeds* your capacity in order to *improve* your capacity. This might mean setting a challenging goal for yourself and adopting a "can do" attitude, also known as a "growth mindset." You might realize that you need to be shown how to paddleboard by someone who is proficient at performing this activity and then to practise the required movements yourself.

Awareness can be a powerful first step toward increasing your capacity!

Section 2.1 Review

1. Give one example of a personal, environmental, and task-specific factor that will influence how you move while performing a chore, sport, or other activity.
2. Describe your demands—the physical activities you need or want to perform each day.
3. List two ways in which you could increase your capacity to handle your demands better.

2.2

2.2 Movement Features and Patterns

Regardless of your age, developmental stage, interests, or daily routine, you probably want to improve your physical performance in some areas for one reason or another. Your everyday physical activities might vary from hiking to playing sports, to regular chores such as washing dishes or doing laundry. Many of us want to progress from simple to more complex activities for a variety of reasons, and as the demands of daily life increase, we strive to increase our capacity to meet those demands.

Building our capacity to move competently begins with awareness. Have you ever thought about how you jump, run, walk up the stairs, get up off a chair, or perform other everyday activities? For instance, do you always bend at your back or your hips when you pick something up off the floor? Developing the awareness to assess your own movement can be sharpened by understanding a few key attributes or "movement features" that will be examined in this section.

The Seven Key Movement Features

As a first step in improving your movement competence, it is important to know which features of a movement pattern matter. When performing activities such as jumping for a rebound, lifting a backpack, or sitting in a chair while studying, which aspects of your movement will influence your performance, your susceptibility to injury, or your long-term health?

Paying attention to **the seven key movement features**, which are shown and described in detail on the following page, can help you build your capacity and enhance your overall quality of life.

Simply becoming aware of these key movement features could change your movement behaviours, alter your daily movement habits, and improve your enjoyment of life.

The **seven key movement features** are

1. Knees in line with the feet and hips
2. Body weight centred over mid-foot
3. Normal low back curvature (avoid rounding and arching)
4. Normal low back curvature (avoid bending sideways—the shoulders and hips remain parallel)
5. Shoulders and hips rotate together
6. Shoulders down and away from the ears
7. Shoulders back (elbow and shoulder move in the same direction)

Improving your performance and reducing injury risk

Integrating or "ingraining" the seven key movement features into your daily activities so that they become habits will go a long way to preventing injuries to your joints, bones, muscles, ligaments, and tendons.

Integrating the seven key features into your daily routines will also help you improve your performance.

These key movement features are relevant to everyone, everywhere. They provide a common framework that you, your friends, and your family can use to understand and improve your movement competence in ways that are meaningful to you. Take a look at the next page to see these seven key features in action.

Every time you lift an object from the ground, for example, the importance of the seven key features comes into play.

Movement Matters!

The Seven Key Movement Features

KNEES

1 In line

Knee in line with hip/foot

What to look for:

1. Body from the front
2. Line from hip to toes
3. Position of knee in relation to line
   - Medial to the line
   - **On the line**
   - Lateral to the line

Coaching tips:

- Grip the floor with the toes
- Push the knees out
- Point knees in direction of toes

2 Mid-foot

Body weight over mid-foot

What to look for:

1. Body from the side
2. Line through the middle of foot
3. Position of weight in relation to line
   - In front of the line (toes)
   - **On the line (arch)**
   - Behind the line (heel)

Coaching tips:

- Push through the floor
- Grip the floor with the toes
- Hinge at the hips, lean forward

LOWER BACK

3 & 4 Straight

Normal low back curve

What to look for:

1. Body from front, back, or side
2. Two lines through hips/upper back
3. Distance between the two lines
   - Closer than standing
   - **Same as standing**
   - Farther apart than standing

Coaching tips:

- Stiffen trunk
- Let trunk move with hips
- Dowel touches head, back, hips

5 Aligned

Hips and shoulders aligned

What to look for:

1. Body from front, back, or side
2. Two lines through hips/upper back
3. Alignment of the two lines
   - Shoulders rotate more than hips
   - **Shoulders in line with hips**
   - Hips rotate more than shoulders

Coaching tips:

- Use upper/lower body together
- Rotate with hips
- Practice with one hand

SHOULDERS

6 Down

Shoulders away from ears

What to look for:

1. Body from front, back, or side
2. Two lines through ears/shoulders
3. Distance between the two lines
   - Closer than standing
   - **Same as standing**
   - Farther apart than standing

Coaching tips:

- Elbows down/close to body
- Treat motions as push and pull
- Hold shoulders back

7 Back

Elbow and shoulder together

What to look for:

1. Body from front, back, or side
2. Line from shoulder to elbow
3. Movement at both ends of line
   - Move in opposite direction
   - **Move in same direction**
   - Only one end moves

Coaching tips:

- Rotate thumbs out when pulling
- Pull shoulder blades together
- Limit how far elbows are pulled back

Figure adapted with kind permission of Dr. David Frost.

Fundamental Movement Patterns

Have you ever wondered why some elite or professional athletes have enjoyed such long careers and have managed to avoid career-ending injuries, while others have not? Similarly, have you ever wondered why some of your adult role models have managed to stay fit, healthy, and injury-free, while others have experienced poor health or been hurt?

The answers to these questions are complex. However, one potential reason for many of the success stories you hear about is that these individuals are often very competent movers.

Learning to move better

The good news is that we can all learn to move better, regardless of our life's pursuits and current abilities. We can learn to move more competently at school, at home, at work, and at play. In order to become better movers, however, we need a way to categorize or describe the various recreational, sport-related, or work-related activities that we perform.

All human movement, no matter how complex, involves variations of general or **fundamental movement patterns**. These patterns are commonly listed as:

- push
- pull
- squat
- lunge
- hinge

These patterns can be used to describe and help us better understand activities that we perform daily, such as tying our shoes, lifting objects, and playing our favourite games and activities. We push or pull to open doors, and we squat or lunge to pick up objects from the floor. We hinge every time we bend at the waist.

By reading what follows, you will learn how these fundamental movement patterns give us a framework for describing, observing, and evaluating how we perform the complex skills involved in our sport-, work-, or life-related activities. Whether you wish to be an elite athlete or to perform everyday tasks safely and efficiently, learning how to perform these patterns properly—in particular, by maintaining the seven key features—will help you attain your goal.

The Benefits of Moving Well

People who move well know how to recruit their muscles to move their joints in a manner that reduces the incidence of injury and improves their performance. Moving well enables them to do the things they love to do in ways that are pain- and injury-free. Who among us doesn't want that?

Push

Push

A **push movement pattern** often involves moving an external object away from your body or pushing your body away from an object or surface, as in a push-up. Most descriptions of pushing as a fundamental movement pattern refer to the upper body only.

In performing a push pattern, however, actual movement is not always necessary. A front plank is a push pattern, for example, as is holding a picture up against a wall before hanging it.

The push-up is an effective exercise for improving core stability and upper-body pushing strength. Push-ups can strengthen the chest, shoulders, triceps, and abdominal muscles (see Chapter 4).

The push-up is also an excellent exercise for improving control of key feature number 3, which focuses on keeping your lower back straight and avoiding arching or rounding.

Properly performed pushing exercises require precise levels of motor control, functional strength, and body alignment that can be achieved through practice and repetition.

Pushing a small suitcase overhead to stow it away in a closet and pushing a grocery cart, lawnmower, snow shovel, or a snow blower are examples of pushing movements used in daily life.

Pushing tactics in football and rugby are examples of pushing movements used in sports. When an offensive lineman pushes against a defensive lineman to create space for a throwing or running play, the offensive lineman is using a push pattern.

Pull

A **pull movement pattern** is the opposite of a push movement pattern: generally, you pull an object toward your body, or pull your body toward an object. Like pushing, pulling is typically used to describe the upper body only.

As for pushing, movement is not necessary to use a pull movement pattern. Pulling is the act of contracting against a load or resistance. Hanging from monkey bars, performing an isometric biceps curl, and carrying groceries in both hands are all examples of a pull pattern.

A single-arm tubing row, shown here, is a variation of a pull pattern. This exercise can help improve control of key feature number 7—keeping the shoulders back and elbow and shoulder aligned in the same direction.

As everyday examples, we use a pull pattern when we lower window shades and pull open fridge doors. We use a pull pattern when kayaking, sailing, wind-surfing, and rock climbing. Shooting a bow and arrow involves both pushing and pulling patterns.

Squat

Squat

Frequently, a **squat movement pattern** requires lowering your body weight by bending your ankles and knees. A squat movement pattern is unique to the lower body compared to pushing and pulling.

Doing a squat exercise like the one shown here builds overall leg strength, especially in the muscles that affect the hips, knees, and ankles.

To perform a squat exercise properly, start by using your own body weight as resistance. You can then increase the level of difficulty by adding further resistance using dowelling, dumbbells, barbells, or kettlebells.

This exercise can help improve control of key feature number 2—body weight over mid-foot—to enhance performance and reduce risk of injury.

We use a squat pattern every time we get in and out of a car, sit down, and get up off a chair. Baseball catchers, wrestlers, and football players use a squat pattern when performing their sport-specific activities. Jumping for a rebound in basketball is a squat pattern, as are all two-foot jumps. Snowboarding, skateboarding, and surfing all involve a squat pattern.

Lunge

The **lunge movement pattern** generally involves one leg extended or bent in front of the body while the other leg is extended or bent behind the body. This pattern includes any form of gait: walking, running, skipping, and so on. Like the squat pattern, the lunge pattern is specific to the lower body.

You can do a lunge exercise in any direction—forward, backward, and sideways. The forward lunge exercise, shown here, is an excellent way to build strength in the muscles that affect the hips, knees, and ankles, depending on how it is performed. Safe and effective performance of a lunge exercise involves integrating and maintaining control of key feature number 1: keeping your knees in line with your hips and your feet.

Activities such as gardening, tying your shoelaces, and picking something up off the ground all involve the lunge pattern. Key feature number 1 is relevant here: whether you are running after a ball or cross-country skiing, your knees should always be in line with your hips and your feet.

Pitching in baseball, hitting a ball in cricket, and performing a dig in volleyball all require players to use a lunge pattern.

Hinge

The **hinge movement pattern** (also known as the "hip hinge pattern") describes any movement that involves flexion and extension of the hips. Ideally, the spine will be kept in a neutral position to prevent injury, maximize performance, or improve quality of life.

For example, a basic understanding and use of this pattern can help prevent lower back injuries when you are picking objects off the ground, going from a sitting position to a standing position, moving furniture, or even brushing your teeth. Think back to key features number 3 (no arching or rounding), number 4 (no lateral bend), and number 5 (no twisting).

The hip hinge is important for performance as well. It is the basis of the athletic-ready stance, it is critical to the vertical jump, and it is the dominant pattern in sports such as rowing. Track athletes also begin their race by adopting a hinge pattern to position themselves in the blocks. Baseball players hinge when accelerating forward to chase down a ground ball. Basketball players hinge when dribbling the ball to avoid defenders.

Section 2.2 Review

1. Why would you encourage someone to maintain the seven key features while performing daily activities?
2. Why is it helpful to categorize our activities by key feature and movement pattern?
3. Give an everyday example that involves each fundamental movement pattern.

Fundamental movement patterns are everywhere! This student is using a **pulling** and a **pushing** movement pattern to place his books into his locker.

2.3 Learning Movement Skills

How do we learn, and then refine or improve, our movement skills?

A **skill** is the ability we have developed to perform an activity well, especially because we have practised it. Learning a skill usually involves a gradual rather than an abrupt transition or change in the learner's performance.

The Stages of Learning a Skill

Whether in physical activities, sports, or any other area, experts such as teachers, coaches, and psychologists typically break down learning a skill into three stages:

1. **cognitive**—understanding the basics of the skill in question
2. **associative**—refining the skill by learning from your mistakes
3. **autonomic**—performing the skill as though it is almost automatic

These stages provide insight into what is involved in learning and improving skills. In real life, these stages are not separate and discrete; they overlap and often do not follow an exact progression.

Building skills, building proficiency

Let's apply these stages to the example of learning a tennis serve.

- **Cognitive stage.** Often we are shown (or we read about) what is involved in performing a proficient tennis serve, and then we try it out. Trying it out reinforces our understanding so that we form a general idea of what is involved in a tennis serve. This thinking process occurs in the early stages of developing any skill, from learning a gymnastics tumble to learning to play chess to playing a new piece on a musical instrument.
- **Associative stage.** Next, we practise the skill continuously, preferably with a mentor, coach, or teammate, until the technique has been learned. This can take a long time, depending on the level of complexity of the skill. This stage involves not only practice but also reinforcement and continuous rethinking. On the other hand, we sometimes end up learning a skill on our own though trial and error, exploring a range of movement solutions to achieve a specific task objective (in this case, putting the tennis ball in the square on the other side of the net).
- **Autonomic stage.** Finally, the skill begins to become almost automatic. At this stage, not a lot of conscious thought goes into performing the basic action itself, although other thoughts about speed and placement may come into play on the tennis court. The person is able to "just do" the skill. Many highly skilled tennis players in this final stage of learning can serve with great precision almost automatically.

It is important, however, to distinguish between "automatic" and "good." Simply because someone has rehearsed a particular skill for years does not always mean that they are proficient. Sometimes the movement skills that have been rehearsed are inefficient. This is why so many of us can develop "bad habits" when learning movement skills. Repeatedly performing a skill in an incorrect manner (because it has become automatic) can lead to injury and less-than-perfect performance.

This is where the seven key features and the fundamental movement patterns can play a beneficial role. They can help us correct incorrect practice by increasing our awareness of our own movement behaviours so we can make conscious improvements. Perfect practice makes perfect!

If you wanted to learn archery, what specific things would you need to learn, and how would you go about learning them? The skills required to be a proficient archer require the same stages of learning (cognitive, associative, and autonomic) described here, along with awareness, practice, and perseverance.

Types of Movement Skills

Many movement skills fall into one of three categories: stability (in this context, whole-body stability), locomotion, and manipulation:

- **Stability** skills involve the body balancing in one place (static balance; e.g., standing on a balance beam) or balancing in motion (dynamic balance; e.g., doing a rotation on the beam).
- **Locomotion** skills involve the body moving in any direction (e.g., walking, running, jumping, and hopping).
- **Manipulation** skills include throwing and catching skills or skills related to striking with the hands, the feet, or an implement (e.g., kicking, volleying, batting, and dribbling).

Refining your skills

Learning certain movement skills and becoming reasonably proficient at them do not happen without effort. To gain a level of proficiency means going through the stages of acquiring a skill at the pace that makes the most sense. Often, the key to success is practice and more practice.

Depending on the skill, the learning process will take time. Maximizing how that time is used lies behind the notion of **deliberate practice**.

- Deliberate practice is purposeful and systematic.
- It involves focused attention and having a specific goal of improvement in mind.
- Deliberate practice is mindful repetition.
- It involves constant feedback, thinking, and reflection about how to improve.

Again, this is where the seven key features can play a helpful role. For example, using key feature number 1 (knees in line with hips and feet) can prevent the knees from collapsing when a jump is performed.

No one truly knows the influence of human genetics on performance. What we do know for sure is that genes do not entirely determine performance. It is similar to being dealt a hand while playing cards. You will have a stronger chance if you happen to be dealt a better hand, but you also need to play the hand well to win. Deliberate practice is about learning to play well with whatever "innate talents" you may have.

It would be difficult to find anyone who has achieved a level of skill proficiency in any field who has not put in the time. Wayne Gretzky, Canada's most famous hockey player, freely acknowledges that he was not naturally gifted in terms of size and speed. He has said that everything he did in hockey he worked hard to achieve. As he put it, "the only way a kid is going to practise is if it's total fun...and it was for me."

Ultimate is just one example of a game that involves moving from stability to instability, to locomotion, and to manipulation all at once.

The importance of feedback and support

In many cases, you cannot learn a skill entirely on your own; at least, it will be more difficult to do so. You often need feedback and support from your classmates and from your teacher or coach. This is especially true when learning skills related to physical activities, games, and sports.

Teachers and coaches have vast experience that they can share with you. They know how to break a skill down into its component parts (key features, patterns, and/or phases, if applicable), how to help you improve your movement competence, and how to help you stay motivated.

There are also technological tools at your disposal to provide feedback. Slow-motion video, for example, is relatively inexpensive yet sophisticated. You can record yourself or a friend performing a skill and analyze your movement to see what is going well or not so well. Knowing what to look for—starting with the key features—and having a strong support network make learning with such tools easier and more fun.

Teachers and coaches are there to support your goals, assess your skill development, and help you stay motivated.

The Phases of Performing a Skill

Not all movement skills can be broken down into distinct phases. Riding a bicycle and brushing your teeth are but two examples. However, breaking a discrete movement skill such as throwing or kicking into its various phases is a useful way to identify your strengths and weaknesses with a view to further improvement. Teachers and coaches do this all the time.

A teacher or coach will focus on how a student performs during each phase of a skill, identify strengths and weaknesses, and offer advice as to what the student can do to execute that phase more effectively.

The four **phases of a movement skill** are usually identified as:

- the preparation phase
- the force production phase
- the critical instant phase
- the recovery and follow-through phase

Let's briefly look at each phase in turn, continuing with the tennis serve as well as a few other examples.

The preparation phase

The preparation phase involves getting a secure footing and a firm grip on the racquet, then beginning to bring the joints and muscles into action. The quadriceps and gluteal muscles of the hip and thigh play an important role in generating power on the serve, as does the swinging of the racquet. "Winding up" is another term for the preparation phase in tennis.

The force production phase

Power on the tennis serve is produced from the hips, legs, shoulder, elbow, and wrist action occurring in a well-coordinated sequence. Uncoiling the various positions reached in the preparation stage and timing them accurately are the keys to a powerful serve.

The critical instant phase

In a tennis serve, the "critical instant" is when the entire wrist finally snaps into play and the tennis ball is struck—all the momentum built up in the swing is transferred to the tennis ball at that point. In a jump shot in basketball, the critical instant is when the ball finally leaves the fingers. For a slap-shot in hockey, the critical instant is the moment when the hockey stick makes contact with the puck.

The recovery and follow-through phase

Typically, experienced tennis players will have both feet off the ground when they finally strike the ball on the serve. Finishing the serving motion, landing, and then regaining balance are important aspects of the recovery and follow-though phase. Coaches and teachers will be alert to this phase, providing advice to ensure that their player is ready for the return shot.

Movement Skill Transferability

Many people seem able to acquire a new movement skill almost naturally. More often than not, this is because they have built on the component parts of a skill—key features along with fundamental movement patterns—that then transfer readily to a similar skill. For example, a skill they have learned that relies on a squat pattern may be relevant in the context of another activity. Therefore, rehearsing the first skill repeatedly may also influence the performance of the second skill.

Skill transferability can occur when activities involve similar fundamental movement patterns and key features. For example, the pushing, pulling, and lunging movement patterns used in snowshoeing and cross-country skiing are quite similar to each other. Both activities also involve controlling the position of the knees in relation to the hips and feet (key feature number 1). Thus, the skills involved in these two activities are likely to be transferable.

Skill transferability is more likely to take place across activities of a similar nature, such as the net games of volleyball and tennis. The tennis serve and the volleyball overhand serve are different, but there are obvious similarities. Ice hockey and field hockey are also quite different, but they are similar in many respects.

The fundamental movement patterns (push, pull, squat, lunge, and hinge) prepare us to perform other activities that involve these patterns. These fundamental movement patterns are the component parts of all the movement skills that we will perform in sports and in other contexts.

Experiencing a variety of fundamental movement patterns is especially important in the younger years, but we can benefit from such experience at any stage of our lives.

You can see skill transferability in action when you compare, for example, a volleyball serve to a tennis serve or snowshoeing to cross-country skiing.

Fundamental Sports Skills

Sport for Life has identified a series of **fundamental sports skills** that they believe are important to learn, especially in the early years. The hope is that once a certain level of competence has been established the following skills become transferable:

- throwing
- catching
- striking
- running
- jumping
- kicking
- agility, balance, and coordination ("ABCs")

Being competent in these skills may help to facilitate your ability to participate in a wide range of sports and activities. Gaining proficiency in performing these skills is part of becoming an all-round, competent mover.

Sport for Life has created a list of suggested sports and activities that showcase skill transferability. Can you think of others?

If you can ▶ **run** you might enjoy ▶ sepak takraw, soccer, basketball, volleyball, track & field, squash, rugby, badminton, tennis, cricket

If you can ▶ **throw** you might enjoy ▶ baseball, softball, bowling, soccer, goalball, football, rugby, tchoukball

If you can ▶ **swim** you might enjoy ▶ swimming, diving, water polo, scuba diving, kayaking, sailing, surfing

If you can ▶ **wheel** you might enjoy ▶ bocce, basketball, rugby, racing, power soccer, curling, tennis

Building Personal Confidence

Personal confidence is an important part of tackling new skills of any kind. Some people find that competence in one skill can increase their confidence in trying to learn a related skill or an entirely new one.

Personal confidence comes from knowing how to do something reasonably well—something to build on, as it were. Once you have gained a degree of proficiency in a particular skill, you may find that you feel confident enough to go on to learn other skills and perhaps help classmates, friends, or family members learn those skills as well.

Consider the following example. The physical ability to throw an effective underhand pitch in softball may not directly transfer to performing a jump-shot in basketball. Nevertheless, the confidence that comes from being able to throw an underhand pitch might give you the confidence to approach the task of learning a jump-shot and becoming proficient at it.

On the other hand, some people have all the confidence in the world but lack competence. Confidence can sometimes actually impede the development of competence. This accounts for why people get hurt on occasion while exercising or playing sports. Conversely, some people have developed a lot of competence but lack the motivation or the confidence in their abilities to engage in a sport, game, or activity—perhaps because they were told at an early age that they were not good enough.

Confidence and competence emerge by focusing on the things that really matter—starting with key features and fundamental movement patterns.

Section 2.3 Review

1. What are the three stages of skill acquisition? Describe each stage with reference to learning a new movement skill.
2. Watch a classmate perform a sport skill. Analyze your classmate's movement during each phase of the skill.
3. Give an example of a movement skill (sport or otherwise) that can readily transfer to a different activity.

Acquiring any skill, from the least to most complex, may give you the confidence to tackle acquiring new ones.

2.4 Movement Principles

How can you become a more competent mover? To answer this question, let's review what you have learned so far.

- You have looked at the concepts of demands and capacity in order to provide the context for why movement matters to you. Demands tell us what our lives look like, and capacity tells us whether we have the ability, motivation, awareness, and so on to perform activities safely and effectively.
- You have learned about observing and assessing your own and other people's movements in terms of seven key features and movement patterns.

This section describes three **movement principles** that you can apply to improve the way you move. Knowing about and applying these principles can help you build your movement competence in various contexts—daily life, school, sports, or work—depending on your current capacity and place on your physical literacy journey.

Before looking at the three movement principles, let's start with a few general recommendations.

Improvement is all about focus

Improving our movement competence involves exploration and figuring things out—giving ourselves opportunities to feel what it is like to experience movement that is proficient, fun, and enjoyable. We can get better at movement through exposure to a wide variety of experiences and trying out different ways of moving. However, we can also develop some bad habits, such as rounding or arching our backs when lifting.

Here are some recommendations for reinforcing the seven key features and building a "movement library" that can be applied to any number of activities in sport, work, or life.

- It is important to challenge yourself—but start slowly. Begin with small steps and progress gradually toward your goals.
- Focus on movements, not muscles. Develop an appreciation for how a movement looks before thinking about the muscles involved. Which muscles are involved will depend on how the movement is performed.
- Always link your movements back to the seven key features and fundamental movement patterns. Check to see whether you are maintaining the relevant key features every time you move.
- Train with a purpose. Focus on what you really want to do. Revisit the demands that life places on you, and train not just for the sake of training, but with those specific demands in mind.
- Improve the transfer of movement skills by emphasizing the seven key features. Keep going back to those basics and keep it simple. Become aware of the seven key features in everything you do so they become a habit.
- Focus on the process and cultivating enjoyment while developing physical literacy. Ultimately, it is all about having fun!

While there are a number of movement principles that shape the way we move, knowing what to look for—the seven key features, for example—is a great place to start. Remember that it is important to keep your attention focused first and foremost on what you look like when you move and on the factors that influence how you move. In addition to the person, the environment, and the task, these factors always include the seven key features.

Movement Principles

Principle 1: Stability increases as the centre of gravity becomes lower, the base of support becomes larger, the line of gravity moves nearer to the centre of the base of support, and the mass becomes greater.

Maintaining Stability

Stability, in the context of physical activity, refers to one's body being in a state of balance. Even walking requires stability. We all need to maintain and control our balance, or whole-body stability, to perform tasks and participate in physical activities and sports.

Among other things, stability depends on these four factors:

- **Mass:** the quantity of matter contained within an object or body
- **Centre of mass:** an imaginary point around which an individual's mass is concentrated. (When we stand upright with our arms hanging at our sides, our centre of mass is located in the middle of our bodies at about the level of the navel.)
- **Base of support:** the supporting area beneath an object or body
- **Position of the centre of mass:** a position relative to the base of support as defined by the line of gravity—an imaginary vertical line that passes through the centre of mass to the ground

In general, whole-body stability increases when *mass* increases, because the more mass an individual has, the greater the resistance to going from a state of rest to a state of motion, or from a state of motion to a state of rest. This accounts for the large amounts of *mass* that often characterize the bodies of wrestlers and offensive and defensive linemen in football.

When lining up prior to the snap of the football, linemen crouch to lower their *centre of mass*. This makes the linemen more stable and better able to stand their ground when they are blocked or contacted by oncoming opponents. The *stability* of the linemen is also enhanced when they broaden their *base of support* by crouching down and putting one hand in contact with the ground. This is called a three-point stance.

Stability and instability work together

Lowering the *centre of mass* and keeping it within the *base of support* improves the chances that a wrestler will be stable when contacted by an opponent. If the position of the *centre of mass* moves outside the *base of support*, however, it becomes much easier for an opponent to knock the wrestler off balance.

Stability and instability affect how dancers, surfers, gymnasts, skateboarders, cyclists, circus performers, skaters, and many others move.

Here are two examples.

- **Surfing.** A surfer will be most stable when she bends her knees, crouches low, and keeps her feet wide apart, thus lowering her centre of mass while producing a stable base of support for herself.

  If the position of the surfer's centre of mass moves, or is moved, outside the base of support, the surfer will find herself in an unstable position. Even a slight shift in the position of the surfer's centre of mass will cause the surfer to fall off the board.

- **Cross-country skiing or sit-skiing.** If you are cross-country skiing or sit-skiing, you need to work constantly to maintain your balance. As you change speed, turn, and react to the unevenness of the ground, you have to absorb a variety of forces and redistribute your body weight. The most important factor to consider is the effect of your body's centre of gravity on your stability.

  When cross-country skiing, keep your knees slightly bent and your centre of gravity as low as possible and directly above your point of contact with the ground. Otherwise, you will lose your balance and take a spill!

When this surfer needs to gain or regain her balance, lowering her body's centre of mass over a wide base of support helps to increase stability as she rides the waves.

Types of Movement at Joints

The other two movement principles you will learn about involve joint movements. Movements at joints can be described in terms of the types of actions involved. Some of these terms—for example, flexion and extension—have become part of our normal English vocabulary. Other terms are more technical and are used mainly by teachers, coaches, and exercise professionals. Some of the more common terms used when describing movement at joints are explained below.

Flexion/extension

- **Flexion** is the action of bending at a joint such that the joint angle decreases. An example of flexion is when you bend your elbow to bring your palm up toward your face.
- **Extension** is the opposite of flexion. It occurs when you increase the joint angle. When you straighten your arm from the flexed position, you are extending your arm.

Abduction/adduction

- **Abduction** occurs when you move a body segment to the side and away from your body. An example of abduction is when you move your arm out to the side and bring it level with your shoulder.
- **Adduction** is the opposite of abduction and occurs when you move a body segment toward your body. You adduct your arm when you bring it back down to your side.

Supination/pronation

- **Supination** is rotating the wrist such that the palm of your hand is facing forward. When you catch a softball underhanded with one hand, you must supinate your wrist.
- **Pronation** occurs in the opposite direction of supination. When you dribble a basketball, you first have to pronate your wrist.

Dorsiflexion/plantar flexion

- **Plantar flexion** is also specific to the ankle joint. It occurs when you point your toes.
- **Dorsiflexion** occurs when you bend at the ankle to bring the top of your foot closer to your shin. It is essential when walking or jumping.

Inversion/Eversion

- **Inversion** is a result of standing on the outer edge of your foot. It is normally what happens when you twist your ankle.
- **Eversion** also is associated with the ankle joint. Eversion is a result of standing on the inner edge of your foot.

Internal rotation/external rotation

- **External rotation** results when you twist or turn a body part outward from the midline, for example when you turn your toes outward.
- **Internal rotation** results when you twist or turn a body part inward toward the midline, for example when you turn your toes inward.

Circumduction

- **Circumduction** is a combination of flexion, extension, abduction, and adduction all wrapped up into one movement. An example of this occurs in softball, when a pitcher throws the ball with a windmill action.

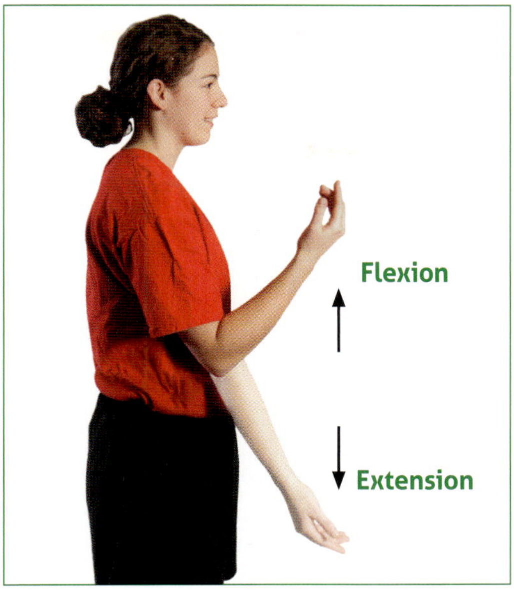
Flexion
Extension

Abduction
Adduction

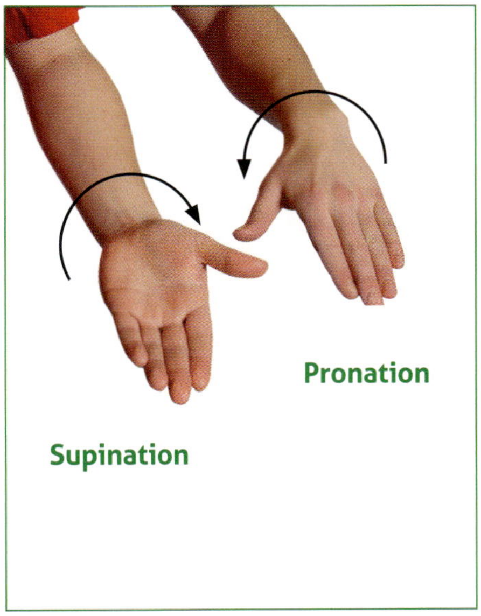
Pronation
Supination

Dorsiflexion
Plantar flexion

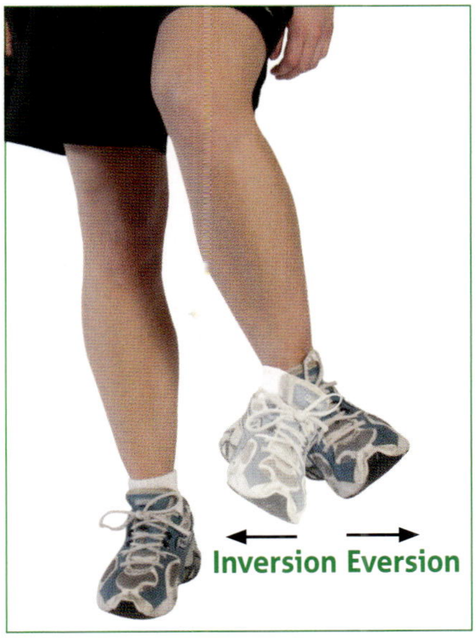
Inversion Eversion

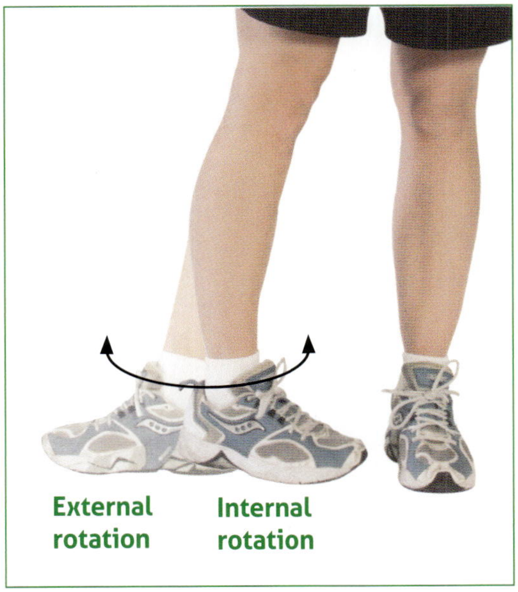
External rotation
Internal rotation

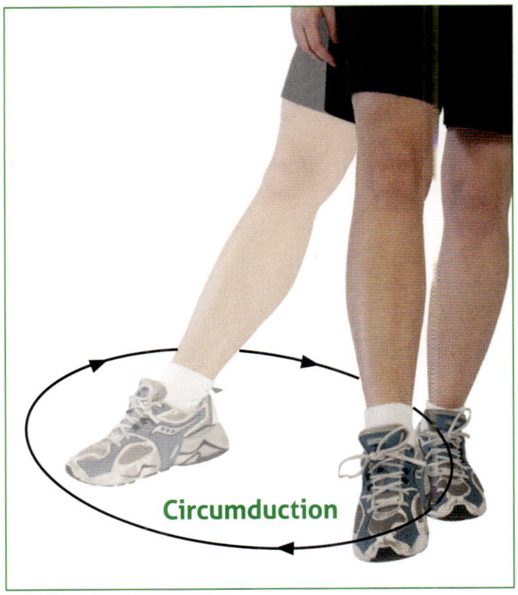
Circumduction

Movement Principles

Principle 2: The production of maximum force requires the use of all the joints that can be used.

Principle 3: The production of maximum velocity requires the use of joints in order—from largest to smallest.

Maximizing Effort

Muscles pull. They cannot push. Movement occurs because skeletal muscles cross over joints, the junction where long bones meet, creating lever mechanisms. These levers work just like any other mechanical lever, creating a "mechanical advantage" (leverage). It is these levers at joints that facilitate human movement.

Maximum effort requires that all the joints that can be engaged in a movement are used in performing that movement **(principle 2)** and that they are used in order from largest to smallest **(principle 3).**

Joint range of motion

The most common type of joint in the body is the synovial joint. This is the type of joint that allows the most movement. Typical synovial joints are the knee, the shoulder, and the ankle.

If the muscles and tendons around a synovial joint are injured (say, by inflammation) or if the joint is injured (say, by cartilage damage), **joint range of motion** is impaired. If the joint's range of motion is restricted, full movement cannot occur.

High levels of physical force are generated at joints, and they are highly susceptible to injury. The leverage produced is a product of the length of the lever arm (the moveable bone), the angle of the muscle attached to the bone, and the strength of the muscle itself.

A complex movement (for example, riding a bike) involves a combination of movements involving several joints. To ensure a smooth and efficient movement and to achieve maximum effort, all the joints that affect the completion of that movement must be engaged, and ideally these joints must be in good working order with a full range of motion.

The javelin throw is an excellent example of maximum effort and range of motion. Here we see an athlete in the IAAF World Junior Championships that took place in Moncton, New Brunswick, in 2010.

Sequencing joint movements from largest to smallest (principle 3)

The third movement principle states that maximum velocity is achieved not only by using all the joints available but also by sequencing them in the right order, normally from largest to smallest.

Let's look at a few examples in a little more detail to gain a better understanding of how this movement principle works.

- **Baseball.** When a baseball is released by a pitcher, the ball has a certain velocity. The sequencing of joint movements from largest to smallest (from legs, hips, and shoulder to elbow, wrist, and fingers) will increase the ball's velocity as it leaves the pitcher's hand. More coordinated sequencing of all the muscles involved in throwing the ball will therefore result in a faster pitch.
- **Weightlifting.** Let's now consider Olympic weightlifting. The weight itself has a certain amount of *inertia* (the resistance of an object to any change in its state of motion). The weightlifter has to overcome this inertia in order to lift the weight. Poor technique (resulting from not using all the available joints or not sequencing them properly from largest to smallest) will mean that the lifter will not be able to produce enough effort to lift the weight. Being able to sequence joint movements so as to maximize effort will go a long way to helping the weightlifter overcome the inertia and lift the weight.
- **Bobsledding.** In Olympic bobsledding, the riders run alongside the sled, keeping their upper bodies stiff as they push with all their strength and weight against the sled before jumping on board. The better the pushing technique (the more they can engage their largest joints and then the smallest ones), the more forces generated by their lower bodies can be transferred to the sled. This transfer of forces will result in the sled gaining velocity as it starts its way down the hill.

If a joint's range of motion is impaired, the full execution of the movement will be restricted, and maximum effort will not be achieved. Likewise, proper sequencing of joint movements, which improves with experience and practice, plays a critical role in allowing you to exert maximum effort in the execution of a movement.

Section 2.4 Review

1 Describe one way in which our need to balance could influence the way we move.

2 In trying to jump as high as possible, why would the range of motion and sequencing of your hips, knees, and ankles matter?

3 Describe one way in which each movement principle in Section 2.4 influences how you move.

2.5

2.5 Game Strategies and Tactics

This section looks at the components of a wide range of physical activities that take place in both indoor and outdoor environments. It describes some basic strategies and tactics that you can apply to enhance your movement competence, performance, and enjoyment if you choose to try these activities on your own or with friends.

An approach called **Teaching Games for Understanding (TGfU)** is based on the concept of teaching games—by actually *playing* games! Instead of learning isolated, sport-specific technical skills (related to volleyball or soccer, for example), you gain skills and knowledge that you can apply to different activities and sports by playing a variety of games associated with six different categories.

By offering choice and flexibility in how you and your friends practise and demonstrate movement skills, the **TGfU** approach aims to provide the best possible chance for the greatest number of participants to succeed.

Game and Activity Categories

The first four categories shown below represent games and activities that are similar in structure. If you learn the rules, basic strategies, and tactical solutions associated with one or more of these categories, you can participate in a wider range of games, activities, and sports of your choice. Your knowledge and skills will transfer from one activity to another within a particular category. For example, learning a tactic such as getting and retaining possession of an object can transfer to and from lacrosse, soccer, handball, water polo, and wheelchair basketball.

- In **territory activities**, participants invade an opponent's territory to score.
- In **net/wall activities**, a participant propels an object into space and tries to prevent an opponent from returning it.
- In **striking/fielding activities**, the participant strikes an object to remove it from defenders in the field.
- In **target activities**, a participant propels an object, preferably with a high degree of accuracy, at a target.
- In **individual activities** and **outdoor activities**, participants who are not drawn to team sports can develop fitness and movement skills related to control of body rhythm, movement aesthetics, creativity, sequencing, and stability, either individually or with others.

TERRITORY ACTIVITIES	NET/WALL ACTIVITIES	STRIKING/ FIELDING	TARGET ACTIVITIES	INDIVIDUAL ACTIVITIES	OUTDOOR ACTIVITIES
Basketball	Badminton	Baseball	Archery	Aquatics	BMX biking
Handball	Pickleball	Choctaw stickball	Bocce	Athletics	Camping
Hockey	Sepak takraw	Cricket	Bowling	Dance	Orienteering
Lacrosse	Squash	Kickball	Curling	Gymnastics	Skateboarding
Soccer	Table Tennis	Softball	Darts	Judo	Skiing
Tchoukball	Tennis		Golf	Karate	Snowshoeing
Water polo	Volleyball		Horseshoes	Taekwondo	
Wheelchair basketball	Wheelchair volleyball		Shuffleboard	Yoga	

TERRITORY ACTIVITIES

Basketball

Handball

Hockey

Lacrosse

Soccer

Tchoukball

Water polo

Wheelchair basketball

Territory Activities

Territory activities are some of the most common games that we play. They include sports such as soccer, basketball, ultimate, ice hockey, field hockey, rugby, football, and lacrosse, just to mention a few. When Canadian-American Dr. James Naismith invented basketball in 1891, he did so by using his knowledge of various other territory games.

Territory games require many different types of manipulation skills. Players must be able to send objects away (throw an ultimate disc), receive objects (trap a soccer ball), and travel with objects (stick handle a field hockey ball) with accuracy to be successful. Many of the basic strategies and skills that are used during territory activities are very similar to each other—for example, carrying the ball, passing the ball to a teammate, and moving to an open space.

If you understand the basic rules, skills, and tactics of territory activities, it will make you better at the territory activities that you already play. It will also help you learn to play new territory games more quickly, as many of the skills and activities can be transferred from one game to another.

Basic strategies and tactics

Within territory activities, there are *three basic tactical problems* when your team is on *offence* (in possession of the object) and *three basic tactical problems* when your team is on *defence* (when the other team has possession of the object).

While *on offence*, teams are trying to

- maintain possession of the object;
- create space on the playing area; and
- attack the goal in order to score points.

Conversely, teams *on defence* are trying to

- regain possession of the object;
- defend space on the playing area; and
- defend the goal in order to prevent the other team from scoring.

Solutions to these tactical problems are very similar across the different territory activities. For example, a player with the object might **1)** try to shield it away from defenders, **2)** try to deke out opponents by moving around them, or **3)** make a short pass to a teammate who is not defended by an opponent. Offensive teammates who do not have the object can provide support by **1)** moving to an open space and **2)** communicating to the player who has possession of the object ("I'm open," "Shoot," "Pass").

These solutions to the tactical problem of maintaining possession apply to almost every type of territory activity. If you understand the basic skills and the importance of providing support to your teammates in one sport, you will be a better player across all territory activities.

Here we see how a player attacks the goal in tchoukball, a territory team sport.

NET/WALL ACTIVITIES

Badminton

Pickleball

Sepak takraw

Squash

Table Tennis

Tennis

Volleyball

Wheelchair volleyball

Net/Wall Activities

Net/wall activities are popular activities that include sports such as volleyball, badminton, tennis, table tennis, squash, racquetball, wall ball, and handball. For competition or recreation—from sandy beach volleyball, to outdoor tennis, to the local squash club—opportunities to take part in these sports are everywhere.

In all net/wall activities, players attempt to hit a ball or object over the net or against the wall in such a way that it cannot be returned by the opposing player. The basic tactical problems and their solutions remain similar.

Net/wall games can be played either as a singles game or as a team game. In some net/wall activities (tennis, squash, racquetball), the ball is allowed to bounce once on the playing surface before it is returned. In others (volleyball, badminton, sepak takraw [or kick volleyball]), players try to prevent the ball or object from landing in their court.

The advantage of having a basic understanding of the *strategies* and *tactics* involved in one net/wall game is that many are common among all such games.

Basic strategies and tactics

To be successful in net/wall games, players and teams must be able to send an object over a net or against a wall into the open space. They must also be able to prevent their opposition from putting the object into the open space on their court.

- The fast-paced nature of net/wall games means that players need to use advanced sending-away skills. In addition to the initial contact with the ball or object (the serve), players must also be prepared to hit a fast-moving object from an opposing player (the return).
- Players use tactical skills (such as bumping, the overhand smash, the forehand, the lob, and the spike) to return objects. Players must also combine locomotor skills (such as running, jumping, diving, and blocking) with sending-away skills.
- Players soon realize that there are areas on the court from which it is difficult to return a shot. These areas include the sidelines, corners, spaces between players, and the front and back of the court.
- Players can use different tactics to exploit these areas. For example, a tennis player may use a drop shot to bring an opponent close to the net, which creates space at the back of the court. If the opponent is able to return the drop shot, the first player can then lob over the player so that the ball lands at the back of the court where the space was created.

Volleyball is a fun team activity that can be played either indoors or outdoors.

STRIKING/ FIELDING

Baseball

Choctaw stickball

Cricket

Kickball

Softball

Striking/Fielding Activities

Striking/fielding activities such as baseball and cricket have become synonymous with many cultures around the world. Baseball, for example, is one of the most popular sports in North America. Similar games (stickball, slow-pitch, softball, and fastball) emerged in North America because of baseball's popularity. Although gaining popularity here, cricket tends to be the dominant striking/fielding game in countries such as England, Kenya, India, Pakistan, and Australia.

In striking/fielding games, a player on the defensive team delivers the ball to a player on the batting (or offensive) team. The batter attempts to strike the ball and score by running between safe areas (bases and wickets) without the ball being caught or by reaching the safe area before the defensive team can deliver the ball to a specified area.

Although striking/fielding games are played around the world, they are all bound by many common rules, skills, and tactics that, if understood, can allow us to play them all successfully.

Basic strategies and tactics

In addition to proficient locomotor skills such as running, sliding, and jumping, players must be able to send away objects and receive objects with proficiency when at bat and when in the field. Offensive players must be able to strike a moving ball.

- Defensive players such as the pitcher or the bowler will make hitting the ball difficult for the batter by throwing it quickly, changing its speed (a fast pitch followed by a slower pitch), changing its location (close to the ground, close to the batter, away from the batter), or changing its flight pattern (in baseball, a curve ball compared to a fastball).
- To score runs in striking/fielding games, players must be able to hit the ball into the open space and away from fielders. To prevent the batting team from scoring, fielders attempt to cover as much space as possible. Ultimately, fielders try to position themselves so that they are able to catch the ball in the air.
- When a ball does hit the ground, fielders must decide on where to throw the ball. In baseball, for example, sometimes this is an easy decision (no base runners, throw to first base). At other times, they may have to decide whether to attempt a difficult throw to get the lead runner out (and prevent a run being scored) or make an easier throw to a different base to help ensure an out.
- On balls hit deep into the outfield, fielders must try to support each other by either backing up a teammate when they are attempting to field a ball or by providing a "cut-off point."

From little league to major league, baseball's popularity is undisputed.

TARGET ACTIVITIES

Archery

Bocce

Bowling

Curling

Darts

Golf

Horseshoes

Shuffleboard

Target Activities

Target activities—for example, bowling and golf—are among the most well-known sporting activities. Other well-known target games include archery, billiards, bocce, croquet, curling, darts, horseshoe pitching, lawn bowling, and shuffleboard.

In all target games, players score points by projecting an object with accuracy toward a target (for example, rolling a bowling ball toward bowling pins). Out of the various activity categories, target games have the least simultaneously occurring action. Players can often focus on making their shots without having to worry about interference by opponents (as in territory activities) or having to collect or return a moving object (as in net/wall and striking/fielding games).

This is not to say that target activities are easy to play. Anyone who has played or watched golf knows that it is not easy to hit a golf ball so that it avoids obstacles (trees, water, and sand traps) and eventually ends up in a hole that measures just under 11 cm.

Not only do target activities require a high degree of skill, but they also challenge players to make good decisions when planning their shots. Many skills learned by playing target activities can also be useful in other sports and activities.

Basic strategies and tactics

Target activities require players to send an object away with a high degree of accuracy. Players can do so with their hand (e.g., deliver a curling rock, roll a bocce ball) or with an implement (e.g., hit the cue ball with a pool cue, strike a ball with a croquet mallet).

- Sometimes this involves a clear shot at the target, such as in five-pin bowling or darts.
- At other times it might mean having to take an *indirect pathway* so that the object either bounces off another object (hitting the cue ball off the side rail in billiards) or making the object curl around an obstacle by putting some spin on it (an in- or out-turn in curling).
- In target activities, the athletic focus is on players *mastering the best stance* to send the object away effectively. Target games can still work well as team sports where players must combine their efforts to achieve success.
- In some target games, such as golf, bowling, and archery, players do not attempt to prevent their opponents from scoring. In others, such as curling, lawn bowling, and shuffleboard, *strategic play is important.* Players can prevent the other team from scoring either by setting up guards that protect previous shots that are in scoring positions or by knocking away their opponent's objects that are close to the target.

Archery is an age-old target activity that has a strong following today.

INDIVIDUAL ACTIVITIES

Aquatics

Athletics

Dance

Gymnastics

Judo

Karate

Taekwondo

Yoga

Individual Activities

Individual activities include physical and recreational activities that develop body rhythm, creativity, sequencing, and stability. Examples of individual activities include track and field, wrestling/combative sports, gymnastics, aquatics, aerobics, yoga, Pilates, and dance.

Most people engage in individual activities to have fun and experience improvement in their health and fitness. Some turn to them for spiritual growth, while others get involved for the sheer sake of competing with themselves to see what their bodies can accomplish.

Many professional and recreational athletes use individual activities to develop various elements of fitness that are dominant in their sport. For example, to increase the strength of their abdominal and deep back muscles, they incorporate Pilates or yoga into their training regimens. Those looking to develop balance and coordination enroll in dance or gymnastics. In fact, some professional athletes take ballet to increase muscular endurance, strength, balance, flexibility, and coordination.

Basic strategies and tactics

Individual activities each involve a unique skill set. Most are not team sports and do not require much specialized equipment. However, because many different activities fall into this category, it is difficult to generalize.

- The skills involved in *track and field* include running, sprinting, and hurdling. The field skills include throwing weighted objects of varying sizes and shapes as far as you can. The long, high, and triple jumps, along with pole vaulting, are other field skills.
- *Wrestling/combative sports* and *gymnastics* require good tumbling and landing skills. Wrestlers grab and throw their opponents to the mat, while gymnasts perform complicated tumbling feats in combination. Wrestlers receive points for throwing or pinning their opponent to the ground. In gymnastics, scoring is determined by a panel of judges who look for mandatory skill elements that are put together in sequence.
- *Aquatics* is more than just swimming. Synchronized swimming, backstroke, the butterfly, and diving all require completely different skills. At national and international competitions, swimmers rely on technology to give them a tactical advantage. The invention of full body swimsuits keeps swimmers more buoyant and reduces drag, which in turn increases speed.
- The activities most difficult to categorize are *aerobics, yoga, Pilates,* and *dance.* Although dance and aerobics competitions exist, all of these activities remain, for the most part, non-competitive. While these activities are accessible to beginners, they offer rewards for participants who take the time to gain skill and develop their strength, flexibility, and body awareness.

Dance is a remarkably expressive way to improve stability and control.

OUTDOOR ACTIVITIES

BMX biking

Camping

Orienteering

Skateboarding

Skiing

Snowshoeing

Outdoor Activities

Outdoor activities can be closely associated with life in Canada. Whether it is the thrill of skiing down a hill or blazing through trails in provincial parks, being outdoors affords us the opportunity to be "at one" with nature while being active.

Many physical education programs offer outdoor education, yet not every student takes advantage of them. Activities such as camping, canoeing, hiking, orienteering, or downhill or cross-country skiing are fun and are also a great way to get active.

The next time your school offers a ski or camping trip, be encouraged to sign up, especially if you have never done it before. You might discover a part of yourself you never knew existed!

Basic strategies and tactics

The greatest thing about outdoor activities is that you can go at your own pace. If you are looking for competition, both orienteering and skiing (downhill and cross-country) offer it at various levels.

- **Orienteering.** The basic skills involved in orienteering are map and compass reading. Learning how to interpret what is on a map and visually land-marking those spots on the course are skills an orienteer must acquire. Movement skills depend on the type of orienteering that is being done. The most common types are walking or running.
- **Skiing.** The key skills in cross-country skiing are "the classic technique" (striding and gliding) and "skating" (similar to ice or in-line skating). Cross-country skiing, according to many experts, is the best all-around cardiorespiratory exercise. All beginner downhill skiers must learn the skill of "snowplowing." It teaches how to control your speed and how to stop. Once you master the snowplow, you can try more difficult maneuvers.
- **Camping.** Many basic survival skills are practised when camping: building a campfire, pitching a tent, cooking your own food, and sometimes even purifying water to drink. Often you must work as a team to get the campsite set up before nightfall or a rainstorm. "No trace camping," which basically means leaving no garbage behind, is enforced in most areas so that others can enjoy the outdoors long after you are gone.

Orienteering is a great way to challenge the body and mind in an outdoor setting.

Modifying Your Games and Activities

When we are learning how to play a new activity, game, or sport, or when we are acquiring a new skill, there is nothing more frustrating than not being able to succeed at it. Similarly, if you already have a strong skill set or playing ability, frustration can set in when you are waiting for others to catch up. You may have experienced these scenarios in your Physical Education classes at some point. After all, not everyone is at the same skill level. Therefore, the challenge is to find a middle path that meets everyone's needs and abilities so that we can all feel challenged while learning new activities and skills with our classmates and friends. This is where modifying our games or activities can really make a difference.

Practising one skill component at a time

Accommodating all students can be accomplished by modifying or breaking down the activity, game, sport, or skill we are trying to learn into bite-sized pieces, practising one component at a time, and then building on our increasing competence. Any modifications that are introduced need to be challenging for all students. Here is where you can play a vital role in your own learning. You can make recommendations to your teacher about modifications to various games and activities in order to maximize the level of challenge and fun for yourself and others.

Let's look at some suggested modifications that can be used to learn sending and receiving skills for net/wall games.

Suggested modifications related to sending and receiving skills

- Start by hitting a large soft sponge ball with just your hand to keep it up in the air. Try to beat your personal best each time. If the sponge ball is too hard to keep up in the air, use a beach ball or balloon.
- Hit the large soft sponge ball off a wall using only your hand. You are allowed one bounce off the ground before you hit it off the wall again. Try to beat your personal best each time.
- With a partner and using just your open hand and the same (or a smaller) ball, try hitting the ball back and forth to each other, allowing only one bounce before the other hits it back. See how many successful rallies (back and forth) you can have. Try to break your record each time you start a new rally.
- Now try using an oversized racquet, repeating the progressions above, or add new challenges that you and your partner devise.

These recommendations are suggestions only, and they are by no means the only possible modifications to aid progression in refining your sending and receiving skills. Your teacher (and you) will have many more ideas; the key is to communicate with your teacher and participate actively in the learning process. Doing so will ensure that everyone will experience greater enjoyment, engagement, and fun, regardless of ability.

Section 2.5 Review

1 Why is it useful to learn basic strategies and tactics related to the various game categories?

2 Which game category or categories appeal to you most, and why?

3 List three possible modifications to assist the acquisition of throwing skills in target games.

Mike's Story

"Understanding how the body moves makes my job as a firefighter much easier and safer. I know how to get maximal force with minimal effort in tough situations, such as breaking down walls with an axe or rescuing someone using the Jaws of Life."
— Mike Doherty

Chapter 2 Review

Knowledge and Understanding

1 Give three examples of movement competence (a) in everyday life; and (b) in physical activities or sports. For each example, list the benefits of moving competently.

2 In your own words, define the term *skill transferability,* giving one or two examples.

3 Distinguish between key movement features and fundamental movement patterns, using examples.

Thinking

4 What is the value of learning about basic strategies and tactics in the various categories of games and activities?

5 If a friend were having difficulty learning a new skill related to dance or some other physical activity, what recommendations could you make to help your friend feel successful?

6 Give an example of how you could apply movement principles related to stability or maximum effort to improve your performance of a specific movement skill.

Communication

7 Write a brief summary detailing how you might improve your movement competence each day.

8 Make a three-panelled drawing or film a brief video to show the three stages of learning a new movement skill of your choice.

9 Draw a simple, labelled diagram with a caption stating what a skateboarder can do to maintain stability. Use a stick figure if you wish.

Application

10 Describe and, if possible, demonstrate the four phases of a movement skill that you perform as part of a favourite physical activity, sport, or recreational pursuit.

11 Research and outline three basic strategies and tactics related to a game, sport, or activity other than the ones described in this chapter.

12 With a partner or in a small group, brainstorm and record some suggestions for modifying a basketball game, a game of bowling, or another activity of your choice to suit the abilities of a class of Grade 3 students.

Fitness Measurements and Appraisals

3

Miryam's Story

Why is it important to select fitness appraisals that are just right for you?

You do not have to be a great athlete to get fit—or to perform fitness appraisals. Appraisals let you figure out your current fitness level so you can set appropriate fitness goals.

This chapter introduces a range of appraisals, many of which were developed by the Canadian Society for Exercise Physiology (CSEP). These appraisals are standardized for ages 15 to 69—everyone is scored the same way—and they cover all health-related aspects of fitness.

As you perform fitness appraisals over the next few years, the results will fluctuate. Your fitness scores will depend on your physical growth, whether you exercise regularly, what you eat, and how much rest you get.

Fitness appraisals are not about comparing yourself to others—instead, they can be used to help you navigate your own journey of improvement.

Learning Objectives

In this chapter, you will...

- learn about aerobic fitness and cardiorespiratory appraisals, including the importance of finding the right tests for you
- follow safety instructions from your teacher when performing cardiorespiratory appraisals
- learn how to find your resting heart rate and to calculate your maximal heart rate, heart rate reserve, and target heart rate zone
- learn how to perform the modified Canadian Aerobic Fitness Test and other common cardiorespiratory appraisals
- distinguish between muscular strength and muscular endurance
- learn what musculoskeletal fitness means and how to perform six CSEP-PATH musculoskeletal fitness tests
- identify some common performance-level appraisals that measure and improve speed, agility, and coordination
- learn about body composition and body composition appraisals
- identify primary influences on body image, including self-esteem.

▶ **Miryam Khokhar** was four years old when she discovered that she loves playing cricket. She has gone on to receive the Most Promising Female Cricketer award by the Toronto District Cricket Association. Dedicated to training, working hard, and encouraging other young players, she has led the Ontario Cricket Academy women's team and captained men's teams as well.

Key Terms

- health-related fitness
- skill-related fitness
- CSEP-PATH
- Canadian 24-Hour Movement Guidelines for Children and Youth
- aerobic fitness
- VO_2 max
- cardiorespiratory appraisals
- Resting Heart Rate (RHR)
- Target Heart Rate Zone
- musculoskeletal fitness
- muscular strength
- muscular endurance
- flexibility
- performance-level appraisals
- body composition
- body mass index (BMI)
- body image
- self-esteem

3.1 Health-Related and Skill-Related Fitness

You need regular exercise, a well-balanced diet, and enough sleep and rest to get fit and stay fit, but your fitness level can vary. At any time, you may be more fit in one way than in another—such as having good muscular strength but weak cardiorespiratory fitness. You may also choose to focus on different types of fitness at different times.

Fitness has two dimensions: **1)** If you are "**health fit**," your heart, lungs, muscles, and bones are in good working order. You may have a condition that limits or challenges your health fitness, so think of being health fit within the context of your own body. **2)** If you are "**skill fit**," you can participate in a sport or other physical activity at a relatively high level. Similarly, you may have a condition that limits or challenges your skill fitness, so consider this too according to your own body.

What Is Health-Related Fitness?

Health-related fitness is all about wellness and achieving a high quality of life. Everyone needs to obtain a certain level of personal fitness in order to carry out everyday activities and feel good about themselves. We cannot all be—nor do we all want to be—elite athletes. Most of us just want to be healthy. Being "**health fit**" is something that everyone can improve on simply by healthy eating and making a commitment to regular exercise. Health-related fitness focuses on core health in five areas:

Cardiorespiratory fitness refers to the ability of the heart and lungs to supply oxygen to the muscles. It gives you the energy and the endurance you need for everyday activities such as climbing stairs or running for the bus. Track and field, aerobics, swimming, and dance all build cardiorespiratory fitness.

Muscular strength is the ability to exert force or move a heavy weight. We use it daily, such as when we push or pull a heavy door to open it. Activities that build strength include ice hockey, football, lacrosse, and resistance training.

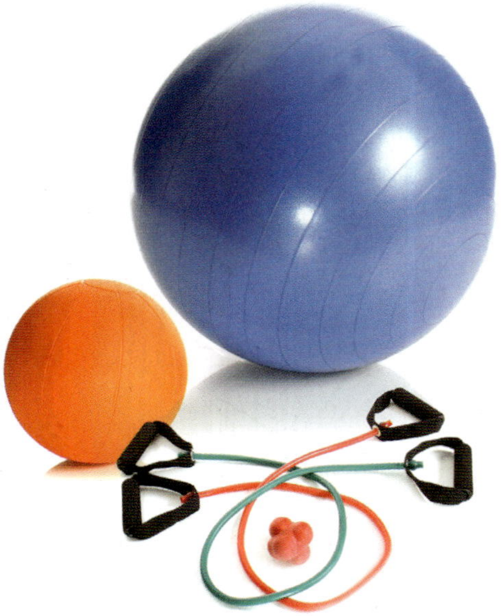

Muscular endurance is the ability of muscles to work over a long time, such as hitting a ball over and over in a game of tennis. Wrestling, aquatics, cycling, soccer, and cross-country skiing all develop endurance.

Flexibility is the capacity of muscles to stretch. Flexibility prevents injuries when the body is pushed beyond its usual limits, such as if you fall while skateboarding. Some activities that increase flexibility include martial arts, dance, yoga, tai chi, and qi gong.

Body composition refers to the distribution of muscle and fat throughout the body. A body with a healthy composition has enough fat to give it energy and enough muscle to perform a variety of activities.

What Is Skill-Related Fitness?

Skill is the ability to do something efficiently and well. In the context of physical activity, you may be skillful at a tennis serve or a basketball jump shot. Developing certain skills can take time and practice—and that helps build patience and discipline.

If you are getting better at a particular sport, it usually means you are improving in several skill areas at once. **Skill-related fitness** usually centres on six components: agility, balance, coordination, power, reaction time, and speed.

Agility is the ability to change direction rapidly and efficiently. Basketball and hockey players are very agile; their feet go one way, their upper bodies the other, and their hands another. Dance, football, soccer, handball, parkour, ultimate, volleyball, and tchoukball all require agility.

Balance allows you to maintain whole-body stability when moving or standing still so you do not fall over when playing racquetball or even just walking. Activities that build balance include yoga, skiing, skateboarding, mountain biking, slacklining, and fencing.

Coordination is the ability to combine agility and balance while moving. Performing two unrelated tasks at the same time, such as running and dribbling a basketball, takes coordination. Field hockey, handball, and gymnastics all build coordination.

Power refers to applying maximum effort in the minimum time. A downhill ski race start, a roundhouse karate kick, a sprint start, a basketball dunk, and a swimming race start all take power to get the body or a body part moving at top speed.

Reaction time refers to how quickly you can respond to a stimulus. Soccer and hockey goalies, for example, must react to an oncoming ball or puck in fractions of a second. Sports that need quick reaction time include table tennis, badminton, and karate.

Speed refers to covering a distance as quickly as possible. It is the most important skill at the competitive level in swimming or cycling. Baseball, soccer, football, track and field, and hockey all require speed.

CANADIAN 24-HOUR MOVEMENT GUIDELINES FOR CHILDREN AND YOUTH

An Integration of Physical Activity, Sedentary Behaviour, and Sleep

GUIDELINES

For optimal health benefits, children and youth (aged 5–17 years) should achieve high levels of physical activity, low levels of sedentary behaviour, and sufficient sleep each day.

A healthy 24 hours includes:

SWEAT

MODERATE TO VIGOROUS PHYSICAL ACTIVITY

An accumulation of at least 60 minutes per day of moderate to vigorous physical activity involving a variety of aerobic activities. Vigorous physical activities, and muscle and bone strengthening activities should each be incorporated at least 3 days per week;

STEP

LIGHT PHYSICAL ACTIVITY

Several hours of a variety of structured and unstructured light physical activities;

SLEEP

SLEEP

Uninterrupted 9 to 11 hours of sleep per night for those aged 5–13 years and 8 to 10 hours per night for those aged 14–17 years, with consistent bed and wake-up times;

SIT

SEDENTARY BEHAVIOUR

No more than 2 hours per day of recreational screen time;

Limited sitting for extended periods.

Preserving sufficient sleep, trading indoor time for outdoor time, and replacing sedentary behaviours and light physical activity with additional moderate to vigorous physical activity can provide greater health benefits.

Source: Reproduced with permission of the Canadian Society for Exercise Physiology (CSEP)

CSEP-Physical Activity Training for Health (CSEP-PATH)

The Canadian Society for Exercise Physiology (CSEP) has developed evidence-based fitness appraisals known as CSEP-Physical Activity Training for Health, or **CSEP-PATH**, to emphasize the health benefits of physical activity.

Founded in 1967, the Canadian Society for Exercise Physiology is the "gold standard" for exercise physiology and health and fitness training in Canada. CSEP was created to provide leadership in research, education, and training to improve health outcomes for everyone.

The CSEP-PATH to fitness and health

The procedures that make up CSEP-PATH appraisals involve a series of physical tests and measurements. Some of them, such as height or body composition, do not involve any physical exertion, but most do.

- The CSEP-PATH **aerobic fitness assessment** tests heart and lung capacity and is based on your heart rate response to various possible tests. A person's interests and capabilities determine which test to use.
- The CSEP-PATH **musculoskeletal fitness assessment** tests muscle strength, power, and endurance, as well as flexibility and balance.

The CSEP-PATH guidelines allow exercise professionals who are trained through CSEP to design a personalized exercise program to suit each and every individual, including persons with disabilities, children, youth, pregnant women, older adults, and persons with chronic illnesses.

Many Health and Physical Education teachers across Canada are certified exercise professionals with CSEP, and most will understand and be able to apply the CSEP-PATH appraisals.

Canadian 24-Hour Movement Guidelines

CSEP has also published **Canadian 24-Hour Movement Guidelines for Children and Youth**. These guidelines were developed by CSEP, the Conference Board of Canada, HALO-CHEO, ParticipACTION, and the Public Health Agency of Canada, with input from research experts and stakeholders across Canada and around the world.

The guidelines make recommendations, based on sound research evidence, as to how much young people should ideally **"sweat, step, sleep, and sit"** each day. The guidelines call for at least 60 minutes per day of moderate to vigorous physical activity, no more than two hours a day of recreational screen time, limited sitting for extended periods, and at least 9–11 hours of sleep per night for children 5–13 years, and 8–10 hours of sleep per night for those aged 14–17 years.

Section 3.1 Review

1 What are the main components of health-related fitness and skill-related fitness?

2 What do the CSEP-PATH fitness appraisals emphasize?

3 In a typical day, how many hours do you sweat, step, sleep, and sit?

Health Benefit Ratings

Within each CSEP-PATH test category, the results have health benefit ratings, so you can see at a glance where you stand in the fitness rankings for your age group:

- **Excellent** is associated with optimal health benefits.
- **Very good** is associated with considerable health benefits.
- **Good** is associated with many health benefits.
- **Fair** is associated with some health benefits but also some risks.
- **Needs** improvement is associated with considerable health risks.

After each test, you can record your results and then compare them to the appropriate health benefit ratings chart.

Your results will give you personalized benchmarks as you build an fitness program suited just for you.

3.2 Cardiorespiratory Appraisals

Highly aerobic physical activities such as basketball, cross-country skiing, and ultimate improve the health of your heart and lungs. Before you put on your running shoes, however, it is important to know the condition of your cardiorespiratory system.

Aerobic fitness is a general term for the efficiency of your heart, lungs, blood vessels, and exercising muscles. It refers to your ability to sustain physical effort.

Aerobic fitness increases the amount of oxygen that is delivered to your muscles. More oxygen allows them to work harder and longer. If you have no health issues, any activity that raises your heart rate moderately and keeps it raised for a period of time will improve your aerobic fitness.

Choosing Appraisals that Are Right for You

The amount of oxygen consumed during intense—or maximal—effort is a common indicator of aerobic fitness. Exercise scientists call this **VO_2 max**. The higher your **VO_2 max score**, the stronger your cardiorespiratory system, because your working muscles receive and use more oxygen.

Cardiorespiratory appraisals are probably the most important of all fitness appraisals. They measure the efficiency of your heart and lungs to take in and deliver oxygen to your muscles and to remove waste products (lactic acid and carbon dioxide). When you increase your cardiorespiratory fitness, you can complete daily activities more easily, and the energy you get also makes you feel more positive.

Most appraisals outlined in this chapter are appropriate for all levels of fitness. If you are not sure which ones to use, ask your teacher. If medical reasons mean that you cannot participate in any of the appraisals, let your teacher know.

Safety Guidelines

Follow the movement preparation and safety instructions provided by your teacher, and heed this advice as well:

- Don't do an appraisal without medical clearance if you have joint injuries or a cardiorespiratory illness.
- Don't perform an appraisal in hot and humid weather.
- Don't exercise for six hours before an appraisal or perform heavy exercise the day before.
- Don't eat, smoke, or consume a caffeinated drink for two hours before an appraisal.
- Don't drink anything for 15 minutes before a session.
- Wear appropriate footwear and clothing.

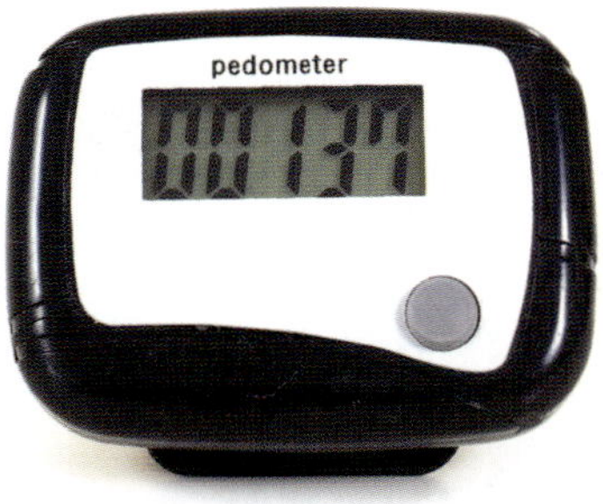

Finding your Resting Heart Rate

Heart rates vary from person to person, but the normal range for your **Resting Heart Rate (RHR)**—the number of times your heart beats per minute when you are at rest—is 70–80 beats per minute (bpm).

A rate of 50–60 bpm generally indicates a strong heart. Some endurance athletes, such as Olympic-level cross-country skiers, have Resting Heart Rates in the low 40s.

The difference in heart rates comes from the strength of the heart's left ventricle, which is the chamber that pumps oxygen-rich blood to the body

Genetics plays a role in your Resting Heart Rate, but regular aerobic exercise and a healthy diet have a strong influence as well.

Finding your pulse

To find your **Resting Heart Rate (RHR)**, you need to find your pulse. The carotid artery on your neck and the radial artery on your wrist are the two main spots. Find one of them using your index and middle finger—not your thumb, because the thumb has its own pulse.

For one minute, count the number of times you feel the artery pulse against your fingers, or count for 10 seconds and then multiply the result by six.

The way to take your resting pulse most accurately is to do so for three mornings in a row, just after waking up. Add the results together and divide by three to get the average.

Technology such as wearable fitness monitoring devices can help you determine and track your heart rate while exercising and at rest.

Staying in the Zone

Your **Target Heart Rate Zone** is the range within which you get the most aerobic benefit from a workout. You can find it using the **Heart Rate Reserve (HRR)** method.

Think of your **HRR** as the capacity of your heart to pump blood to your body over and above what you need when you are at rest. It is measured in beats per minute. To find your **HRR**, you need your **Maximal Heart Rate (MHR)**, your **Resting Heart Rate (RHR)**, and a simple calculation.

Maximal Heart Rate (MHR)

You can find your **Maximal Heart Rate** by subtracting your age from 220.

Maximal Heart Rate (MHR) = 220 bpm – age

For example, 15-year-old Jasmine's MHR is 205 bpm (220 – 15 = 205).

Heart Rate Reserve (HRR)

You can find your **Heart Rate Reserve** by subtracting your Resting Heart Rate (RHR) from your Maximal Heart Rate (MHR).

Heart Rate Reserve (HRR) = MHR – RHR

15-year-old Jasmine's MHR is 205 and her RHR is 75, so her HRR is 130 bpm (205 – 75 = 130).

Finding the limits of your Target Heart Rate Zone

To find the limits of your **Target Heart Rate Zone**, first you will need to calculate your recommended HRR range for exercising. CSEP-PATH recommends that you exercise at 50 to 85 percent of your HRR.

Remembering that Jasmine's HRR is 130 bpm, her heart rate at 50 percent of her HRR would be 65 bpm (130 × 0.5) and 110.5 bpm (130 × 0.85) would be 85 percent of her HRR while she is exercising.

Then, to find the lower and upper limits of your **Target Heart Rate Zone**, add your RHR to these numbers:

Lower limit = (50% of HRR) + RHR
Upper limit = (85% of HRR) + RHR

Remembering that Jasmine's Resting Heart Rate (RHR) is 75, her **Target Heart Rate Zone** looks like this:

Lower limit = 65 + 75 = 140 bpm
Upper limit = 110.5 + 75 = 185.5 bpm

During an active aerobic session, Jasmine should have a heart rate between 140 and 186 (rounded up from 185.5) beats per minute if she has been exercising at a healthy aerobic intensity. Above that range she may be working too hard, and below it she will not get the maximum benefit.

O'CONNOR
ATHLETICS

mCAFT

Modified Canadian Aerobic Fitness Test

The **Modified Canadian Aerobic Fitness Test (mCAFT)** is one of the CSEP-PATH appraisals. It is a multi-stage test used to estimate VO_2 max for people aged 15–69 years. The mCAFT is a sub-maximal appraisal, which means that you do not need to go "all out."

- The mCAFT involves completing one or more three-minute sessions of stepping up and back down a small set of steps until you reach the predetermined ceiling heart rate for your age group. Your ceiling heart rate (the level at which the appraisal must stop) is set at 85 percent of the maximal heart rate for your age group.
- The pace (stepping cadence, or steps per minute) at which you perform the test is set by an audio recording. The recording also tells you when to stop and take your pulse to see if you have reached your ceiling heart rate. The pace increases with every session of the test until you reach your ceiling heart rate. At that point, you stop and record the stepping stage you have reached.
- The mCAFT has a two-step and a one-step technique. Everyone begins with the two-step technique. CSEP-PATH recommends using a heart rate monitor while you perform this appraisal.
- Before you start, practise the stepping sequence first without, and then with, the audio recording. Practise finding your heart rate within each window of time allowed on the recording.

Ready, Set, Go!

- Maintain a constant stepping tempo throughout the test, and step so that both feet end up on the top step with your legs and back straight.
- At the signal given on the recording each time, stop to determine your heart rate by taking your pulse until you reach your ceiling heart rate.
- When you reach your ceiling heart rate, stop and write down the stage you have reached (refer to Table 3.1, column one).
- Depending on the stage you have reached, the amount of oxygen you have consumed (your O_2 cost) can be determined from Table 3.1. Once you know your O_2 cost, you can calculate your estimated VO_2 max score using the formula shown just above Table 3.1.

Your goal is to see improvement in your VO_2 max score over time. Your teacher may have access to performance standards ("norms") so that you can see the results for your age group if you wish.

Safety Precaution

If you cannot take this or any other appraisal for medical reasons, let your teacher know ahead of time.

The Two-Step Test

The CSEP-PATH manual explains how to build a set of steps like the ones shown here, but the mCAFT can also be performed on most staircases.

NOTE: For persons aged 15-19, the starting stage cadence (number of steps per minute) is 3 for females and 4 for males (see the table below).

85% Maximal Heart Rate	=	0.85 (220 – age)
Estimated VO_2 max	=	[17.2 + (1.29 × (O_2 cost) – (0.09 × wt. in kg) – (0.18 × age in years)]

Table 3.1 **mCAFT Stepping Cadence and O_2 Cost**

	Females		Males	
Stage	Stepping Cadence (Pace)	O_2 Cost (ml/kg/min)	Stepping Cadence (Pace)	O_2 Cost (ml/kg/min)
1	66	15.9	66	15.9
2	84	18.0	84	18.0
3	102	22.0	102	22.0
4	114	24.5	114	24.5
5	120	26.3	132	29.5
6	132	29.5	144	33.6
7	144	33.6	118*	36.2
8	118*	36.2	132*	40.1

* One-step procedure

12-Minute Run

The **12-Minute Run** (also known as the Cooper Test) was designed for military use by American researcher Dr. Kenneth H. Cooper in 1968. It assesses aerobic capacity by measuring how far someone can run in 12 minutes.

This appraisal is suitable for all fitness levels, but make sure you prepare properly. Choose a pace that you are comfortable with so you can cover the greatest distance. If you are a beginner or less fit, it is okay to walk or jog during any part of the appraisal.

Ready, Set, Go!

- Select a running surface that is marked off every 100 metres. Choose a partner to help you keep track of your laps (and vice versa).
- Your teacher will let you know how much time you have been running after each lap. Try to adjust your speed to help you last 12 minutes.
- At the 10-minute mark, your teacher will let you know the time remaining. Pick up the pace, if you can, until the whistle blows.

Record the distance you have covered, and see if you can improve on that number the next time. Your teacher may have access to performance standards (norms) that will show how your results compare with average scores in your age group.

Breath Sound Check

Developed by Professor Bob Goode and his team at the University of Toronto, the **Breath Sound Check** monitors the intensity of aerobic activity.

The test is based on the idea that to gain at least the minimum benefit from aerobic activity, you should be able to hear your own breathing while you exercise. This is how it works:

- Jog slowly or walk briskly for one minute.
- Gradually increase the pace so you can just start to hear your breathing, and then maintain that pace. You are now in the breath sound check zone.
- As you become more fit, you will have to jog more quickly or for longer before you can hear your breathing.

Rockport Walking Test

The **Rockport Walking Test** lets you determine your VO_2 max based on how quickly you can walk one mile (1.6 km). This test is an excellent cardiorespiratory appraisal for those who find running a challenge.

Ready, Set, Go!

- Measure out a one-mile (1.6 km) course. You can use the school track or any uninterrupted course.
- Walk one mile as quickly as possible without speed walking.
- As soon as you have finished, check your heart rate monitor device or take your heart rate manually.
- Record the time it takes you to walk the mile and your heart rate when you have finished, then estimate your VO_2 max using the formula below.

Your goal should be to see improvement in your VO_2 max over time. Again, your teacher may refer you to standards that will show how your results compare with averages in your age group.

Estimating Your VO_2 max

Here's how you calculate your estimated VO_2 max (it is a long equation, but easy to calculate):

Estimated VO_2 max = 132.853 – (0.0769 × your weight [pounds])
– (0.3877 × your age [years])
+ (6.315 × gender [male = 1, female = 0])
– (3.2649 × time to walk 1 mile [minutes and 100ths of minutes])
– (0.1565 × heart rate at the end of mile [bpm])

Example: Jerome

- Weight: 132 lbs
- Age: 16
- Gender: male (1)
- Time to walk one mile: 12 minutes, 30 seconds (12.50)
- Heart rate at the end of mile: 180 bpm

Now let's calculate Jerome's estimated VO_2 max:

= 132.853 – (0.0769 × 132 [weight]) – (0.3877 × 16 [age]) + (6.315 × 1 [gender]) – (3.2649 × 12.50 [time]) – (0.1565 × 180 [heart rate])

= 132.853 – 10.1508 – 6.2032 + 6.315 – 40.81125 – 28.17

= 53.83275

Talk Test

The **Talk Test** was developed by Professor Bob Goode and his team at the University of Toronto to monitor the intensity of aerobic activity.

The principle is simple:

- You should be able to carry on a conversation with some effort during aerobic activity.
- If you are out of breath and having difficulty talking, then you are working too hard.
- If you can speak too easily, then you are not working hard enough.

Beep

Beep Test

In 1982, Dr. Luc Léger and his team at the Université de Montréal developed a 20-metre shuttle-run appraisal. An audio recording determines how quickly participants run by making a "beep" sound at shorter and shorter intervals.

Today, this appraisal is referred to as the **Beep Test** because of the sound that tells the runner to change direction. You can make your own recording using Beep Test software.

A Maximal Appraisal

The Beep Test gives results that compare with high-tech appraisals conducted in laboratory settings. It is a very accurate way to measure your maximal oxygen consumption, or VO_2 max.

The Beep Test is a maximal appraisal, which means that at some point you go "all out." This appraisal should be performed only under the supervision of qualified instructors. If you are in good condition, this is the test for you. If you are not sure, consult your teacher to find another test that suits you better.

Williams Swimming Beep Test

This aerobic fitness test was developed by English swimming coach Graham Williams. Many swimmers can be tested at once, using minimal time and pool space.

The test is based on a 1500-metre swim, with speed levels that increase every 100 metres.

Similar to the running Beep Test, participants swim to a recording of beeps that sound at shorter intervals as the test progresses.

Swimmers are scored by the speed level they reach and by the number of segments they complete before they can no longer keep up with the recording.

Ready, Set, Go!

- Choose a flat, non-slip surface with a 20-metre length, such as a gymnasium, hallway, or tennis court. Use the same place to repeat the test later in the year for the most accurate and consistent results.
- Use a tape measure to mark off two parallel lines 20 metres apart, and place cones at the end points of both lines. (If running indoors, ensure there is a slow-down area a safe distance from an encroaching wall.)
- At the first beep, briskly walk or lightly jog from the starting line to the 20-metre line before the next beep. If you get there before the next beep, wait! Do not head back to the first line until you hear the beep again. The pace picks up and soon you will be sprinting back and forth.
- The test ends when you cannot reach 20 metres for two consecutive beeps.

How well did you do?
Record the number of the last stage you completed. Your goal should be to see improvement each time you perform the appraisal. Your teacher may have access to general performance standards (norms) that can show you how your results compare with average scores on this appraisal in your age group.

The Beep Test is a maximal appraisal and should be performed only under the supervision of qualified instructors.

Wheelchair Aerobic Test

The **Wheelchair Aerobic Test** is a simple appraisal that assesses the aerobic fitness of people who use wheelchairs. One of the advantages of this appraisal is that several people can be tested at once, using their own wheelchairs. Participants are encouraged to push themselves as hard as they can.

Ready, set, go!

- Place cones at set intervals (for example, every 50 metres) around a 400-metre running track.
- Wheel around the track for 12 minutes and record your distance to the nearest 100 metres.

Your goal should be to see improvement in the distance covered each time you perform this appraisal. Your teacher may also have access to general performance standards (or norms) that will show you how your results compare with average scores on this appraisal for your age group.

10-Metre Shuttle Test

The **10-Metre Shuttle Test** is an aerobic fitness appraisal for children with cerebral palsy at Level I or Level II in the Gross Motor Function Classification System. It is a variation of the 20-metre Beep Test. An audio recording determines how quickly participants run by playing a "beep" sound at shorter and shorter intervals.

Ready, Set, Go!

- Mark two parallel lines 10 metres apart with tape on a flat, non-slip surface. Place cones at the end points of both lines.
- Walk or run from one line to the other and back and continue until you are unable to keep up with the recording.
- Your score is determined by the number of shuttles you have completed before you were unable to keep up with the recording.

Record the number of shuttles you have completed, and see if you can better that number the next time. Again, your teacher may be able to refer you to performance standards for this appraisal.

Yo-Yo Intermittent Recovery Test

Danish soccer physiologist Jens Bangsbo designed this maximal appraisal for soccer players, but it is also useful for sports such as tennis, handball, and basketball. The test assesses a person's ability to perform intensive bursts of activity followed by short recovery periods repeatedly over a fixed period.

This appraisal is designed for recreational players at two levels: Level 1 is for people with little training; Level 2 is for people who are better trained. Level 2 starts at a faster speed, but both levels use a "beep" recording to increase the speed as the test progresses.

The **Yo-Yo Intermittent Test** usually takes 6–20 minutes to complete at Level 1 and 2–10 minutes at Level 2.

Ready, Set, Go!

- Use cones to mark out parallel lines, 5 metres and 20 metres apart, on a flat, non-slip surface, as shown in the figure below.
- Beginning at the start line, run to the line of cones 20 metres away when instructed by the recording, and return when you hear the beep.
- Between each 20-metre shuttle (out and back), walk or jog around the cone that is 5 metres away, then return to the starting point. This active recovery period lasts 10 seconds.
- The test ends when you cannot complete a shuttle two times in a row.

Record the total distance covered before you were unable to keep up with the recording, and see if you can better that number the next time. Your teacher may be able to refer you to standards for this appraisal so that you can see how your results compare with those of others in your age group.

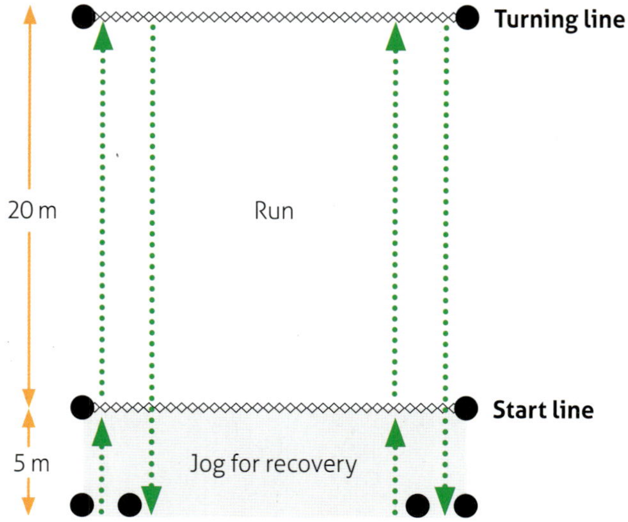

30–15 Intermittent Fitness Test

Dr. Martin Buchheit designed the **30–15 Intermittent Fitness Test** for players of team and racquet sports that involve intermittent play, such as soccer, football, futsal, basketball, rugby, netball, handball, field hockey, badminton, and tennis. It consists of 30-second shuttle runs interspersed with 15-second passive recovery periods.

Ready, Set, Go!

- Mark out a course on a flat, non-slip surface over a straight line for 40 metres. Use cones or tape of one colour to designate the A (0 metre), B (20 metre), and C (40 metre) marks. Use a different colour of cones or tape to mark points 3 metres in from each end. (If running indoors, ensure there is a slow-down area a safe distance from the end wall.)
- Start at point A. At the first beep, run toward points B and C. At the next beep you should be close to point B, and by the following beep you should be within the 3-metre zone at the point C end—and ideally at the 40-metre mark.
- Run back toward point A. At the next beep, you should be close to point B, and so on.
- Continue this pattern until the end of the 30-second running stage (indicated by a different beep). Then walk slowly *in the same direction* as you have been running for a 15-second passive recovery stage until you reach the next mark (A, B, or C).
- Listen for spoken instructions to tell you whether to begin the next 30-second running stage at A, B, or C.
- If you are on a marked point when a running stage concludes, stay on that point and wait for the next stage to begin.
- Each running stage increases the pace by 0.5 kilometres per hour. Keep running until you are too tired to continue or until you cannot be within the 3-metre end zone at the beep on three successive occasions.

Record your running pace (in km/h) when you stop, and see if you can better that pace the next time. Again, your teacher may refer you to standards that can show how your results compare with averages for your age group.

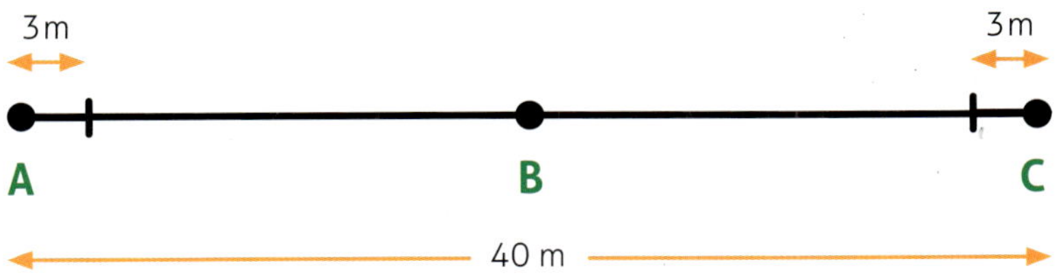

Section 3.2 Review

1. What does a high VO_2 max score indicate?
2. Demonstrate how to find your pulse.
3. Briefly describe two cardiorespiratory appraisals that worked well for you, and explain why.

3.3

3.3 Muscular Strength and Endurance Appraisals

The appraisals in this section are part of the Canadian Society of Exercise Physiology's new CSEP-PATH program. They measure musculoskeletal fitness, so you can work on improving it.

Some of these appraisals focus on specific muscles or muscle groups; others involve many muscles at the same time. You can use your results to design a program that meets your fitness needs.

Musculoskeletal Fitness

Musculoskeletal fitness refers to muscular strength and muscular endurance, as well as to the mobility of your joints.

- **Muscular strength** refers to how much force a muscle can exert in a single contraction.
- **Muscular endurance** refers to a muscle's ability to perform repeatedly without fatigue.

In the context of physical activity, **flexibility** refers to the capacity of muscles to stretch, which can influence a joint's range of motion (ROM).

Grip Strength

The **Grip Strength** appraisal measures the strength of your forearm muscles, which research suggests is also a good indicator of overall muscular strength. This makes sense, because most intense physical activities require a firm grip. Carrying groceries, lifting boxes, shovelling snow, mountain biking, and rock climbing all take grip strength.

This appraisal uses a hand dynamometer, which can be adjusted to suit your hand size. Readings are often expressed in kilograms.

Ready, Set, Go!

- Hold the dynamometer between the second joint of your fingers and the base of your thumb.
- Stand with your arm extended away from your body, palm facing your thigh.
- While exhaling, squeeze as hard as you can on the dynamometer without moving your arm position. Neither your hand nor the dynamometer should touch anything else.
- Check and record the score on the dynamometer to the nearest kilogram. Measure each hand twice, alternating hands.

Record your maximum score for each hand (or combine the maximum scores to get your two-hand total), and see if you can better your results the next time. Your teacher may be able to refer you to performance standards for this appraisal so that you can compare your results to averages in your age group.

Push-Ups

Push-ups are a good all-round indicator of upper-body strength. They use your chest muscle (pectoralis major), your shoulders, and your triceps. The Push-Ups appraisal involves performing as many push-ups as you can consecutively with no time limit. Incorrect repetitions do not count, so practise the proper technique before you begin.

Ready, Set, Go!

- Lie with your stomach and chest on a mat, legs together, hands pointing forward and positioned under your shoulders.
- Push up by fully extending your arms, elbows out from the side.
- Keeping your upper body in a straight line, lower your body until your chin almost touches the mat. Stomach and thighs do not touch the mat.
- Breathe normally during all phases of the push-up. Avoid holding your breath, and do not strain.
- Stop if you feel any pain or discomfort, or once you cannot maintain the proper technique over two consecutive repetitions.

Record the number of push-ups you completed using the proper technique, and see if you can better that number the next time. Your teacher may also be able to refer you to performance standards for this appraisal so that you can see average scores for your age group.

The modified push-up is pictured on the left; the standard push-up is shown below.

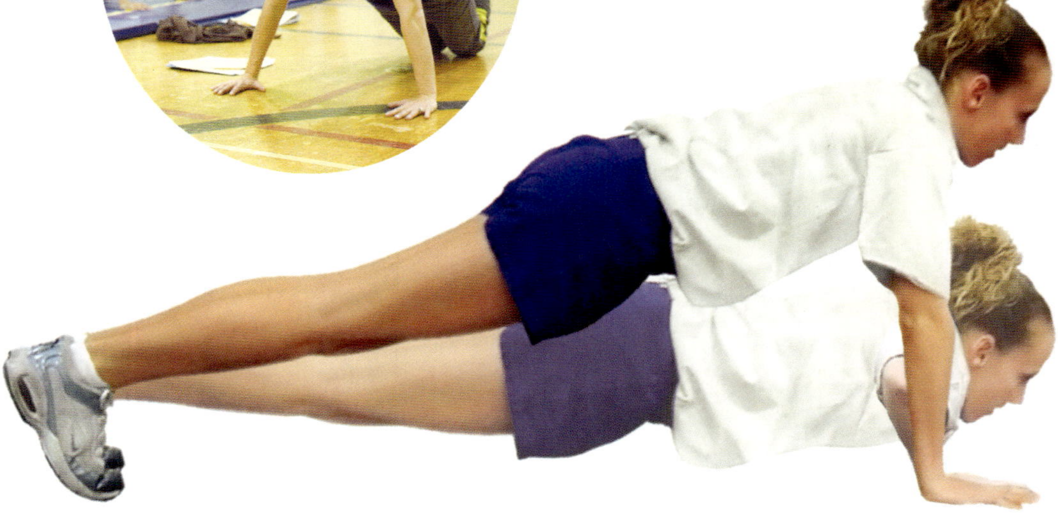

Sit and Reach

The **Sit and Reach** appraisal measures hamstring and lower back flexibility using a flexometer. This device measures how far you can reach forward when you are in a sitting position.

Ready, Set, Go!

- Without shoes, sit in front of the flexometer, legs fully extended, with the soles of your feet placed flat against the box. Ensure that the balls of your feet rest against the upper crossboards without extending beyond them. Keep the inner edges of your feet about 15 centimetres (6 in.) apart.
- With legs fully extended, arms evenly stretched, hands one over the other with palms facing down, bend and reach forward while exhaling to push the sliding marker along the scale as far as you can with your fingertips.
- Do not use a bouncing or jerking motion, and do not bend your knees because the trial does not count if you do.
- Hold this position of maximum flexion for about two seconds while breathing normally, then relax.
- Record your position to the nearest 0.5 centimetre, then repeat.

Use the higher number as your final score, and see if you can better that number the next time. Again, your teacher may be able to refer you to performance standards for this appraisal that show average results for your age group.

Sit + Reach

Vertical Jump

The **Vertical Jump** appraisal measures power—the ability to exert a large amount of force quickly. Power is especially important in physical activities and sports that involve jumping, throwing, and rapid lifting.

Although the Vertical Jump provides a good estimate of power in the legs, it uses almost all the major muscles in the body. When performed properly, it activates your gluteus maximus, quadriceps, and calf muscles as well as your abdominals, deltoids, and back muscles.

Ready, Set, Go!

- Stand sideways to a wall on which height has been marked off in centimetres. With feet flat on the floor, reach as high as you can with fingers fully extended. Have a partner record this beginning height.
- At a safe distance from the wall, move into a semi-squat position. Without doing any run-up or pre-jump, jump as high as possible, touching the tape at the peak of the movement.
- Have your partner record how high you reached. Complete the test three times. Rest 10–15 seconds between each trial.
- Subtract the beginning height from your best result, and record the difference, which is your jump height.

Your goal should be to see improvement each time you perform the appraisal. Your teacher may also be able to refer you to performance standards that will show average scores for your age group.

Estimating Peak Leg Power (PLP)

You can also calculate your **Peak Leg Power (PLP)** from this appraisal if you know your body weight. To calculate your PLP (in watts), enter your jump height and weight in kilograms into the formula below.

PLP = (60.7 × jump height in cm) + (45.3 × weight in kg) – 2055

Peak Leg Power (Watts)

Ages 15–19	Males	Females
Excellent	≧ 4,644	≧ 3,167
Very Good	4,185–4,643	2,795–3,166
Good	3,858–4,184	2,399–2,794
Fair	3,323–3,857	2,156–2,398
Need Improvement	≦ 3,322	≦ 2,155

Table reproduced with permission of the Canadian Society for Exercise Physiology.

Back Extension

The **Back Extension** appraisal is a good way to assess core strength. It tests the muscular endurance of your back muscles.

CSEP-PATH recommends a screening test before attempting the back extension appraisal:

- Lie face down on a mat.
- Extend your right leg up and then place it back down.
- Extend your left leg up and back.
- Repeat these movements while extending the opposite arm.
- If you feel any discomfort or pain, do not perform this appraisal.

Ready, Set, Go!

- Lie with your lower body on a bench or short table, with your hips (iliac crest) positioned at the edge of the platform and the hips, shoulders, and head aligned, keep your hands braced on the floor to support your upper body. Have one partner hold down your legs throughout the appraisal.
- When you are securely in position, lift your hands from the floor and cross them in front of your chest. Contracting your abdominal muscles will help support your upper body.
- With another partner timing you, hold this horizontal position for as long as possible to a maximum of three minutes (180 seconds). Stop if you feel too physically stressed or if you are unable to keep your body perfectly straight.
- Turn onto your back and lie with both knees bent for one minute to relax the back muscles.

Record the length of time you were able to hold the horizontal position. Your teacher may be able to refer you to performance standards for this appraisal.

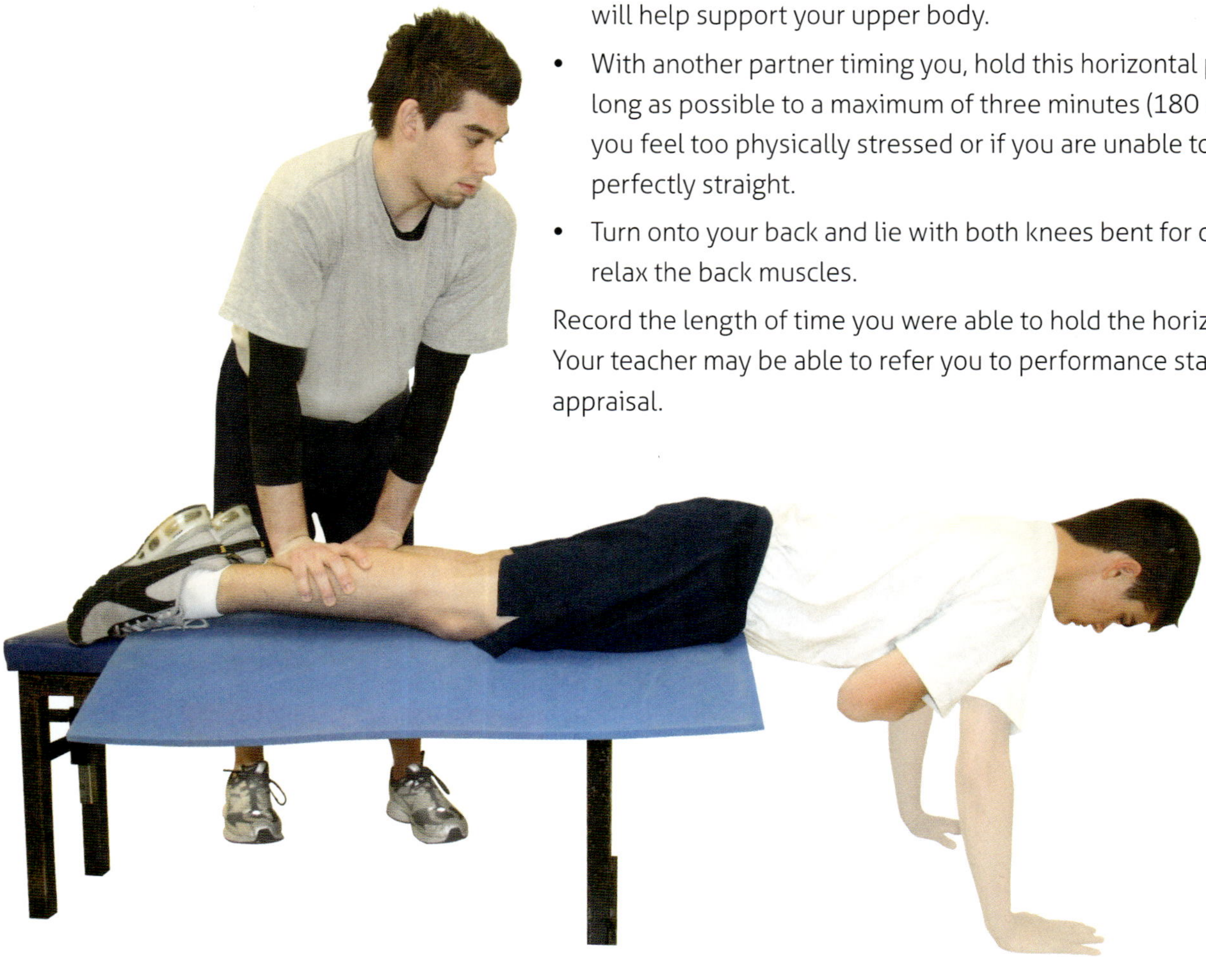

One-Leg Stance

The **One-Leg Stance** appraisal assesses postural stability and balance. Almost every sport and daily activity—such as walking or taking a flight of stairs—involves balancing when you shift from one leg to the other.

This appraisal is useful for all ages. It is easy to administer as part of a fitness assessment program because all you need is a chair, a stopwatch, and a partner.

Ready, Set, Go!

- Stand barefoot behind or beside a sturdy chair with your hands crossed in front of your chest. The floor surface should be flat and stable.
- With eyes open, stand on one leg, lifting the other foot so that it is near but not touching the ankle of the standing leg.
- Try to hold this position for up to 45 seconds with your partner timing you from when you raise your foot. Grasp the chair if you start to lose your balance.
- Timing stops when (1) you move or uncross your arms; (2) your raised foot moves toward or away from the standing limb or touches the floor; (3) you move your weight-bearing foot to maintain balance; or (4) you reach 45 seconds.
- Repeat using the other leg.
- With eyes closed, repeat the test for each leg using the same criteria. If you lose balance during the first three seconds, allow a second try to account for any set-up error.
- Perform the test on one leg with eyes open and then with eyes closed. Then repeat the test on the other leg.

Record all trial times, and see if you can better those numbers the next time you take the appraisal. Again, your teacher may be able to refer you to performance standards for this appraisal.

Section 3.3 Review

1 Distinguish between the terms *muscular strength* and *muscular endurance.*

2 Which of the musculoskeletal appraisals did you find most challenging, and why?

3 Choose one musculoskeletal appraisal and create safety guidelines for it. Ask for your teacher's feedback.

Balance

3.4 Performance-Level Appraisals

Performance-level appraisals focus on specific movement skills such as speed, agility, and coordination. They measure and improve particular aspects of physical performance rather than overall health. Many of these performance-level tests are used by universities and professional sports teams to identify and recruit athletes.

Dot Drill

The **Dot Drill** is part of the Bigger Faster Stronger (BFS) program developed by strength coach Dr. Greg Shepard. This appraisal assesses quickness, agility, and muscular endurance. Perform it on a flat, non-slip surface on five large dots arranged in a rectangle.

Ready, Set, Go!

The drill has five directional, sequenced patterns, repeated in quick succession. You will need to practise the moves so that you can complete the appraisal. Your partner starts timing as soon as you begin the first pattern.

Your goal should be to see improvement each time you perform the appraisal. Your teacher may be able to refer you to performance standards for your age group.

Up and back

- Start with your right foot on A and your left foot on B.
- Jump quickly to C with both feet coming together.
- Jump and split feet to D and E.
- Return the same way backward, landing with your feet on A and B.

Right foot/left foot/both feet

- From your position at A and B, jump to C using only your right foot.
- Jump on your right foot to D, E, C, B, and A, in that order.
- Repeat the pattern with your **left foot,** then with **both feet**.

Turn around

- Both feet should now be on A. Now jump to C with both feet.
- Jump to D and E, landing with your left foot on E and right foot on D.
- Now quickly jump while turning 180 degrees clockwise, landing with your left foot on D and your right foot on E.
- Jump to C with both feet.
- Jump to A and B, landing with your left foot on A and right foot on B.
- Jump and spin counterclockwise 180 degrees, landing with your left foot on B and right foot on A.

Dot Drill

Agility

Illinois Agility Run

Agility is the ability to change direction quickly and efficiently without losing your balance. Agility is important for sports such as squash, football, soccer, and tennis, and can also improve performance during recreational activities.

The **Illinois Agility Run** is a good appraisal for activities or sports that involve changing direction and weaving around objects or opponents.

Ready, Set, Go!

- Select a flat, non-slip surface at least 15 metres long and 8 metres wide. Place a cone in each corner of a 10 × 5 metre rectangle within the area. Place four more cones 3.3 metres apart along a line down the centre.
- Lie in a push-up position at the start point in one corner (bottom left in the diagram). On command, push yourself up with your hands and sprint to the closest cone at the far line (top left). Go around it and back to the middle cone closest to your start (bottom middle). Without stopping, weave around the middle cones.
- Sprint to the other corner of the far line (top right), go around the cone, and then sprint to the finish (bottom right).
- Record the time it takes you to complete the course, and see if you can better that number the next time. Your teacher may be able to refer you to performance standards for this appraisal.

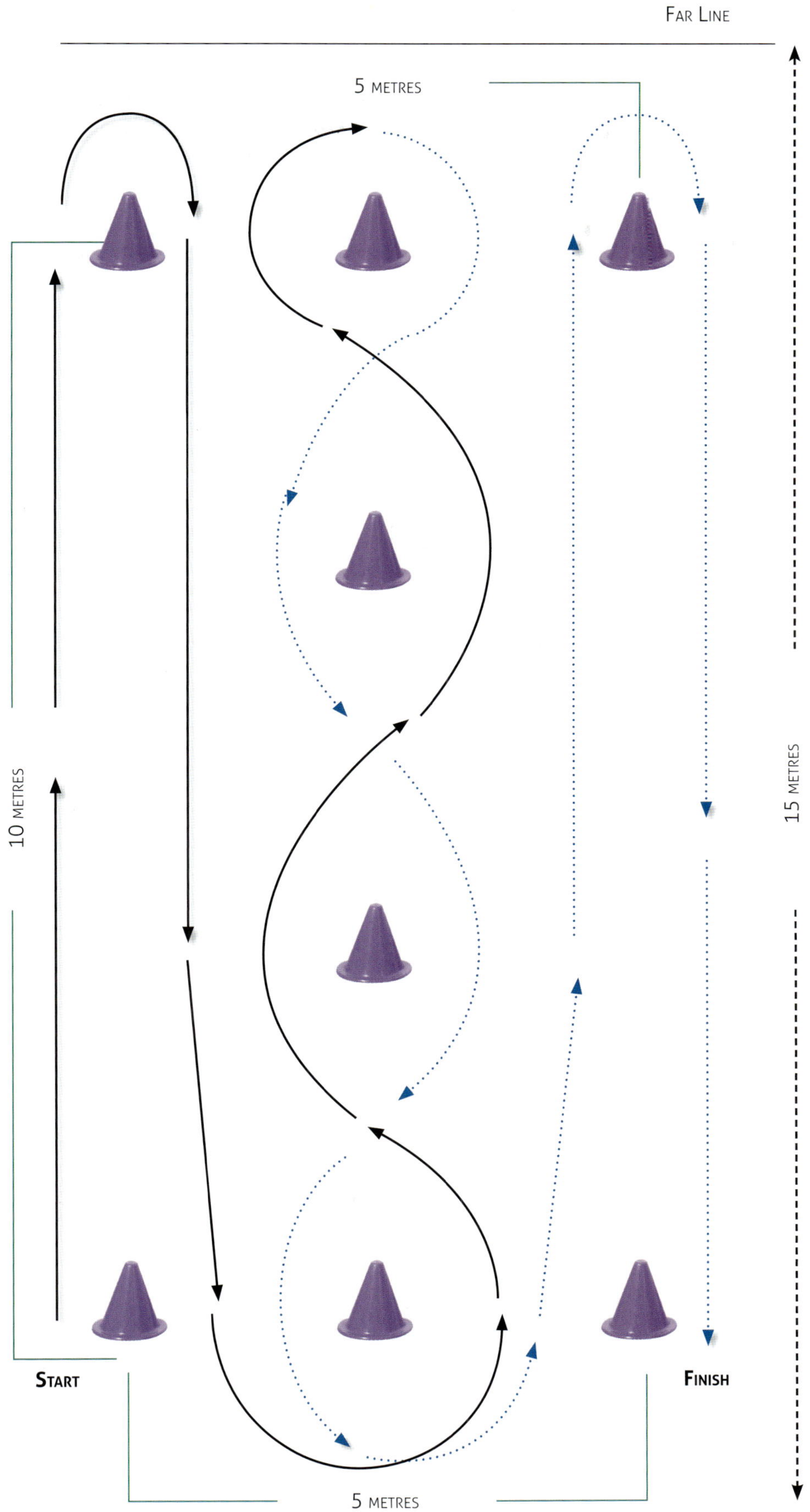
Far Line
5 metres
10 metres
15 metres
Start
Finish
5 metres

Agility T-Test

The **Agility T-Test** requires a tape measure, four cones, and a stopwatch. You will be timed as you run through this appraisal, so practise running backward before you begin.

Ready, Set, Go!

- On a flat, non-slip surface, mark a T-shaped course with cones. Cone A is at the bottom of the T. Ten metres away from cone A, place cones B, C, and D in a line perpendicular to cone A, as shown in the diagram.
- Start at A. On your partner's command, sprint to B and touch the top of the cone with your right hand.
- Still facing forward, shuffle left sideways to C and touch its top, this time with your left hand.
- Shuffle sideways to the right to D and touch its top with your right hand, then shuffle back to B, touch its top with your left hand, and then run backward to A.
- Your partner stops the watch as you pass A.

Take the test three times, and use the best time as your final score. Your teacher may be able to refer you to performance standards for the Agility T-Test appraisal.

Hexagon Drill

The **Hexagon Drill** focuses primarily on testing your ability to move quickly while maintaining balance. It involves making two-footed jumps, back and forth, over the sides of a hexagon. Avoid this drill if you have any pre-existing foot or ankle injuries.

Ready, Set, Go!

- Mark a hexagon on a flat, non-slip surface using chalk or tape. Make each side 24 inches (61 cm) and each angle 120 degrees. Imagine (or label) the sides as A, B, C, D, E, and F.
- Stand in the middle of the hexagon, feet hip-width apart, toes pointing forward, and arms by your sides.
- On command, jump forward across line A, then backward over the same line, back into the middle of the hexagon.
- Continue to face line A. This time, with feet together, jump over line B with both feet, then back to the middle. Then jump over line C and back to the middle, then over lines D, E, and F, following the same pattern, always with your feet facing forward toward line A. Once you have jumped over and back on all six sides, you have completed one full circuit.
- Complete three full circuits. If you jump over the wrong line or land on a line, you must restart the test.

Record your average time per circuit as your final score, and see if you can better that number the next time. Again, your teacher may be able to refer you to performance standards for the Hexagon Drill.

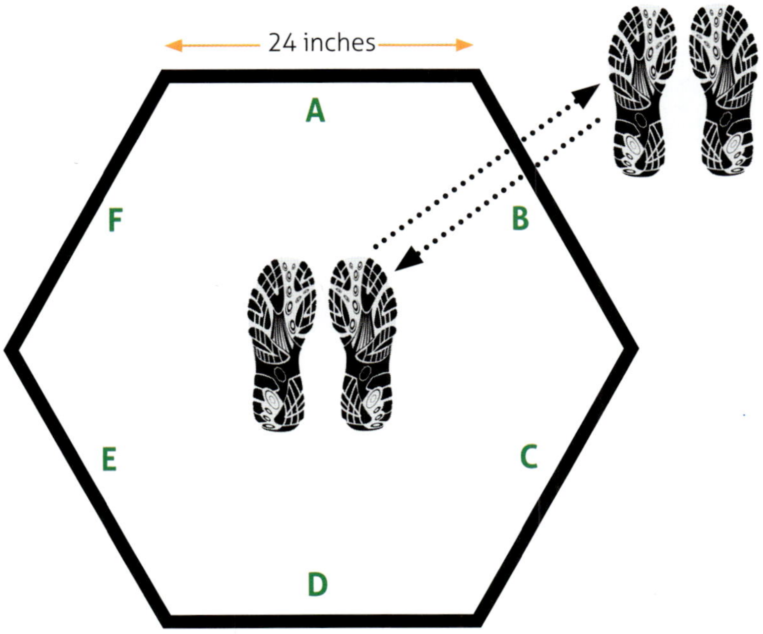

20-Yard and 40-Yard Sprints

The **40-Yard Sprint** (or Dash) was developed by the Dallas Cowboys of the National Football League in the late 1960s, but this appraisal is important for any sport in which athletes have to accelerate from a stationary position and reach top speed as quickly as possible.

The test can be performed indoors or outdoors. (If running indoors, ensure there is a slow-down area a safe distance from an encroaching wall.) You will need two partners to record your times.

Ready, Set, Go!

- Measure off 20 yards (18.29 m) and 40 yards (36.58 m) on a flat, non-slip surface, and mark the distances with cones. Have one partner stand at the 20-yard mark and the other at the 40-yard mark.
- Stand at the start in a sprint or standing position.
- On command, run as quickly as possible past the 40-yard mark.
- Have your partners record your time at the 20-yard and 40-yard marks. These are your final scores.

Your goal should be to see improvement in your scores each time you perform the appraisal. Your teacher may be able to refer you to performance standards for this appraisal.

Flexed-Arm Hang and Chin-Ups

The **Flexed-Arm Hang and Chin-Ups** appraisals measure the muscular strength and endurance of the forearms, arms, and shoulders.

The major difference between them is that Chin-Ups (also called Pull-Ups) are dynamic and the Flexed-Arm Hang is not. It involves an isometric contraction—the elbow angle and muscle length do not change.

Both appraisals use a horizontal bar about 4 centimetres in diameter, positioned at a height that allows you to hang without touching the ground. If you cannot perform one to five Chin-Ups on your own, you should probably try the Flexed-Arm Hang first.

Flexed-Arm Hang: Ready, Set, Go!

- Grasp the bar using an underhand grip (palms toward you, thumbs wrapped around the bar).
- With the help of two spotters, one in front and one behind, pull yourself up until your chin is above the bar.
- Hold this position for as long as possible.
- Stop if your chin touches the bar, if your head tilts backward to keep your chin above the bar, or if your chin falls below the level of the bar.
- Record your time, and refer to it the next time you do the appraisal to see how much you have improved.

Chin-Ups: Ready, Set, Go!

- Grasp the bar using an underhand grip.
- Pull yourself up until your chin is over the bar, then lower yourself until your arms are straight.
- Perform as many repetitions as possible without swinging your legs to gain momentum.

Record your results, and refer to them the next time you do the appraisal to see how much you have improved. Again, your teacher may be able to refer you to performance norms for this appraisal.

Chin-Ups

Shoulder Taps

The **Shoulder Taps** appraisal assesses the strength of the core muscles of the abdomen and back, which support the spine and keep the body stable during all forms of movement. This appraisal also assesses the strength of the upper body, which can make movements such as opening a door or completing a chest pass in basketball easier.

Ready, Set, Go!

- Begin in high plank position, with both hands on the floor or a mat, arms extended but slightly bent at the elbows, and wrists directly under the shoulders.
- Keep your back straight, not arched or sagging.
- Have a partner place a pool noodle along your spine.
- Slowly lift your right hand off the floor and tap your left shoulder.
- Return your right hand to the floor.
- Redistribute your weight, lift your left hand off the floor, and touch your right shoulder.
- Continue until the pool noodle falls off your back.

Record the number of shoulder taps you were able to perform, and see if you can better that number the next time you take the appraisal. Your teacher may also be able to refer you to performance standards for this appraisal.

Wall-Ball Toss

The **Wall-Ball Toss** appraisal measures hand–eye coordination. Coordination is the ability to use the nervous and musculoskeletal systems to control complex movements. This skill is important in sports such as tennis and baseball.

This appraisal requires you to throw a tennis ball against a wall from waist level and catch it with the opposite hand. For a 30-second count, a score of 30 or above is considered "very good" to "excellent." For a 60-second count, 60 or more is "very good" to "excellent."

Ready, Set, Go!

- Mark a line on the floor 1.5 metres from a smooth wall. Most gymnasium walls will work well. Stand behind the line and throw the ball against the wall underhand, catching it with your other hand.
- Alternate hands—throw left, catch right; throw right and catch left—for 30 or 60 seconds.
- Count each successful catch, and do not use your body to catch the ball. If you drop the ball or catch it in the wrong hand, pick it up as quickly as you can and continue.

Record the number of successful catches, and see if you can better that number the next time. Again, your teacher may be able to refer you to performance standards for this appraisal.

Long Jump

Standing Long Jump

Many sports—such as track and field, basketball, and volleyball—require leg strength. The **Standing Long Jump** is a good way to assess leg strength, helping you to determine how effective your training program is.

This appraisal requires an appropriate surface, such as a gymnasium floor. You could also benefit from having a partner to mark your landing and record your results.

Ready, Set, Go!

- Mark a starting line for your jump.
- Place your feet behind the line and crouch down.
- Swing your arms up behind you, then swing them forward as you jump horizontally as far as possible, landing with both feet.
- Have your partner or teacher measure and record the distance from the starting line to your closer heel.
- Repeat the appraisal two more times.

Record your longest recorded distance as your final score, and see if you can better that number the next time. Your teacher may be able to refer you to performance standards for this appraisal.

Section 3.4 Review

1. What is the main purpose of performance-level appraisals?
2. Which of the performance-level appraisals did you find most beneficial, and why?
3. What might motivate you or a friend to improve your performance-related fitness?

3.5 Understanding Body Composition

Fat protects organs, insulates body tissue, provides energy, and helps break down certain vitamins. That means it is essential to keeping our bodies healthy.

Body composition refers to the distribution of fat throughout the body in relation to bone, muscle, and other tissue. Body composition assessments help medical professionals identify potential health problems. Excess body fat can signal increased risk of type 2 diabetes, high blood pressure, coronary artery disease, stroke, and certain forms of cancer.

Body composition assessments alone do not give an accurate picture of overall fitness. They should always be combined with cardiorespiratory and muscular strength and endurance assessments.

Talk to your Health and Physical Education teacher if you wish to know more about the body composition assessments described below—how they are conducted, their relative usefulness, and their limitations.

Body Composition Assessments

Qualified exercise professionals or health care practitioners will trust their own professional judgment when selecting which of the following body composition assessments to use or recommend for specific individuals.

Waist Circumference. A qualified exercise professional or health care practitioner records an adult's waist measurement and then refers to a table of standards to determine the individual's health risk rating. Evidence suggests that abdominal fat is a more important determinant of health outcomes than overall body fat.

Body Mass Index (BMI). One of the most widely used body composition appraisals is the **Body Mass Index (BMI)**. Your BMI score gives a rough indication of whether your body weight, or mass, is appropriate for your height.

For adults, CSEP-PATH recommends using BMI in combination with waist circumference. Together they provide a better appraisal of health benefits and risks related to the amount of body fat and fat distribution. To assess the body composition of people younger than 20, however, CSEP-PATH recommends using only BMI while taking age and gender into account. To assess the risks related to weight for the same age group, the World Health Organization's BMI-for-age growth charts can also be used.

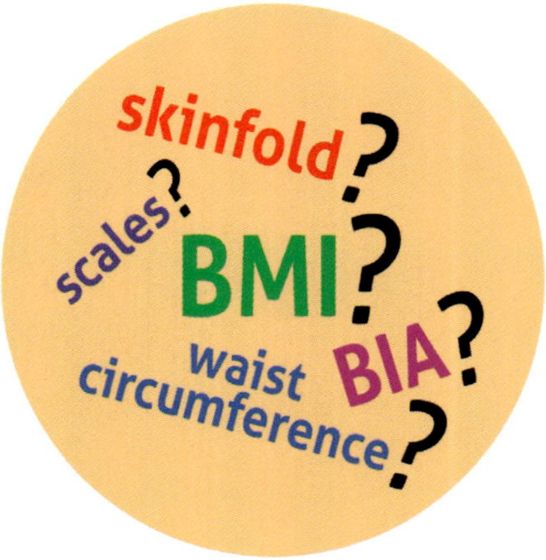

BMI does not distinguish between body fat and dense muscle. It does not directly measure body fat or take into account where fat is located in the body, so it is not useful for very muscular individuals, such as elite or recreational athletes.

Skinfold measurements. This assessment involves multiple measures at standardized sites on the body using a device called a skinfold caliper. These measurements are intended to provide an estimate of subcutaneous fat (fat located just underneath the skin), which is proportional to a person's total amount of body fat.

Measurement errors increase with skinfold thicknesses, however, and a great deal of training and regular practice are required to approach acceptable accuracy.

Bioelectrical Impedance Analysis (BIA). This assessment provides an estimation of body fat percentage using a device that passes a low-level electrical current through the body to measure the impedance, or resistance, to the flow of electricity. The higher the amount of water in the body, the less resistance there is to the electrical current. Fat tissue has lower water content than fat-free tissue. Therefore, the greater the amount of fat tissue, the greater the resistance to the electrical current.

One limitation of this technique is that it provides an estimation of total body fat percentage but no information on the *distribution* of body fat, which is the most significant predictor of health benefits and risks.

Body-fat scales. These digital bathroom scales measure your weight and claim to indicate the percentage of your weight that comes from fat versus muscle, bone, and water. Some of these scales also calculate your BMI, and some allow you to upload information to an app so you can track measurements over time. However, body-fat scales also provide no information on body-fat distribution.

MRI and CAT Scans

All of the body composition assessment techniques described here have limitations and do not work for everyone.

Newer, more sophisticated techniques such as magnetic resonance imaging (MRI) and computer-aided tomography (CAT) scans, although expensive, are now considered "gold standard" methods used by qualified medical or exercise professionals to assess a person's body composition.

Body Composition and Body Image

Each of us has a mental picture of our own body—our **body image**. Your body image may be positive or negative, and it can also fluctuate. It includes what you think and how you feel about the look, size, or shape of your body, or parts or features of your body, how you see yourself, and how you think you look to others.

It is important to understand that body composition appraisals are not judgments about appearance or personal worth—they are tools to help you understand certain aspects of your health and fitness. Therefore it is best not to confuse talking about body composition with a judgment on anyone's size or shape or to let an assessment of your body composition distort your body image in any way.

The influence of self-esteem on body image

Body image is one component of **self-esteem**. Self-esteem describes how valued or worthy a person feels. How we see ourselves affects our self-esteem—and our self-esteem affects how we see ourselves.

People with strong self-esteem feel confident and consider themselves deserving of success and achievement. People with low self-esteem may feel unworthy of the opportunities life has to offer. Fortunately, we can all learn how to develop strong self-esteem and feel good about our unique talents and potential.

Body image is dynamic. The way that you view your body 10 or 15 years from now may very well differ from how you see yourself today. A number of factors, some obvious and some subtle, influence our body image, including the messages we receive from society and the media, our family and friends, and our life experiences.

Influences on our body image are everywhere and can sometimes be destabilizing. Seek advice from a counsellor or health care professional if you are experiencing anxiety related to body image or self-esteem.

The impact of media and advertising

Every day, we are exposed to countless media images featuring "perfect" bodies—but many of these images have been altered digitally.

Media messaging and cultural pressures to achieve an "ideal" body shape or size can be extremely damaging to our self-esteem.

A global fashion, cosmetics, and weight-loss industry worth billions of dollars depends on people's insecurities about the way they look. Many of us respond by comparing ourselves to the often exaggerated media images we see. Sometimes we are tempted to believe that if we buy a certain product, we will look or be like the models in the advertising for that product or like the celebrities who endorse it.

It is important to question all the messages you see in the media telling you that "thin" and "fit" are the same thing. *Active people and fit, healthy bodies come in many different shapes and sizes.*

The role of relationships

Sometimes, with the best of intentions, family members and friends push us to lose weight, go on a diet, or get more toned. It can be difficult to feel happy with our own bodies if other people in our lives are reinforcing unrealistic ideals about body image.

On the other hand, family and friends can help us feel more secure and boost our self-worth by letting us know that how we look is fine and by encouraging healthy behaviours instead. This reduces the pressure to look a certain way and encourages an approach to wellness that is not focused on looks.

What our experiences teach us

Experience also affects our body image and self-esteem. Experiences that demonstrate resilience and physical strength—for example, overcoming an illness or participating in a fitness activity—can help you to see your body as a valuable asset that is worthy of your care.

With experience, you will come to realize that *physical fitness is not about how thin or muscular you are.* Fitness is about your body's ability to do strenuous activity over a period of time—primarily your cardiorespiratory and musculoskeletal health. It is also about having fun as you participate in a range of physical activities, sports, and games that are challenging, relaxing, and enjoyable.

While teachers and coaches are among those who can help us understand our strengths and develop a positive body image, ultimately we are in charge of how we see ourselves. Regardless of body type, we can all achieve good overall health. Attitude and motivation are key factors. If you have any concerns, consult a qualified exercise professional or a family doctor who specializes in the health aspects of body composition.

Section 3.5 Review

1. In your own words, define the term *body composition.*
2. Briefly describe some influences, both positive and negative, on a person's body image.
3. What might you say to reassure a friend who is concerned about body image?

Miryam's Story

"Never let the fear of getting out keep you from playing the game."
— Miryam Khokhar

Chapter 3 Review

Knowledge and Understanding

1 What does a healthy 24 hours look like according to the Canadian Society for Exercise Physiology?

2 Define the terms *aerobic fitness* and *musculoskeletal fitness*, giving examples.

Thinking

3 Compare and contrast health-related fitness and skill-related fitness using a Venn diagram, a table, or simple sketches.

4 Based on your cardiorespiratory appraisals, list the appropriate steps to maintain or improve your current level of fitness.

5 Interview someone who has chosen a career in the fitness industry (preferably a CSEP-certified professional). Ask the person you interview to describe the most effective fitness appraisals to use when working with clients. Be prepared to present your interview in class.

Communication

6 Create a poster or write a blog that presents compelling reasons for following safety guidelines during fitness appraisals.

7 Take your heart rate during a strenuous exercise session to see if you are exercising in your Target Heart Rate Zone. Explain why it is important to get your heart rate into this zone when exercising.

8 Identify which of the fitness appraisals described in this chapter you would choose for yourself, and explain why.

9 Engage in a group discussion about what steps individuals can take to help ensure their body can do everything they want to achieve. What supports might they look for?

10 Explain why the body composition appraisal known as the body mass index (BMI) does not work for everyone.

Application

11 What changes, if any, would you recommend to your family members to ensure that they follow CSEP's Canadian 24-Hour Movement Guidelines for Children and Youth?

12 Browse through five or six popular magazines and document any instances where you feel that the advertising or stories in these magazines might negatively influence a person's body image. Explain why in each instance.

Fitness Planning and Injury Prevention

4

Angel's Story

What things do you need to take into account when designing your own personal fitness plan?

The most successful people—innovators, actors, athletes, business leaders, to name a few—set goals to stay motivated and focused. You can do the same.

In this chapter, you will learn some techniques to develop and apply realistic goals to your fitness and exercise routine. This key skill will also help you set other types of personal goals to keep all aspects of your life on track.

The chapter also describes some common injuries related to physical activity, along with ways to prevent them. The choices you make about exercise safety can make physical activity effective and fun.

You will also be introduced to exercises that work the major muscles and muscle groups to help you improve your core strength, flexibility, balance, and endurance.

Learning Objectives

In this chapter, you will...

- explore the SMART approach to goal setting and how to apply it to your fitness and exercise routine
- examine common barriers to reaching fitness goals and the strategies to overcome them
- examine the individuality principle, the overload principle, the progression principle, the specificity principle, and the reversibility principle
- learn how the FITT principle can help you develop a realistic fitness plan
- elaborate your own fitness plan, using the strategies and techniques outlined
- learn to put safety first in a variety of settings
- explore some basic principles and key concepts related to functional fitness training and resistance training
- examine and attempt a number of health-related fitness exercises that target specific muscles or muscle groups

Key Terms

- short-term goals
- long-term goals
- SMART goal setting
- action plan
- individuality principle
- overload principle
- progression principle
- specificity principle
- reversibility principle
- FITT principle
- strain
- delayed onset muscle soreness (DOMS)
- tendonitis
- SHARP
- PIER
- ligaments
- sprain
- dislocation/separation
- fracture
- shin splint
- stress fracture
- concussion
- functional fitness training
- resistance training
- repetitions/sets
- multiple-repetition maximum

▶ **Angel Blainey** follows a strenuous but enjoyable personal training program. She is a synchro swimmer and competitive skier whose goal is to participate in the World Winter Games. Angel is a cancer survivor who has donated the sales of a cookbook she wrote—almost $40,000—to the oncology and Down syndrome programs at SickKids Hospital in Toronto.

4.1 Setting and Reaching Fitness Goals

Habits can be difficult to break, but clear, attainable goals and good planning can help you change the way you do things. Just knowing that you can succeed is a strong motivator.

Personal fitness planning involves two types of goals:

- **Short-term goals** are specific and can be completed in a few hours, days, or weeks. Measuring your progress in a single workout, or even over a series of exercise sessions, is an example of a short-term fitness goal.
- **Long-term goals** express what you want to achieve over a longer period. Reaching a particular body weight over a semester or even a few years is a long-term fitness goal. Learning to perform a specific skill over a period of time, such as an overhand tennis serve or a yoga position, is another example.

When it comes to goal setting, "short" and "long" are relative terms. Short-term goals should be part of long-term goals, which in turn can form part of longer-term goals.

Being SMART about Goal Setting

Getting started is often the hardest part of setting goals. To set a goal you need a plan—and to make a plan you need motivation. The **SMART** strategy can help.

SMART refers to five key elements of effective goal setting: make your goals **S**pecific, **M**eaningful and **M**easurable, **A**ction oriented, **R**ealistic, and **T**ime bound. Try the **SMART** method the next time you have to set short- or long-term goals, whether they are related to physical fitness or any other aspect of your life.

Specific—Is your goal clear?

A vague goal such as "I want to get in shape" may not provide motivation because it does not indicate how you can achieve it or for what reason. A more specific goal such as "I want to run 20 minutes a day, non-stop, to prepare for my five-kilometre run" is more action-oriented.

Meaningful and measurable—How will you know?

Choose goals that are meaningful to you, and measure your results. If, for example, you want to run a 5 or a 10 km road race by the end of the year even if you are not prepared for it now, you need progressive short-term goals that measure gradual improvement. You might decide, "After one week I will not be out of breath when I run for 10 minutes straight."

Goals must involve something that can be measured. If you cannot measure a goal, then you will not be able to describe your success.

Action oriented—What are the steps?

Your goal must involve taking action. "I want to get in shape this year" is a non-action-oriented goal. To turn it into an action-oriented goal, you could decide, "To get in shape this year, I will not eat junk food more than once a week, and I will eat breakfast every day. I'll walk to school twice a week and join one intramural activity each semester."

Realistic—How likely are you to reach your goal?

Do not try the impossible. A goal is realistic and attainable if it involves a convenient location and appropriate equipment, if it is within your physical and mental capabilities, and if it is something you want to accomplish. To set yourself up for success, you need achievable goals.

Time bound—How long will it take?

A firm timeline, with the time or date you expect to reach your goal and the steps that you need to take, will make your goals easier to reach. Successfully completing short-term goals along the way will keep you on the right track and will boost your confidence.

Setting Your Goals

Consider the following factors when setting personal health and fitness goals:

- your motivation
- your current fitness level
- the influence of peers and friends
- the availability of equipment and facilities
- school, work, and family commitments

Creating a Fitness Action Plan

An **action plan** can help you achieve your health and fitness goals, or any other personal goals—from getting good grades to developing fulfilling relationships. An action plan has four stages:

1. Set SMART goals.
2. Develop action steps.
3. Identify barriers and solutions.
4. Celebrate your success.

Set SMART goals

Visualize your goal. It does not have to be large or difficult, but it has to be personal—something that serves your purpose. Separate the short- and long-term aspects and figure out how they relate to one another.

Then ask, "Is my goal **S**pecific, **M**eaningful and **m**easurable, **A**ction oriented, **R**ealistic, and **T**ime bound?" Is it, in other words, a truly SMART goal?

Develop action steps

List all the smaller things that need to happen in order for you to reach the larger goal. Develop flexible deadlines for each step. What will you do tomorrow? Next week? Next month? By the end of the school year?

Identify barriers and find solutions

Remember that sticking to your program is not an all-or-nothing deal. Sometimes unexpected events may throw you off your schedule, and your plan needs to be flexible enough to cope.

In Chapter 1, you read about the IDEAL model of decision making. It offers a good sequence of steps if you have to make difficult decisions about how to continue your fitness program. Could someone from your school, home, or community lend a hand?

Celebrate your success

What will be different when you reach your goal? Monitor your progress by keeping a log of your results, and seek feedback from teachers, coaches, friends, parents, or guardians. If people see you trying, they will be willing to help, and you can benefit from their advice.

Significantly changing your approach to health and fitness is worth celebrating. Even the most modest celebration will encourage you to stay on the path to fitness success.

Getting Motivated

Many people starting a fitness program notice that they make great progress in the first few weeks. Then, the grind begins. Exercising on a regular basis takes motivation.

Realizing that you are actually moving closer to your goal is a great incentive, so it's a good idea to keep track of your progress. For example, monitoring your resting heart rate every morning over four to five weeks of aerobic training could reveal a drop of about five to ten beats per minute.

What else can help you stick to your fitness plan?

Ownership. Make sure the goals are your own, not your friends' or your teachers'.

Variety. Varying activities and environments can help keep you motivated while producing the same training results. Ice skating, snowshoeing, tobogganing, swimming, skateboarding, kayaking, or canoeing adds variety and gets you out of the gym or fitness room.

A training partner or a change of equipment or workout time can also make fitness training more enjoyable.

Challenge. Think both big and small. Small victories feed the drive to achieve big things.

Revision. Sometimes you will be successful, and sometimes you will not. Either way, it's a good idea to ask from time to time, "Are the goals I set originally still good ones?" If not, revise them to make them more attainable.

Reinforcement. Praise yourself for anything you do to move closer to your goal. Acknowledge successes as you meet your short-term objectives.

Reward. Treat yourself in some memorable way when you achieve a significant long-term goal. Organize a night out with friends, for example, or plan a special meal with your family.

Section 4.1 Review

1 What is the difference between short-term and long-term fitness goals? What is the relationship between the two types of goals?

2 Name each component of the SMART approach to goal setting, and give examples of each.

3 What are the four stages of creating a fitness action plan?

4.2

4.2 Training Principles

Your fitness program should be tailored to your needs and goals, but the underlying principles apply to everyone. Understanding five key training principles will help you maximize the effectiveness of your plan and minimize the potential for injury:

- individuality
- overload
- progression
- specificity
- reversibility

The Individuality Principle

The **individuality principle** acknowledges that we all have different training needs and respond differently to a given training protocol.

This principle recognizes that everyone has a unique physical and psychological makeup and that many factors affect our training needs: pre-training fitness, physical development, eating habits, heredity, social, economic and cultural influences, physical challenges, the quality of our training routines, and whether we follow training principles.

The Overload Principle

When you give your body more to do than it is used to, you create an overload. The **overload principle** means that unless there is some sort of overload, the activity will not lead to significant improvement.

This principle underlies most fitness activity. Your body gradually adapts to the additional demands put on it—the heart and lungs adapt in response to aerobic activities, the abdominal muscles adapt to crunches, the legs adapt to squats. As they do so, your cardiorespiratory system and muscles become stronger and more efficient.

The Progression Principle

When you begin fitness training, you may see fairly rapid improvement—and probably soreness—but the rate at which you improve gradually slows down and the gains become more evenly paced. This is known as the **progression principle**. This training principle states that fitness improves gradually as we progressively add to the overload. This principle also underlines that you should not (and cannot) train hard all the time. It is not physically possible, nor is it wise.

The Specificity Principle

Your fitness can improve in response to the type of physical activity you do. Your muscle strength can improve when you lift resistance objects such as weights. Aerobic improvements can come from activities such as cycling, swimming, or jogging. Your flexibility can improve when you stretch.

In sports, the maximum training effect sometimes comes from mimicking the type of effort the sport demands. This is known as the **specificity principle**. The more closely the training activity focuses on a particular aspect of fitness or skill, the more benefit it will give you in that area.

Of course, you can gain upper-body strength from swimming or aerobic benefits from a strength class. In fact, our favourite activities sometimes produce several different fitness benefits. In general, though, improvement comes from practising a specific activity repeatedly, safely, and properly.

The Reversibility Principle

A short break in your routine is not a serious problem—you may even need a break in order to move on to larger goals. If you stop for a long time, however, you start to lose the gains you have made. This process is sometimes called "detraining." What you have done can easily become undone, in which case you will have to start all over again.

The fact that your body's response to training is not permanent is known as the **reversibility principle**. Some strength gains may begin to decrease in as little as three days, and a few months without regular activity will put you back to where you were before starting your program.

The secret is to make activity an integral part of your life. That way, you will always be in shape.

Section 4.2 Review

1 List some factors that influence an individual's training needs.

2 Name and briefly define the five fitness principles described in this section.

3 The amount of overload must gradually be increased for improvement to continue. Which fitness principle does this statement reflect?

4.3

4.3 Designing Your Fitness Program

Your most important fitness goal should be to become committed to a healthy, active lifestyle. This means establishing a realistic balance of healthy eating, adequate sleep and rest, and daily physical activity.

There are many factors to keep in mind when designing a fitness training program for yourself, and there are some well-structured, proven methods to help you. One of these methods is known as the **FITT principle**.

An Effective Training Program

The **FITT principle** is a well-known approach to designing a balanced fitness training program. **FITT** stands for the four elements of any good training plan: **F**requency, **I**ntensity, **T**ime, and **T**ype of activity.

- **Frequency** refers to how often you do an exercise, and that is just as important as the type of exercise you do. A single exercise session can provide gains, but building your fitness takes regular activity, usually three times a week or more. Keep in mind that after a particularly long or challenging workout, you may need to wait one or two days before resuming a similar workout.
- **Intensity** is a measure of how hard you are working while you are doing an exercise. Scientists who study the effect of exercise on the body have come up with simple methods to determine just how hard your heart, lungs, and muscles are working when they are exercised. For your cardiorespiratory system, these measurements are based on your heart rate. For your muscles, they are based on how much weight a set of muscles can lift using the proper technique.
- **Time** refers to how long you exercise. The duration of the activity will depend on the intensity, your goals, and the time you have available.
- **Type** refers to the nature of your exercise. Unless you are training for a specific activity or sport—and therefore need to be doing plenty of exercises specific to that activity or sport—most experts recommend a training program that includes a variety of activities. Maintaining variety keeps you motivated and prevents injuries due to overtraining.

When designing a fitness program, you can incorporate these five phases:

1. *a movement preparation routine* to prepare your body and avoid injury
2. *aerobic conditioning* to strengthen your heart and lungs
3. *muscular conditioning* to build up strength through resistance training
4. *flexibility exercises* to maintain your range of motion
5. *a cool-down phase* to allow recovery and relieve muscle tightness

The FITT Principle

This table matches the four elements of the FITT principle against the main components of a balanced fitness program.

	Cardiorespiratory	Flexibility	Muscular endurance	Muscular strength
F Frequency	• 3–5 times per week • Increase frequency as you get into better shape	• Should be a regular part of your warm-up and cool-down • Increase frequency as you get into better shape	• Daily for some muscle groups • Perform 3–4 times per week • Increase frequency as you get into better shape	• Perform 3 times per week • Different muscle groups each time you work out • Increase frequency as you get into better shape
I Intensity	• 50–65% of heart rate reserve • Increase intensity as you get into better shape	• Stretch all major muscles and joints; hold for 15–30 seconds • Perform 1–3 repetitions • Increase intensity as you get into better shape	• Less than 50% of your predicted 1-rep max • Start with body weight then add resistance • 15 or more reps/1–3 sets • Increase intensity as you get into better shape	• 60–80% of 1-rep max • 8–12 reps/1–3 sets • Increase intensity as you get into better shape
T Time	• 20–60 minutes of continuous activity • Increase the time as you get into better shape	• 10–20 minutes • Increase the time as you get into better shape	• 30–60 minutes • Increase the time as you get into better shape	• 15–60 minutes • Increase the time as you get into better shape
T Type	• Running, cycling, swimming, and activities that use large muscles	• Perform static stretches and controlled dynamic stretches	• Resistance training (body weight/tubing/ medicine balls/free weights)	• Resistance training (body weight/tubing/ medicine balls/free weights)

Source: Adapted with permission from "Ontario Health and Physical Education Curriculum Support: Grades K–10," Ontario Physical Health Education Association (OPHEA), Toronto;

Overcoming Barriers

We all experience barriers to maintain a healthy active lifestyle, but many strategies can help us overcome them. Here are some of the most common barriers we face when it comes to following a fitness program and suggestions on how to overcome them.

"I don't have time."

- Examine the inactive parts of your day to see if you can add exercise to them, such as walking to school or getting off the bus one or two stops earlier. Every step of walking is better than every second of sitting.
- Make adjustments to your free time, such as spending less time on social media.

"The facilities are too far away."

- Find areas in your home that you can use instead of distant facilities, such as your bedroom, living room, or basement.
- Turn everyday activities into exercise, such as taking the stairs rather than an escalator.

"I have heavy school and work commitments."

- Review your timetable with your guidance counsellor or teacher to find ways to include Health and Physical Education every year.
- Take regular fitness breaks while studying. Three sets of 10 to 12 push-ups, lunges, or squats will help circulate blood to your brain, making you more alert as well as stronger.

"I'm never going to reach my goal!"

- Revise your original goal, possibly scaling it back a little.
- Post your goal somewhere you will see it often, such as in your locker.
- Look for support from friends, relatives, and training partners.

"I'm embarrassed because I'm not in great shape."

- Focus on the health benefits. People today recognize that fitness comes in all shapes and sizes.
- Discuss your goals and concerns with a friend, teacher, or elder.

"This exercise program is boring!"

- Try different equipment, such as medicine balls instead of weights.
- Work out with a friend.
- Listen to music while you work out.
- Take your activities outdoors, such as playing ball in the park or hiking with a friend.
- Vary your routine a little. Most of all, have fun!

Evaluating Your Progress

When you are following a personal fitness plan, you should aim to evaluate your progress regularly. Visual tools can be especially helpful in monitoring your progress, so you may find that a goal-setting worksheet is a useful tool. You can use the worksheet not only to record your progress but also to identify the people you may want to call upon to support you.

It is also always worthwhile to reflect on which elements of your fitness program you would keep the same and on what you would do differently when it comes time to set new goals.

Staying motivated

Staying motivated can be the most challenging part of incorporating more activity into your schedule, but try not to let the occasional bad day get you down. Do not let missing a day of activity turn into an excuse to stop.

Getting input from a trusted adult, mentor, or your closest friends can help you stay motivated, inspired, and on task—even on days when you are not feeling your best.

Do not forget to celebrate successes and come up with strategies to overcome any real or potential barriers. If you are not having fun, it's time to revise or replace your fitness goals. Add more short-term goals, reward yourself as you reach each one, and try to keep active every day.

Section 4.3 Review

1. What does the acronym *FITT* stand for in the context of fitness planning?
2. Give two examples of how the intensity of an exercise can be measured.
3. How many minutes of continuous activity are recommended in order to get aerobic benefits?

4.4 Injuries and Injury Prevention

Many common injuries that occur during physical activity involve the muscles, ligaments, and tendons. These include muscle and tendon strains and tears, muscle soreness, and tendonitis.

Muscle and Tendon Strains and Tears

A **strain** is caused by twisting, pulling, or overstretching a muscle or tendon. If strains remain untreated, tears in the muscle or tendon fibres may get worse. Strains can be either acute or chronic.

- **Acute strains** appear suddenly and can be severe. They can occur during contact sports or when heavy objects are lifted improperly.
- **Chronic strains** occur over an extended period. They usually result from prolonged overuse and repetitive movement of the muscles and tendons while not giving them enough time to rest.

Strains and tears fall into three categories of severity:

- First-degree injuries are the least severe. They usually take a day or a few days to heal if you rest and take proper measures.
- Second-degree injuries are moderate and more severe. They require the attention of a rehabilitation professional.
- Third-degree injuries are the most severe and may need surgery and rehabilitation. They can take 6 to 12 months to repair fully.

Muscle and tendon injuries need time to heal. It is important not to make the injury worse by continuing to exercise strenuously. If the condition is severe, then it is important to seek medical advice as soon as possible.

Delayed Onset Muscle Soreness

Delayed onset muscle soreness (DOMS) refers to the feeling of muscle pain a day or two after intense exercise beyond your usual level—how sore you are depends on the type and intensity of activity.

DOMS is not the same as the immediate and acute pain of a pulled or strained muscle. It is believed to result from microscopic tearing deep within the muscle fibres. Swelling can also occur in and around the affected muscle.

The soreness usually disappears within about 72 hours after appearing. Any steps that increase blood flow to the affected muscles (such as low-intensity activity, massage, hot baths, or a sauna) may help to reduce the soreness.

Proper movement preparation and cool-down exercises can also help to minimize soreness. You should consult your doctor if you feel sore for more than a few days.

Tendonitis

Prolonged or abnormal use of a tendon can irritate it, causing inflammation known as **tendonitis**. Most tendonitis can be avoided by doing proper movement preparation exercises, always moving well, resting the area sufficiently, and increasing physical activity slowly.

Tendonitis has various symptoms:

- pain or tenderness of the tendon
- stiffness and pain that restrict use of the tendon
- occasionally, mild swelling, numbness, or a tingling sensation at the joint

Tendonitis is usually named after the affected tendon or joint. For example, tendonitis of the Achilles tendon—the tissue that connects the calf muscles to the heel bone—is known as *Achilles tendonitis*. Tendonitis caused by excessive use of the lateral forearm and elbow is often referred to as *tennis elbow*. The illustration below shows the different muscles and tendons affected in cases of tennis elbow and golfer's elbow, which are similar injuries.

Early treatment involves rest, cold and heat therapy, and sometimes very temporary splints. A doctor may also prescribe medicated creams. Numerous other treatment options are available.

Preventing Injuries

Following a personal safety and injury prevention plan can prevent many common injuries. Assess the risks of an activity and make decisions such as:

- identifying ways to stay safe
- deciding whether to check in with an adult
- determining whether the challenge is within your skill set
- choosing the safest options

Apply procedures that maximize your safety and that of others, such as:

- wearing appropriate and properly fitting protective equipment
- checking the activity area for hazards prior to participation
- following the rules of the sport, e.g., no head hits
- using proper stretching techniques during cool-down activities
- always putting safety first

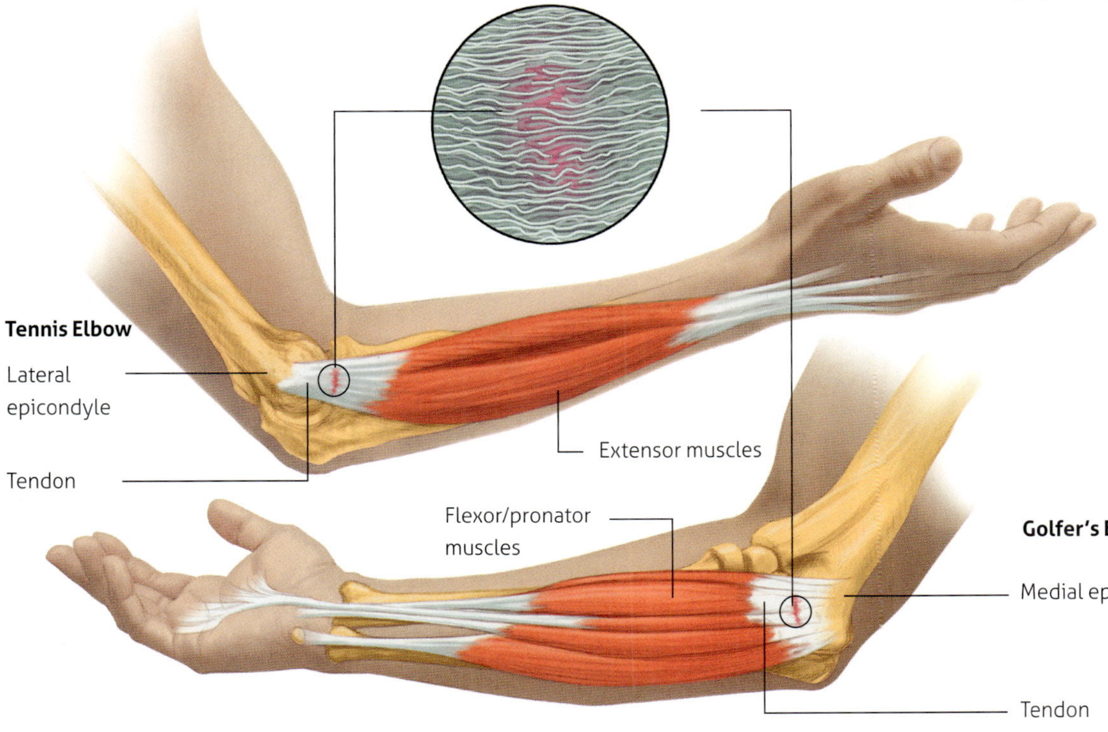

Tennis elbow (lateral epicondylitis) occurs when one of the tendons that connects the forearm to the humerus becomes inflamed. **Golfer's elbow** (medial epicondylitis) is a similar injury, only on the inside of the elbow.

SHARP and PIER

It is important to recognize the signs of an injury so you can take immediate action to stop further damage. The well-known acronyms **SHARP** and **PIER** can help you to recognize and treat minor injuries.

SHARP

Use **SHARP** to remember the signs of injury. In the event of injury, the affected area will show one or more of these signs:

- **S**welling, either instantly or over time
- **H**eat, as more blood flows to the area
- **A**lteration, as the joint may not function properly
- **R**edness, as more blood flows to the area
- **P**ain, if the area is moved or touched

PIER

Keep **PIER** in mind to help you limit the damage from a sports- or activity-related injury.

- **P**ressure should be applied to the affected area using a tensor wrap or special tape, after ice has been applied.
- **I**ce should be placed on the injured area, with a piece of paper towel or cloth between the ice and the skin to avoid skin damage. Keep ice on for 10 to 20 minutes, take it off for the same length of time, and apply again. Repeated icings will help reduce swelling.
- **E**levate the injured area while it is being iced, as this will also help reduce swelling.
- **R**estrict movement with a tensor, sling, or crutches to allow the affected area to rest.

Ligament and Joint Injuries

In Chapter 2, you learned about movement at joints. Joints can sustain various kinds of injury during physical activity or sport.

Ligaments are connective tissues that attach bone to bone. Like rope, they do not stretch much. When ligaments are pulled to their limit they tear, damaging some of their fibres. The severity of the tear depends on the amount of force placed on the ligament. Once ligaments are torn, the entire joint can become unstable.

Sprains

When a ligament is overstretched or torn, the result is a **sprain**. Similar to strains, which occur in muscles and tendons, sprains are classified by severity:

- First-degree sprains can be treated easily, since only a few fibres are torn.
- Second-degree sprains involve more widespread damage and need more attention.
- Third-degree sprains usually mean that the entire ligament is torn, and you might need surgery to repair or reconstruct the ligament.

Sprains can happen when the joint is hit away from its centre, causing an overstretch of the ligament. An awkward landing can also produce a sprain, such as landing on the outside of your ankle when you go for a lay-up in basketball. This is commonly referred to as rolling over on your ankle.

Dislocations and separations

A bone can become displaced from its joint, creating a **dislocation**. Dislocations are often caused by a collision or a fall, and they are common in finger and shoulder joints. Do not attempt to put the bone back into place—you could do more damage.

When ligaments are torn, the bones that they attach to may separate. The most common type of **separation** is a shoulder separation—when the strong ligaments that attach the collar bone (clavicle) to the shoulder blade (scapula) are torn.

Dislocations and separations vary in degree of severity depending on the amount of tearing the ligaments sustain. Be sure to inform your teacher, coach, parents, or guardian if you injure yourself in one of these ways. The sooner you receive medical diagnosis and treatment, the sooner you will be back up and active again!

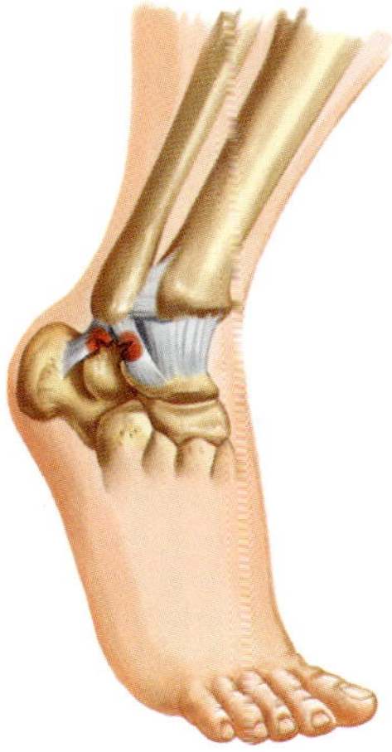

Ligaments do not stretch very far, so when they stretch too much, a sprain occurs. Sprains often occur in the ankle joints.

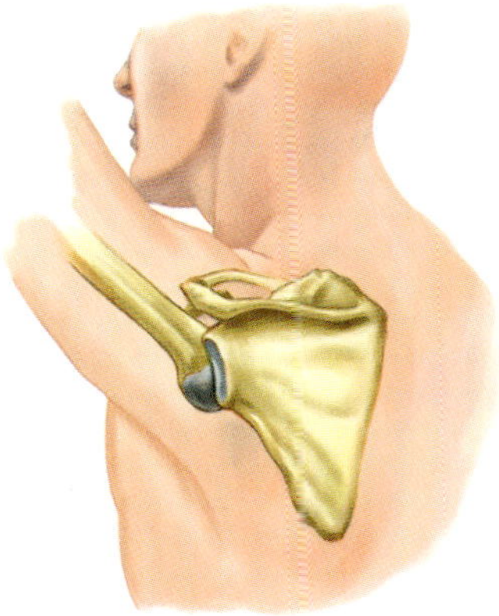

A rough collision or fall can cause a bone to be displaced from its joint. This is called dislocation and occurs often in shoulder or finger joints.

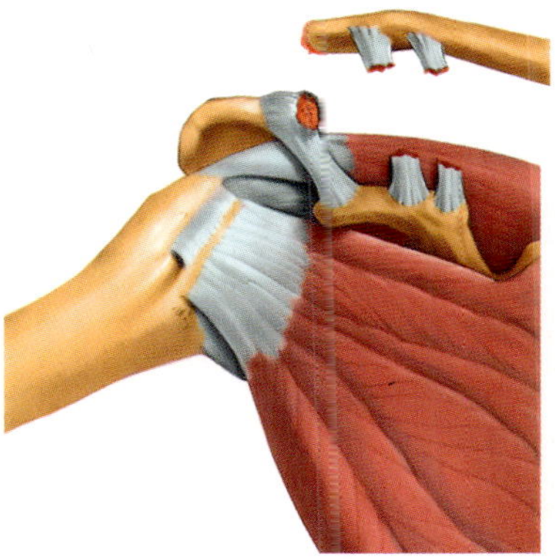

Your clavicle is attached to your shoulder blade by strong ligaments. When the ligaments tear due to a fall, the bones may separate. This is known as a shoulder separation.

Safety Is Everyone's Responsibility

Movement preparation and cool-downs reduce the risk of injury, but there are other potential hazards. Some small but crucial precautions can help keep indoor and outdoor environments and activities safe.

Safety in the Gym

Custodians keep gym floors clean to allow good traction and decrease the risk of slips and falls. You can assist in making participation in a gym safer for yourself and others:

- Visually check for hazardous conditions (e.g., furniture or equipment carts in activity areas).
- Report hazardous conditions to your teacher.
- Follow school protocols (e.g., keeping a safe distance away when sliding doors are being opened and closed).
- Adhere to school rules related to food and beverages in the gym.
- Wear appropriate footwear for activities.
- Enter the gym only when supervised.

Safety on the Field

We share our playing fields with the whole community, so keep these tips in mind:

- Visually check for hazardous conditions (e.g., trip hazards, holes, broken glass, garbage, animal feces).
- Report hazardous conditions to your teacher.
- Wear appropriate footwear for the activity and surface conditions.
- After use of the playing field, remove all non-essential items (e.g., equipment or garbage).
- If the field is wet, the activity should be moved or cancelled.

Safety in the Water and on the Ice

- Entering the water or diving is not permitted until permission to do so is specifically communicated by your teacher and lifeguards are present.
- Follow procedures outlined by your teacher if you or another swimmer gets into trouble.
- Never swim alone.
- Read and obey all water safety signs.
- Wear your Personal Flotation Device (PFD) at all times when boating.
- Walking or skating on frozen bodies of water is not permitted until permission to do so is specifically communicated by your teacher.

Fractures

Because bones bear the weight of our bodies, they are vulnerable to breaking, but they usually heal well and rarely break in the same spot twice. The medical term for a broken bone is a **fracture**. There are three types of fractures:

- **A simple (or closed) fracture** can be seen on an X-ray as a break or crack in the bone, but the bone does not split apart or break the skin.
- **A compound (or open) fracture** breaks the bone into separate pieces that puncture the skin, usually as a result of a hit or fall.
- **A comminuted fracture** occurs when the bone has been shattered into many pieces, as might happen in a major automobile crash.

No matter the type, a fracture requires immediate medical attention. The main indications that a bone has fractured include the following:

- hearing or feeling a crack or snap
- feeling sick or dizzy and vomiting
- the limb looking deformed
- the bone breaking through the skin

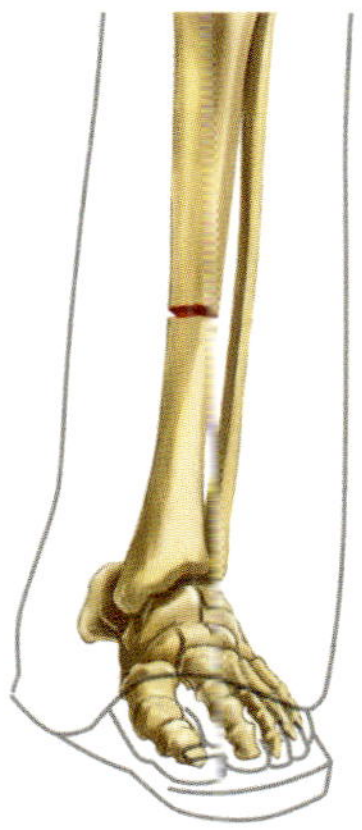

When a simple fracture occurs, a bone breaks but does not split apart; the break can be seen on an X-ray.

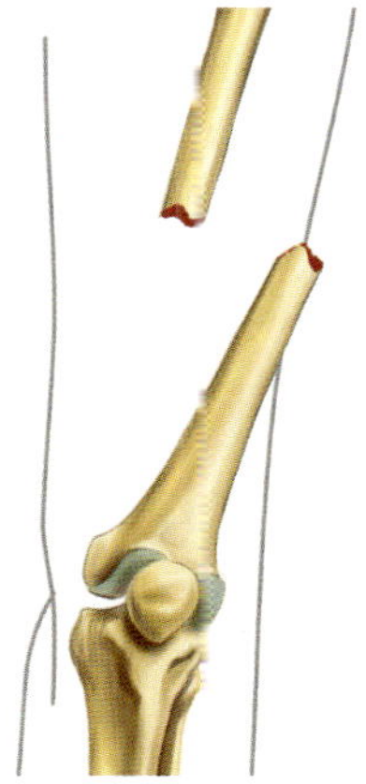

If a bone breaks into separate pieces and protrudes through the skin, that is called a compound (open) fracture.

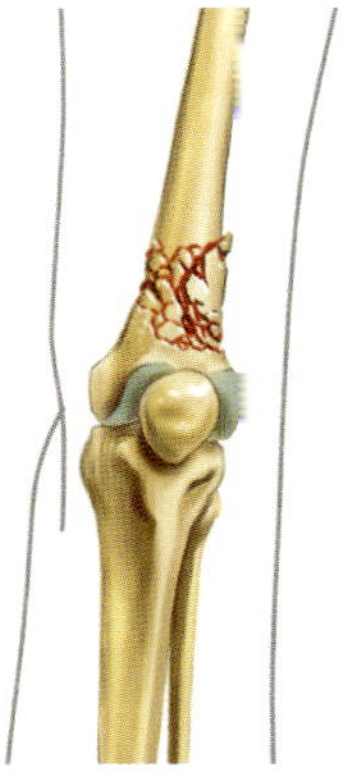

If a bone breaks or shatters into many pieces, a comminuted fracture has occurred.

Shin splints and stress fractures

There are two common lower leg injuries or conditions that frequently affect people who engage in moderate to heavy physical activity:

- **Shin splints** are microscopic tears in the connective tissue between the tibia and fibula, along the front shaft of the shin bone. The pain of shin splints is concentrated in the lower leg between the knee and the ankle. If untreated, shin splints can lead to stress fractures.
- **Stress fractures** are tiny cracks in the bone (for example, the tibia). Although they are often undetectable on an X-ray, stress fractures are very painful and can take a long time to heal.

Shin splits and stress fractures can happen if you do not build up to physical activity gradually enough; when you run, jog, or skip on hard surfaces; or when you use inappropriate or worn-out shoes.

You may be more likely to develop shin splints if you participate in strenuous physical activities or stop-start sports such as tennis, racquetball, soccer, or basketball.

If you seek medical attention immediately, you may avoid much of the pain associated with shin splints and stress fractures and also be able to return to your normal level of activity sooner.

In the meantime, you can apply the PIER principle to lessen the swelling and discomfort.

If a Concussion Occurs

After a hit, fall, or collision with another person or object in which you experience signs or symptoms of a concussion, here is what to do:

- Stop participating in the activity immediately.
- Inform your teacher, coach, or parent/guardian immediately.
- Follow the concussion procedures provided by your teacher/coach.
- If you observe a sign of concussion or if your classmate or teammate tells you about a symptom that he or she is experiencing, inform your teacher or coach immediately.

It is up to you to report any symptoms of a concussion that you might be experiencing, and to report any signs of a concussion that you observe in others. Be sure to get medical treatment if you sustain a concussion, and always follow the doctor's instructions closely.

Concussions

A **concussion** is a traumatic brain injury that causes changes in how the brain functions, leading to signs and symptoms that can emerge immediately or over the course of 24–72 hours.

Here are some important facts about concussions:

- A concussion may be caused either by a direct blow to the head, face, neck, or elsewhere on the body. The blow results in an impulsive force transmitted to the head that causes the brain to move rapidly and hit the walls of the skull.
- A concussion can occur even if there has been no loss of consciousness—in fact, most concussions occur without a loss of consciousness.
- A concussion cannot normally be seen on X-rays, standard CT scans, or MRIs.
- A concussion is typically expected to result in symptoms lasting up to 4 weeks in anyone 18 years of age or under. However, in some cases, symptoms may be prolonged.

Signs and symptoms of a concussion

Concussions are always a serious matter and medical attention is always required, so it is important to learn about the signs and symptoms of a concussion.

- A sign is something that is observed by another person (e.g., vomiting, slurred speech, loss of consciousness, or a dazed or vacant look).
- A symptom is something that a person feels or reports (e.g., ringing in the ears, seeing stars, or dizziness).
- Signs and symptoms can be physical (e.g., headache, dizziness), cognitive (e.g., difficulty concentrating or remembering), emotional/behavioural (e.g., depression, irritability), and/or sleep-related (e.g., drowsiness or difficulty falling asleep).
- Signs and symptoms can be present immediately or they can develop over a number of minutes or hours.

It is vitally important for you to learn the signs and symptoms of a concussion as presented to you by your teacher or coach.

Why should I report my symptoms?

Participating in an activity or sport while experiencing the symptoms of a concussion is dangerous. It often makes symptoms worse and it can lead to a longer recovery and a delay in your return to normal activity.

While your brain is still healing, you are much more likely to have another concussion. A repeat concussion can result in permanent damage to your brain and can even be fatal. Don't let anyone pressure you into continuing to participate in an activity if you have sustained a concussion.

Concussion prevention strategies

These strategies will help minimize the risks of sustaining a concussion:

- Understand the seriousness of concussions and know the signs and symptoms of a concussion.
- Know the dangers of participating in an activity while experiencing the signs and symptoms of a concussion, and the potential catastrophic and long-term consequences of a concussion.
- Follow your teacher's or coach's instructions for reducing the risks of a concussion associated with a particular activity or sport and how to minimize those risks, including sport-specific prevention strategies (e.g., follow a safe tackling program in tackle football).
- Attend safety clinics/information sessions offered by teachers/coaches.
- Avoid hits to the head and follow your coach's rules for safety, the rules of the sport, rules for fair play, and rules for the mutual safety of others.
- Wear properly fitted protective equipment.
- Follow the principles of head injury prevention (e.g., keeping the head up and avoiding collisions).
- Participate in contact activities with the understanding that helmets do not prevent concussions.

Section 4.4 Review

1 List four safety measures to help you prevent injuries.

2 What do the acronyms *SHARP* and *PIER* stand for?

3 Distinguish between the signs and the symptoms of a concussion, giving examples.

4.5 Exercises for Fitness and Health

Not all types of exercise produce the same results. It is up to you to decide which type of exercises—which movement pattern or combination of patterns—will help you meet your fitness goals.

The final part of this section features exercises for functional fitness training and resistance training. With the help of your teacher, find the exercises that are right for you and go for it, but be sure to follow proper form—movement matters!

Functional Fitness Training

Functional fitness training means training multiple muscle groups at the same time rather than isolating and working on a single muscle or muscle group. This kind of training takes a "head-to-toe" approach. It is designed to develop your strength, endurance, balance, and coordination.

Functional fitness exercises use compound movements that combine multiple muscle groups to produce pushing, pulling, squatting, lunging, and hinging patterns. This is the way in which many athletes train to perform at a high level.

Functional fitness training is also an excellent way to prepare your body to perform optimally each day. Training in these movement patterns helps us become better movers when we perform everyday activities—running to catch up to a friend, climbing stairs, picking up something you dropped—and avoid pain, injury, and discomfort.

Resistance Training

Resistance training involves imposing a demand (resistance) on the musculoskeletal system.

The biceps curl is classic example of resistance training. This kind of training is essential in bodybuilding, but note that the biceps muscle rarely works in isolation in everyday life—or during physical activity or sport.

The load in resistance training may come from an external object, such as a medicine ball or dumbbell. Or you may use your own body weight as a form of resistance, such as with a push-up or pull-up.

Benefitting from resistance training

You do not need to lift excessive weight to get the benefits of resistance training. Any resistance will improve your muscular strength and muscular endurance. The number of repetitions and sets you perform determines the gains for your muscles, as will load, speed, and tempo.

- **Repetitions** (or reps) are the number of times you continuously perform a resistance training exercise. If you lift a barbell once, that is one rep. If you lift it 25 times consecutively, that is 25 reps.
- **Sets** are the number of times you perform a certain number of reps. If you lift a barbell for 25 reps, then rest, and perform another 25 reps, you will have done two sets of 25 reps.

The important thing is to use appropriate resistance so as not to injure your muscles and joints. Make sure that your demand does not exceed your capacity. Always avoid lifts that are at or near your maximum ability. Remember, too, that resistance training is only one part of a balanced fitness program.

Safe Training Techniques

When performing exercises for fitness and health, always ensure that the exercise you are attempting is appropriate for you, that you are comfortable with the equipment, and that the conditions you are working in are safe.

The remainder of this chapter contains various strength and conditioning exercises that you can draw upon. To get the best results, begin slowly. Practise the first exercise in each category before attempting the next two, as they will be a little more challenging.

Executing the proper technique helps you get the most out of the exercise and minimize your risk of injury. Be sure to adhere to the **seven key features** described in Chapter 2.

There are four key training techniques:

Body position

Maintaining correct body alignment is the best way to avoid injury. That is why exercise instructors tell you to keep your back straight or not to bounce or rock.

Stop the exercise immediately, and inform your teacher if you cannot maintain the required technique, or if you feel discomfort or pain.

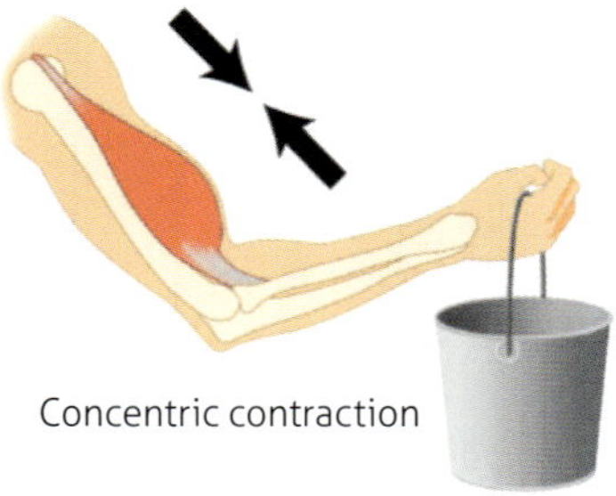

Concentric contraction

Breathing

Make sure to breathe normally while performing the lift.

Holding your breath while using resistance places pressure on the major arteries in the chest and limits the availability of oxygen to your brain. This could cause you to pass out.

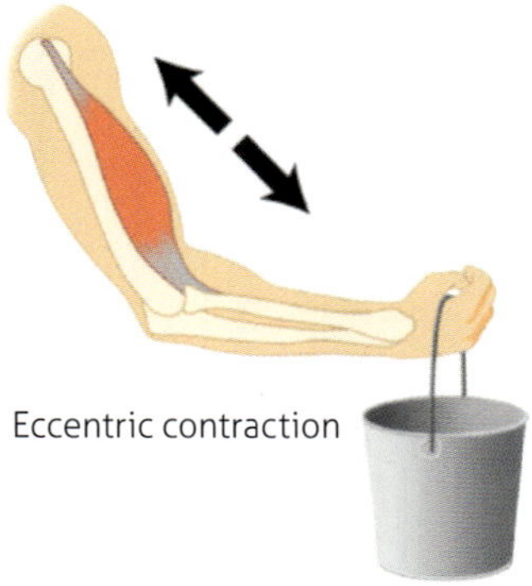

Eccentric contraction

Types of muscle contraction

Skeletal muscles are attached to the bones by tendons and other tissues. Understanding the three types of skeletal muscle contraction will help you use your muscles effectively.

- A **concentric contraction** occurs when your muscle shortens while working. Bend your elbow and watch what happens to your biceps muscle: it rolls up into a ball (shortens) as it contracts.
- An **eccentric contraction** occurs when a muscle lengthens while working, such as when you fully flex your elbow and then slowly lower your arm. In this example, the biceps is flexing and lowering your forearm.
- An **isometric contraction** occurs when the muscle force is equal to the resistance, so the muscle length does not change. If you push or pull against an immovable object, such as a wall, your muscles contract, but they stay the same length.

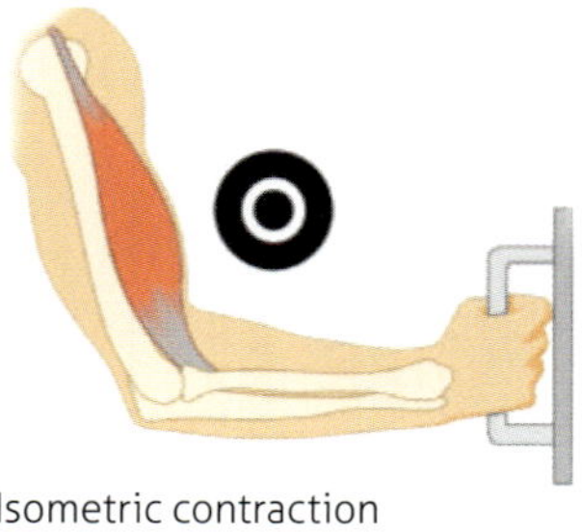

Isometric contraction

Grip

The **supinated grip** (underhand grip) and the **pronated grip** (overhand grip) are recommended for different exercises. Both involve wrapping your thumb around the bar.

The so-called monkey grip—holding the bar with only your four fingers—is *never* recommended. This grip is unstable and could make you drop the weight and injure yourself or others.

Tempo and Phases

You need to maintain a certain tempo, or speed, each time you perform an exercise. Tempo is the amount of time it takes you to perform all the phases of the exercise.

For example, a push-up has four phases: lower, bottom, up, and top. An example of a tempo could be 4-0-2-3. You lower your body weight for 4 seconds; there is no pause (0) at the bottom; you lift your body weight in 2 seconds; and then you hold and squeeze at the top for 3 seconds.

Supinated grip (underhand grip)

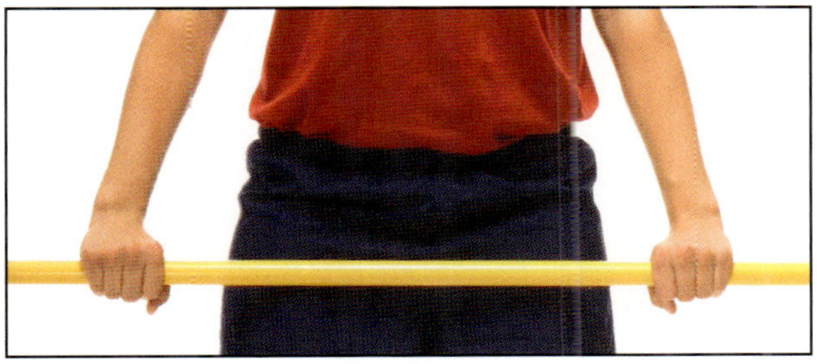

Pronated grip (overhand grip)

Monkey grip (thumb not wrapped around the bar)—*not recommended when lifting a barbell under any circumstances!*

How Much Should You Lift?

Before professional fitness trainers develop a resistance training program for a client, they can find out the maximum amount of weight the person can lift. This is known as the **one-repetition maximum**—or your **1-rep max**.

Finding your 1-rep max by going all out is unwise, as you can risk injury to your bones, muscles, and joints. However, there is an alternative. The **multiple-repetition maximum** method lets you safely and effectively predict the maximum weight you can lift once.

Multiple-repetition maximum

Under the supervision of your teacher, follow these steps:

1. With three classmates of similar ability, select a resistance exercise that all of you want to try, such as the bench press.
2. Select light weights that each of you can lift safely and easily for 15–20 reps. Take turns preparing, so that each person gets adequate rest.
3. Estimate a weight that each of you thinks you can lift for 10 reps with some difficulty. Take turns, while the other three act as spotters, supporting the one lifting the weights.
4. Adjust the weight until you find a load that you can lift for 10 reps with some difficulty. Never try to lift more than is appropriate for you.

Once you know your 10-rep maximum, your teacher can refer to a standardized chart to give you your estimated 1-rep max. Your teacher will likely ask you to work within a certain percentage of your predicted maximum so as to avoid overtraining and injury.

Safety in the Strength Conditioning Room

Good procedures keep you safe in the strength conditioning room.

- Prior to entering the fitness room, check to ensure that it is being supervised. Only students training are permitted in the room—no spectators. There should be two students minimum at any one time.
- Wear suitable clothing and tie back long hair.
- Don't bring any food or drink except a water bottle.
- Tell your teacher if the fitness room has been left unlocked.
- Inform your teacher when equipment needs to be repaired, e.g., when there are tears or rips in cables and resistance tubing.
- Keep fingers and feet clear of moving machines, and report jammed weight stacks to the teacher.
- Don't try to clear weight jams by removing pins or plugs yourself.
- Always work out with a training buddy, and ask others to help if you need additional spotters.
- Respect your classmates' space and avoid horseplay at all times.
- When you are finished, wipe sweat from machines and mats with a towel, and return all weights to their original location.

Helping hands

Consider the following points when you and your fitness partner take turns spotting each other (spotting is the act of supporting another person during a particular exercise):

- Make sure you both know the proper lifting techniques, especially for exercises using dumbbells, barbells, and kettlebells.
- Learn the spotting technique demonstrated by your teacher.
- Check how many repetitions your partner wants to complete, and pay close attention while you are spotting.
- Stop the exercise if it's being performed incorrectly or if it's causing undue stress. Partners should emphasize correct body alignment.
- Avoid distractions and be sure to stand close enough to the lifter.
- Inform your teacher immediately if an injury occurs.

Exercises for fitness and health

Now it's time to get moving! You and your teacher can choose which of the following exercises are right for you. Some isolate muscles and others require the use of many muscles at once. Make sure to implement your safety action plan and follow the techniques exactly as described.

Breathe normally throughout every exercise, and practise each one for the number of repetitions and sets or the amount of time determined by you and your teacher. Always perform an equal number of repetitions for each side of the body, and make sure to rest between sets.

Section 4.5 Review

1 What is the difference between a repetition and a set?

2 Using words or drawings, demonstrate at least three ways to ensure your safety when exercising.

3 After trying some or all of the exercises in the following section, choose three favourites and explain their benefits.

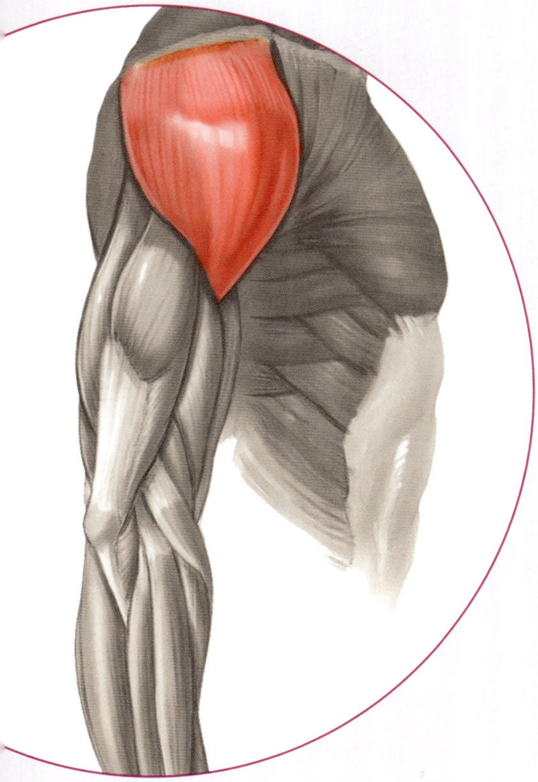

Shoulder Exercises

The **deltoid** is a small but powerful muscle on the end of the shoulder, forming a rounded contour with the shoulder joint itself. The deltoid muscle is named after the Greek letter *delta*, which, like the muscle itself, is triangular in shape.

The deltoid is made up of three distinct parts (or heads), each responsible for specific movements that help the shoulder move in many directions. The three heads have different origins, but they all converge to an insertion point on the middle and outside of the humerus (the upper arm bone).

Overall, the deltoid muscle is responsible for flexing and extending the arm at the shoulder, and it helps to prevent shoulder dislocation.

Lateral Shoulder Raise

The lateral shoulder raise works the outside, or lateral, part of the deltoid and is an excellent exercise for beginner and expert alike.

This exercise can be done with various equipment, but start with lightweight tubing or lightweight dumbbells to avoid putting undue stress on the muscles in the area. Use tubing that provides greater tension, or slightly heavier dumbbells, to increase the difficulty as your strength improves.

- Place the tubing securely under the middle of both feet while holding one handle firmly in each hand using an overhand (pronated) grip.
- Never lift your toes or heels off the ground, as this may cause the tubing to slip.
- Keeping your back straight, knees slightly bent, and feet shoulder-width apart, raise your arms to shoulder height.
- Return to the start position slowly, keeping tension on the tubing.

Rear Deltoid Raises

The posterior, or rear, of the deltoid is probably the most neglected part of the muscle. Rear deltoid exercises should be incorporated into your routine to ensure that you are working all parts of the muscle.

The best way to train this area of the body is by using lightweight tubing or lightweight dumbbells.

- Step forward with one leg and place the tubing securely under your front foot while holding one handle firmly in one hand.
- Bend forward and place your non-lifting hand on your front knee, keeping your back straight throughout the motion.
- Slowly extend your lifting arm backward, moving only at the shoulder joint.
- Pause briefly at the top of the motion, then return to the start position, keeping tension on the tubing at all times.
- After completing the number of repetitions determined by you and your teacher, switch position and repeat on the other side.

Single-Leg Shoulder Press

While working your shoulder muscles, this exercise also challenges your total body balance and control and strengthens your core muscles.

- Stand on your right leg, holding light dumbbells in both hands.
- Raise both arms to shoulder level with your elbows pointing outward.
- Extend one arm high above your head and then bring it down smoothly while extending your other arm high above your head.
- Continue alternating arms for the number of repetitions and sets determined by you and your teacher.
- Repeat, this time standing on your left leg.

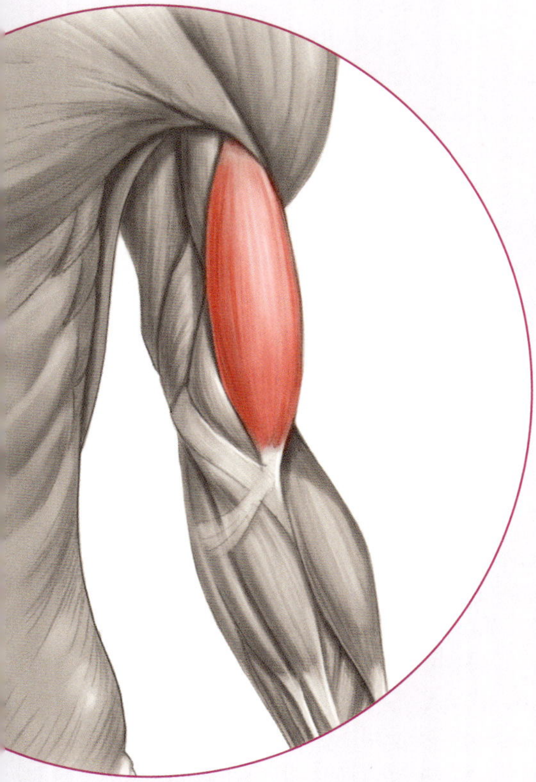

Biceps Exercises

The most powerful muscle of the upper arm is the **biceps brachii** (the biceps). This "two-headed" muscle (*bi-* means two, *ceps* is from the Latin for head) is also perhaps the most well-known elbow flexor.

While the biceps crosses both the shoulder and elbow joints and has many different roles, its main function is elbow flexion. At the elbow, the biceps converges into two tendons, each attaching to one of the two long bones of the forearm (the radius and ulna).

The biceps can be strengthened through resistance exercise, for example through the well-known biceps curl (using dumbbells, barbells, or resistance tubing) and the chin-up.

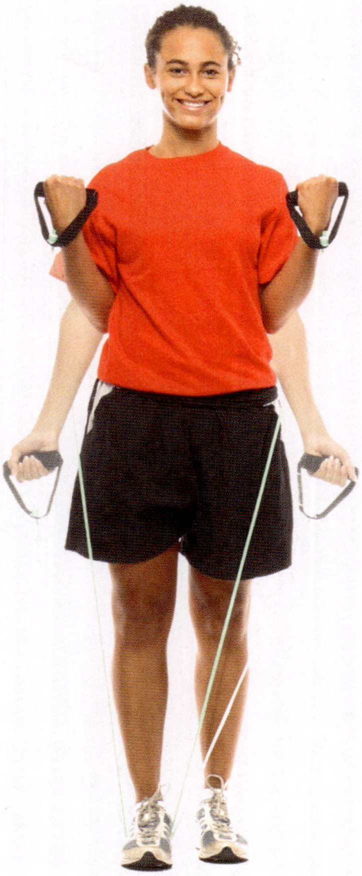

Standing Tubing Curls

This exercise requires you to keep your back straight and your knees slightly bent at all times and to avoid rocking back and forth. After a few weeks and with your teacher's approval, you can slowly increase the load either by using thicker tubing for greater tension or by switching to dumbbells, barbells, or kettlebells.

- Place the tubing securely under one foot, and move the other foot slightly back. Never lift your toe or heel off the ground as this may cause the tubing to slip.
- Extend your arms fully, and hold one handle firmly in each hand using an underhand (supinated) grip.
- Slowly flex your elbows until your hands are at approximately shoulder level, keeping your elbows close to your body.
- Slowly return to the start position, keeping tension on the tubing at all times.

Stability Ball Concentration Curls

The challenge in this variation is to keep your upper body still. You need to keep your back straight at all times and avoid rocking back and forth. Do not perform this exercise until you can sit on a stability ball without losing your balance.

- Place yourself comfortably on the ball with your legs apart and a light dumbbell in one hand.
- Bend forward and place your lifting elbow against your inner thigh and your non-lifting hand on the other thigh.
- Slowly raise the dumbbell toward your chest without taking your elbow away from your thigh.
- Pause briefly at the top of the motion, then return to the start position.
- After completing the number of repetitions and sets determined by you and your teacher, switch arms and repeat on the other side.

Chin-Ups

Chin-ups enhance the muscular strength and endurance of the forearms, arms, back, and shoulders. When performing chin-ups, do not try to gain momentum by swinging your legs or your back.

- Grasp the bar using an underhand grip (palms facing you, thumbs wrapped around the bar).
- Pull your body up until your chin is over the bar, then lower yourself until your arms are straight without locking your elbows.

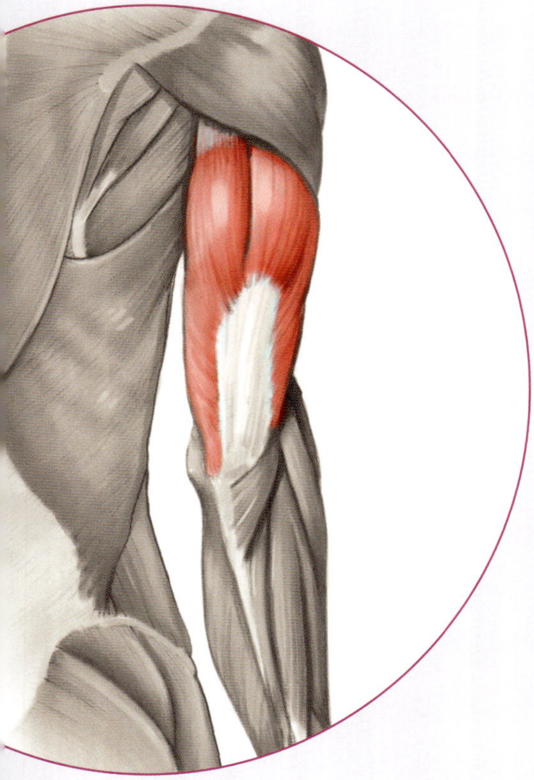

Triceps Exercises

The **triceps brachii**, at the back of the upper arm, is named after the number of heads it has (*tri-* means three). This muscle is principally responsible for extension (straightening) of the elbow joint.

The triceps brachii acts in unison with the biceps—one contracts, the other relaxes. The three branches have different origins (on the collar bone and humerus) and converge into a tendon that inserts onto the ulna, one of the two long bones of the forearm.

Throwing actions in darts, baseball, or racquet sports involve the triceps. Examples of other exercises that involve elbow extension include pushing and pressing movements, such as the triceps kickbacks and the overhead medicine ball toss.

Standing Triceps Extension

For this exercise you need to keep a straight back and your knees slightly bent and to extend your arm fully. To get the most out of the standing triceps extension, pick the tubing tension that best suits you.

- Firmly grasp the tubing at one end just below the handle, bending your arm at the elbow and with your knuckles at ear level.
- Grip the tubing securely at chest level with your other hand.
- Your knuckles should be at ear level, with your arm bent at the elbow.
- Slowly extend your arm upward at a 45-degree angle, bending only at the elbow in order to work the triceps fully.
- Pause briefly at the top of the motion, then slowly return to the start position keeping tension on the tubing at all times.
- After completing the number of repetitions and sets determined by you and your teacher, repeat with the other arm.
- To increase the level of difficulty, you can use tubing that offers more resistance.

Triceps Kickbacks

This exercise, which is sometimes referred to as "donkey kickbacks," can be performed using tubing or dumbbells. You may want to use a wall mirror to make sure you are using the proper technique.

- Bend forward slightly, with your legs slightly apart.
- Keep your back straight and place your non-lifting hand on your knee.
- Raise your lifting arm until you have a 90-degree bend at your elbow.
- Keeping your shoulder fixed, slowly extend your arm backward by bending only at the elbow.
- Pause briefly at the top of the motion, when your arm is parallel to the ground.
- Slowly return the dumbbell to the start position.
- After completing the number of repetitions and sets determined by you and your teacher, switch position and repeat on the other side.

Overhead Medicine Ball Toss

The overhead medicine ball toss not only challenges the core muscles but also works your shoulder muscles and triceps.

- Stand about half a metre away from a wall, with your feet staggered and a medicine ball held above and slightly behind your head.
- Throw the ball at the wall with both hands, aiming for a point that is above your hands when your arms are straight, then catch the ball with both hands.
- Try to keep the movement only in your upper body, and keep your arms above your head.
- Periodically switch the position of your feet, but make sure your feet stay firmly planted at all times.

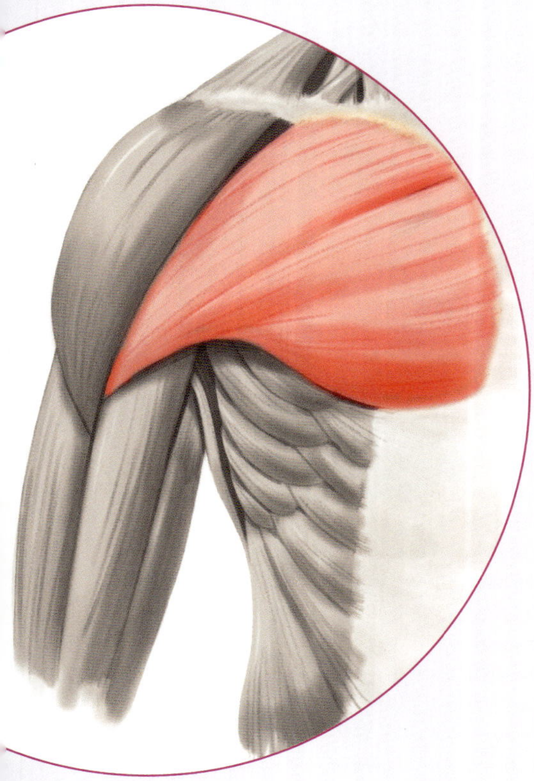

Chest Exercises

The **pectoralis major** is the fan-shaped muscle that covers the upper part of the chest (*pectus* is Latin for breast). The pectoralis major has a "sibling" muscle called pectoralis minor, and together these two muscles make up the pectoral muscle group (the "pecs").

The pectoral muscles primarily control the movement of the arm at the shoulder joint. They have various origin points and converge to a tendon that inserts into a groove at the top of the humerus (upper arm bone).

Exercises such as push-ups and barbell and dumbbell bench presses can strengthen pectoralis major. Strengthening the "pecs" will not only improve your tennis forehand but will also help you to lift yourself out of a swimming pool more easily.

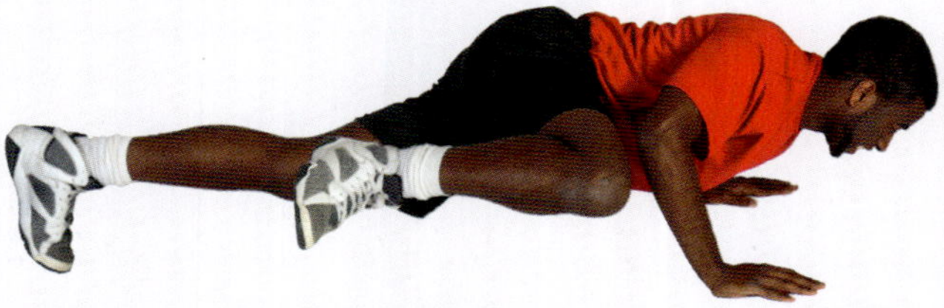

Spiderman Push-Ups

Spiderman push-ups strengthen the triceps, pectoral muscles, and core muscles. You might want to perform this exercise on a mat rather than on the floor.

- Begin in high plank (push-up) position, with your arms straight. Place your feet shoulder-width apart and your hands slightly farther apart.
- Bend your elbows and lower your body toward the floor, while bending your right leg to bring the knee toward your right elbow. Focus on keeping your back straight and your core engaged.
- Push up, straightening your arms and extending your right leg back into the start position to place your toes back on the mat.
- Lower your body again, this time bending the left knee to bring it up toward your left elbow, then returning to the start position.
- Try to perform the exercise continuously, without pausing.

Squat and Press

This dynamic full-body movement engages the chest muscles at several different levels, challenging them to adapt to different types of stress and helping to improve balance and coordination. This exercise is excellent for developing functional pushing strength for sports such as lacrosse and rugby or for activities such as shovelling snow.

- Wrap resistance tubing around a fixed pole.
- Standing facing away from the pole, firmly grasp one of the tubing handles in each hand using a pronated grip (palm facing down).
- Walk forward until the tubing is taut.
- Keep the feet slightly more than shoulder-width apart and the knees slightly flexed. Your arms should be fully flexed and elbows parallel to the floor.
- Squat down until your thighs are parallel to the floor, while extending your arms and pushing the tubing away from your body.
- Rise out of the squat and slowly bring your hands back beside your shoulders.

Staggered Hands Push-Ups

This variation on a standard push-up adds challenge to both the chest muscles and the shoulder muscles. It also helps to balance the strength of all your core muscles.

- Assume the standard push-up position (or modified push-up position), but move one hand forward about half a hand's length and the other hand back the same distance.
- Rotate the heel of your back hand slightly outward to reduce the stress on your wrist.
- Keep your back straight so your body is aligned; otherwise, staggering your hands can sometimes cause you to tilt to one side.
- Once you are in position, perform push-ups as you normally would.
- After completing the number of repetitions and sets determined by you and your teacher, switch the positions of your hands and repeat.

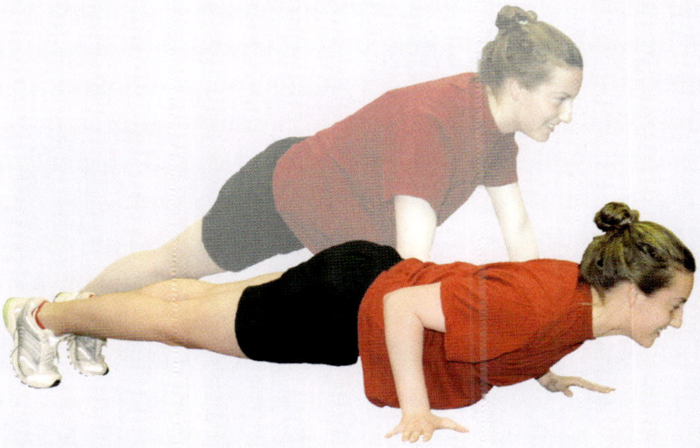

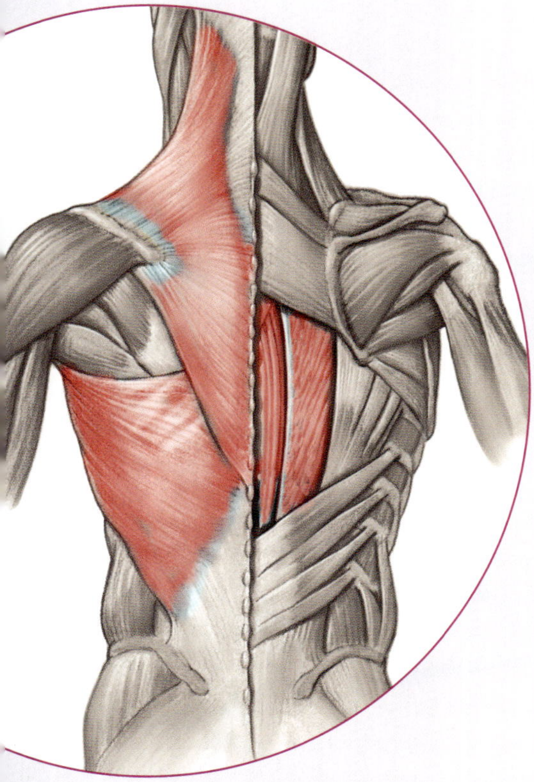

Posterior Core Exercises

There are many important muscles and muscle groups in the upper back region. The major ones are the **trapezius**, **latissimus dorsi**, and the **erector spinae** group.

The **trapezius** covers the upper back, the **latissimus dorsi** covers most of the lower back, and both serve to connect the upper limb to the vertebral column. The **erector spinae** group lies underneath these two, serves to straighten and rotate the back, and consists of three muscles (longissimus, spinalis, and intercostalis) that run along the length of the spine and the back of the ribs.

Each of these back muscles plays an important and unique role in posture and overall movement.

Bird Dog

This exercise primarily targets the three powerful muscles that run up and down your spine: the iliocostalis, longissimus, and spinalis. Together these make up the erector spinae group and, as the name implies, they help to keep the spine erect.

Ideally, the bird dog should be performed on a mat, with one leg and one hand on the mat at all times.

- Place your hands and knees on a mat with your hands shoulder-width apart.
- Raise your right arm and left leg at the same time. Your back should form a straight line with your raised arm and leg.
- Repeat, this time raising your left arm and right leg.

Dynamic Back Bridge

This exercise helps strengthen the gluteal (buttock), lower back, and core muscles, which help support the spine and keep the body stable during all forms of movement. A strong core improves balance, reduces back pain, and makes walking, lifting, and bending easier.

- Lie on your back on a mat.
- Bend your knees, drawing your heels up so they are approximately 30 centimetres from the gluteals. Keep the soles of your feet on the mat.
- Extend both arms at your sides with your palms down.
- In one controlled, fluid motion, contract the core and gluteal muscles to raise the buttocks and lower back off the mat, and lift the right foot off the floor with the leg fully extended. At the same time, raise the left arm while keeping it straight, stopping when it is just in front of the ear.

- Hold this position for a second, using the opposite arm and leg to maintain balance before slowly returning to the start position.
- Repeat the exercise, this time raising your left leg and right arm.

Pull-Ups

Pull-ups strengthen the core muscles and the major muscles of the back, which play an important role in posture. Good posture helps improve movement, and that reduces the risk of injury. (Note that if you do not have access to an equalizer bar, you can use a squat rack.)

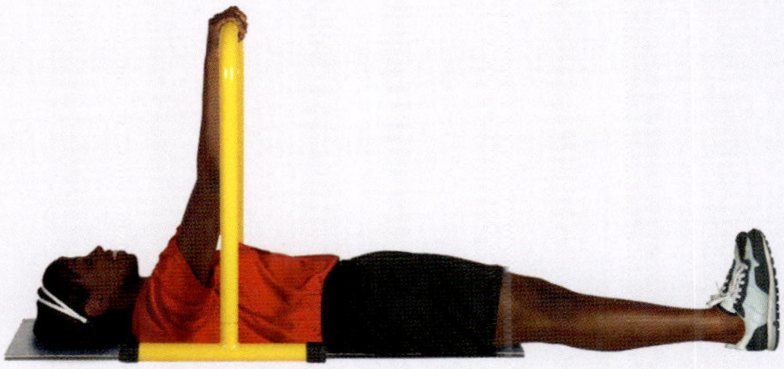

- Lie on the mat with the bar centred over your chest and both your legs fully extended.
- Extend your arms and grab the bar with an overhand grip so your thumbs are slightly more than shoulder-width apart.
- While contracting your core, use your back muscles and then your arms to pull your chest up to the bar. Your heels will be the only point of contact with the floor.

- Focus on keeping your whole body in a straight line, with no sagging in the middle. Keep your head level—do not tuck your chin in or allow your head to drop back.
- Slowly lower your body, stopping just before touching the mat.

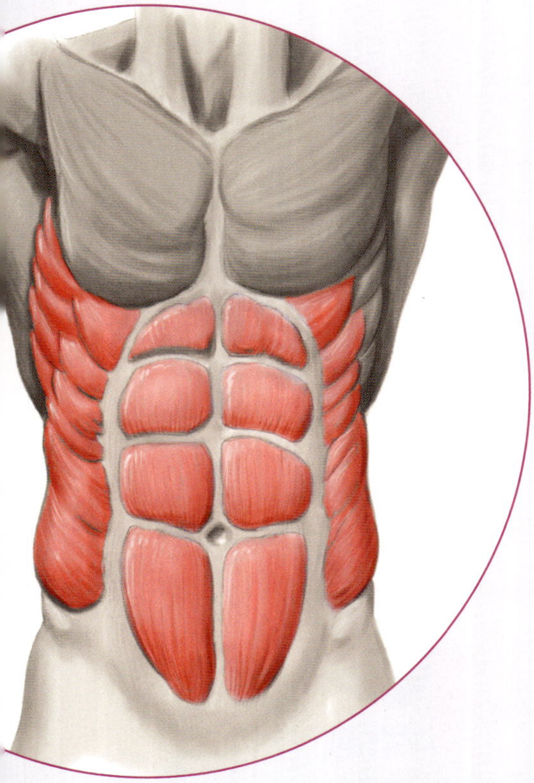

Anterior Core Exercises

Between the shoulder and hip joints are the anterior (or front) core muscles. The most well known of these are **rectus abdominis** (the "abs") and the **external obliques**.

These anterior muscles work in conjunction with those of the posterior core to help stabilize the body. This is essential both for everyday activities and high-level athletic performance.

Strengthening the abdominal core involves more than just developing good-looking "abs." The primary role of these muscles is to stabilize the spine. They also help with ensuring proper posture and with breathing, coughing, and even sneezing.

The McGill Crunch

The McGill crunch is named after Dr. Stuart McGill, a professor of biomechanics and a world-renowned back specialist. This isometric exercise works many of the anterior core muscles.

- Lie on a mat, with your hands under your lower back (palms down) and one knee bent at 90 degrees.
- In a smooth motion, lift only your head and shoulders off the ground while breathing normally throughout the motion.
- Hold this position for a few seconds, then rest, switching bent legs before you begin the next repetitions.
- To increase the level of difficulty, you can raise your elbows off the floor along with your shoulders and head.

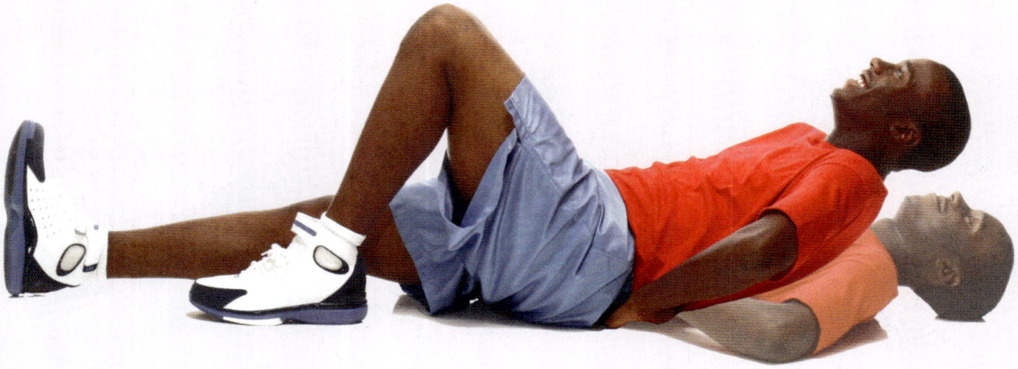

Front Plank

This exercise engages all of the anterior and posterior core muscles, as well as most of the hip, leg, and ankle muscles. To get maximum benefit from this exercise, ensure that your elbows are aligned directly underneath your shoulders and keep your entire body as straight as possible. Be sure not to allow your back to sway. Place a mat under your elbows if you perform this exercise on a hard surface.

- While kneeling, place both hands on the floor, and then lower your body to place both forearms on the floor.
- Straighten out one leg and then the other until your body is fully extended, making sure that your toes are curled up toward your ankles.
- Keep your body fully extended, with your shoulders, back, hips, and legs forming a straight line.
- Hold this position for the desired number of seconds, rest, and then repeat.

Side Planks

Side planks challenge the external obliques and all the core muscles running along the sides of your body. The external obliques are important core muscles and should be included in all types of fitness programs.

- Lie on your left side on a mat, with your legs straight and your left forearm resting on the mat.
- Raise your hips off the mat until your back and legs form a straight line.
- Hold this position for the number of seconds, then return to resting position.
- Repeat, this time lying on your right side with your right forearm resting on the mat.

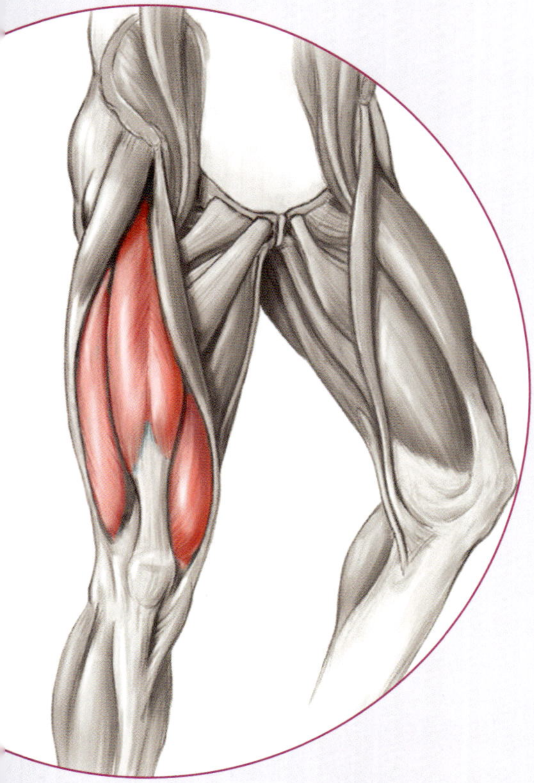

Quadriceps Exercises

The **quadriceps** ("quads") are four muscles located on the front of the thigh. They work to extend (that is, straighten) the knee. One of these muscles (the **rectus femoris**) also flexes the hip.

The **rectus femoris** covers most of the other three muscles. The **vastus lateralis** is on the outer (lateral) side, and the **vastus medialis** is on the on the inner (medial) side. Lastly, the **vastus intermedius** lies underneath the rectus femoris.

Each muscle originates in a different place, but they come together at the quadriceps tendon. This tendon wraps around the patella (knee cap) and attaches to the tibia (shin bone) by means of the patellar ligament.

Goblet Squats

Goblet squats are excellent work for your quadriceps and gluteals. Holding a kettlebell (or dumbbell) in front of you challenges the posterior and anterior core muscles and lower leg muscles. All these muscles work together to keep you balanced while developing strength, coordination, and endurance.

- Grasp the handle of the kettlebell in both hands, holding it under your chin at chest height. Your elbows should be pointing toward the floor.
- Place your feet shoulder-width apart with the toes facing forward. Keep your body upright with the spine aligned in a neutral position—the shoulders back and chest out.
- Keeping the kettlebell at chest height, perform a squat, shifting your body weight toward your heels while keeping your chest and head up and your back straight.
- Keep your knees aligned with the ankles, not coming past the toes, as you squat. Shifting your weight toward your heels will help you keep this posture. You should be able to wiggle your toes at the bottom of the squat.
- After a brief pause, return to standing position.

Single-Leg Squats

Single-leg squats are very good at strengthening the quads. Begin by bending only slightly at the knee, and progress to bending more deeply as you get stronger. Start with your own body weight, then add other forms of resistance, such as dumbbells.

- Stand on your right leg with your arms raised to shoulder level and extended out to the sides. Keep your head and back straight, and your right foot flat on the ground.
- With your left leg raised off the floor, slowly bend at the knee and hips while simultaneously bringing your arms forward.
- Pause briefly, then return to the upright position, keeping your left leg raised.
- After completing the number of repetitions determined by you and your teacher, switch to your other leg and repeat the exercise.

Wall Squat

The wall squat is really the sum of two exercises: a squat and a lateral lunge. This exercise will improve your lateral (side-to-side) range of motion and strengthen the muscles around your hip joints.

- Stand about 30 centimetres away from a wall, facing the wall, legs well apart, and hands on hips.
- Squat, pushing your hips back and allowing the wall to stop your knees from moving too far forward.
- Moving sideways, shift your weight to your right leg until your left leg is fairly straight.
- Without returning to standing position, shift your weight to your left leg until your right leg is fairly straight.
- Shift your weight back to the centre, then return to the standing position.
- Vary the direction in which you first lunge as you continue for the number of repetitions and sets determined by you and your teacher.

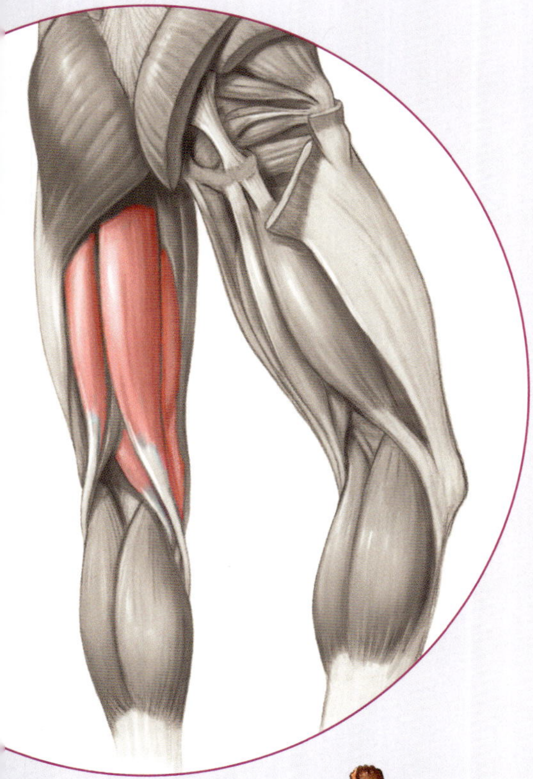

Hamstring Exercises

The **hamstrings**, three powerful muscles at the back of the thigh, serve to complement the quadriceps at the front. The three hamstring muscles are **semitendinosus**, **biceps femoris**, and **semimembranosus**.

The hamstrings flex the knee and extend the hip—movements that are extremely important in daily life and in sports.

So, why that unusual word—*hamstrings*? The word *ham* (or *hom*) in Old English referred to the hollow bend at the back of the knee and *string* refers to tendons. Hence, the string-like muscles at the back of the thigh came to be known collectively as the hamstrings.

High-Arm Lunges

High-arm lunges are an excellent lower-body exercise that targets the hamstrings, quadriceps, and hip extensors (mainly the gluteus maximus) while increasing core strength. A strong core improves agility and helps transfer more power to the legs, helping you to perform explosive movements such as running and jumping.

This exercise develops balance and coordination for everyday activities and can also be used to train for the specific movements required in field, court, ice, track, and water sports.

- Begin in a standing position, with your back straight and your shoulders directly aligned with the hips. Throughout the exercise, focus on keeping your chest up and not hunching forward.
- Take one long step forward with your left foot to enter into lunge position. Your left knee should be bent to 90 degrees and aligned with the ankle; your right leg is extended behind the body, with the knee bent and close to the floor.
- As you step forward, firmly extend your right arm straight up from the shoulder with your right hand in a closed fist. Keep your left arm down at your side.
- Next, take a long step forward with your right foot, entering into lunge position with your right leg forward. At the same time, firmly extend your left arm straight up from your shoulder and bring your right arm down to your side.

Stability Ball Leg Curls

This advanced exercise should be done only when you have mastered the lunge and the dynamic back bridge. Make sure your legs have undergone good movement preparation, and use a mat as a cushion for your back.

- Lie on your back next to a stability ball, hands out to the side for balance.
- Raise your feet so that your lower calves are on top of the ball.
- Keeping your hips high, roll the ball toward your body by bending your knees until they are at a 90-degree angle.
- Slowly return to the start position by extending your knees.

Medicine Ball Step-Ups

This exercise includes many movements that we perform throughout the day. It combines hip, shoulder, and ankle movements that help strengthen the muscles in these areas while challenging your balance and coordination.

- Stand with your feet shoulder-width apart and your back straight, facing a sturdy stepping platform and holding a medicine ball high above your head.
- Step on the platform with your left foot while swinging the ball down to chest level.
- Bring your right knee up to hip level without putting your right foot on the platform.
- Pause briefly, then bring your right foot back down to the floor while bringing the ball back over your head. Then bring your left foot back to the floor.
- Repeat, this time stepping on the platform with your right foot first.

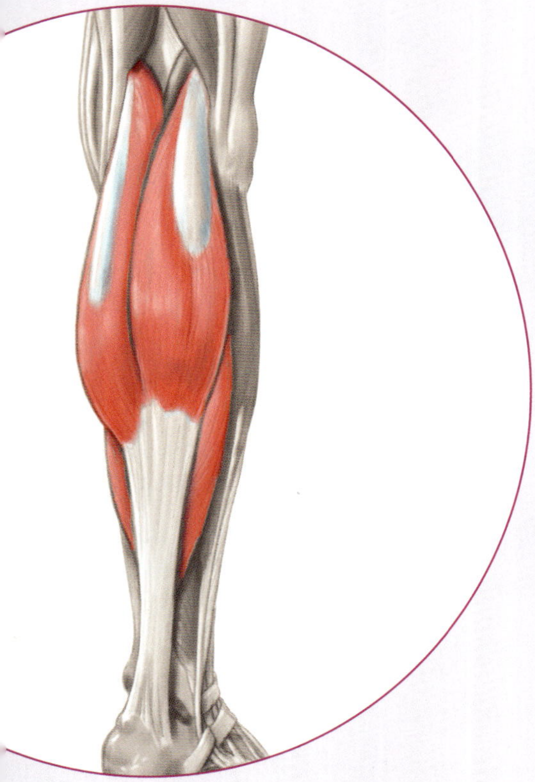

Lower Leg Exercises

The **gastrocnemius** (the "calf") and **soleus** are powerful flexors of the ankle joint. The soleus, the smaller of the two, is located "deep" in relation to the gastrocnemius.

Some anatomists consider these muscles to be a single muscle because the two parts share a common insertion on the heel bone by means of the Achilles tendon.

The gastrocnemius and soleus carry your entire body weight most of the time. Each time you plant your foot at the beginning of a step or come up on your toes at the end of a step, your calf muscles shift into gear.

Calf Raises

A stable raised platform or step is all you need to perform calf raises. If you need to, you can position the platform close to a wall or railing so you can hold on in order to keep your balance. As you improve, you can introduce other forms of resistance, such as a light dumbbell.

- Place your feet slightly apart on the edge of a step or raised platform.
- Allow your heel to drop slightly below the step without losing your balance.
- Slowly come up on your toes without bending at the knees or hips.
- Once you have reached the top of the movement, slowly and smoothly return to the start position. Never bounce.

X-Pattern Footwork

X-pattern footwork helps you to increase your foot speed and agility, which are needed in invasion/territory and net/wall games such as football, soccer, basketball, and volleyball. It also helps improve coordination and balance, regardless of your athletic level.

Make sure to keep your back straight throughout the exercise.

- Place agility slats in an × on the floor, or use tape to create an ×.
- With your knees slightly bent, put your right foot in the top right quadrant and your left foot in the bottom left quadrant.
- Jump in the air and bring your left foot forward and your right foot back. Land with your right foot in the back right quadrant and your left foot in the top left quadrant.
- As soon as your feet touch the floor, jump again, landing with your feet back in the start position.

The Shark

The shark is an advanced gastrocnemius exercise that should be performed only once you have mastered calf raises. This exercise improves overall body balance and control.

- Use tape to construct a 3 × 3 grid of nine squares on the floor.
- Stand on your right leg in the middle square with your arms at your sides and your back straight.
- Hop into another square and back to the middle square. Repeat for each square in turn.
- Switch to your left leg and repeat the sequence.

Angel's Story

"Try not to let anything get in your way or discourage you. Just keep working at it."
— Angel Blainey

Chapter 4 Review

Knowledge and Understanding

1 Give some examples of obstacles that people frequently encounter when trying to adhere to a fitness plan, and suggest a strategy to overcome each obstacle.

2 Describe five factors that affect an individual's personal physical fitness, and explain the benefits of developing fitness as part of a healthy, active life.

3 What kinds of activities can maintain your cardiorespiratory fitness?

4 Make a labelled diagram depicting the five different training principles described in this chapter.

Thinking

5 What are some reasons to plan and implement a balanced fitness program?

6 Investigate your school or community centre's guidelines, policies, and messages about preventing injuries such as concussions. Present your findings in a brief report to the class.

7 Identify which exercises covered in this chapter can improve functional fitness.

Communication

8 Using text or labelled drawings, give some examples of commonly used protective equipment or preventive measures to maximize safety and to minimize risk and injuries related to physical activities and sports.

9 Choose three exercises from this chapter and list **a)** which movement pattern each exercise represents, and **b)** which key movement features each exercise predominantly uses.

Application

10 Think of ways in which individuals can track their fitness goals. Select the methods that appeal to you, and explain why.

11 Choose three of the exercises in this chapter and record in a journal the number of reps and sets that you perform. Continue with these exercises for one month, recording your results each time. Then review your results and compare the number of reps and sets that you did each time you performed the exercises. Describe any improvements you observe.

12 Design an exercise routine to help you develop a muscle or muscle group that is emphasized in your favourite activity or sport. Your routine can focus on either functional fitness or single-muscle exercise. Make a presentation to your class that describes and explains the steps involved in this exercise routine.

Healthy Eating

5

Ella's Story

Which factors in your life support healthy eating choices and behaviours, and which ones sidetrack you from healthy eating?

Just like a car, your body runs on fuel—the food you eat. The better the quality of fuel you put into your body, the smoother the ride and the longer the trip.

Achieving the right nutritional balance is key. This means providing your body with all the nutrients and energy it needs to build and repair itself. Establishing good eating habits and healthy meal planning now will benefit you for your entire life.

Physical, emotional, social, cultural, and environmental factors all affect our eating habits. Find out how you can use Canada's Food Guide, nutrition labels on food packaging, and other sources of information to come up with your own healthy eating plan to suit your activity level, your food preferences, and, ideally, your family's needs.

Learning Objectives

In this chapter, you will...

- review some basic concepts related to nutrition
- explore the energy balance equation and how it helps us maintain healthy eating habits and an active lifestyle
- review how *Canada's Food Guide* and *Canada's Physical Activity Guide to Healthy Active Living* can help us balance food intake and activity level
- use the information on nutrition labels to make healthy choices
- analyze various factors that influence your food choices and eating habits, and change or maintain your choices and habits accordingly
- examine the nutritional aspects of several current food and beverage trends
- develop your own healthy eating plan to help maintain the well-being of you and your family

Key Terms

- nutrition
- macronutrients
- energy nutrients
- carbohydrates
- fats
- proteins
- micronutrients
- vitamins
- minerals
- calorie
- total daily caloric need
- energy balance equation
- Resting Metabolic Rate (RMR)
- Harris-Benedict formula
- Canada's Food Guide
- Nutrition Facts Table
- List of Ingredients
- % Daily Value
- nutrient content claims
- satiety cues
- Canada's Physical Activity Guide to Healthy Active Living
- body image
- self-esteem
- eating disorders
- vegetarianism
- dietary supplements

▶ **Ella Finkelstein** has been involved with the EatFit program since she was a young teen. EatFit aims to help change the physical and mental health of communities "one recipe/activity at a time." The team, which so far has travelled to communities across Nunavut and Northern Ontario, consists of teachers, chefs, yoga instructors, fitness and health professionals, and students like Ella—people who are all passionate about the well-being of children and youth.

5.1 Meeting Your Nutrient and Energy Needs

Nutrition is the science of how your body uses the components of food to grow and to maintain and repair itself. Nutrients are the chemical elements and compounds that are essential for life.

Your body needs more than 50 nutrients daily in order to function properly, and each one helps it to perform a specific task. The 50 nutrients belong to six general categories:

- carbohydrates
- fats
- proteins
- minerals
- vitamins
- water

Nutrients work within the body in different ways. For example, the vitamin category is made up of 13 different vitamins, each with a particular function in the body. Proteins, on the other hand, are formed from 20 organic compounds called amino acids, and each protein has a unique role to play.

Macronutrients

Macronutrients are the nutrients that we need in relatively large amounts every day. In addition to water, the macronutrients are carbohydrates, proteins, and fats. These three macronutrients are also known as the **energy nutrients** because they provide our bodies with energy.

- **Carbohydrates** should provide most of your total daily caloric intake. The body converts carbohydrates into a sugar called glucose, which it can use to fuel physical activity. There are two types of carbohydrates: simple and complex. Orange juice is an example of a simple carbohydrate. Sources of complex carbohydrates are grain products (bread, pasta, cereal, and rice), vegetables, fruits, and legumes (beans, peas, and lentils). Complex carbohydrates provide a slow, steady source of energy for our bodies.
- **Proteins** can be found in all the body's cells: muscles, tendons, hair, skin, nails, and so on. Proteins play a role in sight, hearing, taste, and smell. They also form enzymes that help digest food, fight infection, and build blood. Proteins can act as an energy source but usually only if the body is short of carbohydrates and fat.
- **Fats** are especially useful during prolonged physical activity because they are a concentrated source of energy. You should think of fats as a type of nutrient that the body needs to stay healthy. They also help the body to absorb the vitamins it needs.

Micronutrients

Micronutrients—vitamins and minerals—are chemical elements or substances that are required only in trace amounts. Unlike macronutrients, vitamins and minerals do not contain energy (calories). Vitamins and minerals enable the body to produce enzymes and hormones and help the body use the energy provided by carbohydrates, proteins, and fats.

- **Vitamins** are chemicals that the body needs to build and maintain cells and to release energy from macronutrients. Vitamins are either water soluble or fat soluble, meaning that they are absorbed by being dissolved, or broken down, in water or in fat.
- **Minerals** help make bones, proteins, and blood. Minerals are inorganic substances. For example, calcium, which the body gets from dairy products, is important to the structure of bones and teeth. Iron, found in some meat and some dark-green vegetables, helps carry oxygen to body tissues.

Vitamins and minerals are called "micronutrients" because they are needed only in extremely small amounts. While they are only needed in tiny amounts, micronutrients are essential for good health, and micronutrient deficiencies can result in serious health problems.

Why Variety Is Key

No single food can provide all the nutrients we need—even foods we think of as healthy, such as broccoli or bananas.

Most foods provide a few nutrients but very little or none of others, so it is important to eat a wide variety of foods.

Some foods have very few nutrients but high amounts of energy, often in the form of simple sugars.

Eating too much or not enough of any food, whether it is considered health food or junk food, can harm your health. You need small amounts of each and every nutrient every single day.

Measuring Food Energy

Nutritionists measure the energy we get from energy nutrients in units called calories. A **calorie** is a measure of heat—technically, it is the amount of energy needed to raise the temperature of 1 gram of pure water by 1 degree Celsius.

In a dietary context, what we call a calorie is in fact a *kilocalorie* (1,000 calories). Calories are a measure of the amount of energy that food will produce as it is processed by the body. This energy can also be measured in metric units—one food calorie equals 4,186 joules.

The three energy nutrients supply energy (calories) in different amounts:

- 1 gram of carbohydrate provides 4 food calories.
- 1 gram of protein provides 4 food calories.
- 1 gram of fat provides 9 food calories.

It is generally recommended that we get 45–65 percent of our calories from carbohydrates, 10–30 percent from protein, and 25–35 percent from fats.

Body size, sex, genetics, age, and physical activity level all influence your **total daily caloric need**—the number of calories you need to stay healthy and maintain an appropriate body weight.

For example, a teenaged male athlete needs more calories than an inactive older male. Similarly, because they are still growing, teenaged girls need more calories than older women do.

We do not all have exactly the same daily caloric needs. Extremely active individuals obviously have higher energy requirements than less active individuals.

The Energy Balance Equation

To stay at a healthy body weight, we need to balance energy intake with energy expenditure. The **energy balance equation** treats our caloric intake as *energy in*. The number of calories we burn over the course of an entire day is called our energy expenditure—or *energy out*. The energy equation is often depicted as a scale.

- When energy intake is equal to energy expenditure, the body's energy needs are met, and our weight does not change. We are said to be in neutral energy balance.
- If we take in fewer calories than we burn off through activity, the body loses weight. This is called negative energy balance.
- If we take in more calories than we expend through physical activity, we are in *positive energy balance* and will gain weight.

Physical activity significantly increases energy expenditure, thus making it easier to balance energy intake from the foods we eat. For this reason, individuals who are physically active every day are more likely to maintain a healthy body weight.

Achieving the right energy and nutritional balance means providing your body with all the right foods it needs to build and repair itself and to move around, thus allowing you to do all the things you want to do.

Keeping active and making healthy eating choices every day will definitely help you enjoy life!

Caloric intake—*energy in*—should be balanced with energy expenditure through activity—*energy out*.

The Harris-Benedict Formula

To estimate your total daily caloric need, you will need to know your **Resting Metabolic Rate (RMR)**—the amount of energy your body uses when it is completely at rest.

The terms **Resting Metabolic Rate** and **Basal Metabolic Rate** are often used interchangeably. Basal Metabolic Rate is generally the preferred term when a precise measurement is attempted under strict laboratory conditions.

Individual **RMR** varies depending on height, weight, age, and sex. The **Harris-Benedict formula** has been found to be an accurate method for estimating RMR, using different weightings for males and females.

The Harris-Benedict equation was formulated by American scientists James Harris (a botanist) and Francis Benedict (a chemist and physiologist). Their research was originally published in 1919. The equation has been updated and refined over the years and is widely used by nutritionists as a way of estimating metabolic rate at rest and determining an individual's daily caloric needs.

Estimating RMR for males

For males, the formula for estimating Resting Metabolic Rate (RMR) is as follows:

$$\mathbf{RMR = 66.5 + (5 \times height\ [cm]) + (13.7 \times weight\ [kg]) - (6.8 \times age\ [years])}$$

For example, Dev is 160 cm tall, weighs 68.4 kg, and is 14 years old. Here is how we calculate his RMR:

$$= 66.5 + (5 \times 160) + (13.7 \times 68.4) - (6.8 \times 14)$$

$$= 66.5 + 800 + 937.08 - 95.2$$

= 1,708 calories/day

Estimating RMR for females

For females, the formula for estimating Resting Metabolic Rate (RMR) is as follows:

$$\mathbf{RMR = 655 + (1.9 \times height\ [cm]) + (9.5 \times weight\ [kg]) - (4.7 \times age\ [years])}$$

For example, Talia is 153 cm tall, weighs 55.0 kg, and is 15 years old. Here is how we calculate her RMR:

$$= 655 + (1.9 \times 153) + (9.5 \times 55.0) - (4.7 \times 15)$$

$$= 655 + 290.7 + 522.5 - 70.5$$

= 1,398 calories/day

Estimating Total Daily Caloric Need

The Harris-Benedict formula shown on the facing page is a precise way to estimate **Resting Metabolic Rate (RMR)**, but there is also a quick formula. It is designed for adults, but give both methods a try and then compare them.

The quick calculation multiplies weight in kilograms by 24.2 for males or 22.0 for females. The examples we used for the Harris-Benedict formula—Dev (68.4 kg) and Talia (55.0 kg)—give the following results:

Dev's RMR = 68.4 × 24.2 = 1,655 calories/day
Talia's RMR = 55.0 × 22.0 = 1,210 calories/day

Once you know your **RMR**, you can estimate your total caloric need according to your level of physical activity. Table 5.1 shows how to make sure you are taking in the right number of calories every day.

Simply multiply your **RMR** by the appropriate activity factor. If your **RMR** is 1,400 calories and you are moderately active, for example, you need 2,170 calories per day (1,400 x 1.55).

Section 5.1 Review

1 Explain why we need both macronutrients and micronutrients in our diet.

2 List four factors that influence your total daily caloric need.

3 Make a simple labelled sketch to illustrate the energy balance equation. Use a stick person in your sketch if you like.

Table 5.1 **Calculating Total Daily Caloric Need**

Activity level	Physical activity	Activity factor*
Sedentary	Little or no exercise	1.2
Lightly active	Light exercise or sports 1–3 days per week	1.375
Moderately active	Moderate exercise or sports 3–5 days per week	1.55
Very active	Hard exercise or sports 6–7 days per week	1.725
Extra active	Very hard daily exercise or sports	1.9

* Multiply your RMR by this number to find your total daily caloric need.

Understanding your caloric need, based on your RMR and your level of daily activity, will help you to plan and regulate your daily meals.

5.2 Canada's Food Guide and Regulated Food Labelling

Canada's Food Guide provides Canadians with recommendations for healthy eating based on current scientific evidence. The guide was first introduced in 1942 during a period of wartime rations. The 1942 version was called the Official Food Rules. In 1944, the guide was revised and renamed Canada's Food Rules. In 1962, the guidelines were again revised and renamed Canada's Food Guide.

The All-New Canada's Food Guide

Over the years, Canada's Food Guide has gone through many changes in name, appearance, and message, but it has never veered from its original purpose—promoting reliable nutrition information for everyone. The publication—now a set of related publications—is available in 12 languages. It also includes a separate guide that reflects the values, traditions, and food choices of First Nations, Inuit, and Métis.

Canada's Food Guide is based on what nutritionists refer to as the "total diet," which recognizes that no single food or single meal determines the quality of your diet. Announcing the new Canada's Food Guide for 2018–19, the federal Minister of Health noted that "the classic one-size-fits-all guide no longer meets the needs of Canadians."

More healthy choices for everyone

The new Canada's Food Guide recognizes that we no longer produce and consume food the way we used to. The food we eat now comes through a chain that stretches all over the world. The new guide reflects the multitude of food preferences among Canadians today. In effect, the new guide better reflects the multicultural nature of Canada itself.

The new guide focuses on encouraging everyone to consume more nutrition-dense foods and to stay away from harmful saturated fats, sodium, and sugar. It also underlines the importance of knowledge and skills relating to health and nutrition. We are advised to shop for nutritious foods, plan and cook healthy meals, and share meals with family and friends. All this, Health Canada notes, "can help reinforce positive eating habits and help children develop healthy attitudes towards food."

The new guidelines also introduce, for the first time, a strong environmental message, turning its attention toward the impact of mass food production methods—such as greenhouse gas emissions, water quality, food waste, animal welfare, and soil degradation. Many such harmful effects, it says, can be lessened with the promotion of healthy eating and greater consumer knowledge and awareness.

Health Canada's guiding principles for healthy eating

Health Canada outlines the following guiding principles for healthy eating, which are to be incorporated into the new Canada's Food Guide and its many supporting publications over the coming years:

1 **A variety of nutritious foods and beverages are the foundation for healthy eating.** Health Canada therefore recommends:
   - regular intake of vegetables, fruit, whole grains, and protein-rich foods—especially plant-based sources of protein
   - inclusion of foods that contain mostly unsaturated fat, instead of foods that contain mostly saturated fat
   - regular intake of water

2 **Processed or prepared foods and beverages high in sodium, sugars, or saturated fat undermine healthy eating.** Health Canada therefore recommends:
   - limited intake of processed or prepared foods high in sodium, sugars, or saturated fat
   - avoidance of processed or prepared beverages high in sugars

3 **Knowledge and skills are needed to navigate the complex food environment and support healthy eating.** Health Canada therefore recommends:
   - selecting nutritious foods when shopping or eating out
   - planning and preparing healthy meals and snacks
   - sharing meals with family and friends whenever possible

Using the Food Guide

Unlike fad diets in books and magazines and on the internet, Canada's Food Guide is based on up-to-date and reliable nutrition research.

Here are some tips to get you started using the guide:

- Create a record of everything you eat and drink for one or two weeks.
- Compare your record with Canada's Food Guide.
- Set a healthy eating goal that makes one change at a time.
- Do a progress check after one week to see if your choices improved.
- Revise your plan until you have a balanced and healthy one that works for you.

Which tip or tips would work for you?

The food that goes on our plates today varies from one region to another and from one person to another, reflecting that there is no single "Canadian food menu." The new Canada's Food Guide reflects the changing composition of the Canadian population and includes a good representation of cultural diversity and eating choices.

Regulated Food Labelling in Canada

Canada has a highly regulated system for providing nutritional information to consumers. These regulations make nutrition labelling mandatory on most food packaging so we can make better informed choices about the kinds of foods we buy.

Reading the Nutrition Facts table

At the top of the **Nutrition Facts table** is the serving size, which tells you the amount of food on which the nutrient information is based. When reading the label, keep in mind that many products contain more than one serving in a package and that some labels give information for half a package even if the product looks like just one serving.

The key to using the Nutrition Facts table is the **% Daily Value (% DV)** column. This column tells you how much, or how little, of a nutrient the serving size contains in relation to what a person needs every day. *The recommended daily values are based on two sets of standards:*

1. reference standards for fat, saturated and trans fats, cholesterol, carbohydrate, fibre, potassium, sodium
2. recommended daily intakes (RDIs) for vitamins and minerals

Daily values for carbohydrates, total fat, and saturated and trans fat are based on a 2,000-calorie diet since this calorie intake meets the average needs of adults.

Because it is expressed as a percentage, % DV works whether or not you know exactly what your daily requirements are. The % DV column of the Nutrition Facts table makes it easy for you to find out how nutritious a product is, to modify your intake of specific nutrients, to manage a special diet, and to compare similar food products.

The Nutrition Facts Table

Canada has federal regulations and requirements for food labels. Companies producing and selling food products must ensure that their labels meet these requirements. Some features of the Nutrition Facts table are shown here.

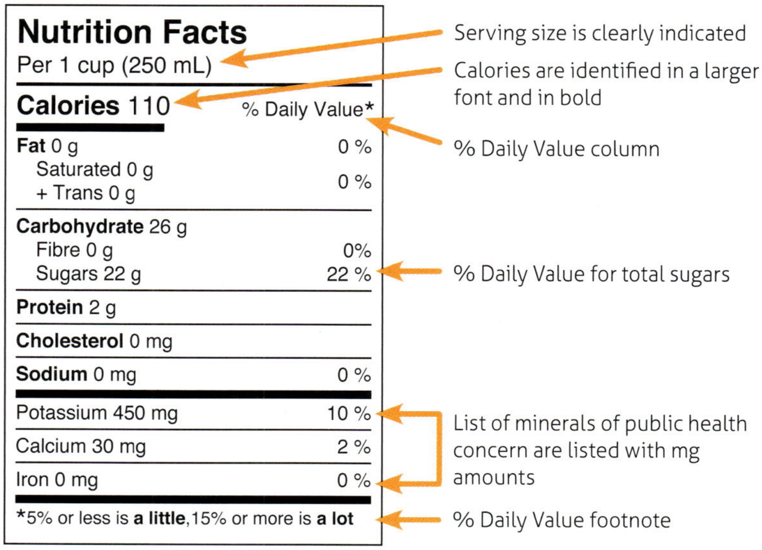

Food labelling changes

The food label is undergoing changes over the next few years, with major improvements to the Nutrition Facts table and the list of ingredients.

The changes to the Nutrition Facts table include

- making the serving size more consistent so that it is easier to compare similar foods and it reflects the amount typically consumed in one sitting
- making the information on serving size and calories easier to find and read by increasing the font size
- revising the % daily values based on updated science
- adding a new % daily value for total sugars
- updating the nutrients list to add potassium because it is important for healthy blood pressure
- removing vitamins A and C because most Canadians get enough of these nutrients in their diets
- adding the amounts in milligrams (mg) for potassium, calcium, and iron
- adding a footnote about % daily value as this will help consumers understand how much sugar and other nutrients are in their food

Changes to the **list of ingredients** will make it easier to find, read, and understand. These changes include

- grouping sugars-based ingredients in brackets after the name "sugars" so as to help consumers identify the sources of sugars added to a food
- listing food colours by their common names
- making the text in black font on a white or neutral background
- creating minimum type height requirements for ingredients
- using bullets or commas to separate ingredients

Marketing Fast Food to Youth

In its report titled *The Kids Are Not Alright*, the Heart and Stroke Foundation of Canada makes a case for greater federal regulation of advertising junk food to children and teens.

Marketing high-fat foods, sweetened cereals, and sugary soft drinks matters a great deal since these young people are establishing lifelong food preferences and eating habits.

The province of Québec, for example, has banned the advertising of fast food since 1980. The Québec regulations are credited with lowering the rates of obesity in that province.

Other countries, such as Sweden, Finland, and Greece, have strict controls on marketing to children and youth, and both France and Britain have legislation underway.

Do you support government regulation of fast-food advertising to children and teens? Why or why not?

List of Ingredients

Like the Nutrition Facts table, Canada also has federal regulations and requirements for the way ingredients on food products are listed. Some features of the list of ingredients are shown here.

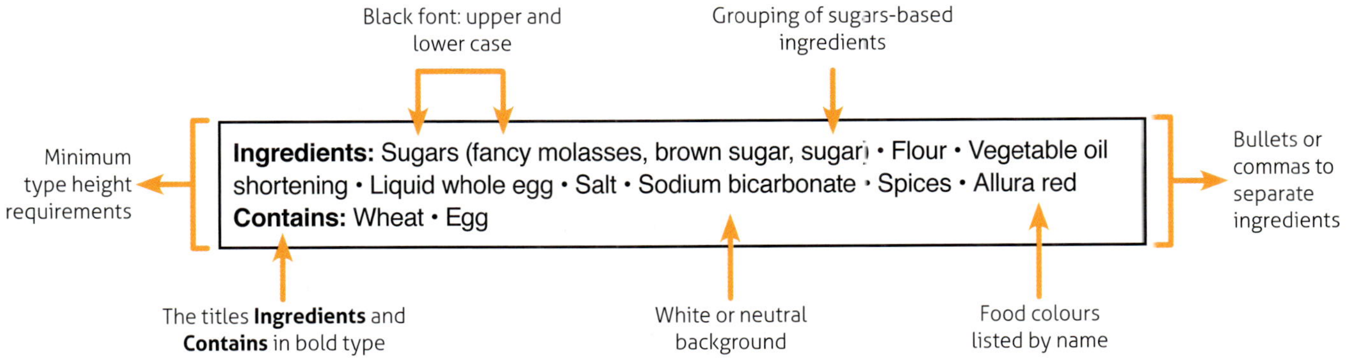

After September 15, 2018, it will be illegal in Canada to sell any foods that contain partially hydrogenated oils (PHOs). PHOs are the main source of artificial trans fats in Canadian diets.

The Fats of Life

Fat has a bad reputation—you may think of it as bad for your heart, bad for your weight, bad for your health. However, fat is necessary for many important functions, helping the body to build cells, operate the immune system, produce hormones, and absorb some vitamins.

As Table 5.2 shows, there are different kinds of fats—polyunsaturated, monounsaturated, saturated, and trans fats—and they have different effects on the body.

Fats and cholesterol are related, so many dietary discussions talk about them together. Cholesterol is manufactured naturally in humans and other animals, and it is essential to body functions. However, too much saturated fat and trans fats can cause cholesterol to build up in the body.

There are two types of cholesterol:

- **HDL**, or good, cholesterol picks up the other type of cholesterol in your blood and carries it to the liver to be excreted from the body.
- **LDL**, or bad, cholesterol can build up on the walls of your arteries, obstructing blood flow and increasing the risk of heart problems.

The goal is to have a relatively high level of HDL and a relatively low level of LDL. We can do this by avoiding trans fats and saturated fats while consuming some polyunsaturated fats and monounsaturated fats.

Table 5.2 **The Effect of Fat on Cholesterol**

Type of fat	Function	Form	Found in
Polyunsaturated fats (good)	Helps lower LDL in the blood	Liquid at room temperature	• Corn, soybean, sunflower, safflower, sesame oils • Some mayonnaise and soft margarine brands • Grain products • Fish, seafood
Monounsaturated fats (good)	Lowers LDL and raises HDL in the blood	Usually liquid at room temperature	• Canola, olive, peanut, safflower, grapeseed, sesame oils • Soft margarines containing these oils • Seeds, nuts • Avocados • Popcorn, whole grain wheat, cereal, oatmeal
Saturated fats (not so good)	Usually raises the levels of LDL in the blood	Solid at room temperature	• Palm oil and coconut oil (used in prepared foods such as cookies, cakes, coffee creamers) • Hard margarines • Lard, meat, poultry • Butter, cheese, sour cream, ice cream
Trans fats (bad)	Raises LDL and decreases HDL in the blood	Hydrogenation converts liquid vegetable oils into solid or semi-solid fats	• Hydrogenated oils, shortening • Some margarines • Baked goods, cookies, crackers, many brands of potato chips

Nutrition Content Claims on Food Packages

Food labels often contain **nutrient content claims**. These claims, when used, must follow specific rules from Health Canada to make sure they are consistent and not misleading. There are two types of claims:

- A **nutrient content claim** describes the amount of a nutrient such as calories, fats, and fibre in a food product. For example, "a source of fibre" or "trans fat free" are nutrient content claims.
- A **health claim** describes the potential health effects of a food product if consumed within a healthy diet. For example, "A healthy diet rich in vegetables and fruit may help reduce the risk of some types of cancer" is a health claim.

What do they mean?

Health Canada has a list of nutrient content claims that companies can use on a food label. If you use these food claims when choosing a food product, it is important to know what they mean. For example:

- **"Fat free"** means the food must have less than 0.5 grams of fat per serving.
- **"Low sodium"** means the food must have less than 140 milligrams of sodium per serving.
- **"High source of fibre"** means the food must have at least 4 grams of fibre per serving.

Health Canada also has an approved list of health-related claims, as well as the criteria the food product needs to meet in order to use the claim. Some claims may need to be checked by Health Canada before they can go on a label.

Companies can also make general health claims, such as "healthy," "smart," and "nutritious." These claims cannot be misleading and, depending on the claim, some additional criteria may apply. For example, a "nutritious" claim can only be used on a food that contains at least one nutrient from the Nutrition Facts table.

What claims cannot be made?

Companies cannot make nutrition or health claims unless the label includes a Nutrition Facts table. In addition, a company cannot make a claim about a nutrient that does not appear in the Nutrition Facts table. For example, if a company claims a food product is "a good source of vitamin D," then vitamin D must be included in the Nutrition Facts table for that item.

Companies are not permitted to alter approved nutrition content and health claims to make them sound more appealing. Claims such as "ultra low fat" or "extra high protein" are not permitted.

Section 5.2 Review

1 What determines the quality of a person's daily diet?

2 Name two important ways Canada's Food Guide can be useful to you.

3 State three important pieces of information on a Nutrition Facts table.

5.3 What Influences Our Eating Habits?

Nutritional, or physiological, needs are not the only influences on what we choose to eat. We are also influenced by

- physical/biological factors such as hunger, appetite, and taste
- economic factors such as income, and cost and availability of food
- marketing factors such as advertising campaigns for food products
- environmental factors such as education, cooking skills, and time
- social factors such as family, peers, and habitual meal patterns
- psychological factors such as stress and mood
- cultural attitudes, beliefs, and knowledge about food

These influences change at different stages of life and vary from one individual or group of people to the next. Understanding the factors that affect what and how we eat can help us make healthier eating choices.

Physical and Biological Factors

- **Daily energy and nutritional needs.** Our bodies need energy and nutrients so that we can perform all the tasks of daily living.
- **Level of physical activity.** Hydration and nutritional needs will vary depending on whether we do light, moderate, or vigorous physical activity on any given day.
- **Developmental stage.** Daily energy intake is influenced by a person's physical stage of development, such as whether you are still growing.
- **Food allergies and sensitivities.** Allergic reactions to foods such as nuts or shellfish, or sensitivities to foods containing lactose (in dairy) or gluten (in wheat) can restrict what we eat.
- **Hunger and satiety.** Metabolic cues enable the human body to stop eating, while sensory cues make people want more food based on how good it tastes. Our bodies give us **satiety cues**—satisfaction signals—to tell us when we are hungry and when we are full.
- **Energy density.** The macronutrients generate satiety signals. Foods with high energy density have weak satiety signals, and foods with low energy density have strong signals. Fat gives us the weakest satiety signals, carbohydrates have an intermediate effect, and protein is the most satiating. Eating foods that are high fat and/or high sugar without the additional bulk that lets us know we are full can lead to *passive overconsumption*, when we consume excess energy unintentionally.
- **Portion size.** The volume of food we eat, or portion size, can give us an important satiety signal. Many people do not know how to recognize an appropriate portion size and can unintentionally consume excess energy.

Tips to Avoid Overeating

When you are heading for a snack, stop to decide whether you are actually hungry or if you are just bored or eating out of habit.

It can take about 20 minutes for your body to realize it is full. Try to eat slowly and savour your food. Chew five to ten bites for soft foods and 25 to 30 bites for vegetables and meats. This will give your body more time to tell you when it has had enough.

Drinking a glass of water or two before a meal can help curb your appetite.

Use a portion plate to help you eat the right amount if you have trouble understanding your body's satiety cues. Portion plates show you roughly how much space each type of food should take up on a standard-sized plate for each meal (breakfast, lunch, and dinner).

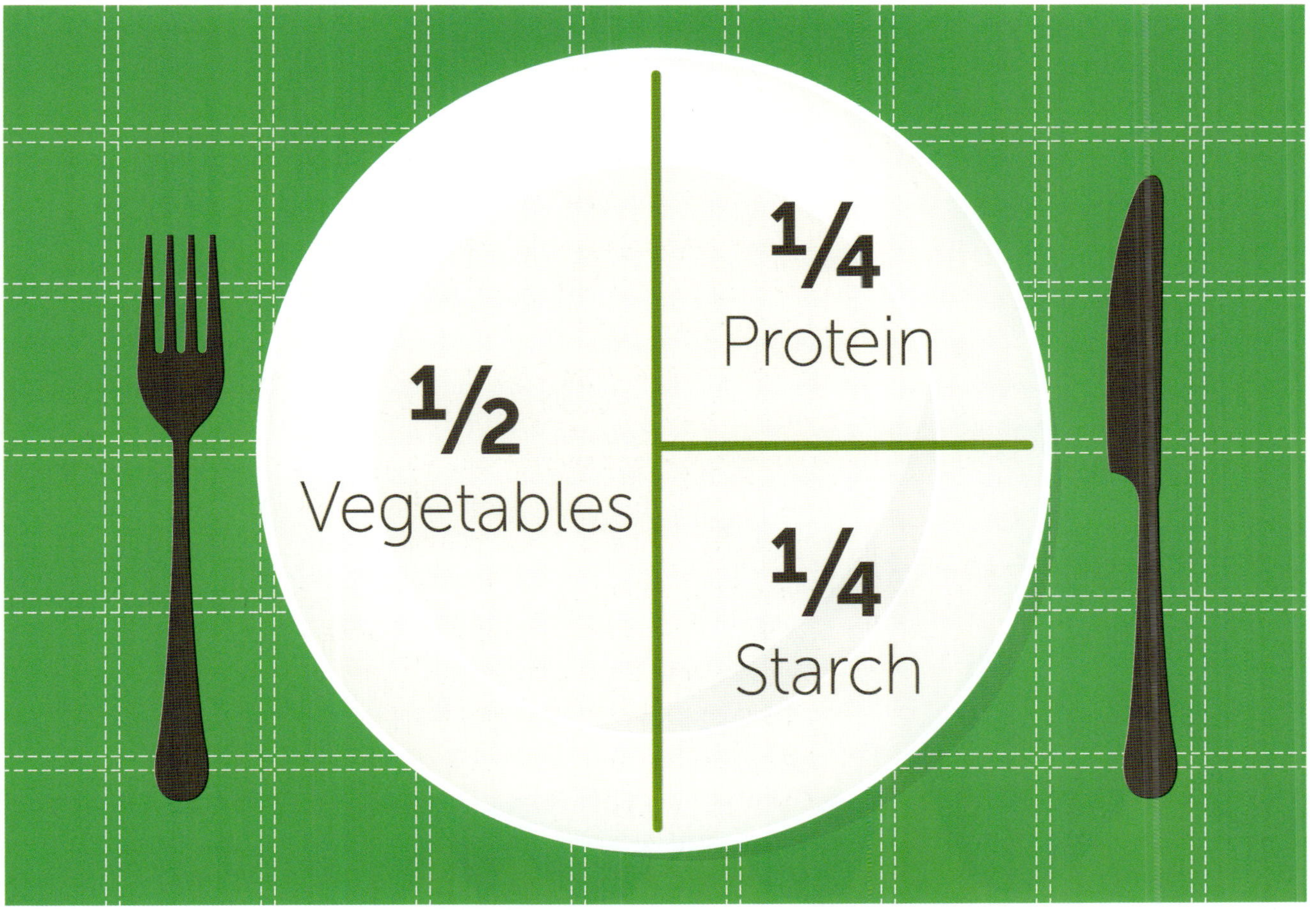

Portion plates can be a useful way to limit and proportion the types of food you eat. The ratios (like the one shown here) can vary from one meal to the next (breakfast, lunch, and dinner), and what is right for you might not be what's right for others. It is always best to consult with your doctor or nutrition expert before making significant changes to your eating habits.

Food Intake and Physical Activity Level

It is important to match food intake and physical activity level, which can vary according to your goals for healthy active living. Figuring out your activity level not only helps you achieve that balance, but also is a good way to plan for a more active lifestyle.

To analyze your current activity level, keep a journal for seven consecutive days noting your physical activities from when you get up until you go to bed:

- Record all the activities you do that involve continuous movement.
- Record whether the activity is light, moderate, or vigorous.
- Estimate how many minutes you spend doing each activity.
- Record the time of day you do each activity.

Canada's Physical Activity Guide to Healthy Active Living
Keeping a journal will help you become aware of your activity patterns. Then you can see how you are doing in relation to **Canada's Physical Activity Guide to Healthy Active Living**, developed by the Canadian Society for Exercise Physiology (CSEP). The guide indicates how much activity we should strive for every day.

It recommends that young people start with five- to ten-minute periods of physical activity and slowly work up to at least 60 minutes of moderate activity and 30 minutes of vigorous activity every day.

The guide also suggests that children and youth decrease the time they spend on sedentary activities—such as watching TV, playing video games, and browsing social media—by at least 30 minutes per day.

If we do not get regular physical activity, it can be difficult to keep our food intake at the same level as our energy expenditure. The more active we are, the easier it is to maintain a healthy body weight—and to stay healthy.

Emotional Factors

Our emotions can have a strong influence on our eating habits. It is important to be aware of the signs of emotional eating so that we can regulate our emotions and maintain healthy eating habits—not eating too much and not restricting our food intake to an unhealthy extent.

Psychological hunger

True hunger becomes gradually more intense and is accompanied by a rumbling stomach and lower energy, but strong emotions such as anger, guilt, loneliness, or happiness can sometimes make you feel hungry.

This is known as psychological hunger, and it can lead to emotional eating which in turn leads to overeating. When you eat to satisfy your emotions, it can be hard to stop—even if your stomach is full.

Food cravings

Trying to restrict your intake of certain foods can make you want those foods more, leading to food cravings. A depressed mood also appears to influence the severity of cravings.

Women more commonly report food cravings than men do. This is especially the case during the premenstrual phase, when total food intake increases and the basal metabolic rate changes.

Stress

Stress is the most common reason for emotional eating because it floods the body with the hormone *cortisol*—the same mechanism that makes us crave sugary, fatty, and salty foods.

The effect of stress on food intake depends on the individual, the stressor and the circumstances. Some people eat more than they normally do when they experience stress and some eat less.

Boredom and fatigue

When we have nothing else to do, we sometimes find ourselves opening the kitchen cabinets or the refrigerator in search of something to eat. We also sometimes confuse fatigue with hunger and reach for a quick "energy boost" in the form of food when we are overtired.

Habit

Sometimes we eat when we come home from school or work just because it is a pattern we have developed. We do not think about what time it is or whether we are about to have a meal.

Body image

Many people struggle with their **body image** and **self-esteem** and may think frequently or obsessively about being either too heavy or too thin. This can lead to unhealthy eating habits based on emotions rather than physical needs.

Too Little or Too Much?

Inadequate diets can lead to two different problems:

- **Undernutrition** occurs when the body does not get enough micronutrients.
- **Overnutrition** occurs when the body gets too many macronutrients, leading to being overweight or obese.

These problems require different forms of intervention.

Social and Cultural Factors

What we eat is shaped by social and cultural circumstances. Even when we eat alone, our food choices are influenced by the attitudes and habits we develop through interaction with others.

Other people affect our eating behaviour either directly (by feeding us) or indirectly (by modelling eating behaviour). This influence can be conscious—such as when parents or guardians teach their beliefs—or subconscious.

Socioeconomic factors that affect the way we eat

Studies also show that differences in **household income** are connected to differences in food and nutrient intake. Household income and food prices are important aspects of food choice, especially for people living on a restricted income.

People with small budgets may be reluctant to buy new foods for fear the family will reject them and waste them. However, developing nutrition knowledge and learning cooking skills can encourage people to prepare varied meals using unprocessed ingredients such as fresh vegetables or legumes.

Household income certainly plays a significant role in the food we consume, in what we can and cannot afford to buy. Making the most out of our budgets and understanding trends in food prices can help us make good choices at the grocery store when planning a nutritious diet.

Cultural factors that affect the way we eat

Several other less obvious, cultural factors affect the way we eat.

- **Social supports.** Support from family, friends, and co-workers can improve our eating habits. Feeling that we belong to a supportive group can encourage us to make and sustain healthy dietary changes.
- **Pressure about appearance.** Parents or guardians, siblings, and friends sometimes put pressure on young people to look a certain way, and the focus is often on dieting and exercise. The healthier approach is to eat well-balanced meals and stay physically active without being obsessed with having a "perfect" body.
- **Family meal patterns.** People often eat in front of the TV, in the car, and even standing up in the kitchen. On the other hand, many cultures value the benefits of planning, preparing, and eating meals together as a family. Home meals are often more nutritious and economical than fast food or restaurant food. Eating at home can teach young people the basics of meal preparation and expose them to a wide variety of dishes, and with fewer distractions we can enjoy food more.
- **Social settings.** Where we eat affects what we eat. You may be more likely to eat junk food at a sporting event or the movies. A potluck meal with friends might offer foods you have not tried before.
- **Cultural or religious practices.** Culture and religion play a major role in what, when, and how much we eat, and in how we prepare, serve, and share food. Some cultures exclude foods such as meat or milk. In some countries, people eat from individual plates, and in others they eat from a shared bowl. Many cultures teach parents to give food to children first if there is not enough.
- **Media and advertising.** Advertisements bombard us with images of sugary drinks and high-fat snacks like potato chips. The media shape our eating habits, but we can resist the influence. Try stocking up on healthy snacks such as low-fat popcorn, apples, carrot or celery sticks, yogurt, boiled eggs, and whole-grain crackers.
- **Cost, availability, and convenience.** Dietary guidelines call for as many as eight to ten servings of fresh fruit and vegetables each day. Of course, fresh produce can be expensive, and it is not readily available in all communities. The Dietitians of Canada website offers excellent tips to plan nutritious meals on a budget and from what you have on hand.
- **Nutrition fads.** Products to promote quick weight loss or muscle gain are everywhere, but they can be expensive and the results rarely last. Crash dieting or drastically restricting your caloric intake can also put strain on the body. It is far better to follow a well-balanced meal plan endorsed by a registered dietitian.

Food Deserts

We must all strive to make the best healthy food choices we can based on personal and external factors. Many people in Canada live in "food deserts" where food choices are limited to, for example, convenience stores or fast food establishments. Community non-profit organizations such as Building Roots and Second Harvest in Toronto are working to make fresh healthy foods more readily available to people living in food deserts.

Environmental Factors

An increasing proportion of food is eaten outside the home. Healthy food options are sometimes limited in work and school environments. This is particularly true for people who work irregular hours or who have special requirements, such as vegetarian or vegan foods.

At the same time, awareness of the ethical and environmental impact of what we eat is on the rise. The good news is that consumer demand for healthier choices is having an impact on the foods available for sale.

Market researchers for food companies are smart to pay attention to the growing desire among Canadians for healthy menu and grocery options.

A heightened awareness of environmental impacts

It was not long ago that the thought of eating strawberries in winter in Canada would have seemed ludicrous. It used to be that you would eat whatever was in season locally, and that was that. Today, an abundance of produce from all over the world is constantly available.

Shipping fruits and vegetables from places as distant as South America or Australia can be extremely taxing on the environment. The trucks and tankers used to transport fresh produce all produce a large amount of greenhouse gases. The total amount of greenhouse gases produced to directly and indirectly support human activities is usually expressed in equivalent tonnes of carbon dioxide (CO_2).

People are starting to examine all of their behaviours, including how they eat, to see how they can reduce their environmental impact, or *carbon footprint*.

Eating local

As a result of this heightened awareness of both food quality and the environmental impact of food choices, many people now try to eat as much locally sourced food as possible. Some people will eat only food that comes from very close to their home. The short distance from field to table often means fresher and better tasting food.

Lots of cities and towns have farmers' markets, and several grocery store chains stock local seasonal fruits and vegetables. Community gardens, food stands, and restaurants that offer locally grown ingredients are also becoming popular. Many people prefer to purchase food by starting within their own immediate community and then proceeding to buy food produced in their own province or country.

Even small changes, like adding one locally sourced meal a week, can improve the environmental impact of your food choices.

Eating organically produced foods

The word *organic* refers to the way farmers produce foodstuffs such as fruits, vegetables, grains, dairy, and meat. Using natural fertilizers to nourish the soil and plants and using crop rotation or mulch instead of pesticides to manage weeds are examples of organic farming practices.

Why do people choose organic food?

- Organic farming practices attempt to reduce pollution and conserve water and soil quality.
- Organic produce may taste better.
- Organic food may limit the consumer's exposure to pesticide residues and food additives such as preservatives, monosodium glutamate, and artificial sweeteners, colouring, and flavouring.

Are there any disadvantages to choosing organic food?

- Organic foods typically cost more than their conventional counterparts, partly because organic farming practices are more expensive.
- Organic fruits and vegetables may spoil more quickly because they are not treated with waxes or preservatives.
- Organic produce may look less than perfect, coming in odd shapes, varying colours, or smaller sizes.

However it looks or tastes, organic food must meet the same quality and safety standards as conventionally produced food.

Farmers' markets, like the one in Montreal shown here, provide easy access to locally grown produce.

What Causes Unhealthy Eating?

Usually several risk factors interact to increase a person's chances of unhealthy eating habits:

- having family members with a history of unhealthy eating
- personality traits such as perfectionism, obsessiveness, negative self-evaluation, anxiety, and/or inflexibility, combined with an overvaluation of appearance
- being in a profession such as dance that involves pressure to be thin
- living in a society that perceives a thin body as ideal
- childhood adversity, including abuse or the death of close relatives or friends

Seek help from a health care professional if you are experiencing problems related to eating or body image.

Eating Disorders

Eating patterns can range from healthy eating to disordered eating (having some unhealthy thoughts or behaviours related to food) and all the way to diagnosed eating disorders. People may be at different places on the continuum at different points in their lives.

Eating disorders are serious conditions that affect both physical and mental health. They occur when someone manipulates food intake and body weight in an often unconscious attempt to feel a sense of self-control and achievement, and to regulate mood.

According to medical criteria, there are three main eating disorders:

- **Anorexia nervosa** is a form of self-starvation characterized by drastic weight loss. Many people with anorexia overexercise as well.
- **Bulimia nervosa** is a condition characterized by cycles of bingeing and purging—inducing vomiting or taking large quantities of laxatives. These behaviours are attempts to regulate body weight and emotions that are often overwhelming.
- **Binge eating** involves consistent overeating. People with a binge eating disorder do not purge and are therefore frequently overweight.

People are considered to have an eating disorder when their thoughts and behaviours associated with eating are so uncontrolled that they interfere with their daily lives. Although anyone can have an eating disorder, they are most common among young females. Only 5 to 10 percent of people with eating disorders are male.

Treatment for eating disorders

Eating disorders are complex illnesses and almost always require professional attention. There are many theories about what causes disorders such as compulsive overeating, but no one truly knows for sure. Sometimes a person with an eating disorder such as anorexia or bulimia starts out just trying to lose some weight or get in shape. However, the urge to eat less, to purge, or to overexercise can become compulsive and extremely hard to stop.

Eating disorders are very common among teens. Intervention options depend on the person and the person's family, and many incorporate journalling, therapy, and working with dietitians and doctors.

Since the behaviours associated with an eating disorder can become gradually worse and more ingrained, it is best to seek help as early as possible. Possible interventions include

- individual, family, or group psychological counselling
- medications (in some instances)
- support groups

Therapy, or counselling, plays a very important role in recovery. In many cases, family or group therapy is key to eating healthily again. Family members can help loved ones learn to accept their body shape and size based on their culture, genetic inheritance, and lifestyle.

Health care professionals sometimes work as an interdisciplinary team to address eating disorders, abnormal eating habits, and problems with body image and self-esteem:

- **Mental health professionals.** Psychiatrists, psychologists, and social workers help the person to change behaviours and deal with the issues that can contribute to an eating disorder, such as low self-esteem.
- **Registered dietitians.** Dietitians help people who are struggling with abnormal eating habits and perceptions of their weight by teaching them about a balanced diet that provides adequate amounts of nutrients and energy, and by encouraging them to enjoy healthy food.
- **Nurse practitioners.** Nurses with special training in eating disorder management offer mental health support and medical care in both the hospital and the community to people experiencing eating disorders.
- **Physical therapists, occupational therapists, and certified personal fitness trainers.** These professionals help people with eating disorders to be active and productive in healthy ways that are not tied to weight loss alone.

If you are concerned about your eating habits, or have a friend or family member who is struggling with an eating disorder, do not hesitate to ask for help. A teacher, family doctor, school nurse, elder, or guidance counsellor can connect you to options available in your community.

Section 5.3 Review

1 List simple steps you can take to ensure you do not consume too much or too little food.

2 State some environmental factors that might affect a person's food choices.

3 Which factors that affect food choices and eating habits do you think exert the most influence on you and your family? Why?

5.4 Dietary Trends and Practices

Our society tends to be obsessed with health and diet trends. In recent years, for example, relatively unusual foods such as chia seeds, kale, and pomegranates have caught on with consumers.

Various food trends are worth noting, but before deciding to follow a particular way of eating it is a good idea to consult a doctor who specializes in nutrition or a registered dietitian.

Natural foods. Today's consumers are reading the small print on food labels. Foods with fewer ingredients tend to be healthier.

Clean eating. Many people try to avoid artificial ingredients and packaged or processed foods in favour of natural foods.

Less red meat. More and more studies indicate that red meat can lead to diseases because of its saturated fat and cholesterol content. A Harvard School of Public Health study, for example, suggests that even moderate regular consumption of red meat poses serious health risks. The Mediterranean diet advises eating meat only once a month. The high environmental cost of production is another reason why people may avoid or reduce consumption of red meat.

Gluten- and wheat-free foods. Some people avoid gluten because of health issues such as celiac disease. Others cut out gluten or wheat because they believe that avoiding these foods will help improve their health.

Ancient grains. Quinoa, spelt, freekeh, millet, faro, buckwheat, and amaranth, the so-called ancient grains, have been top trends for the past several years.

Superfoods. There is no legal or medical definition for "superfoods," but some food websites describe these foods as "nutrient powerhouses" that pack large doses of antioxidants, vitamins, and minerals. Some people believe that eating these foods may reduce the risk of chronic disease and prolong life. Examples of superfoods commonly identified are tomatoes, blueberries, apples, kale, black beans, broccoli, spinach, salmon, and oats.

Low fat is now seen as a negative. People who wish to lose weight still favour carbohydrate restrictions, but low-fat foods are no longer seen as healthy. These foods can still have a high-sugar and high-caloric content.

Everyone's an expert. Consumers are getting much of their nutrition information from nutrition blogs, but a lot of this advice comes from non-professionals and could lead to nutritional deficiencies.

To make good choices, consult your doctor or the Dietitians of Canada. If you live in Ontario, Manitoba, or British Columbia, you can call a dietitian at no charge. For details, visit the Dietitians of Canada website.

Vegetarianism and Nutrition

People choose to be vegetarian for various reasons. Some feel a strong ethical commitment to animal rights. Others want the health benefits of **vegetarianism**. For others it is a part of their religious beliefs.

Research suggests that vegetarian diets may reduce the risk of chronic diseases and health conditions such as obesity, heart disease, and some types of cancer.

Planning a well-balanced vegetarian diet—one that provides all the nutrients needed for good health—is the key to reaping these benefits. Overly restrictive diets that eliminate entire groups of foods without adding a vegetarian replacement can lead to nutritional deficiencies.

Shortages of iron, calcium, and zinc are the most noted drawbacks of vegetarian eating. Teenagers, who are growing and active, need higher than average amounts of these nutrients, so they need to be especially careful to plan and eat appropriate vegetarian meals.

Vegetarians who choose a variety of foods each day, in adequate amounts, can get all the nutrients they need.

Table 5.3 **Common Vegetarian Eating Styles**

Type	Foods selected	Foods avoided
Vegan	Vegetables and fruit; grain products; meat alternatives*	Meat and poultry; fish and shellfish; milk and milk products; eggs
Lacto-ovo vegetarian	Vegetables and fruit; grain products; milk and milk products; eggs; meat alternatives*	Meat and poultry; fish and shellfish
Ovo-vegetarian	Vegetables and fruit; grain products; eggs; meat alternatives*	Meat and poultry; fish and shellfish; milk and milk products
Lacto-vegetarian	Vegetables and fruit; grain products; milk and milk products; meat alternatives*	Meat and poultry; fish and shellfish; eggs
Semi-vegetarian	Vegetables and fruit; grain products; milk and milk products; poultry, fish, and shellfish; eggs; meat alternatives*	Red meat

* Tofu, legumes, and nuts are all considered meat alternatives.

What Influences Your Eating Patterns?

How can you use what you know about the factors and trends that influence *what, when, how much,* and *how often* you eat?

Think of ways to maximize the factors influencing you to eat healthily and to minimize the ones persuading you to eat unhealthily. Awareness of *influencing factors* can go a long way to support healthy eating patterns.

Dietary Supplements

In most cases, the foods we eat give us all the nutrients and vitamins we need. Despite that, a huge industry has developed to produce and market products known as **dietary supplements**.

These products are intended to add to, or supplement, the foods we eat. They are taken orally and contain a *dietary ingredient*—vitamins, minerals, herbs or other botanicals, amino acids, or substances such as enzymes and organ tissues.

Hundreds of different dietary supplements are sold as tablets, capsules, liquids, powders, extracts, or concentrates. Some are sold as bars, drinks, or specialty cereals; supplements sold in these forms closely resemble conventional foods.

In general, the dietary supplement industry in Canada and the United States is not as well regulated as it could be. Unlike the government systems that are in place to ensure the safety of drugs, the manufacturers of dietary supplements may make claims that are not always supported by scientific evidence.

As a result, the manufacturers' claims may not be valid because the manufacturers wish to profit as much as possible from the sales of their products—whether or not the products work as they claim they do. Additionally, dietary supplements are not subject to the intense scrutiny by government agencies that drugs undergo.

Become an informed consumer

Ultimately, we are all responsible for the health and lifestyle choices we make. This is especially true where dietary supplements are concerned. Because these products are only loosely regulated, it is up to the buyer to learn as much as possible about a supplement before buying it. Here are some *dos and don'ts* to guide you:

- **Do research the product before buying it.** Find out what the product contains and whether the claims about its effects are valid. Health Canada and your pharmacist are reliable sources of information.
- **Do read the label.** Consider any negative side effects. If anything on the label is unclear, ask your doctor or pharmacist before taking the supplement.
- **Do look for a natural product number (NPN).** Check the label for an eight-digit number preceded by the letters NPN, which stands for *natural product number*. If a product does not have an NPN, it has not been researched or regulated by the Natural Health Products Directorate of Health Canada.
- **Do consult a dietitian.** You may well get the nutritional effect you want through diet alone, without any supplements. A dietitian can help you figure out how.
- **Do talk to your coach, dietitian, or team doctor if you are a competitive athlete.** Most sport organizations recommend that athletes avoid *all* supplements because they may contain a banned substance.
- **Do tell your doctor and pharmacist what you plan to take.** Some supplements have powerful side effects. Others can interfere with other supplements or products you are using. Health care professionals can help you make an informed decision before you take anything.
- **Do report side effects immediately.** If you experience any unusual symptoms after using a supplement, contact your doctor. Even mild side effects are a warning that something is wrong. Symptoms that you should be concerned about include stomach upset, pain, headaches, rashes, dizziness, breathing problems, and tiredness.
- **Don't be persuaded by advertising language.** If something seems too good to be true, it probably is. Phrases such as "miracle product," "breakthrough," and "clinically proven" mean very little.
- **Don't believe everything you read.** Information provided by health and fitness magazines, health food stores, and manufacturers is not always reliable.
- **Don't take more than the recommended dose.** Stick to the dosage your doctor or pharmacist recommends. Taking more will not maximize the benefits—but it will carry the risk of overdose.

In most cases, a balanced diet is the best way to meet your energy and nutrient needs. Think food first.

Energy Drinks and Specialty Coffees

Energy drinks sell a lifestyle. Their ads and packaging design appeal to our sometimes unconscious desire to live fast and miss nothing.

Considering their name, they typically contain surprisingly low amounts of nutrients. Specialty coffees are not much better. Black coffee or tea has little nutritional value, and neither do the added syrups, sugars, and heavy cream.

The caffeine

The one thing these drinks have in common is caffeine, often a lot of it.

Health Canada recommends at most 400 mg of caffeine daily for adults, which equals about three 8-ounce cups of coffee. So-called standard mugs often hold much more than that. What you think of as three cups may actually be closer to five.

For children under 12, no more than 2.5 mg of caffeine per kilogram of body weight is recommended.

These numbers are only guidelines. No one needs caffeine, and consuming too much of it can interfere with the amount and quality of your sleep, not to mention making you feel jittery.

The cost

Another major drawback to speciality caffeinated drinks is the cost. Just a few of these each week can quickly add up. Think how much you would save by buying only unsweetened juice or milk—or simply drinking water for free.

The calories

When you add milk, whipped cream, and mocha sauce to a single expresso, it can substantially add to your daily calorie intake. Let us look at a large specialty coffee drink and a double cheeseburger.

The calories in each one of these items is more than 20 percent of the total calories that Health Canada recommends the average Canadian should consume each day (2,000 calories).

	Iced chocolate coffee with whipped cream (24 oz)	Double cheeseburger
Total fat	19 mg	21 mg
Total carbohydrates	60 mg	35 mg
Total protein	13 mg	25 mg
Calories	463	429
% of a 2,000-calorie diet	23%	21%

The Body Positivity Movement

If you are like most people, you have been exposed to a lot of messages telling you that "thin" and "fit" mean the same, but media messaging is slowly changing to reflect the reality that fit healthy bodies come in different shapes and sizes. This is known as the *body positivity movement*.

Research has shown that families are disposed to certain body traits and health conditions. You and your family members may have a genetic predisposition to being tall or stocky. You may share a tendency to metabolize your food more slowly and store more energy in the form of fat.

Your family also teaches you a lot about eating. If children are fed larger portions of foods that are high in fat and sugar, they tend to develop more body fat. This does not prevent anyone from living an active healthy life, but these food choices can affect body composition and fitness.

How fit you are depends on your body's ability to do sustained strenuous activity—in other words, your cardiorespiratory and musculoskeletal health. It is also about eating well, staying active, and feeling good about yourself and your body.

Eating well

- Give your metabolism a boost by eating breakfast.
- Switch to whole grain bread, cereal, and pasta.
- Eat fruits and vegetables every day.
- Avoid sweetened beverages.

Staying active

- Cut your screen time to two hours per day.
- Find an activity you enjoy and do it often. Team sports are not for everyone.
- Build activity into your daily life. Take the stairs, walk, or ride your bike.

Feeling good about yourself

- Question media messages.
- Notice the benefits of eating well and being active, such as having more energy and feeling less stress.
- Take care of your body instead of trying to reach a certain weight.
- Your mental picture may have little to do with how you really look, and you can project negative feelings about your body. Be kind to yourself, and others will be more likely to see you positively as well.

Section 5.4 Review

1 Of the dietary trends and practices described in this section, which ones do you follow or would you like to follow? Why?

2 List some of the drawbacks of consuming energy drinks or specialty coffee drinks.

3 What can you and your friends do to support the body positivity movement?

5.5

5.5 Developing a Healthy Eating Plan

Now that you have reviewed some basic nutrition principles and healthy eating practices, you can apply your knowledge to develop a healthy eating plan that takes personal and external factors into account. Keep these points in mind:

- Make sure to include all food groups in Canada's Food Guide.
- Adjust your food intake to your activity level, and keep an eye on portion size.
- Try baking, grilling, broiling, steaming, poaching, or microwaving food. These methods are healthier than frying.
- Consider whether fast food fits into your plan. You might have to change how often you eat out and what you order.

As you develop your plan, check out reliable sources of information, such as the Health Canada and Dietitians of Canada (DC) websites.

The DC website lists toll-free numbers, so residents of Ontario, Manitoba, and British Columbia can ask a registered dietitian specific questions about diet and meal planning. The EatRight Ontario website also has a customizable meal planner.

Quick and Easy Meal Planning

There are lots of simple ways to plan healthy meals that save money and are quick and easy to prepare:

- Check the fridge, freezer, and cupboard for what needs to be used up.
- Keep a stock of healthy basics that have little or no added fat, sugar, or sodium.
- Try to limit processed, packaged, ready-to-eat, and take-out foods.
- Try to plan to have at least one serving of vegetables or fruit in each meal.
- Get in the habit of reading flyers to find out what is on special.
- Make a list of your favourite healthy options as "go to" snacks.
- The Foodland Ontario website is just one that has some great seasonal meal ideas. Do not be afraid to try something new!
- Store favourite recipes in a binder to use again.
- Add your ideas to a family grocery list with headings such as "produce," "drinks," and so on. Encourage everyone in your family to add to the list.
- Support your family members in helping to plan simple weekday meals.
- Take responsibility for one task: planning, shopping, cooking, or clean-up.

A healthy meal planning checklist

A healthy meal plan has the following features:

- a variety of interesting flavours, colours, shapes, textures, and temperatures (for example, cooked or raw)
- few processed or pre-cooked foods—home-made whole-wheat pizzas using flat bread, for example
- fresh vegetables and fruits in season, and frozen or canned fruits and vegetables at other times
- at least one dark-green vegetable (for example, bok choy) and one orange vegetable (carrot, sweet potato) or fruit (peaches, cantaloupe) daily
- at least half the daily grain intake using whole grains—brown rice, barley, bulgur, oats, quinoa, couscous, wild rice, popcorn, whole-wheat pitas, cereals, pasta, tortillas, and roti
- 2 percent milk fat or less, or fortified soy beverage
- lean meats with fat trimmed, skinless poultry and meat alternatives such as beans, eggs, or tofu
- at least two servings (125 mL or ½ cup or 75 g) of fish every week

Balance, Variety, Moderation

When it comes to healthy meal planning, three words are your guide:

Balance. Choose foods that together contain all the nutrients the body needs.

Variety. It is much more enjoyable to eat a variety of foods than to eat the same things all the time.

Moderation. Try to eat small amounts of a wide range of nutrient-rich foods every day. If you do eat foods with little nutrition (baked goods, chips, candy), try not to eat too much.

Guidelines for Daily Beverage Choices

- Drink plenty of water to stay hydrated.
- Drink 500 ml (2 cups) of milk or fortified soy beverage each day, or 750 ml (3 cups) if you are 14 to 18 years old.
- Drink no more than six cups of tea or three cups of coffee a day, to a limit of 300–400 mg of caffeine.
- Limit juice to no more than 125 ml (½ cup) for children and 250 ml (1 cup) for teens and adults each day. Try to eat fresh vegetables and fruits instead of drinking 100% juice.
- Avoid sweetened fruit drinks, punch, energy drinks, and soft drinks.

Healthy cooking methods

- Use herbs, spices, onions, and garlic to add flavouring.
- Do not add fat, sugar, or salt.
- Use only a small daily amount of unsaturated fat per person (30–45 ml, or 2–3 tablespoons), from canola, olive, or soybean oil, salad dressing, soft margarine that is low in saturated fat and trans fat free, or mayonnaise.
- Limit butter, lard, and shortening and avoid hard margarine.
- Use lower-fat cooking methods such as baking, poaching, roasting, slow cooking, broiling, grilling, and steaming.

Table 5.4 **Making Healthier Food Choices**

Instead of...	Try...
Potato chips, tortilla chips	• Pretzels, baked crackers, popcorn (small amounts of butter, margarine, or salt) • Raw vegetables and lower-fat dip
Pop, fruit drinks, slushies, energy drinks	• Water, 100% fruit juices, milk, chocolate milk
French fries	• Tossed salad (order salad dressing on the side and use only small amounts) • Baked potato (small amounts of butter, margarine, or salt)
Large hamburger	• Small hamburger or chicken or turkey burger (order any special sauces on the side, and use only small amounts)
Cereals with added sugar	• Whole grain cereals (add fruit if desired)
Breaded, fried chicken burger	• Grilled chicken or turkey burger (order any special sauces on the side and use only small amounts)
Thick pizza with meat toppings	• Thin-crust vegetarian pizza, whole wheat crust, made with minimal oil and cheese
Deli meat submarine sandwich	• Whole wheat bun with leaner meats such as chicken or turkey instead of sausage or salami (mustard, relish, cranberry sauce, or salsa to season)

Tracking Your Eating and Physical Activity

Dietitians of Canada (DC) offers a free online tool called eaTracker for people 14 years old and up to track their eating habits and physical activities. Once you have registered an account and signed in, you can watch a short video that demonstrates all the tools you can use:

- Under the My Food tab, record and analyze the food you eat as well as any supplements you are taking. You will receive feedback on whether you are getting enough of the food groups, on your calorie consumption, and on the amount of each nutrient you are getting.
- Under the My Activities tab, record your daily physical activities. You will find out how many calories you are burning and how your physical activity compares to Canada's Physical Activity Guide to Healthy Active Living.
- Under the My Goals tab, set healthy eating and activity goals. Choose from a list of goals or write one yourself. You can track your weekly progress, plus get weekly emails from EatRight Ontario with tips and motivational messages.
- Under the My Recipes tab, analyze recipes to find the nutritional content of one serving of your recipe.
- Under the My Coach tab, connect with a registered dietitian—for a fee. You can also get free support by talking to the dietitians at EatRight Ontario at 1.877.510.5102. In British Columbia, call toll free 811. In Manitoba, call toll free 1.877.830.2892 or 204.788.8248 in Winnipeg.

Section 5.5 Review

1 Which sources of information about food and nutrition do you consider most trustworthy? Why?

2 List your typical daily beverage consumption, and rate it as healthy or unhealthy based on the criteria in this section.

3 What key points must you keep in mind in developing a healthy eating plan?

Ella's Story

"It's hard to fight the urge to consume salty and sugary foods, but once you get past the cravings and start to eat more fruits and vegetables, it will change how you feel, not only physically but also mentally."
— Ella Finkelstein

Chapter 5 Review

Knowledge and Understanding

1 List the six categories of nutrients that we need in our diet every day, and briefly describe their role in our health.

2 Describe four types of nutritional information that can be found on a food label, and explain how you can use this information to make healthier food choices.

3 Considering the different factors that influence people's eating habits, identify one physical/biological factor, one social/cultural factor, and one environmental factor. Explain why it is important for people to know about these different types of factors.

4 Briefly explain the body positivity movement.

Thinking

5 Compare and contrast the information on the food labels of three pre-packaged meals. Determine the relative nutritional value of each meal. Present the results to your class, explaining the criteria you used.

6 In a group, list and discuss the nutritional pros and cons of vegetarianism for teens. After the discussion, what is the group's consensus?

7 Research the nutrition information that a fast food restaurant chain makes available either online or at the restaurants, with respect to the types of fats contained in various menu items. Is it possible to make a healthy meal choice at this restaurant? Explain your answer.

Communication

8 Create a blog or a short video featuring five benefits of a food trend or practice of your choice.

9 What advice would you give a friend who is considering taking a dietary supplement?

Application

10 Find two cereal boxes. Based on your understanding of % DV, determine which cereal is more nutritious. Be specific in your answer.

11 Investigate the local or organic food available in your community, and develop an appealing and nutritious meal plan that incorporates some of these foods.

12 Evaluate three or four advertisements in both print and online media. Discuss in a group whether you think the advertisements reflect body positivity.

Sexual Health, Development, and Safety

6.1 Human Sexuality and Gender Identities

6.2 Healthy Intimate Relationships

6.3 Factors that Influence Sexual Decision Making

6.4 Developing Your Decision-Making and Communication Skills

6.5 Safeguarding Your Sexual Health

6

Sharicka's Story

Why is it important to develop decision-making and communication skills that positively affect your sexual health and safety?

We are all exposed to information about sex and sexuality every day. Sexual images are used in advertising to sell everything from shampoo to cars. Yet, if you look at the content of these media, it's clear that much of the information presented is either incomplete or incorrect. Some of it can be demeaning and offensive.

People use the term *sexuality* to refer to a number of related ideas, including the physical development of sexual characteristics, gender roles, relations between the sexes, and intimacy, love, and affection. The term is also associated with sexual attraction, sexual contact, sexual decision making, and sexual orientation.

This chapter will examine all of these dimensions of sexuality, with a particular focus on protecting our sexual and emotional health and ensuring that our relationships are safe and positive.

Key Terms

- sexuality
- human rights codes
- sexual orientation
- gender identity
- Intersex
- sexual intimacy
- healthy relationships
- SHARE qualities
- sexual decision making
- consent
- abstinence
- methods of contraception
- sexually transmitted infections (STIs)
- Kids Help Phone

Learning Objectives

In this chapter, you will...

- identify the stages of human sexual development
- describe factors that influence sexual decision making
- demonstrate an understanding of factors that can influence a person's gender identity
- describe some common misconceptions about sexuality
- demonstrate an understanding of the skills and strategies needed to build healthy intimate relationships
- describe the relative effectiveness of various methods of preventing unintended pregnancy or sexually transmitted infections (STIs)
- apply your knowledge of sexual health and safety and decision-making skills to safeguard your sexual health
- identify reliable sources of information and support

▶ **Sharicka Reid**'s cultural influences and family provided great support when she had to make decisions about dating and goal setting as a teenager. She grew up in a household where open communication was encouraged. Today, she benefits from that support in her roles as mother, partner, friend, citizen, and social worker in the field of mental health.

6.1 Human Sexuality and Gender Identities

Sexuality encompasses our physical development as well as our sexual knowledge, attitudes, beliefs, and behaviours. It also involves making important decisions about intimate relationships. As we go through the stages of sexual development, we learn more about ourselves, and we express feelings of love, affection, and pleasure in different ways.

There are no exact times that these changes occur, but the stages are summarized below and in the table that follows.

Stage 1: Infancy (Birth to Age 2)

From birth until about two years old, infants are completely dependent on others. They learn about love through nurturing physical contact, including hugs, kisses, and snuggling with their caregivers, and they begin to notice differences between male and female bodies.

Stage 2: Childhood (Ages 3 to 8)

From the age of three until about eight, children grow increasingly curious about their bodies and about sexuality. They explore these ideas through role-playing games, and they begin asking questions about sex. They also begin to develop a basic sexual identity and sexual orientation, and they may start to become aware of what they consider sexually attractive.

Stage 3: Pre-Adolescence (Ages 9 to 12)

From ages 9 to 12, young people often begin the important transition of puberty. As their bodies produce more sex hormones, pre-teens may start to experience sexual feelings.

Because many children of this age feel awkward about their own bodies, they often want more privacy. They may also develop crushes on friends, classmates, older teens, and even teachers or their favourite celebrities.

Puberty comes at different times for different people, so pre-adolescents may change more quickly or more slowly than their friends.

Stage 4: Adolescence (Ages 13 to 18)

From ages 13 to 18, during adolescence, young people face many physical, social, and emotional changes. As they make the transition from childhood to adulthood, their bodies continue to grow and change.

Many teens begin to date and to develop intimacy with a partner. They typically experience increased sexual feelings and want to be physically close or romantic with another person. At the same time, teens can face peer pressure to experiment sexually, whether they feel ready or not.

Stage 5: Early Adulthood (Ages 19 to 45)

In early adulthood, people often become comfortable with sexuality in general, and their desire for physical intimacy and a sexual relationship increases. Younger adults often choose a long-term partner and make decisions about cohabitation and/or marriage, and sometimes about having children.

Stage 6: Later Adulthood (Ages 46 and up)

In the first part of later adulthood (46–65), people may be raising children with their partner or on their own. Most experience physical and hormonal changes linked to menopause (when a woman's menstrual cycle stops) or andropause (when a man's testosterone level drops). However, sexuality remains an important part of a person's identity during later adulthood.

Sexuality: One Term, Many Dimensions

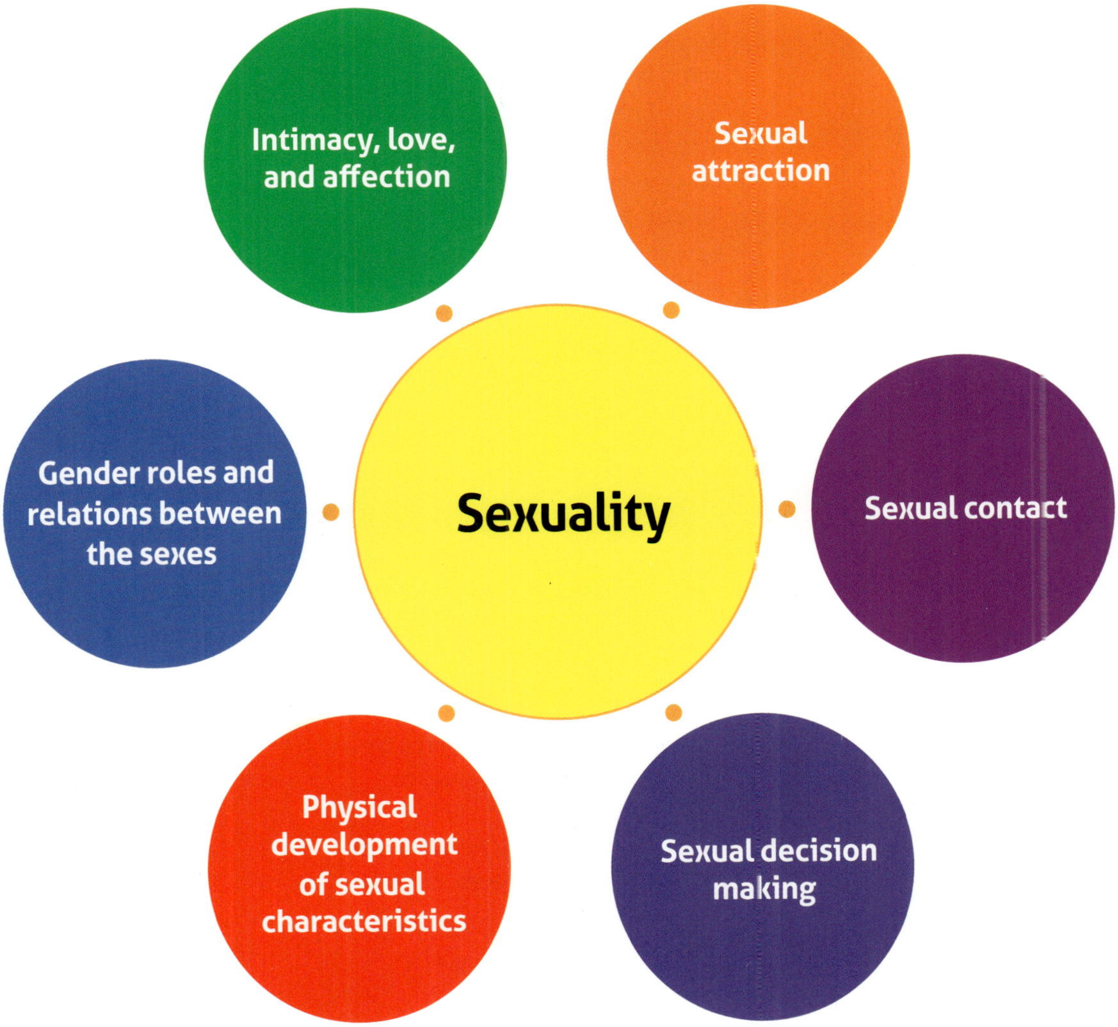

Table 6.1 **The Stages of Human Sexual Development**

	Physical traits	Emotional/mental traits	Social behaviour
Stage 1: Infancy (birth to age 2)			
Infants may...	• have erections or lubricate vaginally • experience pleasure through genital stimulation	• learn about trust through relationships with caregivers • learn about love through nurturing physical contact • gain self-esteem by experiencing kindness and physical closeness	• discover socially expected behaviour differences between genders • explore their own bodies, including their genitals • begin to notice differences between male and female bodies
Stage 2: Childhood (ages 3–8)			
Children may...	• begin to masturbate	• become curious about bodies and learn that they are either male or female • become aware of sex and reproduction and develop a basic sexual identity and orientation • acquire attitudes about sex from caregivers • feel romantic attachment toward a caregiver • possess definite (often stereotypical) ideas about gender roles • begin to be affected by media stories about sexual issues such as abuse	• begin to use language to express needs and feelings • use words related to sexuality • explore the body/sexuality through role-playing games • enjoy learning and talking about body parts and functions • ask questions about birth or pregnancy • seek a strong relationship with same-sex caregiver • mimic adult intimate behaviour • continue to learn about gender roles by observing others • develop strong same-sex friendships and mimic friends' behaviour • engage in name calling and teasing
Stage 3: Pre-adolescence (ages 9–12)			
Pre-teens may...	• begin puberty, including menstruation or sperm production and greater production of sex hormones • experience growing sexual feelings and fantasies • masturbate to orgasm	• feel awkward about their own bodies • struggle with mixed emotions, wonder if they are "normal" • acquire core values from parents and family • become increasingly influenced by peers, particularly with regard to self-image • have romantic feelings for people of the opposite sex, same sex, or both	• develop greater modesty and seek privacy • continue to seek same-sex friendships • take part in sexual exploration with peers • make decisions about sex and drugs

	Physical traits	Emotional/mental traits	Social behaviour
Stage 4: Adolescence (ages 13–18)			
Adolescents may...	• complete the changes of puberty • experience increased sexual feelings and fantasies • desire physical closeness with a partner	• have strong sexual identity/ orientation • place great value on independence • become very concerned about their appearance and attractiveness • become increasingly influenced by peers, partners, family, cultural community	• begin to separate from parents • seek romantic relationships in favour of close friendships • begin to date • sometimes face pressure to be sexually active • develop intimacy with partners • make choices regarding sexual activity and safer sex • experience relationship breakups • sometimes engage in risk-taking activities or face violence in relationships
Stage 5: Early adulthood (ages 19–45)			
Younger adults may...	• experience increased desire for physical intimacy and sexual relationships • report greater sexual satisfaction in their relationships	• become more comfortable with sexual identity/orientation and sexuality in general • become less concerned with conformity • feel less pressure to behave in gender-specific ways in relationships	• make decisions about cohabitation, marriage, children • potentially experience relationship breakups or divorce • develop adult relationships with parents • seek friends of both sexes • make healthy decisions regarding safer sex • complete breast or testicular self-examinations for good health • raise children with partner or on their own
Stage 6: Later adulthood (ages 46 and up)			
Older adults may...	• experience physical and hormonal changes linked to menopause or andropause • continue to explore sexual intimacy and sexual activity with partner(s)	• feel comfortable with sexual identity/ orientation • struggle with negative stereotypes of sexuality and aging	• potentially experience relationship breakups, divorce, death of loved ones • continue to make choices about single/married life, dating, intimate relationships • continue to raise children • develop relationships with adult children and grandchildren • continue to make healthy decisions regarding safer sex • potentially decrease sexual activity after age 65

Respecting Diversity and Promoting Equality

How we feel about ourselves, how we identify ourselves, and who we are attracted to can be complicated. These feelings generally become evident during puberty—a time when our bodies and brains begin to change significantly.

During puberty, our pituitary gland sends signals to our sex glands. These in turn send out sex hormones that affect the growth and function of our reproductive organs and the development of secondary sex characteristics (e.g., facial hair, voice pitch, breast development, and other sex characteristics not directly involved in reproduction). When this occurs, you become more conscious of your emerging gender identity and sexual orientation.

Human rights protection

Today, all Canadian citizens have equal rights and protection under the law. Section 15 of the *Canadian Charter of Rights and Freedoms*, for example, prohibits discrimination on the basis of a person's sex, and the courts have interpreted this to include sexual orientation and gender identity.

The *Canadian Human Rights Act* and various provincial **human rights codes** also prohibit discrimination and harassment on the basis of sexual orientation or gender identity.

Not all countries have such laws. These legal protections are now a part of our rights as Canadian citizens.

Same-sex sexual activity between consenting adults was decriminalized in Canada in 1969 following legislation introduced by then-Justice Minister and Attorney General Pierre Elliott Trudeau (who later became Prime Minister). Pierre Trudeau famously commented at the time: "There's no place for the state in the bedrooms of the nation." Below, his son Justin Trudeau (who became Prime Minister of Canada in 2015) and his family participate in a Pride parade in Vancouver.

Sexual orientation

People can vary in terms of their sexual attraction toward others. These differences are described as a person's **sexual orientation**.

- Someone who experiences his or her sexuality as *heterosexual* feels sexually attracted toward those of the opposite sex.
- A *lesbian* is a woman who is attracted to other women. A *gay* man is attracted to other men. The term *bisexual* refers to people who are attracted to both women and men.
- People who self-identify as *questioning* generally feel some confusion about their sexuality and are unsure of their sexual orientation.
- Members of several groups use the term *queer* as a way of declaring that they are not heterosexual. It is meant to be empowering and to offset prejudice and discrimination.

Gender identity

Most people describe themselves as either male or female, but some people experience **gender identity** differently.

- People who identify as *transgender* do not feel their assigned gender reflects the way they feel inside. They may choose to dress and present themselves as a different gender without undergoing sexual reassignment surgery. Transgender people may also present themselves as having both male and female characteristics.
- People who identify as *transsexual* feel a consistent and overwhelming desire to live as another gender. Transsexuals may consider or pursue hormonal therapy and surgery in order to make the transition to a different gender.
- *Two-spirited* is an Indigenous term that recognizes gender as a continuum and includes sexual or gender identity, social values, and sexual orientation.

Intersex individuals

Intersex is an umbrella term that describes a wide range of naturally occurring bodily variations. Intersex people are born with sex characteristics that do not fit typical notions of male or female bodies. In some cases, such intersex traits are visible at birth while in others they are not apparent until puberty or may not be physically apparent at all.

Intersex relates to a person's biological sex characteristics, which is distinct from a sexual orientation or gender identity. An intersex person may be heterosexual, gay, lesbian, or bisexual, and may identify as female, male, both, or neither.

Intersex people often face stigmatization and discrimination. Increasingly these issues are regarded as human rights abuses and are taken up by international and national human rights and ethics organizations. Intersex organizations also monitor such human rights violations.

Section 6.1 Review

1 Define the following terms: *sexuality, gender identity, sexual orientation.*

2 Distinguish between the terms *transsexual* and *transgender.*

3 Which federal law prohibits discrimination or harassment on the basis of sexual orientation or gender identity?

6.2 Healthy Intimate Relationships

From the moment of birth we long for intimate contact: a loving touch, the sound of a caring voice, or a familiar face looking fondly at us. Intimacy—the expression of deep, faithful love—is essential in a truly loving relationship.

It is also the foundation of good friendship. You have probably shared your deepest secrets with a trusted friend. This closeness is what we call intimacy. Sexual activity is just one possible form of intimacy between loving and committed people.

What Is Sexual Intimacy?

As we establish relationships, we make choices about how intimate we wish to be. We decide how much personal information we share with our partner, how we communicate, and to what extent we want to be physically close. **Sexual intimacy** is a way of expressing intimate feelings for another person.

You can think of sexual activity as a gradual progression from less intimate acts toward more intimate acts if the couple agrees. For the majority of couples, a relationship will begin with a period of sexual abstinence, during which they meet socially and privately and become comfortable with each other.

Over time, romantic relationships often become more intimate. As they grow closer, some couples develop a long-term, committed relationship and/or get married and increase their levels of intimate and sexual activity.

Close friendships can provide emotional support, especially if you are going through a difficult time.

The Importance of Open and Honest Communication

The speed at which a couple might move through the steps of intimacy depends on a wide variety of factors, such as their ages, the amount of time they spend together, and their personal values.

All too often, young people rush through the steps of intimacy. This is unfortunate, because getting to know another person fully, falling in love, and becoming intimate are really special experiences. It takes time to grow as a couple and build a strong relationship.

Ideally, a couple will make decisions about sex together. It is important to become comfortable enough to discuss personal beliefs, thoughts, fears, hopes, and limits openly and honestly, with trust, respect, and mutual consent.

When Relationships Are Unhealthy

Relationships do not have to involve physical violence to be unhealthy. You should question a relationship if you feel pressured to do something you don't want to do in order to make your partner like or love you.

Girls are at a greater risk for sexual or physical assault compared to boys. In Canada, about one in four women between the ages of 18 and 24 experiences violence from her partner.

If you or someone you know is living with violent or abusive behaviour, help is available. Talk with any trusted adult, or call your local health department or Kids Help Phone at 1.800.668.6868.

Evaluating Relationships

Responsible sexual and intimate decisions are most easily made within healthy relationships. Generally, **healthy relationships** cause people to feel good about themselves, while unhealthy relationships cause people to feel unhappy. In healthy relationships, partners respect themselves and one another. They consider each other's feelings and take care of each other.

Often, in unhealthy relationships, one partner mistreats the other. Occasionally, both partners treat each other badly. Sometimes, people who are not being treated well do not recognize that they are being mistreated.

Warning signs of an unhealthy relationship include

- excessive criticism
- threats
- physical violence
- jealousy
- controlling behaviour such as checking in constantly by phone, text, or email

How you feel is perhaps the best sign of whether or not your relationship is healthy. Read through Table 6.2 and consider which qualities apply to the relationships in your life.

Table 6.2 **Healthy Versus Unhealthy Relationships**

In healthy relationships, partners...	In unhealthy relationships, partners...
• feel more happy and relaxed • are more confident • have more positive self-esteem • feel appreciated • are able to talk about sexuality • attempt to understand one another • build intimacy through the honest exchange of ideas • make sexual decisions together • act with mutual respect, consideration, and trust • listen to each other • enjoy equality • spend time together and time apart • demonstrate independence	• feel unhappy • are less sure of themselves • have negative self-esteem • feel disrespected and unappreciated • do not talk about sexuality • do not attempt to understand one another • can be dishonest with each other • do not make sexual decisions together • act with disregard for each other's feelings • frequently argue over important issues • pressure the other into doing something • manipulate each other • use intimidation or threats • hurt or harm each other • depend on the other person for emotional stability

The SHARE Qualities

Every relationship is unique, but healthy relationships have some things in common. These are sometimes referred to as the **SHARE** qualities: **S**afety, **H**onesty, **A**cceptance, **R**espect, and **E**njoyment.

Safety. In a healthy relationship neither person worries about being physically or emotionally hurt by the other. You feel safe making a decision—such as whether or not to have sex—without being afraid of how your partner will react.

Honesty. You and your partner tell each other the truth even when you know that you disagree or that the truth may not be pleasant. You resolve problems honestly and openly, and you are able to admit when you have made a mistake.

Acceptance. You accept each other for who you are. Neither of you tries to "fix" the other. If your partner has qualities you really do not like, you probably should not be with that person.

Respect. You and your partner respect each other's right to have different opinions. Neither of you worries that you will be made fun of or ignored. You do not feel inferior or superior—you each think highly of the other, even if you do not always agree.

Enjoyment. You feel happy and energized when you are together. You can play or be serious, and you enjoy each other's company no matter what you are doing. Even when things are not perfect, you still feel comfortable with each other.

Sometimes a person knows that he or she is not happy in a relationship but does not know what to do about it. The person might feel powerless to improve the situation or might want to leave but feels afraid to do so. Sometimes people think that any relationship is better than being alone.

If any of this applies to you, tell a parent, elder, school counsellor, doctor, social worker, or someone you trust. They can help you find the right kind of counselling for you.

If you think you are in an unhealthy relationship, you probably are. Unhealthy relationships damage your self-esteem. Help yourself by getting out.

What Is the Foundation of a Healthy Relationship?

When we act in ways that align with our beliefs, we normally feel good. This can positively affect our self-esteem. It is only when we build self-esteem that we can also build healthy romantic and sexual relationships.

People with a positive and strong sense of self are more likely to communicate what they want and need to their partner. They are less likely to compromise their values or act in ways that are unsafe or degrading.

When we act in ways we think are wrong, we tend to feel bad. This can negatively affect our self-esteem. We might feel embarrassed or as if someone has taken advantage of us. When people do not value themselves, their health, or their well-being, they may engage in risky behaviours and make poor choices.

Ultimately, the most solid foundation for a healthy relationship is knowing and respecting yourself and your values. It is worth taking time to get to know yourself mentally, emotionally, spiritually, and physically. This will help you figure out what you need and want from a close, exclusive relationship—if that is what you desire.

The impact of exclusive relationships

An **exclusive relationship** affects not only the individuals involved but also all their other relationships. If your friends or family members do not like your partner, it can cause tension and resentment. Spending time with your partner might mean less time for friends, family, homework, and extracurricular activities.

On the positive side, an exclusive relationship can provide emotional support and a sense of security and belonging. We learn more about ourselves, our needs, our strengths, and our vulnerabilities by being in a close relationship.

Dealing with a breakup

One downside is that most exclusive teen relationships end at some point. **Breakups** are a normal occurrence, but they can be an opportunity for personal growth. In the aftermath of a breakup, it's important to focus on survival strategies:

- Show respect for your former partner. Do not criticize or betray confidences.
- Acknowledge your hurt or angry feelings, and talk with your friends or family members about how you feel.
- Seek out new experiences to develop your confidence and self-reliance.

Above all, rely on your support network and trust that the passage of time will help you recover and move forward in the pursuit of your goals and dreams.

Section 6.2 Review

1 What factors affect the speed at which a couple moves through the steps of sexual intimacy?

2 List some qualities of healthy relationships and unhealthy relationships.

3 Compare the advantages and disadvantages of being in an exclusive relationship.

6.3 Factors that Influence Sexual Decision Making

Sexual decision making means making conscious choices about your sexual activity. There is a lot to consider. First, what does sexual activity mean to you? The term covers a broad spectrum of intimate, romantic, or sexual activities.

Young people who have positive relationships with their parents or guardians, who participate in extracurricular activities, and who are well informed about sexuality are best able to make responsible sexual decisions.

- Having strong relationships with your parents or guardians suggests that you feel loved and that you care about what they think. This strong foundation can enable you to think about how your actions affect your family.
- Participating in extracurricular activities requires a commitment to yourself and to a group. This level of commitment indicates that you are able to set goals and priorities for yourself.
- Having accurate sexual health information is essential to making good decisions. If you do not know the risks and benefits of your actions, you will not be able to make responsible, fully informed choices.

A trusting relationship with a parent or other family member can strengthen our ability to make good decisions for ourselves.

Making Decisions for Yourself

Pressure to have sex (or not to have sex) comes from all directions: the media, friends, family, religious and community leaders, and partners.

If you are thinking about having sex, especially for the first time—or even increasing your level of intimacy with a partner—you will need to sift through these influences carefully. Try weighing them against your values and beliefs and discussing your choices with those closest to you.

Ask yourself why you want to take such a big step and why now. Are you trying to fit in with a group? Are you trying to make someone else happy? Is your partner pressuring you? These reasons may lead you to regret your decision later.

It does not matter what your friends are doing. Understanding consequences and making your own decisions are signs of maturity. Sexual activity is not.

Stepping back from a sexual decision

At some point we all make decisions we regret—but we can stop doing something if it makes us unhappy. We can stop smoking or stop eating french fries, for example, and benefit from a healthier choice.

Similarly, you can step back from a sexual decision, and benefit from a carefully considered choice that works better for you.

You may re-evaluate your personal limits. You may decide to re-affirm abstinence within your current relationship or with a new partner. Your partner should respect your choice.

The important thing is to be honest with yourself and your partner about what you need to do in order to feel good about yourself.

Reasons to wait

The following are some good reasons to wait before engaging in sexual activity:

- religious beliefs about marriage and sexuality
- wanting to avoid being the subject of gossip or teasing
- concerns about pregnancy
- concerns about sexually transmitted infections
- lack of trust in your partner or in the relationship
- waiting for the right person
- feeling that you are not old enough
- simply not feeling ready

Asking the Right Questions

- How will my decision make me feel about myself?
- How will my decision impact my other relationships with family and friends?
- Will I experience conflict and pressure in my relationship?
- Will my parents continue to trust me?
- Will I feel responsible and proud of myself?
- Will my decision make me happy?
- Will I regret this decision?

Making Decisions with Consequences in Mind

Each of us develops a sense of self as we move through adolescence and into adulthood. Your sexuality encompasses an important part of who you are—your body, thoughts, values, ideals, morals, and personality.

Our childhood experiences, our personalities, our family values, our education, our cultural standards, our spiritual and religious beliefs, and the information we receive via the media all influence how we view sexuality and the sexual decisions we make. As we mature, our beliefs and feelings change to reflect new ideas and new experiences.

Since sexual decisions are so important, we need to make them with all the possible personal, social, and health consequences in mind. Some sexual behaviour might affect your options in the future. For example, unintended pregnancy might interfere with your educational or career goals.

Above all, be sure to make your own choices, based on what you believe to be healthy and responsible behaviour. You can also seek out people you trust for advice and guidance.

Reflecting on good questions about sexuality and relationships, and finding people you trust to talk with, are positive ways to help you make the decisions that are right for you.

Values, Beliefs, and Sexual Decision Making

When making sexual decisions, consider whether a choice will make you feel ashamed or as if you have something to hide. Feeling that you have to lie is a good indication you should think twice about your course of action.

The sexual choices you make can have serious long-term consequences, so it's important to think about them *before* you are on the spot. After taking all the factors into account, you may decide you are not ready for sexual involvement.

In order to make good decisions about sex, we all need comprehensive information about sexual health, time to consider the options, and opportunities to practise our decision-making skills.

Section 6.3 Review

1 What are some reasons teens might decide to wait until they are older before having sex?

2 List as many factors as you can that influence sexual decision making.

3 Summarize what you consider to be responsible sexual decision making.

Factors Affecting Sexual Decision Making

Physical factors

Increased sex hormones after puberty

Age

Health factors (risk of STIs)

Drugs and/or alcohol (being impaired)

Individual qualities

Personality

Self-esteem, self-image, self-awareness

Personal morality

Culture, ethnicity

Religious or spiritual beliefs

Sexual experiences

Knowledge about sexuality

Social factors

Influence of parents, siblings, teachers

Wish to rebel against parents

Influence of friends and peers

Desire for acceptance and/or popularity

Pressure to conform to social stereotypes

Fear of social stigma

Social prejudices such as homophobia

Plans and goals

Concern over whether your actions break the law

Your relationship

The quality of your relationship

Sense of loyalty to and from your partner

Love

Curiosity about sex

Desire for physical and/or emotional closeness

6.4

6.4 Developing Your Decision-Making and Communication Skills

It is up to you to consider the possible consequences of choices that you might make about sexual activity. You will also need to decide what level of intimacy is acceptable to you.

When the time comes for you to make these decisions, you will need to take into account the beliefs and values of the people who would be most affected by your decision, as well as your own beliefs and values.

Practise Your Communication Skills

Developing strong communication skills is an important part of learning how to talk through sexual decisions with a partner. Good communication skills are essential when it comes to thinking through, defining, and communicating your personal limits and making sexual decisions.

All too often young people rush through the steps of intimacy. This is unfortunate for several reasons—but especially because the process of getting to know another person closely and engaging in intimate behaviour with that person is really special and takes time.

The following strategies are all part of effective communication in relation to sexual decision making:

Refusal. This means saying "no" and sticking to it. Although it can sometimes be difficult, it is important to remember that you are not necessarily rejecting the other person. You are only refusing to participate in a particular activity.

Delay. You might need time to step back and think things over before making a decision that involves some level of sexual intimacy. It is always okay to say "I'm not ready for this yet." In effect, you are indicating that you want to wait and that your partner must respect your decision.

Negotiation. When partners are respectful and mature, they can sometimes find solutions by negotiating. Negotiation involves looking for common ground and engaging in give and take. When negotiating your participation in intimate activities, you need to ensure that both partners are comfortable with a joint decision.

Acceptance. You are responsible for setting clear boundaries. It is best to do this before you are in the position of having to enforce them. Stating your limits consistently and clearly will help to ensure that they are understood and respected.

Practise your communication skills so they become second nature and you will be better able to handle most situations.

Three Types of Communication

Most human communication falls into one of three categories: aggressive, passive, or assertive. As the descriptions below demonstrate, assertive communication tends to be the most effective in building understanding and resolving disagreements between people.

Aggressive communication involves

- putting yourself before others by overpowering, threatening, or bullying them
- not listening to other people's opinions
- taking what you want, but often not receiving respect

Passive communication is characterized by

- putting others first all or most of the time
- always giving in to what others want
- staying silent when something bothers you
- apologizing a lot for no reason
- not being able to defend yourself or others

Assertive communication helps you meet your own needs while respecting other people's needs. It involves

- acting with confidence, without being pushy or bullying
- talking openly as well as listening to other people
- handling differences of opinion with respect

Say it with conviction

The following are four suggestions that can help you practise assertive communication. They will be especially helpful to you when making and stating your decisions relating to sexual activity:

1. Explain the issue using "I" statements:
   "I feel... when... because...."
2. Make a clear request:
   "I would like..." or "I wish you would...."
3. Ask how the other person feels about your request:
   "Is that okay with you?"
4. Accept the other person's feedback with thanks:
   "Great, I appreciate that."

What Is Coercion?

Coercion is when someone pressures the other person to turn "no" into "yes."

This can include pressuring someone into sexting. Coercion also includes getting someone high or intoxicated to persuade the person to have sex. In these conditions, people make decisions they would not normally make.

Getting another person intoxicated or high in order to have sex with the person is breaking the law.

Communicate Assertively!

We need to use our best judgment when applying assertive communication skills, especially when we feel threatened or unsafe. Communication is practised differently across cultures. In some cultures, putting other people's voices before our own or not looking people in the eyes, for example, are signs of respect.

In North America, being assertive in positive ways is generally encouraged. It is taught in schools, and employers often look for assertiveness in job interviews and on the job.

In intimate relationships, assertive communication helps to ensure that both people can voice their needs and opinions, and that both people feel respected. Being an assertive communicator involves:

- speaking clearly and truthfully
- taking the time to say exactly what you want to say
- being receptive to the other person's needs, thoughts, and feelings

Practising assertive communication skills can help you establish clear personal limits and avoid misunderstandings. This is especially helpful with respect to a vitally important aspect of sexual relationships—consent.

What Is "Consent" and Why Does It Matter?

Consent means clearly agreeing to do something or giving permission for something to happen. It is important to understand what consent means and to learn the skills to stand up for ourselves and to show respect for ourselves and others.

Understanding consent can enhance interpersonal communication and respect, which in turn foster healthier relationships with friends, peers, family members, and romantic partners. Consent involves knowing and respecting your own boundaries and those of others. In all situations, understanding what makes you and other persons comfortable or uncomfortable can help ensure that relationships stay healthy and safe.

Respect and honesty in personal relationships

Consent involves developing the skills and the confidence to avoid or leave a situation that feels uncomfortable and respecting the fact that other people have the right to do the same.

In a romantic context, consent is...

- **Freely given.** There is no pressure and no manipulation.
- **Informed.** Partners in a romantic relationship need to reveal any sexually transmitted infections they have had and to be honest about whether they are or have been sexually active with other people.
- **Something you can take back.** It is okay to stop at any time. Saying "yes" once does not mean saying "yes" forever or saying "yes" to other intimate activities.

Consent is a topic that people in a romantic relationship need to discuss, no matter how long they have been in the relationship. Consent is about an individual's right to choose "yes" or to choose "no"—at any time.

When people think about consent, "no means no" often comes to mind. Also, a person cannot give consent if intoxicated or unconscious. Sexual activity without consent is sexual assault!

Section 6.4 Review

1 Why are good communication skills essential when it comes to sexual decision making?

2 List four steps in practising assertive communication.

3 Explain what consent means in the context of romantic relationships.

6.5

6.5 Safeguarding Your Sexual Health

Sexual health education gives you the information you need in order to make responsible choices about sexual activity when you are ready. This includes explaining the possible outcomes of your actions, including any associated physical health risks.

Understanding Health Risks

When it comes to sex, you need to get in the habit of thinking in advance. It is important to understand and weigh the potential risks before you act, just as you do in other aspects of your life. What do you want and what are your limits? It is best to find out before you are faced with a decision.

Sexual activity can have serious health risks:

- unintended pregnancy and becoming a parent before you are prepared to be one
- sexually transmitted infections (STIs), including HIV/AIDS

Either of these outcomes will affect your opportunities for the rest of your life:

- If you become a parent before you are ready, you will face some very difficult choices. Taking care of a child is very demanding, and your desired career or other plans may be more difficult to achieve.
- If you contract an STI, you will require medical treatment. Some infections cannot be cured. Some have other unpleasant consequences.

Table 6.3 **Sexual Decision Making**

Possible desirable outcomes	Possible undesirable outcomes
• Feelings of responsibility and pride • Maintaining trust of parents/guardians • Avoiding pregnancy • Avoiding sexually transmitted infections • Upholding your religious and spiritual values and beliefs • Strengthened confidence in your ability to set limits • Development of strong communication skills and habits	• Unplanned pregnancy • Sexually transmitted infections • Increased stress and worry about your sexual health • Unhappiness about risks to your reputation among your peers • Conflict with your partner or loss of your partner • Parents/guardians not agreeing with your choices, leading to arguments • Invasion of your privacy via social media (e.g., if intimate texts are shared with others)

Abstinence

Abstinence means refraining from any form of sexual activity that could result in pregnancy or the transmission of STIs, including all forms of intercourse. When couples are abstinent, they may kiss and cuddle, but they avoid sexual activities.

Abstinence, when practised correctly and consistently, offers the best protection against STIs and, theoretically, 100 percent protection against pregnancy. Note, however, that some STIs, such as HIV/AIDS and herpes, can be spread by other means, such as breastfeeding, sharing needles, and unsafe tattooing and piercing practices.

For a variety of reasons, including a desire to safeguard sexual health, many young people choose abstinence. When there are strong feelings of sexual attraction between a couple, however, it takes a high level of self-control and clear communication to practise abstinence. It may not always be an easy choice, but it can help young people avoid many of the possible negative outcomes associated with sexual activity.

Contraceptive Methods and Barriers against Infection

Methods of contraception are designed to prevent pregnancy, either by blocking the sperm from reaching the egg or by preventing ovulation.

No method is guaranteed to be 100 percent effective, but using some form of contraception can significantly reduce the risk of pregnancy. In order to make mature decisions that reflect personal, cultural, and perhaps religious values, individuals need to consult reliable sources, such as their family doctor or the Society of Obstetricians and Gynaecologists of Canada, to find out how each method works, the relative effectiveness of each method, and the potential risks associated with each method.

Non-hormonal methods of contraception

Some methods of contraception, such as condoms, offer protection against STIs by physically blocking the exchange of bodily fluids during sexual contact. Condoms for males or females are available without a prescription and, when used correctly, have a high success rate in preventing both pregnancy and STIs. Other non-hormonal methods—which medical authorities report are less effective than condoms in preventing pregnancy—include the sponge, the diaphragm, and the cervical cap.

Hormonal methods of contraception

Hormonal methods include the pill, the implant, the patch, contraceptive injections, and intrauterine contraceptives (IUCs), which are small T-shaped devices that are inserted into a woman's uterus by a health care professional in a clinic. These methods work by preventing ovulation. Data published by medical authorities reveal that they are the most effective form of birth control. If a woman does not ovulate, she cannot become pregnant. A woman needs to visit a doctor for a physical examination and a prescription in order to obtain any of these contraceptives. At present, oral contraceptive pills for men are not available.

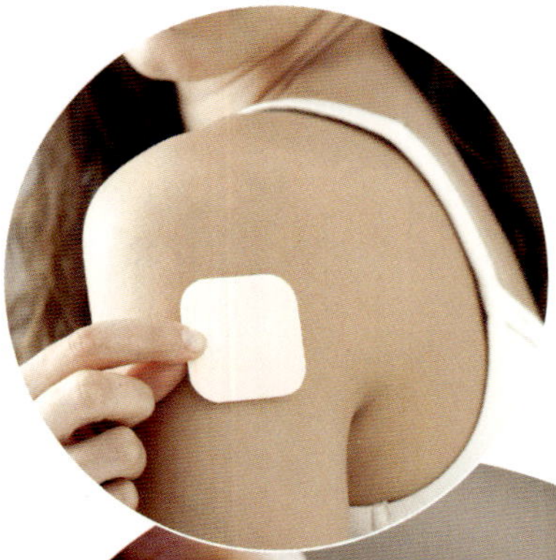

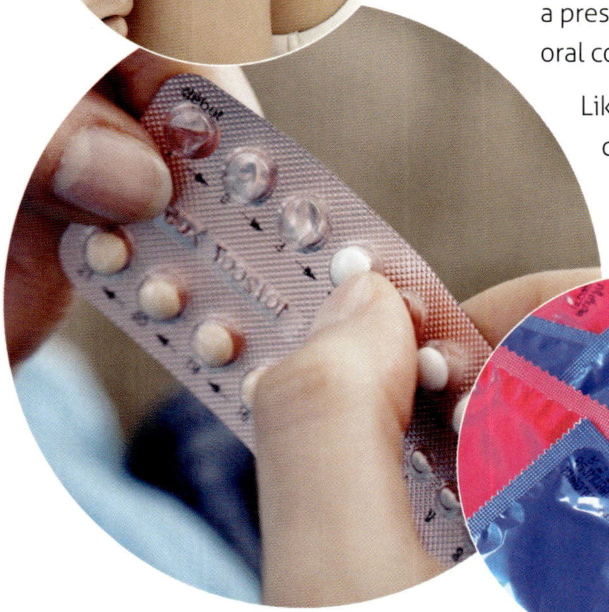

Like all types of contraception, hormonal methods must be used correctly. If a woman takes medication that interferes with how the contraceptive works (such as some antibiotics) or if she does not use the method as instructed, the risk of pregnancy increases. Hormonal methods do not protect against STIs and can have side effects such as acne, headaches, mood issues, or unwanted hair growth.

Used properly, hormonal contraceptives can be highly effective not only in preventing pregnancy but also in regulating a woman's menstrual cycle.

Natural methods of contraception

Natural methods of contraception, also known as *fertility awareness*, do not involve medications or devices to prevent pregnancy but rather rely on behavioural practices and/or making observations about a woman's body and menstrual cycle. The most effective methods require a woman to pay attention to the symptoms that indicate ovulation, such as body temperature and amount of cervical mucus. Couples avoid sexual intercourse on days when an egg is available to be fertilized.

- These methods are not recommended for a young woman whose reproductive system has not fully matured. Her ovulation cycles will not be regular enough to predict when she is likely to be fertile.
- These methods are not recommended outside of a long-term, committed relationship in which partners accept the possibility that an error may result in a pregnancy.
- These methods do not protect against STIs, and require a great deal of attention and discipline from both partners.

When practised correctly and vigilantly by an adult couple who have been properly trained, these techniques can be effective in avoiding unintended pregnancy and in conceiving a child when the time is right.

Society of Obstetricians and Gynaecologists of Canada (SOGC)

The Society of Obstetricians and Gynaecologists of Canada (SOGC), a highly respected leader in the area of reproductive health, describes the various methods of contraception and how they work in a clearly written and illustrated 28-page booklet.

The free booklet, which is available online, also includes research-based information related to the advantages, disadvantages, and relative effectiveness of each method ("typical use failure rate").

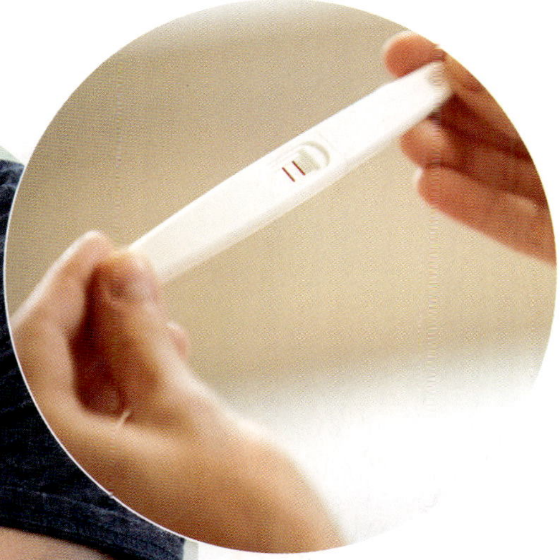

Sexually Transmitted Infections

Sexually transmitted infections (STIs) are caused by bacteria, viruses, or parasites that are transmitted through semen, vaginal fluid, blood, or other body fluids during sexual activity. Safer sex practices can reduce the risk of STIs, but you can never be too careful.

STIs include *asymptomatic* infections—those without any recognizable symptoms. Some STIs have fairly minor symptoms, such as itching, rashes, or sores. Many can be easily treated and have few lasting consequences if they are treated early.

Other infections can have serious health consequences. Some, such as HIV and herpes, cannot be cured, although researchers are working to find effective treatments.

How STIs are spread

STIs are spread in several different ways, not always involving direct sexual contact.

- Almost any kind of sexual activity—not just intercourse—can spread STIs, because the bacteria or viruses travel in semen, vaginal fluids, blood, and sometimes saliva. If you have a tiny cut in or around your mouth, infections can enter your bloodstream even during kissing.
- Infected blood can spread certain STIs. Getting a tattoo or piercing from an unsterile needle, for example, can cause infection.
- Infected women can pass on some STIs to their babies during pregnancy, at childbirth, or during breastfeeding.

The only sure way to avoid contracting an STI is to avoid risky behaviour. Condoms and dental dams (latex barriers used during oral sex) reduce the risk of exposure to infections, but they do not ensure complete protection.

Getting tested and treated

Untreated STIs can cause serious health problems for both sexes, so it's important to get tested if you are sexually active and to get treated early if you contract an infection.

Because each STI is caused by a different bacterial or viral micro-organism, different tests are needed to identify the particular infection. Some infections can be completely cured, while others can only be controlled. Medication can reduce the symptoms but will not make the disease go away.

- **Bacterial infections.** Chlamydia, gonorrhea, syphilis, and other bacterial infections can be cured using specifically prescribed antibiotics. No single drug is effective against all bacteria, and some bacteria now show resistance to standard treatments.
- **Viral infections.** Hepatitis B, genital herpes, genital warts, HIV, and other viral infections often do not have a cure. However, treatment to reduce the symptoms is available.

If you think you may be infected, talk to your doctor, visit a clinic, or contact the local public health department. You owe it to yourself and your partner. All the information you give will be kept private.

How Will I Know?

Since many STIs do not cause obvious symptoms, anyone who engages in sexual activity or who might have come into contact with an infection should be tested regularly.

The following symptoms may appear, alone or in combination:

- different or heavier discharge from the vagina
- discharge from the penis
- a burning feeling when urinating
- sores, particularly around the genitals or anus
- itchiness around the sex organs or anus
- a rash
- swollen glands in the groin

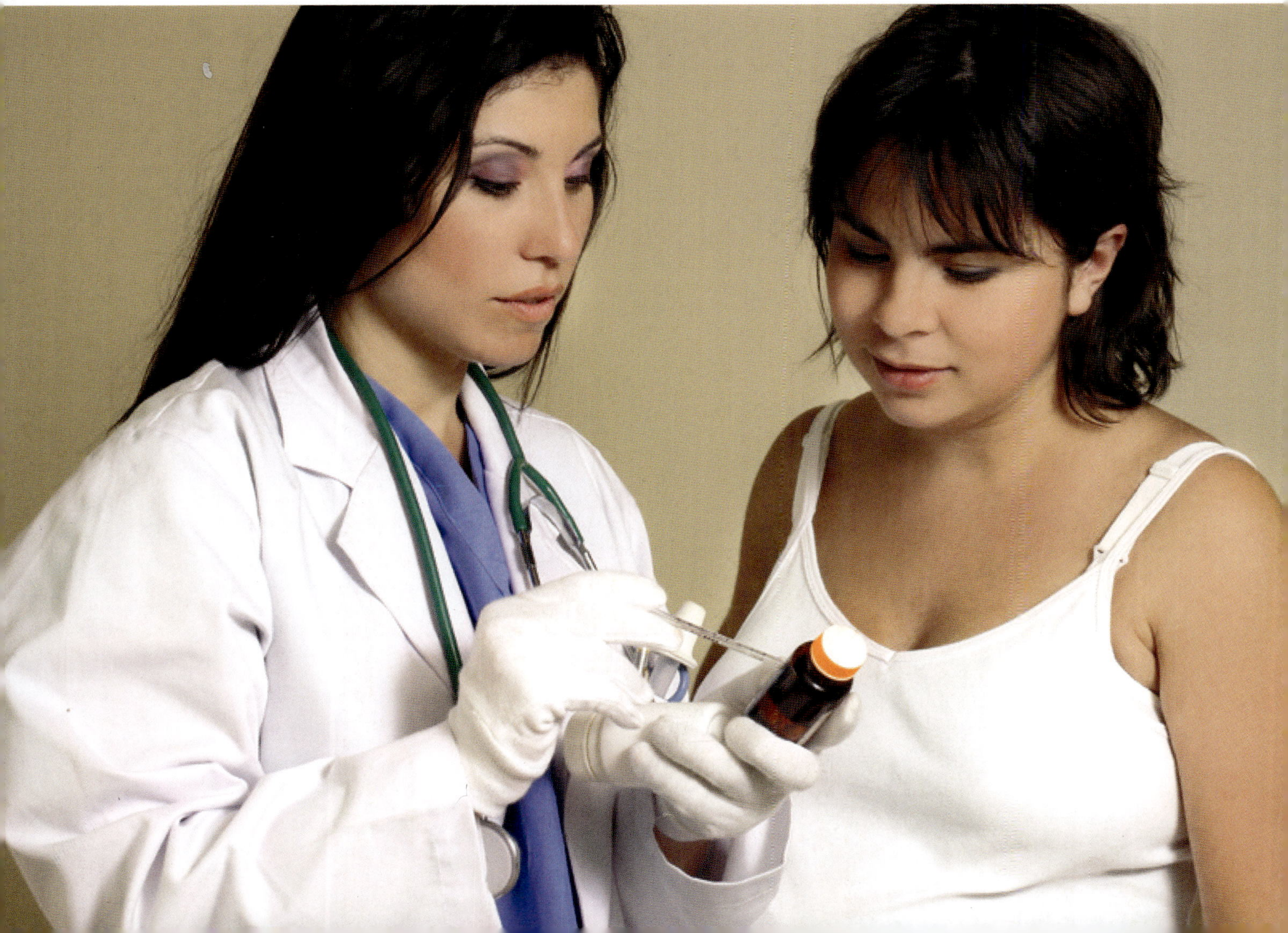

Table 6.4 **Sexually Transmitted Infections**

Infection	How it is transmitted
Chlamydia	• Unprotected sex* • Mother to infant at birth • Hand-to-eye contact
Gonorrhea	• Unprotected sex* • Mother to infant at birth
Hepatitis B	• Unprotected sex* • Sharing items such as needles, razors, eating utensils, toothbrushes • Mother to infant at birth
Herpes simplex virus (HSV, or genital herpes)	• Unprotected sex* • Direct contact with facial or genital sores (touching, kissing, skin-to-skin contact) • Mother to infant at birth
Human immunodeficiency virus/ Acquired immune deficiency syndrome (HIV/AIDS)	• Unprotected sex* • Exchange of blood, semen, vaginal fluids, breast milk • Sharing needles • Mother to infant at birth
Human papillomavirus (HPV, or genital warts)	• Unprotected sex* • Skin-to-skin contact
Pubic lice (crabs)	• Sexual contact • Contact with infected bed linens, towels, clothes
Trichomoniasis (trich)	• Unprotected sex* • Sexual contact
Syphilis	• Unprotected sex* • Direct contact with genital or facial sores (touching, kissing, skin-to-skin contact) • Sharing items such as needles • Mother to infant before birth

* Unprotected sex includes vaginal, oral, and anal intercourse.

Symptoms	Treatment
• Usually no symptoms • Genital discharge or inflammation • Pain during urination and/or intercourse • Pain in testicles or abdomen	• Various antibiotic treatments prescribed by a doctor
• Often no symptoms • Genital discharge • Pain during urination and/or intercourse • Pain in genitals or abdomen	• Antibiotics prescribed by a doctor, often treating chlamydia at the same time
• No symptoms for almost half of those infected • Flu-like symptoms including abdominal pain, fatigue • Darkened urine • Yellowed skin	• Preventative vaccine • No cure, but treatments can prevent infection and condition disappears on its own in some cases
• Usually no symptoms • Facial or genital sores, blisters • Flu-like symptoms including achiness, fever, swollen glands • Pain during urination or inability to urinate	• No cure, but antivirals and topical creams can relieve symptoms • Fewer and weaker outbreaks over time in most cases
• Often no symptoms • Weight loss, fatigue, flu-like symptoms	• No cure, but medication can slow progress from HIV to AIDS
• Usually no symptoms • Genital warts • Some links to cervical cancer	• No cure • Warts can be removed, but virus stays in the body
• Itching or irritation around genitals or infested area • Greyish rash	• Lice killed with a special shampoo • Eggs must be removed by shaving pubic hair or combing it with a fine-toothed comb
• Vaginal discharge and odour • Pain or itching during urination • Spotty bleeding, frequent urination	• Antibiotics for infected person and partner(s)

• Early symptoms
  • a painless sore called a chancre, usually but not always on the genitals
  • swollen glands in the neck, groin, or armpits
• Later symptoms
  • rash
  • flu-like symptoms
  • genital growths
  • swollen glands
  • hair loss
	• Antibiotics, but only if condition is detected early
	• Unless administered early, medication cannot repair damage already done

What to Expect at a Sexual Health Exam

Most people have their first sexual health exam in their mid- to late teens. Others may wait longer, until they are sexually active. Knowing what to expect can help you feel more comfortable with the process. If you have any concerns, try to talk with your doctor or with a public health nurse ahead of time.

Choose a doctor with whom you feel comfortable. A sexual health exam involves sensitive parts of your body, which you may have been taught are private. You need to feel comfortable with the doctor who is touching and looking at your body. Some people prefer to see a doctor of the same sex as they are. You may decide that your family doctor knows you best, or you may wish to find a doctor who has not known you as a child. If you would rather not see your family doctor, you can visit a sexual health clinic or a walk-in clinic instead.

Ask questions. Your doctor is there to help, so do not be afraid to ask questions—it's your body and your sexual health. During puberty, your body and your mind go through a lot of changes, and getting your questions answered can make these changes easier to understand.

Take a friend. Many young people find that it helps to have a friend around for moral support, in the doctor's office or the waiting room. If you are nervous about going alone, invite someone that you know you can trust to accompany you to your appointment.

Relax. Being tense can make an exam last longer and feel more uncomfortable. No matter how unfamiliar things seem to you, doctors have generally seen it all. Keep breathing, and try to relax your muscles as much as possible.

Ask for specific tests. Many people think that a sexual health exam automatically includes tests for sexually transmitted infections, but this is not the case. You must explicitly inform the doctor if you wish to be tested for an STI. Do not worry about being judged. Most doctors are only interested in your health and that of your partner.

Trust your instincts. Doctors may have many years of training, but no one spends as much time with your body as you do. If your doctor says you are fine but you still feel like something is wrong, do not hesitate to get a second opinion from another medical professional.

Develop the habit. It is good to develop the habit of regular sexual health exams because many STIs can be present for long periods of time without symptoms. The sooner any potential problems are detected by a doctor, the sooner they can be treated.

Sources of Information and Support

Parents, guardians, siblings, friends, doctors, nurse practitioners, public health professionals, teachers, counsellors, elders, and religious advisors can often answer your questions about sexuality and intimate relationships. You can also get anonymous, reliable help and information over the phone and online.

- **Kids Help Phone**, at 1.800.668.6868, is a toll-free, anonymous help line for young people. Counsellors can talk with you non-judgmentally about any sexual health matter (including sexual assault, sexual abuse, sexual orientation, and pregnancy) or more general health-related issues (e.g., bullying, drug addiction, physical abuse, and mental health). They can give you plenty of information and refer you to resources. On the Kids Help Phone website, you can browse through sexual health topics or send your question to a counsellor via email.
- On provincial health hotlines, such as Telehealth Ontario at 1.866.767.0000, you can speak to a registered nurse to get quick answers to your questions about sexual health or advice about whether you need to see a doctor.

Several other organizations provide online information and support:

- The Society of Obstetricians and Gynaecologists of Canada
- Action Canada for Sexual Health & Rights
- The Asexual Visibility and Education Network (AVEN)
- Run for Rocky: Benefitting Gay–Straight Alliances
- Canadian AIDS Society
- Egale Youth OUTreach
- Health Canada
- Healthy Teen Network
- PFLAG Canada
- Project Respect
- Sexual assault/domestic violence centres

Section 6.5 Review

1 What steps can you take to safeguard your sexual health?

2 What risks are associated with sexually transmitted infections?

3 If you are nervous about having a sexual health exam, where might you turn for help and advice?

Sharicka's Story

"The most important sexual decision you make should always be for *your* benefit and for your sexual health and safety."
— Sharicka Reid

Chapter 6 Review

Knowledge and Understanding

1 List three ways in which making responsible sexual decisions can benefit you and your family.

2 Choose five factors from the diagram on page 233 and explain why you think they are especially important in sexual decision making.

3 Describe three benefits of developing assertive communication skills.

4 Outline various ways by which sexually transmitted infections can be passed from person to person and how transmission can be prevented.

Thinking

5 Compare and contrast two methods of preventing unintended pregnancy in terms of how they work, as well as their effectiveness, advantages, and disadvantages.

6 Investigate your school's strategies and policies to help prevent or respond to discrimination or harassment related to gender identity and sexual orientation. Evaluate whether you think these strategies and policies are effective.

Communication

7 In a small group, discuss what could be done to educate teens and adults about the dangers of unprotected sexual activity. Brainstorm ways to communicate positive media messages about safe and healthy sexuality.

8 Write a two-minute talk explaining how building a strong sense of self is related to sexual decision making. Be prepared to present your talk in class.

9 Write a blog or create a short video or slide show that encourages teens to make responsible sexual decisions.

Application

10 Identify five components of a healthy intimate relationship, and explain why they are important to you.

11 Work in a small group to brainstorm and refine a list of tips titled "Surviving and Thriving after a Breakup." If there is time, compare your ideas with those of another group.

12 Conduct research on access to sexual health resources, crisis centres, and support services in your community. Compile your findings in a brief report to share in class.

Substance Use and Addictive Behaviours

7

Michel's story

What strategies and skills can you develop to boost your resilience and help you make healthy decisions regarding substance use?

People consume mind- or body-altering substances, or take part in addictive behaviours, for many different reasons. Social pressure, popular culture, or media influences may lead you and your friends to consider experimenting with tobacco, alcohol, other drugs, or performance-enhancing substances.

The consequences of substance use and addiction can be significant for both the individual and society. Addictive behaviours are linked to serious personal and social harms, including injury to self, harm to others, and poor school performance.

Making appropriate choices about substance use and behaviours leading to addiction takes the same decision-making skills you use in other health-related areas.

Learning Objectives

In this chapter, you will...

- describe factors influencing substance use and behaviours leading to addiction
- demonstrate an understanding of the impact of substance use and addictive behaviours on all aspects of health and well-being
- identify public issues related to addiction, and analyze the local, national, and international impact of these issues
- explain the concept of resilience, and identify related protective and risk factors
- explain how skills in decision making, communication, refusal, and coping can help you respond effectively to situations involving substance use or addictive behaviours
- find a variety of social and community supports for individuals whose lives are affected by substance use or addictive behaviours

Key Terms

- substance misuse
- substance abuse
- drug dependence
- physical dependence
- psychological dependence
- tobacco
- e-cigarette
- vaping
- alcohol
- blood alcohol concentration (BAC)
- fetal alcohol spectrum disorder (FASD)
- psychoactive drugs
- marijuana (cannabis)
- hallucinogens
- depressants
- stimulants
- problem gambling
- continuum of gambling risk
- anabolic steroids
- resilience
- protective factors
- risk factors
- harm reduction

▶ **Michel Chikwanine** was just five years old when he was abducted by the military in the Democratic Republic of Congo and forced to become a child soldier. He escaped, but the transition back to normal life was, as he describes it, "very tough." Today, Michel is a motivational speaker and an author who inspires hope, courage, and resilience in others.

7.1 Factors Influencing Substance Use and Addictive Behaviours

During adolescence, young people may experiment with drugs such as alcohol, tobacco, and cannabis, and with body-altering substances such as weight-loss pills or muscle-building supplements.

Whether they are legal or illegal, substances affect the way you think, feel, and behave. Sometimes a substance can make you feel more confident or relaxed, but many mood-altering substances and related behaviours can be addictive. That means it can become very hard to control their use or stop taking them.

Substance Misuse, Substance Abuse, and Addiction

Substance misuse means using a substance in ways that are illegal or not recommended medically. **Substance abuse** refers to excessive use despite the physical, cognitive, emotional, social, legal, spiritual, or economic harm this can do.

In the context of alcohol, for example, **misuse** can impair your judgment, leading you to harm yourself or someone else. **Abuse** usually involves drinking too much over the long term, potentially harming your relationships and causing serious health problems such as liver and kidney disease or alcohol poisoning from binge drinking.

One of the greatest risks of drug abuse is **drug dependence**—also known as addiction or substance use disorder. A person who cannot stop using a substance compulsively despite growing problems in areas such as health, school, family, relationships, or finances has a drug dependence problem.

Physical dependence occurs when a person's body has become used to a drug and undergoes physical symptoms of withdrawal without it. It often does not take long for regular use to turn into dependent use. Some drugs, such as alcohol, tobacco, and heroin, can produce severe physical dependence. Prescription drugs and over-the-counter drugs can also create dependence.

A regular user who stops taking any of these substances can suffer symptoms such as depression, craving, and anxiety from hours to days after the last use of the substance. Withdrawal can make it very difficult to quit a drug habit and, in the case of alcohol, can even be life threatening.

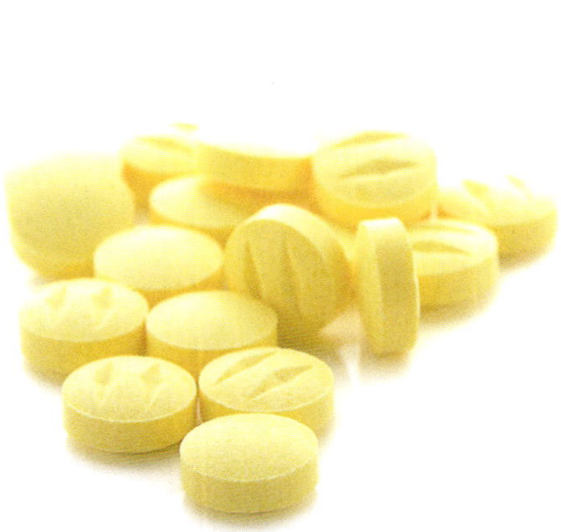

Other drugs do not create physical dependence, but all mood-altering substances can create **psychological dependence**. The person using the drug feels an overwhelming desire to repeat the effects of the drug. Cannabis is one possible example. People who are psychologically dependent feel they have no choice in taking the substance, and therefore they are in serious need of help and professional counselling.

From Non-Use to Dependent Use

Using drugs always comes with risk. Risk can range from very low to very high, and you can experience harm even if it's your first time.

People can move back and forth between types of use with one or more substances. They may depend on one substance and not another. People can struggle with drug use at different levels even if they never become dependent.

- **Non-use.** About one-third of young Canadians choose not to use tobacco, alcohol, or any illegal substance. Non-use is the healthiest choice because it has no risk.
- **Experimental use.** Experimental use may only occur once. Usually the risk is low, but that depends on the drug, the way it is taken, and how much is consumed. It also depends on the individual's personality, mood, and expectations, and on the context. Inexperienced individuals may be at higher risk, such as by unintentionally taking too much of a drug.
- **Social use.** Social drug use involves ongoing, moderate consumption. The risk can be low to moderate, depending on the particular drug and how it is used.
- **Binge use.** Taking a large amount of a substance at one time is binge use, and the risk of harm is high any time a person binges. Binge use of alcohol is considered to be five standard drinks for men and four standard drinks for women.
- **Frequent, heavy use.** Frequent, heavy drug use can lead to problems in one or more areas of a person's life, such as study, work, friendships, and family relations. The risk of significant and lasting harm is high.
- **Dependent use.** Dependent use, or addiction, involves compulsive and excessive drug use that continues despite leading to problems in various areas of life, such as school and relationships. The risk of significant and lasting harm is very high.

Knowing the harms that can arise from using substances can put you in a good position to develop a balanced view of the kind of role you would like to see substances play in your life. Health Canada is the leading agency for implementing Canada's drug policy and it provides well-researched information about all aspects of substance use and misuse that can guide you in making healthy decisions about substance use.

If you feel an overpowering desire to re-experience the effects of a drug, you may have developed a psychological dependence on it. Professional counselling can help you make healthy choices about substance use.

Peer Pressure Can Be Positive

Peer pressure is a two-way street. You can influence your peers, as well as the other way round.

You can have a positive impact by encouraging friends and classmates to avoid illegal or potentially harmful substances—and especially by helping them to avoid situations that will be dangerous to themselves and others, such as drinking and driving.

What Influences Substance Use?

The younger people are the first time they use drugs, the more they are at risk of hazardous use throughout their lives. Various factors can prompt young people to experiment with substances such as alcohol or tobacco.

Popular culture and media
Popular culture and media often glamorize alcohol and other drugs. Advertising, for example, often uses images suggesting good times, popularity, and success in order to sell alcoholic beverages. Unrealistic media images can also persuade teens to try to change their appearance—to use steroids to bulk up their muscles or diet pills to lose weight.

Social factors
Peer pressure can lead teens to smoke or try drugs in order to fit in with a group. Photos that their friends post on social media sites, showing them drinking, smoking, and having fun can seem cool and appealing.

Curiosity and boredom
Teens might wonder how alcohol, tobacco, and other drugs can make them feel. Curiosity can prompt young people to experiment impulsively. Sometimes they are just trying to avoid feeling bored.

Emotional pressure
Many teens experience stress and low self-esteem from time to time. Sometimes they turn to drugs to ease those emotions. Mood-altering substances hold the promise of temporarily improving how they feel, but drug use does not address the underlying issues.

Celebrations and religious observances
Drugs such as alcohol are often a part of family or community celebrations and religious services. At these events, however, the drug tends to be valued more for its symbolic importance than for its effect. We might toast the couple at a wedding, for example.

Mental health problems
People with increased risk of mental health issues due to family history or other circumstances may be at greater risk of dependence if they turn to non-prescription drugs or other illegal substances to relieve their distress. They may begin to rely on substances as a way to cope or to screen out painful experiences.

A more effective approach to help relieve symptoms of mental health problems is proper medical treatment and support. In some cases, people may need carefully prescribed medications to help them manage their mental health.

Environmental factors

Having family members who habitually smoke or drink alcohol may influence young people. They come to see smoking or drinking as a normal, acceptable part of life and as a way to relax or to screen out life's everyday stresses.

Poverty, mental abuse, or physical abuse can prompt some people to use drugs or alcohol as a temporary escape and to relieve feelings of hopelessness.

Other environmental factors include family conflict, lack of support and direction, and divorce or separation. Family transition and instability may also compound stress.

Finally, the quality of a young person's performance and participation at school can be a significant factor in substance use. Expulsion, absence from school, boredom, or a lack of motivation and commitment can increase the likelihood of drug use.

This is why being involved in your school to help build a healthy community that supports all teens is important—it helps to balance out some of these environmental factors that might lead to substance use.

Section 7.1 Review

1 Explain the difference between physical dependence and psychological dependence.

2 Explain the continuum of drug use.

3 Create a graphic organizer showing various factors that influence substance use.

Real friends do not pressure one another to experiment with drugs. They look out for one another's safety and well-being.

7.2 Tobacco and Alcohol

Tobacco and alcohol are controlled mood-altering substances permitted for non-medical use in Canada. Public support for tobacco has decreased steadily over the years, while alcohol is still widely accepted and used.

Smoking and drinking can have serious short- and long-term effects on you and others. It is important to understand what tobacco and alcohol contain, what they do to your body, and the consequences of using them.

Tobacco and the Effects of Smoking

Tobacco is the shredded, dried leaf of the tobacco plant. It can be smoked in cigarettes, cigars, and pipes, or chewed. Tobacco is the only natural source of nicotine, one of the most addictive substances.

Because nicotine is so addictive, even experimental use is risky. Once you start to smoke with any regularity, it's very hard to stop.

Smoking causes your heart rate and blood pressure to go up and your breathing to get faster. First-time smokers may feel dizzy and may even vomit or get diarrhea.

Smoking quickly reduces your fitness and athletic ability. Grade 12 students who are regular smokers and who began smoking by Grade 9 are twice as likely as non-smoking students to report poorer overall health, coughing with phlegm or blood, shortness of breath, and wheezing or gasping.

Smoker's breath is also a problem that you—and others—will notice right away.

Second-hand smoke is harmful, too

Second-hand smoke is exhaled by the smoker—or comes from a smouldering cigarette—and is then inhaled by another person. This process is sometimes called passive smoking.

A person exposed to second-hand smoke is more likely to have respiratory problems than someone who has not been exposed. Health Canada estimates that every year, second-hand smoke causes more than 1,000 deaths from heart attacks and lung cancer in Canadian non-smokers.

It is increasingly clear that second-hand smoke leads to heart disease, especially in people with allergies and those with lung disease. Children whose parents smoke tend to have more ear infections, lung problems such as asthma, and chest infections than the children of non-smokers.

Given scientific evidence about the harmful effects of second-hand smoke, most jurisdictions in Canada outlaw smoking both inside and outside public premises.

E-Cigarettes and Vaping

An electronic cigarette, or **e-cigarette**, is a device with a rechargeable battery, a cartridge, and an LED that lights up at the end when a person inhales.

The e-cigarette heats water, along with a flavour and usually nicotine and other chemicals, to boiling point. Inhaling the vapour that is produced is called "vaping."

E-cigarettes are marketed as a less harmful alternative to combustible cigarettes—ones that you light—because they do not contain carcinogens such as arsenic and vinyl chloride. However, vaping can result in chest pain, a sore throat, and wheezing.

Some social media sites portray vaping as fun, for example with competitive online vape tricks such as blowing smoke into an "O" shape.

Some people believe that e-cigarettes renormalize smoking, which has become less and less socially acceptable over the past 20 years. Vaping makes smoking seem less unappealing.

Critics also suggest that e-cigarettes may act as a gateway to combustible cigarettes. A lot of people report that while they enjoy vaping, they find themselves needing a certain level of nicotine—and vaping does not always satisfy that need.

Apart from their nicotine content, e-cigarettes are not regulated by clear standards and may contain toxic heavy metals. Health Canada discourages their use.

Smokeless Tobacco

Like tobacco smoke, snuff and chewing tobacco contain nicotine, carcinogens, and other harmful substances. Smokeless tobacco is a cause of mouth cancer and other problems affecting the mouth, teeth, and gums.

The Long-Term Consequences of Tobacco Use

Smoking is the greatest cause of poor health in Canada and other industrialized nations. It causes over 40,000 deaths every year in this country—more than 21 percent of all deaths.

- Some 13,000 of those deaths are due to lung cancer caused by smoking. Lung cancer is a deadly disease: more than 50 percent of people with lung cancer die within five years of being diagnosed.
- Smoking can also lead to cancer of the oral cavity, pharynx, larynx, esophagus, pancreas, kidney, bladder, cervix, and large intestine, and to some forms of leukemia.
- Another 9,000 deaths in Canada are the result of respiratory diseases that attack the lungs and other parts of the body.
- More than 18,000 Canadians also die each year from cardiovascular diseases as a result of smoking. These are diseases and injuries of the heart and blood vessels—the veins and arteries.

Most long-term tobacco users are physically and psychologically dependent. This habit leads to addiction and serious health problems. If you have started smoking or chewing tobacco, do not give up on giving it up. Many of the harmful effects can be reversed over time if you quit.

You can receive daily support emails by signing up with Health Canada's online E-Quit program, or call Ontario Smoker's Helpline.

Anatomy of a Cigarette

Did you know that tobacco smoke contains over 4,000 chemicals? Moreover, at least 40 of the chemicals are carcinogenic—that is, they are known to cause cancer.

In Canada, tobacco companies are required by law to indicate on tobacco packages how much of each of the following chemicals is found in the exhaled smoke or tobacco emissions:

- Tar (also found on paved roads and roofs)
- Nicotine (a carcinogenic chemical that comes from the tobacco plant)
- Carbon monoxide (found in exhaust from cars)
- Methane (sewer gas)
- Formaldehyde (used to preserve dead bodies)
- Hydrogen cyanide (used in dyeing and explosives)
- Benzene (a toxic carcinogen)

The Long-Term Health Effects of Tobacco

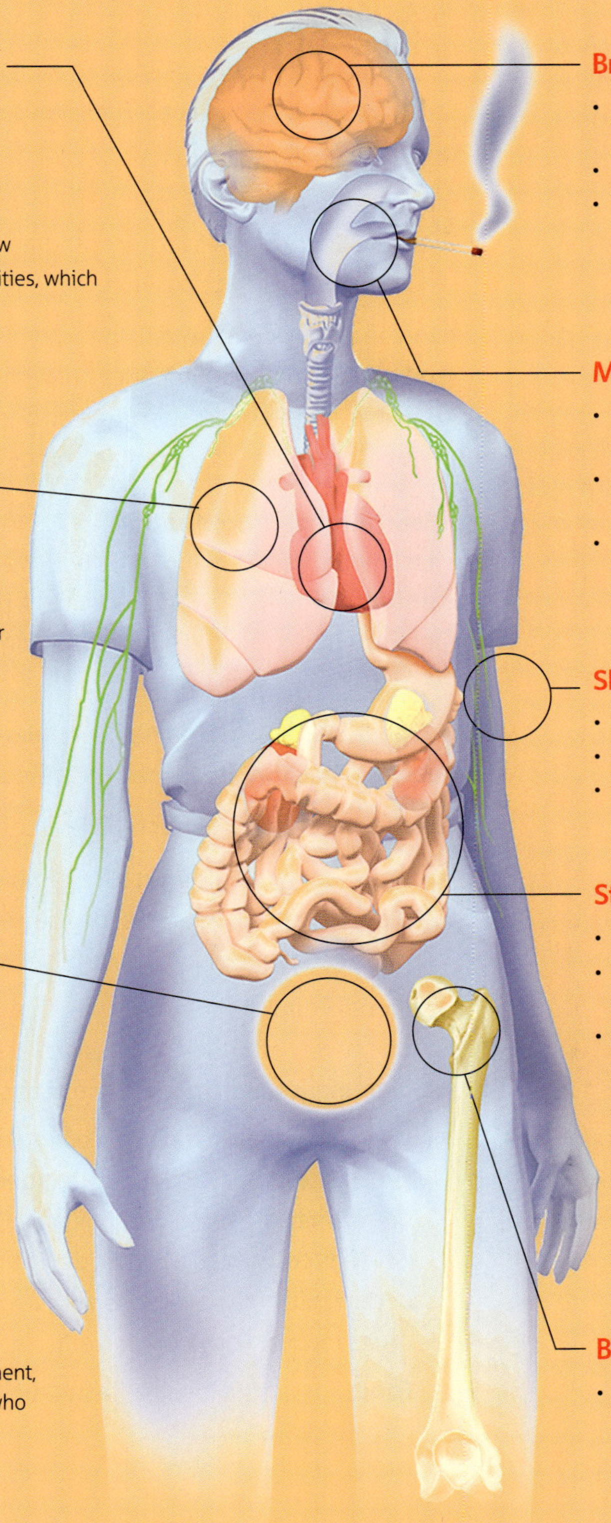

Heart and circulatory system

- Reduces fitness and athletic ability
- Increases risk of heart disease
- Increases risk of heart attack
- Increases blood pressure
- Hardens arteries and decreases blood flow
- Leads to poor blood circulation in extremities, which could lead to amputations

Lungs

- Reduces rate of lung growth
- Increases risk of emphysema and bronchitis
- Destroys tiny hair-like structures in the trachea (cilia) that filter bacteria and other harmful substances, reducing immunity to diseases
- Leads to phlegm buildup and excess coughing
- Increases risk of lung cancer

Reproductive system

Male

- Decreases sperm count
- Decreases sperm movement
- Lowers sex drive

Female

- Adversely affects menstrual cycle
- Increases risk of cervical cancer
- Increases risk of breast cancer
- Leads to early onset of menopause
- Leads to low-birth-weight babies
- Can affect growth, intellectual development, and behaviour of infants with mothers who smoked while pregnant

Brain

- Increases risk of stroke, especially for women using oral contraceptives
- Can lead to nicotine addiction
- Kills brain cells

Mouth and throat

- Increases risk of mouth, throat, and tongue cancer
- Increases risk of larynx and esophagus cancer
- Stains teeth and causes tooth decay and tooth loss

Skin

- Increases skin dryness
- Speeds up aging of skin
- Causes wounds to heal slowly

Stomach and intestines

- Increases risk of ulcers
- Leads to bleeding of the stomach lining
- Increases risk of stomach and intestinal cancer

Bone

- Increases risk of osteoporosis

Alcohol Poisoning

A blood alcohol concentration above 0.40 to 0.60 milligrams of alcohol per 100 millilitres of blood is usually fatal, typically because that much alcohol blocks the brain's control over breathing. This is called alcohol poisoning.

Alcohol and Its Effects

Alcohol for human consumption is made by fermenting or distilling various fruits, vegetables, or grains. Pure ethyl alcohol, which is clear and colourless, is mixed with other ingredients that affect the colour and reduce the alcohol content of the drink.

Alcohol is categorized as a depressant because it depresses, or lowers, the activity of the body's **central nervous system (CNS)**.

Alcohol usually makes a person feel relaxed and less inhibited. Drinking can make some people feel sociable and more self-confident, but others become angry, depressed, or withdrawn. Drinking small amounts can also cause drowsiness or dizziness.

Drinking may seem low risk, but like tobacco, alcohol causes many health and social problems. Statistics on alcohol-related car crashes and physical violence, for example, show that alcohol consumption is a major public heath issue in Canada and many other countries.

Blood alcohol concentration

The amount of alcohol in the bloodstream is referred to as **blood alcohol concentration (BAC)**. BAC measures a person's level of intoxication, and it depends mostly on the amount consumed in a given period.

A person's size, sex, and metabolism also play a role. Smaller people reach a higher BAC from the same quantity of alcohol, and women generally reach a higher BAC than men do after drinking the same amount.

Several other factors affect the level of intoxication:

- **Age.** Young people with little or no experience with alcohol may not be able to predict its effects. They may make risky decisions while intoxicated or drink to the point of *alcohol poisoning*.
- **Mood.** People who drink when they are angry or depressed often do not pay attention to the signs of intoxication. People who are extremely elated may make this mistake as well.
- **Other substance use.** Signs of intoxication can be missed if other substances affect an intoxicated person's self-perception, which is one of many reasons why mixing substances is a bad idea. Someone who has consumed another depressant drug, such as a tranquilizer or painkiller, may overdose with a much lower BAC because the two drugs multiply each other's effects.
- **Food.** A hungry person will metabolize alcohol and feel its effects more quickly.

Overconsumption of alcohol can lead to what many people refer to as a "hangover" the next day, with symptoms consisting of a headache, nausea, dehydradation, dizziness, and fatigue.

Drinking and driving: Know the facts

- The amount of alcohol in the breath is directly related to the amount in the blood, so BAC can be measured with a breathalyzer.
- A single drink may give you a BAC of about 0.02 (20 milligrams per 100 millilitres of blood), but your BAC depends on your body weight, how quickly you drink, and other factors.
- The legal limit for driving in Canada is a BAC of 0.08, and it's a criminal offence to drive over the limit. Also, a BAC of 0.05 to 0.08 can come with provincial penalties.
- In Ontario, Manitoba, New Brunswick, and Nova Scotia, a **zero tolerance** law applies: drivers aged 21 and under cannot consume *any* alcohol before getting behind the wheel.
- New drivers of all ages are also subject to **zero tolerance** until they get their G2 licence.
- Studies have shown that drivers with a BAC above 0.10 are seven times more likely than unimpaired drivers to cause a crash, because both their hand–eye coordination and their judgment are affected. They are also less able to estimate distances, and their reaction time slows down.
- With a BAC over 0.20, a person is very intoxicated and will stumble when walking and slur words when speaking.

MADD Canada

Mothers Against Drunk Driving (MADD Canada) is a volunteer-driven charitable organization whose mission is to stop drunk, drugged, and underage driving.

Each year MADD offers support services to at least 20,000 victims and survivors of impaired-driving crashes across Canada. It also provides programming to educate elementary, middle school, and high school students about the dangers of mixing alcohol and/or drugs with driving.

MADD public education campaigns also focus on improving safety on roads, waterways, and trails.

It is never a good idea to risk getting behind the wheel after drinking.

The Long-Term Health Effects of Alcohol

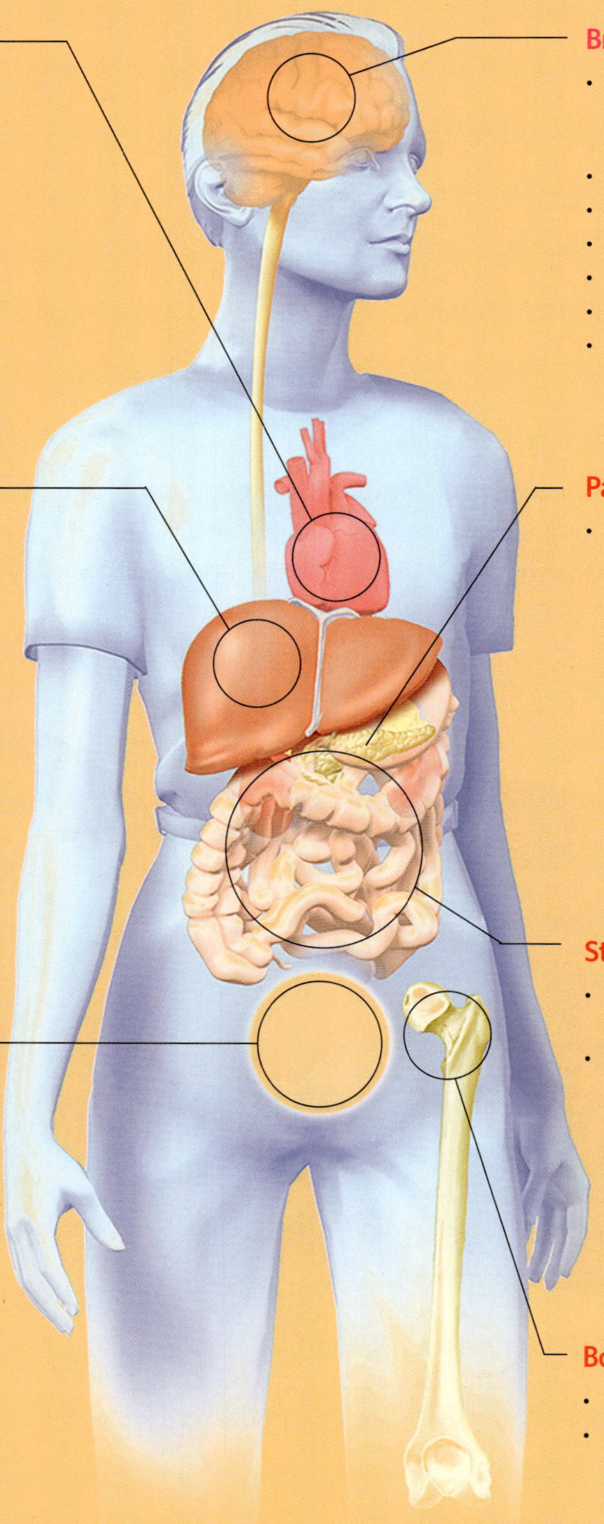

Heart and circulatory system

- Damages heart muscle and can lead to heart failure
- Weakens heart's ability to pump blood
- Increases risk of high blood pressure
- Increases risk of heart attack
- Increases risk of stroke
- Reduces production of red and white blood cells

Liver

- Increases risk of cirrhosis (scar tissue formed in the liver as a result of dead liver cells)
- Increases risk of liver cancer
- Promotes buildup of excess fat in the liver, blocking the flow of blood to liver cells and causing liver damage
- Can cause liver failure, leading to coma or death

Reproductive system

Male

- Decreases sperm count
- Leads to impotence

Female

- Increases reproductive problems such as irregular periods
- Can lead to fetal alcohol spectrum disorder if consumed during pregnancy

Brain

- May lead to physical and psychological dependence on alcohol
- Leads to memory loss
- Disturbs sleep patterns
- Kills brain cells
- Affects normal growth patterns
- Impairs ability to think clearly
- May lead to mood swings and violent behaviour

Pancreas

- Leads to inflammation of the pancreas, blocking pancreatic chemicals from entering the small intestine in order to leave the body and causing them to kill the pancreas, resulting in death in severe cases.

Stomach and intestines

- Leads to ulcers, inflammation, and bleeding
- Leads to loss of appetite and vitamin deficiencies

Bone

- Interferes with calcium absorption
- Leads to osteoporosis

The Effects of Alcohol Abuse

Even though buying and drinking alcohol is legal, people who consume alcohol habitually and compulsively often find that it negatively affects their health, their life expectancy, and their relationships with friends, family members, co-workers, and other members of their community.

Social problems

Alcoholism, or alcohol dependency syndrome, can lead to troubles with the law (for drinking and driving, or other illegal behaviour while intoxicated), with money (from spending too much on alcohol), and on the job (for missing work because of a hangover).

Those who are close to heavy drinkers sometimes describe them as "different people" when they drink. Under the influence of alcohol, these drinkers often behave in anti-social ways and alienate their friends and family.

Safety risks

Alcohol abuse can cause injuries from car accidents, drowning, falls, fire, work-related accidents, or fights—sometimes even leading to death. Pedestrians who are impaired by alcohol may take unnecessary risks when walking near traffic.

Health problems

Long-term heavy drinking (more than two drinks a day on average for men, less for women) leads to many serious health problems. Liver damage, heart disease, ulcers, certain types of cancer, blackouts with memory loss, brain damage, and sexual problems are just some of them. Women are generally affected sooner than men are.

Dependence

When the body becomes accustomed to alcohol, it does not respond as strongly right away. Long-term heavy drinkers may be able to drink steadily without seeming intoxicated.

These drinkers are also likely to be physically and psychologically dependent. When they stop drinking, they may suffer sleeplessness, sweating, vomiting, tremors, seizures, and hallucinations. Withdrawal can lead to death if the symptoms are severe enough.

Fetal alcohol spectrum disorder

Young women need to be aware of the risks associated with consuming alcohol during pregnancy. Drinking during pregnancy exposes the fetus to alcohol and can result in **fetal alcohol spectrum disorder (FASD)**. The child may have reduced growth, experience mental disabilities, and have a different facial makeup. People with FASD need a great deal of support throughout their lives, and some of these individuals experience lifelong challenges in living independently.

Section 7.2 Review

1 Create a table to list some short-term and long-term consequences of tobacco use or excessive alcohol consumption.

2 What factors affect a person's blood alcohol concentration (BAC)?

3 Why should you never drink and drive?

7.3 Marijuana and Other Drugs

Cannabis sativa (Latin for "cultivated hemp") is the plant from which marijuana, sinsemilla, hashish, and hash oil are produced. Tetrahydrocannabinol (THC) is the major psychoactive, or mood-altering, ingredient in these drugs. Marijuana is the most popular form of cannabis.

The medical uses and decriminalization of cannabis have been the subject of much debate. In 2015, the Canadian government announced plans to decriminalize and regulate the use of cannabis by 2018.

Various **psychoactive drugs** are commonly available in Canada. These drugs affect the body's **central nervous system (CNS).** Health Canada classifies them according to the effects they have on us.

- **Marijuana** acts primarily as a hallucinogen but also has depressant and stimulant effects.
- **Hallucinogens** alter a person's perception of reality. These distortions can increase the risk of accidents and injuries. Among hallucinogens are LSD (acid), psilocybin (magic mushrooms), and mescaline.
- **Depressants** lower, or slow down, the activity of the CNS and reduce inhibitions. Depressants are easy to obtain but can be very dangerous. Examples include alcohol, solvents such as glue or gasoline, tranquilizers and sleeping pills, and club drugs.
- **Stimulants** speed up body systems such as the CNS and the cardiorespiratory system. Stimulants include nicotine, caffeine, diet pills, a medication called Ritalin®, cocaine and crack, and methamphetamine (speed).

Even after marijuana has been decriminalized, it will still be illegal to use until a certain age (e.g., 18 in Quebec and 19 in Ontario). Decriminalization and regulation will make marijuana use more acceptable, but health-related concerns will remain.

Drugs and Risk Assessment

Three factors determine the risk associated with drug use: the drug, the person using the drug, and the context.

The drug can be weak or strong; it may be swallowed, sniffed, inhaled, or injected; and it can be taken in different amounts. These factors are all significant aspects of risk.

The user's weight, sex, metabolism, and state of health can play a role. Risk also increases when a person uses drugs to cope with anger, stress, or sadness.

The context in which people use drugs affects the risk. Certain settings or situations always pose a high risk and should be avoided:

- before driving a car, boat, ATV, or snowmobile, or using machinery
- before physical activity such as sports
- before sexual activity, because lack of inhibition may lead to unsafe practices
- when sick or taking medication or other substances

Lack of quality control

Although it's a criminal offence, drug dealers are constantly developing and manufacturing new illegal substances. Unlike legal pharmaceutical laboratories, illegal labs have no guidelines for cleanliness, procedures, or quality control.

Even if the dealer does not purposely add impurities to stretch the supply of a drug, it may become contaminated because the facilities are unsafe.

The risk of overdose

Overdose is always a risk—even with over-the-counter painkillers and alcohol. Because people who use drugs can build a tolerance to some substances, a larger dose becomes necessary to get the same effect, and the risk of overdose rises.

Injecting carries a greater risk than swallowing a drug. Mixing drugs can also make an overdose more likely, because drugs may work together to produce a stronger reaction.

If someone you know appears ill, disoriented, or confused, or is losing consciousness or cannot be revived, an overdose is possible. If you suspect an overdose...

- Do not leave the person unattended.
- Call 911 and remain on the line with the dispatcher.
- Put the person, if unconscious, into the recovery position.
- If the person stops breathing, begin CPR or find someone who can.
- Stay calm.

This photo shows how to put someone into the recovery position.

Short-Term Effects of Marijuana Use

Although it's the most commonly used mood-altering drug in Canada and around the world, less than 3 percent of Canadian teens report using marijuana daily.

- Some people who use marijuana regularly want to escape stress or negative thoughts. Some like the way marijuana makes them feel.
- Some may see it as a ticket to a certain social network. Others may be attracted to its forbidden quality or want to experiment.
- The effects of smoking marijuana are almost immediate and last from two to four hours. If the drug is eaten, the effects appear more gradually, last longer, and can be more intense.
- Typically, using marijuana or cannabis causes red eyes, dry mouth and throat, increased appetite, and problems with concentration and short-term memory.
- Marijuana produces a mix of depressant effects, such as relaxation, and stimulant effects, such as an increased heart rate. Sensory perception seems enhanced, and sense of time and space is distorted.
- Some people experience more intense, unpleasant effects, such as hallucinations, anxiety, and depression. A few experience panic, paranoia, or an increase in psychiatric symptoms that already existed.

Long-Term Effects of Marijuana Use

Although some people may be able to use marijuana occasionally, a person who has developed a full dependency will find it very difficult to control. The more a person uses most drugs, including marijuana, the more likely the person may suffer from long-term negative effects.

- **Respiratory system.** Like tobacco smoke, marijuana smoke damages the respiratory system. The two contain many of the same carcinogens, but marijuana smoke has higher amounts of them and also more tar. Marijuana smokers inhale more deeply and hold the smoke in their lungs longer. If marijuana is smoked with nicotine, these problems are compounded.
- **The brain.** Heavy long-term use of marijuana affects memory, concentration, and the brain's ability to organize and process complex information. Lack of motivation and lack of interest in life also seem to go hand in hand with regular long-term use—although no one knows if this is a direct effect or actually a factor in starting to use marijuana.
- **Mental and emotional health.** Research has shown that marijuana use can make the symptoms of schizophrenia worse in people who already have it. It can bring on the disorder if a person is predisposed to it. Long-term marijuana use may induce schizophrenia in a person who has no predisposition to it.
- **Pregnancy.** A woman's marijuana use during pregnancy can have a negative effect on the mental development of the child.
- **Dependence.** People who use marijuana can develop a tolerance for the drug and will gradually need more to get the same effect. Treatment programs in Canada report that marijuana is the drug of choice for an increasing number of clients.

Withdrawal symptoms may be relatively mild compared to those from other substances but can include anxiety, irritability, insomnia, sweating, and loss of appetite. These symptoms and psychological cravings can make it difficult to quit.

Treatment for marijuana dependence is much like treatment for other substance dependencies. It usually involves working with a counsellor to learn the skills to live well without the use of any substance.

Table 7.1 **The Classification of Drugs—The Risks and Effects**

Class of drug and examples	Short-term effects (can have at least one effect)	Risks and harms (can include some of these)
Cannabis		
• Marijuana • Sinsemilla • Hash • Hash oil	• Increased appetite • Drowsiness • Feelings of relaxation • Feelings of well-being, euphoria	• Anxiety • Panic reactions • Onset of schizophrenia
Hallucinogens		
• Mescaline • Peyote • Psilocybin (magic mushrooms) • Phencyclidine (PCP, or angel dust) • Lysergic acid diethylamide (LSD) • MDMA (methylenedioxymethamphetamine, or ecstasy) • MDA (methylenedioxyamphetamine)	• Muscle twitches • Dizziness, nausea, vomiting • Altered/distorted body image • Visual and auditory distortions, hallucinations • Feelings of enhanced mental capacity • Loss of touch with reality	• Erectile dysfunction • Panic reactions • Psychosis • Flashbacks • Anxiety • Depression • Memory and thinking problems • Poor judgment leading to accidents or death
Central nervous system (CNS) depressants		
• Alcohol • Solvents • Inhalants • Minor tranquilizers (Valium®, Ativan®) • Sleeping medications (Halcion®, Imovane®) • Barbiturates (Tuinal®)	• Slurred speech • Decreased motor skills • Decreased inhibitions • Increased confidence • Feelings of relaxation • Intoxication • Poor judgment • Impaired memory and thinking	• Respiratory problems • Seizures • Liver disease • Heart disease • Increased risk of some cancers • Fetal alcohol spectrum disorder • Brain damage • Fatal overdose
▶ **Opiates/narcotics (a sub-class of CNS depressants)**		
• Various prescription painkillers • Morphine • Codeine • Heroin	• Constipation • Decreased breathing rate • Pinpoint pupils • Pain relief • Drowsiness • Intoxication followed by euphoria	• Pulmonary (lung) problems • Hepatitis (from sharing needles) • HIV/AIDS (from sharing needles) • Increased risk of some cancers • Brain damage • Coma • Death from respiratory failure
Central nervous system (CNS) stimulants		
• Amphetamines (including crystal meth) • Methylphenidate (Ritalin®) • Cocaine and crack cocaine • Nicotine • Caffeine	• Increased heart rate and blood pressure • Decreased appetite • Dilated pupils • Hallucinations • Increased energy • Euphoria • Feelings of enhanced sociability, sexuality, confidence	• Insomnia • Lack of sexual interest • Panic reactions • Extreme anxiety • Paranoid psychosis • Depression • Seizures • HIV/AIDS (from sharing needles) • Heart attack/stroke

Hallucinogens

Hallucinogens include a wide range of naturally occurring substances (for example, mescaline, peyote, and psilocybin, which is found in a species of mushroom) and synthesized substances (for example, LSD, PCP, MDA, and ecstasy). These drugs greatly distort the senses and, as their classification implies, can cause hallucinations. Most of these substances are taken orally.

The effects of LSD

Lysergic acid diethylamide (LSD), commonly known as acid, is one of the most common hallucinogenic drugs. It is extremely powerful—a pill the size of an aspirin could contain 3,000 doses of pure LSD. The drug is a tasteless, odourless, fine white powder that is sold in capsules or tablets.

As is the case with other drugs, the effects of LSD can be unpredictable. Usually, the first effects of the drug are felt 30 to 45 minutes after taking it. People taking LSD may feel several emotions in quick succession—from euphoria (a feeling of intense well-being) to sadness or fear, and back again.

It is not uncommon to experience disorienting sensations that can lead to a "bad trip" involving anxiety and terrifying thoughts and feelings. Because LSD trips last 12 hours or more, a negative experience can be deeply disturbing.

A person cannot overdose or become physically dependent on LSD. However, regular use can lead to experiences of upsetting flashbacks in which the effects of LSD are felt without taking the drug again.

The effects of ecstasy

Ecstasy (methylenedioxymethamphetamine, or MDMA) is considered a hallucinogen, but it also has stimulant effects. It is made in illegal drug labs and goes by names such as E, XTC, Adam, Euphoria, or X. It usually comes in gelatin capsules or coloured tablets that may have a design such as a dove or a diamond on one side. Ecstasy can also come as a powder that people using it can snort or, less commonly, dissolve and inject.

The effects of ecstasy have a great deal to do with the state of mind and health of the person using it. The pupils dilate, the jaw tightens, and blood pressure and heart rate increase. Other effects include nausea, sweating, dry mouth and throat, and loss of appetite.

Some people using ecstasy report a heightened awareness of their surroundings, greater appreciation of music, and more intense sensory experiences.

Long-term ecstasy use may cause short-term memory impairment, depression, mood changes, and disrupted sleep patterns. Other possible long-term effects include flashbacks or psychosis. The signs of an overdose include eye rolling, chest pain, and seizures.

Club Drugs

Club drugs are illegal and dangerous substances associated with some dance clubs and party venues.

Little is known about the long-term effects of these substances, which often contain unknown additives or impurities. Among club drugs are ketamine, GHB, and Rohypnol®.

The latter two, known as rape drugs, are sometimes used intentionally to sedate and then sexually assault an unsuspecting person. Rape is a form of violent sexual assault and is a very serious criminal offence

A Risky Mix

Produced naturally in the leaves and seeds of many plants, caffeine is defined as a drug because it stimulates the CNS, making you more alert.

What happens when you mix highly caffeinated energy drinks with alcohol? In 2016, researchers at the University of Victoria's Centre for Addictions Research of BC conducted the first systematic review of published research on the subject.

They found that of 13 studies that fitted their research criteria, ten made a link between increased risk of injury and drinking a mix of alcohol and energy drinks, compared to drinking alcohol only. The studies included unintentional injuries such as falls or car accidents and intentional ones resulting from fights or other physical violence.

Depressants

Depressants get their name because they depress the activity of the central nervous system (CNS). This class of drugs includes alcohol, some prescribed medications, opiates, and inhalants.

Depressants should never be combined with other substances that cause drowsiness, even cold and allergy medications. Combining some drugs can multiply their effects, slowing breathing and heart rate to the point of death.

To stop taking a depressant after prolonged use can lead to withdrawal. The brain's activity can rebound once use stops, causing seizures. It is always important to consult a physician before stopping a medication.

Barbiturates and tranquilizers

Barbiturates were developed to treat sleep problems, anxiety, high blood pressure, and seizures. Some are used as anesthetics.

Tranquilizers called benzodiazepines are often prescribed for anxiety, nervousness, and sleep problems, and to relax muscles. Although they are safer and have fewer side effects than barbiturates, they are generally recommended only for short-term use because they can lead to dependence.

Opiates

Opiates are a highly addictive sub-class of depressants. Some are produced naturally. Opium and morphine, for example, come from the seed pod of the Asian poppy. Others are produced synthetically in laboratories. Codeine, Demerol®, Dilaudid®, and Percodan® are examples.

Synthesized opiates have valuable medical uses as painkillers (oxycodone) or cough suppressants (codeine), but they should be taken only under medical supervision because it's not uncommon to become dependent.

Heroin is a very powerful opiate. It can be sniffed, smoked, taken orally, or injected under the skin, but it's usually injected directly into a blood vessel—a practice known as mainlining.

Heroin and other opiates slow the body's functions and suppress or reduce physical and emotional pain. Feelings of relaxation, detachment, and reduced anxiety are common effects.

People do successfully give up long-term use of heroin and other opiates, but coming off and staying off these drugs can be difficult.

Inhalants

Inhalants such as paint thinners, modelling glue, gasoline, and cleaning fluids induce euphoria and light-headedness while slowing the body's systems. They can cause brain damage, suffocation, and death.

Stimulants

Stimulants speed up, or excite, the central nervous system (CNS). Examples of stimulants include caffeine, nicotine, cocaine, amphetamine-type stimulants, and a medication called methylphenidate, commonly known as Ritalin®. Stimulants are typically used to increase alertness, decrease appetite, delay fatigue, and produce feelings of well-being. For people with attention deficit hyperactivity disorder (ADHD), however, the stimulant Ritalin® has a calming effect.

Use of stimulant drugs can result in severe psychological and physical dependence, which can make it difficult to stop using them.

Cocaine

Cocaine is a strongly addictive stimulant processed from the leaves of the coca plant. Crack is a smokable form of cocaine made by adding baking soda to a cocaine solution and allowing the mixture to dry.

In Canada, the most common form of cocaine is a fine white crystalline powder that is often diluted with sugar, cornstarch, or talcum powder. It can be sniffed, absorbed through mucous membranes in the mouth, smoked, or injected.

People who use cocaine say they feel more alert, energetic, confident, physically strong, and intelligent. Although they perceive those benefits, they are actually experiencing numerous negative psychological and physical effects as well.

Large doses can cause severe agitation, paranoid thinking, erratic or violent behaviour, muscle spasms, hallucinations, convulsions, and even death. Impurities in street cocaine can bring on a fatal allergic reaction.

People typically experience depression and extreme tiredness after using cocaine. Those who inject cocaine get a short-lived high, so they need to inject several times a day to maintain the high. If they share needles, they greatly increase their risk of contracting HIV and/or hepatitis.

Amphetamine-type stimulants

Amphetamine-type stimulants (ATSs), such as crystal meth, have effects similar to those of cocaine. People using these stimulants may become talkative, restless, or excited. They feel powerful, superior, aggressive, or hostile and may behave in a bizarre, repetitive fashion. ATS drugs can produce a strong dependence.

The Opioid Crisis

Today's opioid crisis has its roots in a massive increase in prescriptions for narcotic painkillers about 20 years ago. Before the mid-1990s, doctors prescribed opioid-based medicine only if the patient was experiencing acute pain—pain at a high level.

Canadian physicians were then advised that such medicines could also treat chronic pain, which is less severe but ongoing. The risk of addiction was thought to be low. Tragically, that was not the case.

By the time physicians realized the risks, thousands of people had become addicted and their withdrawal symptoms were unbearable. Many turned to the streets to get any opioid or opioid variant that would ease their suffering.

The dangers of synthetic opioids

Opioids bind to receptors in the brain and spinal cord, blocking how a person perceives pain. This drug category includes some very dangerous synthetic opioids:

- **OxyContin (oxycodone)**, known on the street as oxycotton, is a semi-synthetic opioid that has been in clinical use since 1916. It is crushed and snorted to deliver a powerful and fast high that many people with addiction prefer to heroin.
- **Fentanyl**, a synthetic opiate first made in 1960, is roughly 50 to 100 times more potent than morphine. You cannot see it, smell it, or taste it, but it can kill you.
- **Carfentanil**, first synthesized in 1974, is related to fentanyl but is 100 times more potent—and 10,000 times stronger than morphine. It is among the most powerful opioids and is used in veterinary medicine to sedate large animals.

Alone or in combination with other drugs, these synthetics have had a devastating impact.

"There has never been a more dangerous time to source drugs on the street," said Dr. David Juurlink, head of clinical pharmacology and toxicology at Sunnybrook Health Sciences Centre in an interview with the CBC.

Fentanyl and carfentanil are cheap and incredibly potent. Drug dealers add them to heroin and other illegal drugs to reduce costs and multiply the effects, which increases profits. For them, quality control is not a big concern, so exactly how much they add is essentially unknown.

The supply chain for fentanyl begins in China, but the problems in Canada start at home. No other country consumes more prescription opioids per capita, according to a 2016 United Nations report.

Confronting the crisis

The appearance of cheap, powerful synthetic opioids alongside overly prescribed painkiller medicine has produced an "epidemic within an epidemic," according to Dr. Juurlink. Canadian health care experts are calling for urgent action to deal with the situation. Education campaigns, clearer direction for physicians, and stiffer penalties for street dealers are among the measures proposed.

The U.S. Centers for Disease Control and Prevention has issued guidelines advising doctors first to try non-drug therapies for chronic pain and to prescribe opioids only in low doses and for short-term use. New draft guidelines for Canadian doctors have been developed at McMaster University in Hamilton. These guidelines suggest restricting opioids to the equivalent of 50 to 90 milligrams of morphine per day, except in rare cases. The previous guidelines from 2010 limited the upper daily dose to 200 milligrams.

Governments and public health agencies across Canada are also warning family physicians to think first before prescribing narcotic painkillers. Canadian medical schools are revising courses to underline for future doctors the dangers of opioids and suggest alternatives for treating patients experiencing chronic pain.

Public health experts are also asking the federal government to set up more safe injection sites. At these sites, people can be supervised and resuscitated if the drug they are taking is contaminated with fentanyl or carfentanil. At these sites as well, qualified professionals can provide addiction counselling and anti-withdrawal drugs to help people who are addicted to opioids.

Section 7.3 Review

1. Name three main factors in the risk level of using drugs.
2. In your opinion, what is the most serious risk associated with drug use?
3. If someone you know appears to have overdosed, what should you do?

7.4 Problem Gambling and Other Addictive Behaviours

Gambling is the decision to risk losing money or other valuables when the outcome is decided by chance. There are many types: casino games, bingo, slot machines, lottery tickets, scratch or pull-tab tickets, card games, sports betting, and various forms of online gambling.

Problem gambling is not about your parents or guardians buying the occasional lottery ticket or going to bingo now and again. It is about risky and recurring behaviours with potentially negative consequences.

Gambling becomes a problem when it...

- interferes with school, work, and other aspects of normal life
- affects family and personal relationships, creating marital problems, family violence, or the loss of friendships
- causes wasteful spending, reckless use of family resources, increasing debt, or loss of home, job, or savings

Problem gambling affects not only finances and family but also a person's mental and physical health and future opportunities. The degree to which gambling is a problem is shown in a **continuum of gambling risk**.

Online Gambling

Online gambling is available 24 hours a day, and people who gamble do not even have to leave the house. Online gambling comes with some complex legal issues in Canada, but many gambling sites are located beyond our borders. You never know who owns them or how they are regulated.

It is not uncommon for teens to find offshore gambling sites and get hooked. It is easy to forget that the virtual money you use to gamble online is actually your own real money. Because it is done in private, online gambling has fewer restraints on how much you lose or how long you play.

Video Lottery Terminals

Provincial and territorial governments have come to rely on revenue from legalized gambling. Video lottery terminals (VLTs) are the single largest source of government gambling revenues and 60 percent of all VLT revenues come from problem gamblers.

VLTs are found in casinos, racetracks, and, depending on the province, in bars, bowling alleys, billiard halls, and other youth-oriented locations.

VLTs are very addictive. They allow people to bet quickly and to bet more than they can afford. VLTs have caused so much harm in some communities that many citizens want a total ban.

Prevention and Early Intervention

Certain social groups are more at risk of becoming problem gamblers than others, for example, older adults, people with low incomes, newcomers to Canada, and young people. Given the high level of risk, you can take proactive steps to avoid gambling altogether, or at least to limit the risks:

- **Get fit, get active.** Stay involved in activities with other people. Take a class, participate in a sport, join a club, or become a volunteer.
- **Treat yourself.** Use your money for something special instead of gambling. Save to get something you really want, or plan a night out with friends.
- **Learn more.** Find sources of reliable information to give you a better idea of how the gambling business works and its potential hazards.
- **Set a strict limit.** It is best not to gamble at all, but if you do decide to gamble, at least restrict the amount of time you spend and the money you bet. If you go over the limit, seek help right away.

Just like the 12 steps of Alcoholics Anonymous (AA), the 12 steps of a Gamblers Anonymous (GA) program can provide a framework for lifelong recovery from a gambling addiction.

The Continuum of Gambling Risk

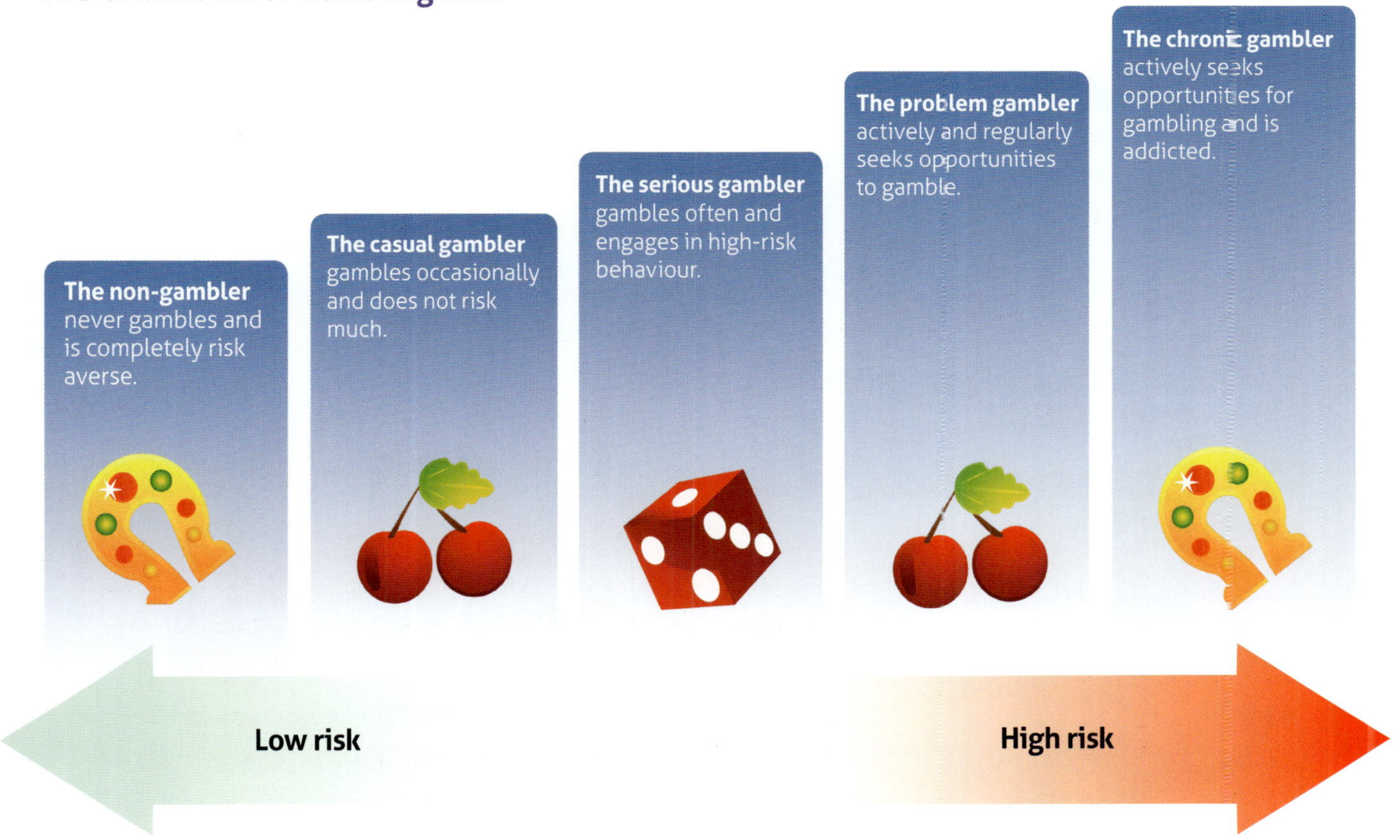

Internet, Video Gaming, and Social Media Addictions

Internet addiction is much more than just a strong desire to be online. Like other addictive behaviours, it's marked by a progressive loss of control, as the person becomes less and less able to avoid or regulate a behaviour.

The core components of internet addiction are similar to those of any other compulsion:

- **Tolerance.** Just like drugs and alcohol, smartphones and tablets can trigger the release of the brain chemical dopamine and alter your mood. Moreover, just like using drugs and alcohol, you can rapidly build up tolerance, so that it takes more and more time to get the same pleasurable reward.
- **Obsession.** You may spend most offline time thinking about past online experiences and planning future online sessions.
- **Social isolation.** You may abandon friends and hobbies in order to focus on online activities.
- **Withdrawal.** You may feel frustration, anxiety, or irritability when unable to go online.
- **Ignoring the consequences.** If you continue to spend time online despite negative consequences such as school difficulties, deteriorating relationships, and even health problems related to poor nutrition, poor personal hygiene, and insufficient sleep, you may be addicted.

If you cannot stop constantly checking your devices, it's time to reassess your technology use. Learning the signs and symptoms of internet and smartphone addiction, as well as ways to break free of unhealthy habits, can help you find a better balance in your life—both online and off.

Remember that social media is not the only way to be social. Try putting your phones down and trying other fun ways to interact with those around you.

Negative Consequences of Online Addiction

An addiction to online activities can have many negative consequences affecting our overall health and quality of life. For one thing, spending long hours sitting in front of a screen poses risks to our physical health and well-being. Doctors today are warning us that "sitting is the new smoking." The risks posed to mental health are serious as well.

Impulse-control problems

- **Online compulsions**. Gaming, gambling, online shopping, or bidding on auction sites can lead to financial and job-related crises. You may buy things you do not need and cannot afford just to experience the excitement of making a winning bid.
- **Fear of missing out.** You may feel pressure to always be online. "Fear of missing out," or FOMO, prompts people to check and respond to messages constantly, and it can contribute to high stress levels.
- **Neglect of real life.** Compulsively surfing the web, playing games, and so on can make you less productive at school and isolate you for hours at a time. You may neglect other aspects of your life, from real-world relationships to outdoor pursuits.

An overloaded brain

- **Worsened attention deficit disorders.** The stream of information from a smartphone can overwhelm the brain and make it difficult to focus on anything for more than a few minutes without feeling compelled to move on to something else.
- **Reduced creative thinking.** Constantly checking and using your smartphone can distract you from important tasks, slow your work, and interrupt the quiet moments that are crucial to creativity and problem solving.
- **Disturbed sleep.** Excessive smartphone use can disrupt sleep, seriously affecting your overall mental health. It can impair your memory, your ability to think clearly, and your cognitive and learning skills.

Preoccupation with self

- **Virtual relationships.** Addiction to social networking, dating apps, texting, and messaging can make virtual relationships more important than real-life ones. Online friends exist in a bubble, however, and you cannot always depend on them. Teens also tend to compare themselves unfavourably with their peers on social media, heightening loneliness and depression.
- **Increased self-absorption.** People who spend a lot of time on social media are more likely to display negative personality traits, such as narcissism. Posting endless selfies and details about your life can make you more self-centred and unable to cope with stress.

Self-Help Tips for Online Addiction

Schedule your smartphone, tablet, or computer use for certain times of day, or reward yourself with time online once you have finished your homework or chores.

- Do not bring your phone, tablet, or laptop to bed.
- Replace online activities with healthy recreational ones. If you are bored or lonely, plan ways to fill time, such as reading or seeing friends face to face.
- Play the "phone stack" game. When having lunch or snacks with friends, ask them to place their smartphones face down on the table. Those who cannot resist checking their phones lose the game!

Cybersex Addiction

Compulsive use of internet pornography and sexting can affect your real-life intimate relationships and overall emotional health. Online pornography and cybersex are accessible, anonymous, and convenient. Using either one compulsively is a type of sexual addiction.

Such addictions deprive an individual of opportunities to learn how to develop and sustain healthy, close relationships with other human beings.

As movies do, online pornography presents a fantasy. When actors have a fist fight, for example, it has no actual effect. However, in real life, broken bones, concussions, or even death could result.

Similarly, the scenes in online pornography are staged. They involve paid actors and do not represent healthy, genuinely intimate relationships.

Seek professional counselling if you are concerned that you may be addicted to online pornography or cybersex.

Steroid Use

Our bodies produce steroids naturally to fight stress and promote growth and development. Some people use steroid pills, gels, creams, or injections in an effort to improve their sports performance or their looks.

Anabolic steroids are artificially produced hormones that are the same as, or similar to, male sex hormones such as testosterone. Anabolic steroids stimulate muscle tissue to grow in response to training by mimicking the effect of naturally produced testosterone on the body.

Steroids became popular because they may improve endurance, strength, and muscle mass. They can be addictive, however, and people using steroids can experience withdrawal symptoms such as loss of appetite, fatigue, restlessness, insomnia, mood swings, and depression when they stop taking anabolic steroids.

Steroids can also have various side effects, including

- acne
- hair loss or premature balding
- weight gain
- stunted growth
- mood swings and increased aggression
- disrupted sleep patterns
- high blood pressure
- greater chance of injuring muscles and tendons
- jaundice or yellowing of the skin
- liver damage
- increased risk of heart disease, blood clots, stroke, and some types of cancer

Anabolic steroid use is illegal and is banned by professional sports organizations and medical associations.

Even so, some athletes take steroids because they think it gives them a competitive edge. As some high-profile cases have shown, if athletes undergo drug testing and are caught using steroids, their careers can go down in flames.

Section 7.4 Review

1 What can a person do to avoid becoming a problem gambler?

2 What strategies can people use to overcome an internet or smartphone addiction?

3 As a society and as individuals, what can we do to help prevent compulsive behaviours such as problem gambling?

Long-term effects of steroids include shrunken testicles, impotence, severe acne, liver damage, and stunted growth.

7.5 Responding to Substance Use and Addictive Behaviours

Positive mental health is closely related to the development of psychological and emotional **resilience**—the ability to recover or "bounce back" when we are confronted with a crisis, a traumatic event, or an unsettling change in our lives.

Resilience is a major factor affecting decisions related to substance use. Also known as durability, resilience gives us the strength to deal with difficult situations and to rebound from challenges and setbacks. It is an important aspect of mental, emotional, and spiritual well-being.

Things that promote resilience, such as strong family ties and close relationships, are known as **protective factors**.

Things that reduce resilience, such as a family history of substance abuse or difficult relationships, are known as **risk factors**.

Boosting protective factors and **limiting risk factors** can help individuals become better able to cope with situations that might draw them into substance use and substance use disorders. Table 7.2 lists some protective factors and some risk factors associated with resilience.

How Can You Strengthen Your Resilience?

Some factors are the result of forces you cannot control, but you can take control of other factors. What are some ways of strengthening your resilience? How can you apply these strategies when making choices about substance use?

- **Find positive ways to cope with stress.** Talking with friends, getting enough sleep, eating well, and taking part in stress-relieving activities such as exercise or meditation can make you less likely to deal with stress in negative ways, such as using alcohol or drugs.
- **Get correct information.** We risk making harmful choices if we do not understand their possible consequences. For example, some people think that it's safe to experiment with prescription drugs because they are not street drugs—but they can be addictive and overdoses can kill.
- **Keep good company.** Seek friends who are not afraid to get the facts for themselves and who are proud of making healthy choices—and become one of those people yourself.
- **Take part in healing and cultural activities.** Connecting with our cultural identity and relying on traditional or ceremonial healing practices can help us build a stronger sense of self and renew our commitment to good health.

We can all learn to manage the protective factors in our lives in order to strengthen our resilience, thereby enhancing our mental health.

Table 7.2 **Risk Factors and Protective Factors Associated with Resilience**

Context	Risk factors	Protective factors
Individual characteristics		
	• Genetic traits • Long-term physical illness • Experience of discrimination based on race, sexuality, gender, or religion • Being easily angered • Communication difficulties • Low self-esteem • Childhood abuse, neglect, or trauma	• A sense of humour • Spiritual faith • Good social skills • A positive attitude about life • Respect for authority • Personal goals • High self-esteem • Good problem-solving skills
Relationships and home life		
	• Family problems • Experience of severe bullying or physical or sexual abuse • Acting as a caregiver, taking on adult responsibilities • Associating with friends who engage in high-risk behaviours, such as experimenting with drugs • Witnessing family conflict and violence • Living in poverty or being homeless	• At least one close relationship • A stable family environment • Involvement with extended family • Opportunities for quality time with parents/guardians • Parental/guardian warmth, support, and clear expectations • Parental/guardian support for education • Stable housing
School and community environment		
	• A learning disability or long-standing school difficulties • Lack of access to recreational activities • Lack of access to basic community services such as housing and clean water • Easy access to alcohol and other substances • Few economic opportunities • Refugee or asylum seeker status • Violence or war in the community	• Strong connections to school • Strong relationships with teachers • Teachers who express high expectations • Participation in a range of sports and/or leisure activities • Involvement in community activities • Peers who value responsibility • A positive role model

Being Prepared to Say "No"

By the time you are in a social situation that involves alcohol or other substances, you may already have formed an opinion about them—but refusing can still be difficult. You may

- not want to be a bystander
- not want to miss bonding with friends
- not want to be teased or ridiculed
- not want to hurt someone's feelings
- not know how to get out of the situation without embarrassing yourself

You need to decide how you will respond to such pressures well before you face them. Thinking ahead of time about what to say and using refusal and assertiveness techniques can help you resist peer pressure to take drugs or drink, or to do something risky online.

You can learn and practise these techniques to protect yourself in risky or difficult social situations, whether face to face or online:

- Keep what you want to say to the point.
- Be polite yet firm in saying no confidently and persuasively.
- Maintain eye contact when you are face to face. Listen carefully to the other person and observe the person's body language.
- Remain calm and do not show anger.

You can also choose friends who are supportive and who do not urge you to drink, smoke, take drugs, or practise other risky behaviours. True friends respect one another's decisions.

Adopting a Harm-Reduction Approach

In Canada, the federal and provincial governments have adopted and promoted a number of strategies to prevent or reduce alcohol- and drug-related problems affecting individuals and society as a whole.

As well, social workers are at the forefront in developing innovative and evidence-based practices to help people with substance use disorders.

Social workers and others in Canadian substance use programs generally adopt a harm-reduction approach. **Harm reduction** focuses on ways to minimize the harmful effects of substance use and addictive behaviours. Harm reduction tactics aim to improve the health and social and economic conditions of individuals and their communities.

Harm reduction may involve abstinence—although abstinence is not necessarily a goal. The approach offers a range of options. These include safer drug use techniques, using legal rather than illegal drugs, and decreasing the amount and/or frequency of use.

Although harm-reduction strategies have been available for decades, the emergence of AIDS and HIV raised their profile, especially in relation to decreasing injection drug use. Harm-reduction strategies promote a non-judgmental attitude to people who use substances and offer them recovery options in a compassionate and non-coercive way.

Reducing the Impact of Substance Use

Substance use contributes to thousands of deaths, illness and disease, accidents and injuries, social and family disorders, damaged relationships, workplace problems, crime, and reduced community safety.

The harm caused by substance use costs taxpayers billions of dollars every year. Direct economic costs come from health care, social welfare programs, and policing. Indirect economic costs include reduced employee productivity.

All substance-use decisions should involve weighing the perceived benefits against the risks. Unfortunately, many people do not think about the consequences, and impulsive decisions can lead to all kinds of problems.

Before you make a decision, stop to consider the short- and long-term consequences for not only your own safety and well-being, but the safety and well-being of your family and friends as well.

Family members and friends can play a vital role in a loved one's recovery from a substance use disorder. The current recovery model favoured by mental health professionals focuses on the person as a whole and untapped strengths rather than on symptoms alone. The recovery model champions a message of hope: it bolsters the idea that renewed health is possible for anyone struggling with a substance use disorder.

Sources of Information and Support

If you are struggling with substance use or an addictive behaviour, you can turn to a friend, family member, teacher, school counsellor, elder, or medical professional for help. This person might refer you to a community treatment or intervention program or to an appropriate support group.

You can also find information and support from many sources such as the following services and organizations:

- At **Kids Help Phone**, 1.800.668.6868, counsellors answer questions from across Canada in both English and French. Calls are free and confidential.
- The **First Nations and Inuit Hope for Wellness Help Line**, 1.855.242.3310, is toll free and open 24 hours a day, every day.
- The **Family Navigation Project** at Sunnybrook Health Sciences Centre in Toronto is a call-in and email service to support families with youth who are struggling with mental health concerns or addictions. Youth 13 to 26 years old or a concerned family member can call 1.800.380.9367.
- The **Canadian Distress Line Network** is made up of distress centres across Canada that offer a variety of services to their communities. You can go online to send an email, or click on the Resources link to find a distress line in your area. They usually offer sympathetic listeners round the clock. You can also call your local health clinic, mental health centre, hospital, doctor, or emergency number for help connecting to a crisis centre.
- **ONTX Ontario Online Text and Crisis Services** allow you to live-chat online or text (741741) with a highly trained responder from 2 p.m. until 2 a.m. daily. These safe one-on-one conversations allow you to ask for help completely confidentially.
- The **Centre for Addiction and Mental Health (CAMH) Child, Youth and Emerging Adult Service** helps young people with mental health and/or addiction problems to function better at home, in school, and with peers.
- The **Canada Safety Council**, a national non-government charitable organization dedicated to safety, considers gambling addiction a community safety and crime prevention issue. It offers a number of preventive strategies.
- The **Family Association for Mental Health Everywhere (FAME)** empowers families and caregivers who have a loved one with a mental health concern by providing support, education, coping skills, and self-care strategies. FAME offers services across the Greater Toronto Area and Peel region. **FAMEkids** supports children aged 7 to 12 and youth aged 13 to 17 who have a family member with a mental health concern. For more information, call 416.207.5032.

Section 7.5 Review

1. Name various ways to strengthen resilience, and explain why it is important.
2. List some side effects of steroid use.
3. Draw a cartoon showing an effective response to a situation involving substance use or addictive behaviour.

Michel's Story

"To build resilience and a strong sense of self, choose self-affirmation rather than self-destructive behaviours, forge positive connections rather than letting friendships take you down the wrong path, and be open to letting other people in who will listen to your story."
— Michel Chikwanine

Chapter 7 Review

Knowledge and Understanding

1 Give three reasons why someone might try using illegal drugs or other harmful substances, and present a counterargument for each reason.

2 List the known physical and psychological consequences of long-term marijuana use.

3 What is the opioid crisis, and what can be done about it?

4 Describe at least three things that can be done to address gaming, internet, or smartphone addiction.

Thinking

5 Why do you think video lottery terminals are commonly referred to as the crack cocaine of gambling? What do you suggest could be done to reduce the risks associated with VLTs?

6 Imagine a friend intends to use illegal drugs for the first time. Give three examples of how this behaviour could put your friend in danger and two ways the behaviour could endanger you as well. What might you say or do to persuade your friend not to use illegal drugs?

7 Your class has been put in charge of promoting drug and alcohol awareness in your school. List four key themes that can be emphasized to help your peers make healthy decisions related to drug and alcohol use.

Communication

8 Make a collage, poster, slide presentation, video, or web-based ad that clearly demonstrates the risks of using one or more of the substances or illegal drugs discussed in this chapter.

9 Conduct and record brief interviews with people you know who seem particularly resilient and ask their permission to share their comments with the class.

Application

10 In groups, discuss various ways in which television, movies, social media, and popular music tend to glamorize drug use. What strategies might help to counterbalance these influences?

11 Act out scenarios with your classmates related to staying safe at a party or other venue where drugs and alcohol are being consumed.

12 Imagine that someone close to you has a dependence on tobacco, alcohol, or another potentially addictive substance. Investigate the resources in your community that the person could draw on to help overcome dependence.

Personal Safety and Emotional Well-Being

8

Josh's Story

What are the most effective strategies for keeping yourself, your loved ones, and your friends physically and emotionally safe?

Adolescence is a time when we have more opportunity to explore our world with much less adult supervision than ever before. At this stage, we are gaining responsibility for making important decisions that affect our well-being and that of the people around us. We are beginning to understand that risk can sometimes be exciting, scary, boring, uncomfortable, educational, and thrilling. Sometimes there are hazards that we can see and feel, but sometimes they are harder to detect. We are beginning to learn the difference between hazards (to be avoided) and risks (to be managed).

Our physical and personal environments can both threaten our safety and bring tremendous joy and learning.

The term *personal safety* refers to several related ideas:

- protection from physical and bodily harm, such as infectious diseases or injury
- protection from environmental dangers such as extreme weather
- protection from threatened or actual violence, aggression, harassment, or abuse such as dating violence or cyberbullying

Fortunately, we can learn some effective skills and strategies to reduce harm, protect our own and others' physical, mental, and social well-being, and prevent or resolve conflicts with others.

Learning Objectives

In this chapter, you will...

- manage risk in your physical and social environments
- develop a personal safety plan
- describe ways to ensure your safety while spending time with friends or outdoors
- demonstrate an understanding of factors that influence mental well-being
- describe some ways to reduce or cope with stress
- describe some warning signs that indicate mental health concerns
- apply strategies to respond to or prevent bullying, harassment, hate crimes, racism, and other forms of violence and discrimination
- identify sources of information and support for everyone

Key Terms

- risk
- hazard
- personal safety plan
- ultraviolet radiation (UVR)
- UV Index
- personal flotation device (PFD)
- stress
- bullying
- cyberbullying
- harassment
- dating violence
- sexual harassment
- hate crime
- racism
- ethnic violence
- homophobia/biphobia/transphobia
- heterosexism
- online communication technologies
- internal conflict
- interpersonal conflict
- intragroup conflict
- intergroup conflict
- anger management strategies
- conflict resolution strategies

▶ **Josh Beckstead** was just 18 months old when an explosion at his home caused third degree burns to most of his body. He has undergone many reconstructive surgeries. A strong and caring network of family, friends, and teachers and an aptitude for sports have contributed to Josh's resilience and positive attitude.

8.1 Ensuring Your Personal Safety

Being physically and socially active is not only good for your health but it brings pleasure and enjoyment as well. Learning to weigh the costs and the benefits of personal choices and actions will help you enjoy healthy active living for a lifetime without serious illness or traumatic injury.

In matters of safety, we need to develop personal risk management skills, particularly as we begin to spend more time away from direct adult supervision. A **risk** is the effect of uncertainty on our objectives; this effect can deviate either positively or negatively from what we expect. We need to recognize and manage potential positive and potential negative outcomes of our decisions and behaviours. We also need to become skilled at recognizing potential hazards at home, at school, at work, at recreation sites, and in public. A **hazard** is any source of potential damage, harm, or adverse health effects on someone or something.

Being aware of your surroundings and learning to tune out distractions that might threaten your physical safety are two important habits you can develop to manage risk and explore your environment successfully.

Many everyday situations call for practical skills and strategies for managing your well-being, some of which are listed below.

Developing a Personal Safety Plan

A **personal safety plan** is a set of protective strategies to build your confidence—so you are less likely to experience harassment or violence—and to guide you if you are unsafe.

- **Go places with friends whenever you can.** It is easier to stay safe or to find help if you are with a group.
- **Remain alert.** Avoid appearing distracted; stay awake on public transit.
- **Appear confident.** Walk confidently rather than timidly. The more confident you look, the less likely you are to be threatened or attacked.
- **Pay attention to your instincts.** If you think you are being followed, go where there are plenty of people and text or call a family member or friend who can pick you up, or call the police.
- **Stay connected.** Make sure people know where you are going and when you are due home. Keep your cell phone charged and with you at all times, hidden from sight. If you and your friends are returning home late at night, text each other when you arrive. If someone does not check in at the expected time, tell an adult right away.
- **Avoid darkly-lit areas.** Be sure to stay in well-lit areas with other people around. Choose major routes and do not take shortcuts.
- **Be prepared.** Keep emergency contact numbers stored in your phone, but write them down and carry them on you as well. Carry enough money with you for public transit, a taxi, or a ride-for-hire.

Reducing risks to your physical health

Your personal and social environments carry various health and safety hazards, but you can adopt some simple habits to minimize those outcomes. Here are a few general guidelines to keep in mind:

- Follow basic health practices such as washing your hands frequently to reduce the likelihood of spreading infectious illnesses. Stay home if you have a cold or the flu, and try to avoid close contact with people who are sneezing and coughing.
- Ask a parent or guardian if your immunizations are up to date, and if they are not, book an appointment with your family doctor. Consider getting a flu shot during flu season. Many pharmacies offer free shots without an appointment.
- If you are thinking of getting a tattoo or a piercing, take a couple of important precautions. Check the health and safety record of the tattoo parlour you have in mind. You could get infected with hepatitis B or C, HIV, or other diseases if the tools are not sterilized properly. Also, piercings need to be cared for and cleaned carefully to prevent bacterial infection.
- Practising good oral hygiene will benefit your overall health. Brush and floss your teeth regularly and try to get in to see a dentist twice a year.
- Listen to music at a moderate volume to avoid damaging your hearing.

Responding to Hazardous Situations

The following three steps can minimize your chance of harm in potentially hazardous situations:

1. **Identify** potential hazards. Is there a piece of broken equipment? Is the protective gear the wrong size or missing? Is the water level shallow or deep? Is the water fast-moving? What are the road conditions like, and do you or a friend feel comfortable driving?
2. **Evaluate** the potential outcomes. Weigh the costs and the benefits of the potential outcomes of the situation. Do you have the information you need to make a healthy decision? How will you address a change in the situation? Is your safety plan flexible?
3. **Act** quickly to remove yourself from hazardous situations. Always have an exit strategy that you can adapt to the circumstances. Know your right to refuse in the workplace if you are asked to do something dangerous that you are not trained for. If a designated driver is under the influence of drugs and/or alcohol, find alternative transportation for you and for that individual. If a friend has consumed too much alcohol and is unconscious, call 911 to get them the help they need. Have enough money and a phone with you to call a taxi or a trusted friend or adult to get you and your friends out of a hazardous situation.

Planning ahead will help you respond appropriately to potentially unsafe situations as well as to emergency situations such as an asthma attack.

Staying Safe Outdoors

Although we may not be aware of the associated hazards because we are around them everyday, sun safety, road safety, sidewalk safety, weather safety, and water safety are important issues.

Sun safety

Ultraviolet radiation (UVR) is the part of sunlight that can cause sunburn, skin damage, and skin cancer. Most solar radiation reaches the earth in the form of UVA rays, and the rest is in UVB rays.

UVR exposure accumulates over time. You can protect your skin from UVR whenever you are outside with these simple tips:

- Stay in the shade whenever you can.
- Cover up with clothing as much as possible.
- Wear a sunhat, a cap with a brim, or a visor.
- Buy a pair of sunglasses that offers good UVA and UVB protection.
- Choose a water- and sweat-proof brand of sunscreen with an SPF (sun protection factor) of 30 or more. Apply the sunscreen 20 minutes before you go outside, and reapply it every two hours.
- Limit your exposure to the sun, especially between 10 a.m. and 3 p.m., when the sun is strongest.

In the short term, being exposed to the sun for too long may cause sunburn or sunstroke. In the long term, you increase your risk of skin cancer and cataracts, and your skin will wrinkle and age more quickly.

You can protect yourself by checking the **UV Index** before you go outdoors and limiting your sun exposure.

Road safety and sidewalk safety

Pedestrian deaths caused by motor vehicles are on the rise, especially in larger Canadian cities. It is vitally important to observe road safety rules while walking, cycling, in-line skating, skateboarding, or using a scooter.

- **Avoid distractions.** Never use headphones on a public road or pathway.
- **Wear protective gear.** Wear a safety helmet that meets Canadian safety standards and protective padding when you are in-line skating, skateboarding, or using a scooter. Fluorescent safety strips and safety lights, especially ones that flash, make you visible to motorists.
- **Safety checks.** Check your bike and other equipment regularly and replace any worn or damaged parts. If you need help, an adult can show you how to check and maintain your equipment.
- **Be aware of others.** Pay close attention to other people in the area, share the route, and do not get too close to other cyclists or pedestrians.

Tanning Beds

Using a tanning bed is just as dangerous as exposure to the sun—if not more so. According to Health Canada, tanning beds and sunlamps can produce five times more UVA rays than we get from sunlight.

The World Health Organization recommends that no one under 18 use artificial tanning methods.

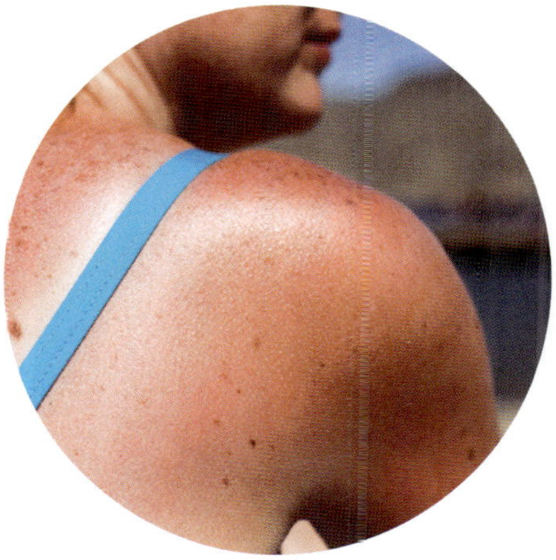

Weather Safety

We live in a country with extreme weather—and too much heat or cold can have serious consequences. Weather-related injuries can be life-threatening and require immediate medical attention.

Hot weather concerns

In hot weather, the body sweats in order to dissipate heat so we can maintain a normal temperature. If we do not drink enough fluids, we get dehydrated. Dehydration is often indicated by dark-yellow urine, a dizzy or light-headed feeling, and a dry, sticky mouth.

- **Heat cramps** occur when we get dehydrated through sweating. The muscles in the legs or abdomen can seize up with cramps.
- **Heat exhaustion** occurs when we exercise in a hot, humid environment without drinking enough fluids. It is characterized by slow, short breaths, a weak pulse, shivering or chills, and clammy skin.
- **Heat stroke** also occurs when we exercise in hot, humid weather. When the body's cooling system shuts down, our core temperature increases. Symptoms include clammy skin and sometimes loss of consciousness.

Cold weather concerns

Normal body temperature is around 37 degrees Celsius (98.6 degrees Fahrenheit). In extreme cold, our body loses heat faster than it can produce heat.

- **Hypothermia** occurs when the body's core temperature drops below 35 degrees Celsius (95 degrees Fahrenheit). Symptoms include chills, shivering, confusion, slow movement, and poor coordination. To prevent hypothermia, wear appropriate clothing on cold days and change into warm clothes immediately after outdoor activity.

Wearing protective clothing is essential to prevent frostbite to fingers, toes, and ears that are exposed to the cold. The affected area becomes frozen and, in severe cases, may have to be amputated.

Water Safety

Every year, Canadian federal and provincial governments spend millions of dollars on campaigns to reduce drowning in oceans, lakes, rivers, and swimming pools and to warn beachgoers of the risks of rogue waves.

Each year as well, tragic and avoidable snowmobile deaths occur across Canada when riders crash through ice and are immersed in cold water. Other immersion deaths involving motor vehicles on ice include ATVs and ice fishing using a road vehicle.

Most of these deaths are preventable if safety rules are followed.

- **At the pool.** Effective supervision of children around water requires watching them constantly. If children are under the age of five, you should stay in the water with them. Take young children with you if you leave the pool area even for a few minutes. Make sure that a resuscitation chart is posted on a wall close by and read it carefully.
- **At the beach.** Always swim within the area that is supervised by a lifeguard. If there is no lifeguard, ask an adult in authority where it is safe to swim. Do not swim alone. Read and obey all water safety signs.
- **Strong currents.** Strong currents can pull swimmers hundreds of metres offshore. If you are caught in a current, stay calm, float on your back with the current, and call or wave for help. If you are a strong swimmer, try to escape the current by swimming parallel to the shore. Alternatively, travel downstream feet first to protect your head.
- **Fast flowing water.** Never swim in water that is flowing quickly. Test the speed by tossing in a twig—but do not go in if you have doubts.
- **Shallow water.** Many people suffer neck or head injuries from diving into shallow water. Always check whether it's safe to swim or dive by asking someone who knows the area, such as a park ranger.
- **Cold water.** Lake water can be much colder than you anticipate, and sudden immersion can cause physical distress and shock. If you start to feel uncomfortably cold, get out of the water right away.
- **River banks.** Do not stand near the edge of river banks—they could give way and you could tumble into the water.
- **Water sports.** Always wear a **personal flotation device (PFD)** such as a life jacket during water sports or while boating—and never drink alcohol while doing any kind of water sport.
- **Know your terrain.** When snowmobiling, survey the area you are riding in and identify any potential danger spots. Avoid snowmobiling in the dark, when it is more difficult to detect unsafe conditions.
- **Verify ice conditions.** Ensure that ice is at least 25 centimetres thick before snowmobiling on it. Snowmobiles are heavy and require thick ice for support.

Section 8.1 Review

1. Suggest effective, attention-catching ways to post safety tips in your school or community.
2. A friend teases you for using sunscreen. What arguments could you make for reducing exposure to UV radiation?
3. Identify all safety hazards associated with an outdoor activity such as canoeing, and suggest ways to minimize them.

8.2 Promoting Positive Mental Health

Most of us experience times or situations when we feel sad, worried, afraid, anxious, or depressed. These occasional feelings are part of being human. For some of us, however, these kinds of feelings can be more severe and long-lasting. When negative feelings such as anxiety or depression don't go away, it's time to reach out for help from others. We can reach out to our friends and family. We can also seek help from a teacher, counsellor, elder, social worker, peer support worker, or medical professional.

The best way to understand mental health is to view it as a *continuum*. Our position on this continuum may shift from time to time depending on events in our lives. Good mental health takes balance—and that means participating in productive daily activities, maintaining fulfilling relationships, adapting to change, and coping with stress.

Factors that Enhance Mental Health

Mental health and emotional and spiritual well-being are enhanced by both external factors and internal factors (or personal characteristics).

External factors include social, economic, and cultural circumstances. A supportive social network, including family, other trusted adults, and friends, is important. We also need to be given clear boundaries and expectations to feel safe and to have a sense of purpose.

Access to a clean environment with plenty of green spaces can also benefit our mental health and well-being.

Poverty can make it more difficult to cope from day to day, although financial stability does not guarantee mental and emotional well-being.

Internal factors can include a strong sense of self, coping and self-monitoring skills, the ability to make healthy choices, and a feeling of cultural pride.

A green ribbon is often used to promote discussion and awareness of mental health issues.

For many First Nations, Inuit, and Métis individuals, for example, understanding one's culture and identity is an important component of spiritual health.

Positive internal factors help build self-esteem, self-confidence, self-discipline, and effective problem-solving and decision-making skills. They help us cope with negative influences, make wiser choices, and avoid getting involved in things that could lead to injury or harm.

Internal factors that enhance mental health can be strengthened by stress and mood management techniques. These include deep breathing, mindfulness, meditation, yoga, qi gong, pryer, or healing ceremonies such as smudging.

Warning Signs of Mental Health Concerns

What warning signs might indicate that someone is not doing well mentally or emotionally? The person may withdraw from relationships, have trouble sleeping or eating, or respond to situations in a new way. Sometimes people turn to substance use to suppress negative feelings.

People struggling with mental or emotional difficulties may experience

- inability to cope with stress
- rapid mood shifts, with greater anger or irritability
- insomnia or sleep disruptions
- feelings of sadness, anxiety, hopelessness, or worthlessness
- recurring negative thoughts about themselves, others, and the future
- thoughts of suicide

What should you do if you see these signs in a friend or family member? First, listen empathetically to the person's worries, and respond with gentle encouragement. Do not tell a distressed individual to "Just snap out of it!" or offer a quick-and-easy fix.

Offer practical and emotional support. Lend a friend a hand completing homework, sit and talk over a cup of tea, go for a walk, or watch a movie together. If warning signs don't go away, offer to accompany the person to a counselling session or a doctor's appointment.

Being supportive, respectful, and attentive with friends is an excellent way of letting them know you are there for them when times are tough.

Coping with Stress

Stress can be both positive and negative. It can motivate you for a big game or an exam, but it can also impair your ability to concentrate, solve problems, or reach goals. How we cope with stress can have a major effect on our mental health and well-being.

One of the most important long-term strategies for managing stress is developing healthy habits—getting enough sleep, following good eating practices, and staying physically active. Here are some tips for reducing or eliminating stress, whether it's anxiety about a major life event or simply the challenges of day-to-day life:

- **Keep moving.** Physical activity is one of the best ways to keep stress away. Physically fit people are better able to handle the long-term effects of stress.
- **Get enough rest and sleep.** When you are overtired, a problem may seem much more serious than it actually is. Schedule breaks and relaxing activities such as music, art, reading, gardening, or cooking.
- **Eat healthy foods.** Start your day off with a good breakfast, do not skip meals, and stay away from so-called energy drinks.
- **Spend time in nature.** Get outside alone or with friends to feel connected to the natural world.
- **Get organized.** Planning and getting organized really help when you have many things to do.
- **Record your strategies.** Keeping a journal to describe what you did to deal with a stressful situation means you can look back later to see how well it worked.
- **Talk to someone.** Instead of keeping your feelings bottled up, talk to a person you trust or respect. Someone else's views can help.
- **Help someone else.** Signing up for a volunteer project is a good idea, but helping others can be as easy as saying hello.
- **Avoid feeling isolated.** Socialize with people who are positive.
- **Practise positive thinking.** Reframing or changing your thoughts to see the positive in a situation can help change our perceptions for the better. Sometimes stepping back from a problem helps us see that things are not as bad as we had thought.
- **Hug a friend or family member.** Make sure you get and give plenty of hugs. Hugging is a wonderful way to help reduce stress.

Worrying is an understandable and expected part of life, but it becomes a problem if a person has ongoing feelings of worthlessness, stops enjoying activities, or feels as if nothing good will ever happen. If you have these feelings and they do not go away, it's important to seek help.

Suicide Prevention

Approximately 3,500 Canadians per year—about ten every day—die by suicide.

The **Canadian Association for Suicide Prevention (CASP)** is a non-profit organization dedicated to suicide prevention. CASP aims to reduce the suicide rate and to minimize the negative consequences of suicides and suicidal behaviour on families and communities.

CASP offers crisis worker certification courses and runs a yearly national conference for researchers, health professionals, and others concerned with suicide prevention.

CASP does not provide counselling, but it can refer you to a crisis centre in your area—as well as support groups for survivors or people affected by suicide.

If a person talks about having suicidal thoughts, even jokingly, take it seriously. Such talk may be a call for help. It is very important to tell a trusted adult about someone's suicidal thoughts and behaviours. You are being a good friend.

Suicide warning signs and how to get help

Many people who have died by suicide gave some or even many indications of their intentions. People may be giving warning signs if they demonstrate any of the following behaviours:

- making a will, giving away favourite things, saying goodbye
- producing poems or drawings about people killing themselves
- writing suicide notes
- obtaining the means to kill themselves
- verbalizing plans either directly ("I'm going to kill myself") or indirectly ("You won't need to worry about me any more")

What you can do to seek help

Suicide is a complicated issue with no easy answers. If you or someone you know is having suicidal thoughts, remember that help is available. Helplines like the **Kids Help Phone** (1.800.668.6868) can provide immediate assistance.

If you or someone close to you feels desperate and needs help immediately, you can also call a **crisis hotline** or go to the **emergency department** of the hospital nearest you. In some communities, **mobile crisis units** can send mental health professionals to your home.

Your family doctor can also refer you to an appropriate **mental health support worker** who can provide long-term counselling services.

Section 8.2 Review

1. Identify some external factors and internal factors that influence mental health.
2. What are some warning signs and symptoms of a mental health concern?
3. Compare things that you and your friends like to do to combat negative stress. Which strategies would you rate as most effective, and why?

8.3 Preventing and Responding to Threatening and Violent Behaviours

Threatening and violent behaviours such as bullying, harassment, dating violence, and hate crimes have countless damaging effects on individuals and on the spirit of a society. Although you may not have been involved in an abusive or violent incident, it is likely that you have witnessed one in some form—perhaps even in your own school or neighbourhood.

The media constantly bombard us with violent images and language, almost to the point where degrading and harming others is presented as a normal part of life. However, we all have a responsibility to try to eliminate all forms of abuse and violence wherever they occur, as a precondition for safe schools and safe communities.

Bullying and Harassment

Bullying is the use of power against another person in intimidating, aggressive, or violent ways. Bullying occurs among people of all ages—in homes, schools, public spaces, and workplaces.

People who bully others believe the people they target are worthless, stupid, unpopular, or just different. Bystanders provide an audience for people who bully and feed their perception of power.

In the past, bullying tended to consist of direct physical aggression, such as pushing, slapping, and hitting. These forms of bullying are considered assault and are increasingly prohibited.

People who are bullying also use more indirect methods such as teasing, taunts, threats, intimidation, extortion, and coercion. Teasing can be focused on race, weight, appearance, sexual orientation, gender, and gender expression.

Some people who bully become experts at excluding peers, spreading rumours, and using emotional blackmail, ostracism, and manipulation. Bullying can also involve inappropriate sexual behaviour.

Cyberbullying—bullying over the internet—is on the rise and is especially difficult to detect and control. (For more on this topic, see Section 8.4 in this chapter.)

When they are made repeatedly, unkind comments, ridicule, taunts, or slurs are a form of **harassment**. They can lead to more serious types of abuse, including physical, sexual, or racial harassment, dating violence, gender-based abuse, or even gang violence.

The consequences of using personal power to humiliate or injure another person become more serious for people who bully as they get older. They become legally accountable for any harm they cause to others.

A blue ribbon is often used to promote awareness and prevention of bullying.

How to handle bullying

Many people who are bullied are too afraid to tell anyone or to fight back. Nevertheless, there are several strategies you can apply if you or someone else is being bullied:

- Try ignoring the person who is bullying and walking away. Losing your temper is often easier than refusing to engage with the person who is bullying, but it's not a good strategy.
- Do not participate! Part of the power of someone who bullies comes from having an audience. Do not laugh at what is happening, and do not let yourself be provoked into taunting someone else.
- If you see bullying or hear it being planned, tell an adult or a person in authority right away.
- Make sure your school recognizes the problem and actively enforces an anti-bullying policy.
- If the bullying has already occurred, encourage the person who has been bullied to talk to an adult. Lending support lets the person know that they are not alone.
- Do not blame yourself—people who bully often choose their victims at random.
- Find people who share your interests and spend time with them. Being bullied can damage your self-confidence. If you and your friends support one another, a bully is more likely to leave you alone.
- Recognize that the person who is bullying also needs help and support. Look for ways to promote and participate in models of conflict resolution that feature "restorative practices." These practices give people who bully an opportunity to ask for forgiveness and make amends to the person or persons they have harmed.

Anti-Bullying Tactics

If you are being bullied...

- Stay calm and act confident, even if you do not feel that way. A bully is less likely to continue if you project self-confidence.
- Do not use derogatory names or become aggressive. It may provoke further violent action.
- Do not carry a weapon. It is illegal, and the weapon may end up being used against you or someone with you.
- Tell someone. School counsellors, teachers, or other adults can often address the problem. If you want to remain anonymous, you can call the **Kids Help Phone** (1.800.668.6868).

The best plan is one that prevents the conflict from becoming worse.

Combatting Sexual Harassment

Sexual harassment is any unwanted sexual behaviour of any kind. It can involve a one-time occurrence or a pattern of behaviour exhibited over a period of time. It can occur in schools, homes, or workplaces, in public places, and on public transit. Some examples of sexual harassment are

- sexually suggestive comments or gestures
- unwelcome sexual invitations or requests
- sexual emails or texts
- unwelcome and/or repeated remarks about a person's body, appearance, gender, or sexual orientation
- a display of sexually offensive pictures
- whistling, cat calls, and other sexually suggestive noises
- winking, throwing kisses, or licking the lips
- inappropriate touching
- exposure of a person's genitals

People of any gender or sexual orientation can experience sexual harassment—from individuals of the same or opposite sex. Victims are not always the target but are affected by the offensive conduct.

Sexual harassment is demeaning and degrading, and therefore cannot be tolerated. It damages a person's dignity and self-esteem and can lead to anxiety, depression, or other mental health issues.

Dealing with sexual harassment

- Harassment should not be ignored because it can lead to violence. If you are being sexually harassed, use refusal and assertive communication skills to tell the person to stop.
- If you can, remove yourself from an unsafe situation and seek out a setting where you feel protected from further physical or verbal harm.
- If telling the person to stop has no effect, report the behaviour immediately to a school counsellor, a parent or guardian, an elder, a doctor or public health nurse, a police officer, or another trusted adult.
- Be sure to document all relevant details related to incidents of harassment to support your version of events, because the person who is harassing you will, in all likelihood, deny that they committed the wrongful actions.
- Be prepared to describe your experiences as calmly, clearly, and consistently as possible to someone in a position of authority who can help you.
- Have faith in your own power and integrity, and do not back down from confronting the individual who has harmed you. Remember that your taking a stand may well help someone else in a similar situation.

Signs of Intimate Partner Violence

- In healthy relationships, partners show respect, support, and affection for each other. In physically, emotionally, or sexually abusive relationships, anger, jealousy, possessiveness, cruelty, and manipulation prevail.
- The perpetrator may be easily frustrated and prone to violent or dangerous behaviour.
- The abused partner might be depressed and may start missing school or work and withdrawing from friends. He or she may have difficulty sleeping or concentrating on schoolwork or other tasks and may have unexplained injuries, such as bruises, cuts, or bite marks.
- Victims of abuse are often afraid of ending the relationship. Some worry that they will never find someone else. Unfortunately, the results of staying in an abusive relationship are potentially much worse.
- Anyone can be at risk of being involved in an abusive relationship, but people who have experienced some form of violence or abuse in the past may be more prone to intimate partner violence or dating violence.

Confronting Dating Violence

Dating violence is any sexual, physical, or psychological attack made by one partner on the other in a dating relationship. Dating violence can happen in both heterosexual and same-sex relationships.

It is important to understand and recognize what an unhealthy dating relationship entails—and how to end it—because dating violence is alarmingly common.

This type of violence is often motivated by lack of respect for a partner, insecurity, a power imbalance, or lack of the skills needed to manage healthy relationships. People who are prone to act violently toward a partner can be set off by external factors such as stress or substance abuse.

Individuals caught in a violent relationship may find it difficult to express what they want or do not want. They may feel pressured into sexual behaviour and risks that they would not normally take.

If you are experiencing dating violence, talk to a trusted adult—and get involved in activities that build your confidence and self-esteem.

Getting Help to Deal with Intimate Partner Violence

If you think you are in an abusive or unhealthy relationship, tell a trusted adult exactly what your partner has done. The adult can help you talk to a parent or guardian, an elder, a counsellor, school authorities, a social worker, or even the police.

Talking openly can be the first step in developing adaptive and coping skills that will lead to a stronger sense of self, greater well-being, and healthier relationships as time goes on.

Responding to and Preventing Hate Crimes

According to the Criminal Code of Canada, a **hate crime** is a crime that is committed against one or more people because they are members of an "identifiable group"—those who can be distinguished by colour, race, religion, ethnic origin, or sexual orientation. The two most common forms of hate crime are racism and homophobia.

Hate crimes are illegal, but sometimes even the threat of sanctions does not stop someone from committing a hateful act. Schools need to take the initiative, focusing on strategies to prevent hate crimes rather than just increase the severity of the punishment.

Students can take part in programs that teach respect for diversity. Find out what your school's policies are, and work with others in the school community to make the policies stronger if necessary.

Whatever happens, do not ignore the crime but, rather, document relevant details and report it. It is not likely to stop without some form of action.

As difficult as it may be, your first step may be to tell the person to stop. If other people have witnessed the incident, find out whether they are willing to back up your report to help put an end to the aggression.

Challenging racism

Racism is a belief in the superiority of a particular race, as well as the prejudice or antagonism that results from this attitude. Violence directed at other groups based on religion or culture is called **ethnic violence**.

When people focus their own fears and hatred on a specific group, they treat the targeted group as less than human. This can open the door to acts of violence or degradation.

Racist attitudes and behaviour never stand up to the test of reason—they are based on ignorance and prejudice rather than on facts. That is why they need to be challenged on every occasion.

Canada takes pride in being a genuinely multicultural society. Our population reflects a vast diversity of cultural heritages and racial groups—the result of centuries of immigration. We can keep our identities, take pride in our ancestries, and feel a sense of belonging. We are able to choose our friends or partners based on who they are, not on what they look like or their ethnic background.

Eliminating homophobia, biphobia, and transphobia

The terms **homophobia** and **biphobia** refer to fear of, or contempt for, other people because of their sexual orientation or gender identity and expression. **Transphobia** is fear of, or contempt for, others because of their gender identification. Like racism, these are considered hate crimes in Canada.

You can help prevent homophobic, biphobic, or transphobic behaviour in the following ways:

- Accept that students in your school may identify as lesbian, gay, bisexual, queer, transgender, gender neutral, or other.
- Think about how you and your friends have formed your attitudes, and acknowledge and discard any biases or prejudices. Biases such as **heterosexism**—the misconception that everyone is or should be heterosexual—do not necessarily indicate homophobia, but they can indicate stereotypes that stigmatize LGBTQ+ individuals.
- Keep your own language inclusive and free of biased or stigma-laden terms, and do not accept sexist or homophobic language in others.
- Show kindness, dignity, acceptance, and respect to students who are being targeted or ostracized, and listen to what they have to say.
- Stand up for anyone who is being disrespected or teased, and use assertive communication skills to tell the abusers to stop. If the situation feels unsafe, help the person to get away or get help.
- Consider participating in gay–straight alliances and other student-led campaigns to promote understanding and respect for diversity.

By taking the initiative to be inclusive and socially responsible, you can help make your school and community a better place for all students.

Section 8.3 Review

1 Identify some strategies for reducing or eliminating bullying and harassment.

2 What are some factors that can motivate dating violence, and what can be done to stop it?

3 Analyze why hate crimes seem to be on the rise, and how this trend might be addressed.

It is important to challenge misconceptions about sexuality in our culture because these misconceptions inflict harm by denying the self-worth of each individual.

8.4

8.4 Safe and Healthy Online Relationships

The instant and universal nature of communication provided by social media offers many benefits. Everything you post online and the following you build can foster intimate relationships—in some cases, with people you might not have met otherwise.

However, electronic communication also poses risks that we need to be aware of—every time we send a text or go online.

Benefits and Risks of Online Technologies

Online communication technologies allow you to connect with more people, more rapidly and more widely. That brings both benefits and risks.

Instant information. Social media can expose you to many more creative ideas and resources than ever before. You can invite lots of input to help solve a problem or find a wealth of information and entertainment.

Digital versus real intimacy. The ease of connecting with others online can be so attractive, however, that we begin to think that these relationships are more intense and more committed than they really are. We might even alienate the people in our daily lives while we pursue intimacy with online friends.

It is important to find the right balance between online and offline relationships for the sake of our personal and social well-being.

Emotional contagion. Social media relationships can also expose you to emotional contagion. If someone in your online social network is angry, lonely, or hostile and takes it out on you, you may be more likely to transmit this mood to others in your digital network.

Negative online behaviours. Similarly, some people interact in more mean-spirited and more critical ways online than they would in real life. This is a significant problem, because negativity, bad manners, and even abuse expressed online can multiply quickly.

Unrealistic comparisons. With the inflow of information about how other people are living their lives, it's easy to feel we cannot compete. We may feel that our successes are less and our failures greater than they are.

Adopting an online persona. We might also feel pressure to adopt a persona, as we know that people are always watching us. It can feel as though we have exchanged a real identity for an online one.

Various studies reveal that social media participation can generate a type of anxiety among teens known as FOMO—fear of missing out.

Online threats to personal safety

Online communication technologies can also expose us to distinct threats to personal safety.

- Given that even "private" online conversations are not really private, it's easy to lose control of information. Online sharing can spread an offhand comment we never intended to broadcast, with a lasting negative impact. Furthermore, *always* refrain from sexting, as you may be setting yourself up for exploitation and humiliation.
- Pornography can be easily downloaded. Its sexual imagery is often disturbing and demeaning, especially to women.
- People you chat with online may not be who they say they are—and they could be sexual predators.
- People can easily bully and harass others online. Internet trolls hide behind their anonymity to post sexist, racist, homophobic, xenophobic (hatred or prejudice against people from other countries), and hate-filled comments—and they rarely experience any consequences.

Not everyone who plays violent video games will exhibit violent behaviour, but continued exposure to violent and aggressive imagery can desensitize people.

Protecting Yourself Online

You can protect yourself online by developing a few good habits:

- Chat online only with people you know and trust. Otherwise, try using an online nickname.
- Do not give out personal information or information that can identify you such as photos or videos.
- Remember that any information you post online is public. Think before you act—and do not talk about private matters, including sex.
- Use security software to protect your computer. Choose passwords that cannot be figured out easily, and never share your passwords.
- Respect other people's privacy online, and avoid sharing or posting any images without consent.
- Stand up for yourself and others in response to online abuse, but remember that it's better to end the contact than to risk escalating the problem.
- If a problem persists, get help. Use safe and anonymous channels set up by your school or community to report abusive incidents, such as sharing sexual images without consent.

Benefitting from Social Media Relationships

Considering the risks, how can you make sure you benefit from your social media relationships?

- **Limit the time you spend on social networks.** While it's tempting to keep checking your online messages, other parts of your life will suffer if you do so too often.
- **Regulate your emotions.** If you find yourself getting irritated, angry, or distressed and you do not know why, it's time to back away from the computer. Spend time outside or connect with someone in your offline life to gain perspective on your reactions.
- **Take care not to compare yourself to others.** It is all too easy to envy other people's lives at the expense of not fully exploring all the opportunities that are open to you.
- **Set guidelines for your online relationships.** Have a clear idea of why and how you want to befriend people in your networks.
- **Maintain a balance between your online and offline life.** Form a real-life network of friends as well—and find lots of fun activities to do together.

Section 8.4 Review

1 Compare the benefits and risks of using online communication technologies.

2 List four strategies to protect your online safety.

3 If you or a friend were a victim of cyberbullying, how would you respond, and why?

8.5 Conflict Resolution and Anger Management

Conflict is an inevitable part of life. It is how you respond that shapes events. Most disputes can be resolved calmly and in a way that benefits both sides. This section looks at the different types of conflict that can arise and strategies that can be used to minimize their effects.

Types of Conflict

There are four different types of conflict: internal, interpersonal, intragroup, and intergroup.

- **Internal conflict.** An internal conflict comes from opposing emotions you feel within yourself. When you can see both sides of an issue, it can be hard to choose which path to take, whom to support, or where to draw the line. For example, you may strongly support animal rights but also see the benefit of breeding programs at zoos to protect endangered species. Internal conflicts may cause you to question some of the core values and beliefs you learned in childhood.
- **Interpersonal conflict.** An interpersonal conflict is a dispute between people. The way you deal with such conflicts will depend to some extent on your relationship with the other person. You probably handle conflict with a parent differently from conflict with a friend, a teacher, or an employer. Managing conflict with someone in a position of authority can be tricky. Make sure you know what your rights are, as well as the rights of the other person. For example, you have the legal right to refuse to do work that is unsafe.
- **Intragroup conflict.** Conflict between members of a group or team falls into the category of intragroup conflict. In these types of conflicts, members within a group disagree on some issue. For example, a group of friends who are organizing a party might disagree over what type of music to play. The group members may base their choices either on loyalty to their friends or on their own personal preferences. Conflict or disagreements ensue.
- **Intergroup conflict.** Intergroup conflict occurs when two groups (or teams) are in opposition to each other. In sports, as in life, healthy competition is normal, but a dispute can have serious consequences if it is not handled appropriately. Team sports have umpires and referees to ensure that conflicts are properly managed. Intergroup conflicts also happen outside of sports, but the "referees" have different names. In the business world, professional mediators often negotiate disputes between different groups. Other kinds of real-world referees include moderators, arbitrators, judges, and negotiators.

Anger Management Strategies

You may have heard the term "fight-or-flight." When we feel threatened, we may react with anger (fight) or run away (flight). Some people feel they cannot hear, focus, process information, or make good choices when they are angry. Aggression can increase dangerously in such circumstances.

How well you channel your own anger and other people's affects how well you can resolve a conflict. **Anger management strategies** such as the ones described here can help:

- **Determine the cause.** You can often control anger better once you identify what is causing it.
- **Use relaxation techniques.** Deep breathing or exercising can help you gain and keep control of what you do and say when you feel angry.
- **Avoid triggers.** Sometimes people behave in ways that are almost guaranteed to make others angry. (That can be intentional, such as when siblings squabble.) Think about what might trigger a conflict, and avoid words or behaviours that are likely to generate anger.
- **Walk away.** A cooling-off period gives you time to calm down and express your anger in ways that are not aggressive or confrontational.
- **Think before you react.** You can control your reactions better by knowing which anger management strategies work best for you. The one strategy that works well for everyone is to stop to think before lashing out in anger against another person. Pause to consider the damage that an angry outburst might cause to a relationship you value or to your sense of self-worth.

Six steps to letting go

People who find it difficult to keep their anger in check may find the following six-step approach to letting go helpful:

- Stop blaming yourself.
- Try not to take things too seriously.
- Deal with your feelings rather than trying to suppress them.
- Put yourself in the other person's shoes.
- Make peace with the past.
- Seek professional help if you find you cannot control your anger.

Resolving Conflicts

Conflict resolution involves many kinds of skills. Problem-solving and decision-making skills can help us to identify the causes of conflict as well as possible solutions.

You can learn and practise **conflict resolution strategies** to help you handle various types of conflict:

- **Choose a good time to talk.** Find a time when no one is angry, upset, or tired and when you will not be interrupted.
- **Think before you speak or act.** Give others time to explain their case, and give yourself time to assess all aspects of the situation.
- **Listen actively.** Let the other person know that you are paying attention by an occasional "uh huh" or a nod. When it's your turn, summarize the other person's points to demonstrate that you have understood.
- **Empathize.** Empathy is the ability to put yourself in other people's shoes and recognize that their needs are as important as yours. Empathy is important in conflicts because it leads to a greater understanding on both sides.
- **Show patience and respect.** Always speak respectfully to the other person. Use non-confrontational body language, and give the other person plenty of physical space.
- **Stay clear, calm, and direct.** It is invaluable to be able to express yourself calmly, clearly, and in a non-threatening way, not only in a conflict but all the time. If you feel anger start to rise, walk away for a few moments to regain your composure. Focus on expressing yourself in ways that will be taken seriously, while showing respect for the other person.
- **Communicate assertively.** Avoid being aggressive or abusive. Always use "I" to say what you think. If necessary, repeat your message so that the other person understands. Maintain eye contact, use confident body language, and control your emotions.
- **Think critically.** Do not accept things at face value. Instead, dig deeper to find the root causes of the problem and to develop workable solutions.
- **Think outside the box.** Try to approach problems from different viewpoints. You may find new solutions that have not been tried before. If the opposing parties brainstorm solutions together, that is even better.
- **Be willing to compromise.** Be open to several options. The key to getting along in a group, small or large, is to find compromises that work for everyone.
- **Stick to your agreement.** Once you find a compromise, you might even write up a contract that both parties promise to honour.

Sources of Information and Support

When it comes to personal safety, mental health, and conflict management, many sources of support are available. You might also seek help from a family member, a coach, your doctor, or any trusted adult with whom you have a good connection.

Most communities have various sources of information and support, such as the following:

- a hospital emergency department
- community services referral agencies
- crisis hotlines
- community health centres
- distress centres
- mental health clinics
- self-help groups
- mosques, churches, parishes, and other religious places of worship
- PARTY (Prevent Alcohol and Risk-Related Trauma in Youth). This is a one-day injury awareness and prevention program at Sunnybrook Health Sciences Centre. This program for youth 15 and older is a vital part of a growing community effort to reduce injury and death in alcohol-, drug-, and risk-related incidents.

Ask your teacher (if you feel comfortable), or go online to learn what steps to take to find the information and support you might need.

Section 8.5 Review

1 Identify the most common causes of conflict.

2 Which three strategies would you recommend to family members or friends to prevent a conflict from getting worse?

3 Without sounding preachy, how could you help a friend who has an out-of-control temper to manage anger better?

Methods of Resolving Conflicts

Collaboration
Solving differences together is always best. Mutual understanding merges and both parties are better off.

Negotiation
Most conflicts can be sorted out with a little give and take on both sides.

Mediation
Mediation means that a third party—an independent person or a peer—gives direction to the disputants.

Confrontation
Confrontation risks escalating a conflict to the point at which aggression is the only possible next stage.

Aggression
Aggression produces only winners and losers—and sometimes neither.

Josh's Story

"To help make the world a more respectful and inclusive place, treat people how you would want to be treated. I'm a people person. I love to make friends. I just go out and be me and that's it."
— Josh Beckstead

Chapter 8 Review

Knowledge and Understanding

1 What is sexual harassment, and how can it be stopped?

2 What can you do to help reduce or eliminate hate crimes or racism in your school or community?

3 Describe four different types of conflict, and list positive ways to respond to each.

Thinking

4 What do you consider to be the most serious outdoor safety risk in your province or territory? Justify your thinking.

5 In a one-page report, evaluate the effectiveness of your school's safety plan with regard to bullying and harassment. Cite specific examples, but be sure to respect privacy and confidentiality.

6 Expand on this chapter's suggestions for healthy ways to benefit from your social media relationships.

Communication

7 In a small group, discuss how to educate teens about the dangers of careless online activity. Ask for permission to post your suggestions on the school's website.

8 In a small group, discuss the most effective strategies to combat online bullying or harassment, and have a group spokesperson present your ideas to the class.

9 Write a short skit or create a short video that demonstrates effective conflict resolution strategies in action.

Application

10 Draw up a five- or six-point personal safety plan for use before, during, and after a social, recreational, or sports event.

11 Outline a plan to address mental health concerns relating to yourself, a friend, or a family member, should any concerns arise.

12 Research some mental health resources, crisis centres, and support services in your community. Compile your findings in a brief report to share in class.

Appendices

ACT High School CPR & AED Student Manual

Saving people — Touching lives

HEALTH PARTNERS

AstraZeneca Canada
Sanofi Canada
Amgen Canada

HIGH SCHOOL CPR & AED STUDENT MANUAL
TABLE OF CONTENTS

Acknowledgments

The guidelines for CPR are based on guideline recommendations from the 2015 International Consensus on CPR and ECC Science with Treatment Recommendations (CoSTR).

"A healthy diet includes..." was borrowed from "Healthy Eating: Healthy Eating Basics," published online by the Heart and Stroke Foundation of Canada. The Chain of Survival™ logo is a registered trademark of the Heart and Stroke Foundation of Canada. Illustrations of heart and lungs were reproduced with permission of St. John Ambulance, Canada.

MODULE 1

THE 4 "Rs" OF CPR

RISK

RECOGNIZE

REACT

RESUSCITATE

Hi There!

INTRODUCTION: CHAIN OF SURVIVAL

Welcome to the world of CPR... Cardiopulmonary Resuscitation. You are going to learn how to help someone who chokes or someone whose heart stops. CPR is the "heart" of any first aid program. (Sorry for the pun).

This CPR course teaches the 4 "Rs" of CPR:

RISK: factors in your life that predispose you to developing heart problems or a stroke;
RECOGNIZE: how to recognize a serious developing emergency;
REACT: what to do when you see a developing emergency;
RESUSCITATE: how to do CPR, how to use an AED and how to help someone who is choking.

Why learn this? Don't paramedics look after pre-hospital cardiac arrests and other serious emergencies? Why you? Well, the key to surviving these emergencies is a chain reaction. It's the **CHAIN OF SURVIVAL**, the emergency response system we need if we are going to improve survival from emergencies:

Healthy Choices
Early Recognition
Early Access
Early CPR
Early Defibrillation
Early Advanced Care
Early Rehabilitation

Someone's life may depend on what you learn in this course. Don't forget that for a minute, but learning it will be fun too. There is a lot of information. It is wisdom you can take home to your family now, and carry with you throughout your life. So let's get into it.

Without Oxygen, Serious Damage to the Brain Starts in 4 to 6 Minutes.

Other organs, like the heart, last longer without oxygen, but only minutes longer.

Nitroglycerin

Many people take nitroglycerin spray when they get angina. It helps open up the circulation and relieves the pain.

THE HEART AND WHEN IT BREAKS

What is a Heart Attack?

Oxygen is carried by blood through a network of blood vessels, nourishing the organs of the body. Without circulating blood, without oxygen, these organs start to die.

Without oxygen, serious damage to the brain starts in 4 to 6 minutes. Other organs, like the heart, last longer without oxygen, but only minutes longer.

Like any tough muscle, the heart needs oxygen delivered to its tissues.

The heart has its own blood vessels that supply its muscle. When one of these arteries gets blocked (e.g. by plaque, which is junk like fat or cholesterol) the area of heart muscle that the artery nourishes is suddenly deprived of circulation... no blood circulating, so no oxygen... the person experiences chest pain.

If the blockage opens up after a little bit, the pain goes away (until next time). This is what is called **angina**.

If the artery stays blocked, the pain remains and the area of affected heart muscle starts to die. This is what most people call a **heart attack**. (**Trivia**... doctors call this a **myocardial infarction)**.

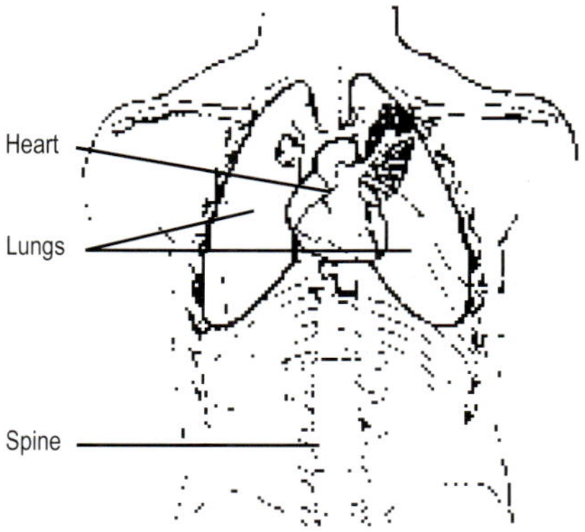

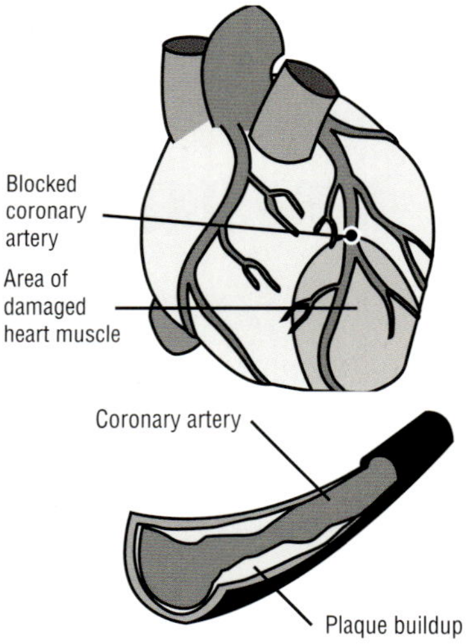

What is Cardiac Arrest?

When a heart stops beating, it is no longer pumping blood to the rest of the body. That heart is in "**cardiac arrest.**"

When the heart muscle is suffering because it can't get oxygen, it gets irritable. (If you choke and can't get air, you'll get irritable too!) The heart's main muscles, the ones around the **ventricles**, lose their rhythmic pumping action and may start to **fibrillate**. This is a squirmy kind of muscle contraction that doesn't pump blood called **ventricular fibrillation** (because it is a ventricle and it is fibrillating). This most common kind of cardiac arrest is also the most treatable.

What is CPR?

Starting **Cardiopulmonary Resuscitation** on a person whose heart has stopped means two things:

1. Pushing on the person's chest forces blood to flow through the body.
2. Mouth-to-mouth breathing provides oxygen to the lungs.

What is Defibrillation?

When you call 911 and start CPR on someone, paramedics or firefighters will be there in a few minutes. They attach a small computerized device (an automated external defibrillator, otherwise known as an AED) to that person. It delivers a special kind of shock to the heart, trying to kickstart it, trying to reset the heart muscle and restore its smooth pumping action. This is called **defibrillation**... ZAP!

Defibrillation A Shocking Thing!!

When you deliver the shock and the heart stops fibrillating, you have de-fibrillated it.

"PAD" Public Access Defibrillation

Look for new, small, easy-to-use defibrillators hanging on walls in lots of places, just like fire extinguishers.

Lifeguards, security guards, even hotel desk clerks and the server in your favourite restaurant are being trained to use them. Seriously!

These are for the general public to use. That is how they get their name.

WHAT IS A STROKE?

If you understand heart attacks, you can figure this out. Remember how arteries to the heart can get blocked by junk, like fat or cholesterol? The area of heart muscle that the artery nourishes suddenly receives no circulation (no blood circulating, so no oxygen) and the person experiences a heart attack.

It is the same in the brain. After a lifetime of burgers and fries, an artery gets blocked up by all that cholesterol. When the area of the brain nourished by that artery has no oxygen, it gets damaged. As a result, a person may have a sudden headache, slurred speech, vision problems or sudden weakness of the face, an arm or leg. That is a **stroke**.

Someone thought, "Hmm, if it happens in the heart and we call it a heart attack, why not call this a '**brain attack**'?"

One kind of stroke is different. Instead of getting clogged up like a usual stroke, a blood vessel bursts. You can't tell without tests at the hospital which kind of stroke it is. No matter which kind of stroke it is, you have to help in the same ways you will learn here.

That part was tough. You learned about blood circulation and oxygen, about hearts that stop when they fibrillate and start when someone defibrillates them. And you learned a little about strokes or "brain attacks".

Now you are ready to learn the 4 "Rs" of CPR. Knowing them lets you make the system move when an emergency occurs.

Let's tackle those 4 "Rs."

MODULE 2

Risk Factors You Can Control

Cigarette smoking
High blood cholesterol
High blood pressure
Diabetes
Obesity
Lack of exercise
Excessive stress
(for some people)

A Healthy Diet Includes:

1. Eating lots of vegetables and fruit.
2. Choosing whole grain foods more often.
3. Eating a variety of foods that provide protein.
4. Avoid highly processed foods.
5. Watch out for sugar-sweetened beverages.

THE 4 "Rs" OF CPR

I. Risk Factors — Heart Disease and Stroke

A risk factor is something that increases the chance of heart disease or stroke. If you have several relatives who have heart trouble, you too may be at risk. This, and simply getting older, are two risk factors you can't do much about.

But you can do something about most risk factors. Let's talk about these and about being "**Heart Healthy**".

Smoking

Smoking causes lung cancer and stinky breath. It is also the leading cause of heart disease in Canada. It is the worst, most direct, most personal, kind of air pollution. Even if you don't smoke, those smokers around you are offering you second-hand air pollution.

High Blood Cholesterol

High blood cholesterol means lots of fat in the blood. Some is produced by our body, while other fat comes from our food. Too much cholesterol can cause heart disease or stroke. To help reduce your chances of having high cholesterol, eat more vegetables, fruits and grain products, limit the amount of fat in your diet and get plenty of physical exercise.

High Blood Pressure

High blood pressure can damage your heart and blood vessels, increasing your chances of having a heart attack or stroke. It means your heart has to work harder to pump blood through those pipes, your blood vessels. It can run in families, but diet and stress may affect it too. Your blood pressure can be too high and you might not know it. You may feel pretty normal but it is still dangerous. Blood pressure should be checked regularly.

Diabetes

Diabetes affects the level of sugar and fat in your blood. It is a problem, but it can be managed. People with diabetes will do better and have fewer complications like heart trouble or stroke if they eat properly and follow their doctor's instructions.

Obesity

Obesity is not good. Your heart has to pump harder all the time to move blood around.

You Were Going to Ask...

So what's the difference if your heart works hard because you are overweight or because you exercise? Why is one good and the other not? Well, a sweaty weightlifter does a workout, hits the showers, rests a day and comes back for more. His muscles get stronger. If he had to lift weights 24 hours a day, his body odour might get stronger, but his muscles, well, they would just wear out.

We Are Not Just Talking About Heart Attacks!

Remember, emergencies needing CPR happen for various reasons. People of all ages drown, get electrocuted or bleed from injuries. With your CPR training, you will be able to assess if a person with one of these problems needs CPR.

Lack of Exercise

Lack of exercise is another risk factor. Remember, your heart is a muscle. It works better if you keep fit and active.

Stress

Stress affects the body in very physical ways. If you are nervous, if your hands are shaking, you can be sure things inside of you are also being affected. If you are stressed for a long period of time, your body may break down. Heart problems can be one of the results.

Lifestyles, Risk Factors — Some Thoughts

You never find parents **encouraging** kids to smoke. They learned the little things about smoking, like the expense and the bad breath! Some have learned about the bigger costs, about wheezing, heart disease or lung cancer.

And what overweight adult wouldn't love to be fit and thin? Yet, unlike smoking, you still find adults who don't know what a healthy diet is. Some kids are growing up with poor diet habits they pick up at home. There is more work to do here.

If some adults in your life smoke or are overweight, it may not be totally their fault. It can be really tough to lose weight or stop smoking. Now, many of those adults have health problems. You can be smarter, developing healthy living habits. You are able to learn more about what to do... and about what not to do. Set your own course.

Well, that is one "R" out of the way. Don't be afraid to go and tell the folks at home what you have learned about Risk factors. You may help someone make wiser choices.

Now let's move on to Recognition...

II. Recognize

"Early Recognition" means realizing someone may be having heart trouble, a stroke or a cardiac arrest.

Signs of a Heart Attack

The 5 "Ps"

Signs of a Heart Attack — Look for the 5 "Ps"

Pain — heaviness, tightness, squeezing or pressure, which may spread to the neck, jaw, shoulders or arms.
Pale — pale skin (that is often sweaty).
Puffing — trouble breathing.
Pooped — feeling very tired.
Puking — feeling sick to the stomach or actually vomiting.

Signs of a Stroke

Signs of a Stroke

If you recognize what might be a stroke: sudden numbness, tingling or weakness of the **F**ace, an **A**rm (or a leg), or **S**peech problems, **T**ime is critical. New treatments for strokes (e.g. clot busters) must be given within a few hours to work.

No driving to the hospital! Call 911 for an ambulance which will take you to the right hospital.

F ace is it drooping?
A rms can you raise both?
S peech is it slurred or jumbled?
T ime to call 9-1-1 right away.

Act F A S T because the quicker you act, the more of the person you save.

Denial and Fear

People often have trouble accepting that they might be experiencing a heart problem or stroke. You might see:

Denial — "I'm too young!" "It will go away with a little rest!" The thought, "It can't be happening to me."

Fear — the person may be terrified inside and afraid to go to the hospital.

Be firm. If the signs are there suggesting a heart attack or stroke, the person needs to be taken by ambulance to a hospital quickly.

It is important that you Recognize that what is happening in front of you may be a real emergency. Remember the signs for a heart attack and the signs for a stroke and don't let yourself be paralyzed by Fear and Denial.

Suspect a Cardiac Arrest?

Occasional gasps?

Treat as if there is no breathing.

Signs of a Possible Cardiac Arrest

If the person is unconscious, tap the shoulders and shout, "Are you alright?" and check for breathing. If there is no response and no breathing, assume the person is in cardiac arrest. If the person still has occasional gasps, treat that as if there is no breathing.

Now let's learn how to React...

MODULE 4

If the Person Has Chest Pain... What Do You Do?

Remember:

"Hazards & Holler"

Then... stay with the person and offer a little PLT

Position — P

Loosen clothing — L

Talk, reassure — T

Alert ! Alert !

People who have been ill often wear a "MedicAlert" bracelet or necklace. It will often have information about the person's allergies, past medical history and medications.

III. React

What if it might be a Heart Attack or Stroke?

Check for hazards — make sure there is nothing around that can hurt you (e.g. electric wires, traffic, fire, glass, gas).

Holler for help if you are alone. If you are still alone, call 911 for an ambulance. If someone hears your call, get that person to call 911 and send someone for an AED.

If a person with chest pain, which might be a heart problem, has Aspirin tablets nearby, suggest chewing or swallowing 2 low dose (81mg) pills, or just a regular Aspirin while waiting for the ambulance. If the person already took Aspirin or has been told not to take it in the past, wait for the paramedics instead.

If you think the person may be suffering a stroke, no Aspirin.

While waiting for the ambulance there are several things you can do to make a person more comfortable:

> **Position the person** so he/she is most comfortable. Usually sitting or lying down will be best but the person will usually tell you what works best;
>
> **Loosen tight clothing** at the neck or waist;
>
> **Talk to the person.** Let him or her know help is on the way. Remember, as much as possible, stay with the person. If the person becomes unconscious, he/she will need your help even more.

What if the person is in cardiac arrest?

Shout for help, call 911, send someone for an AED and start CPR.

What to do until the ambulance gets there?

Paramedics are trying to find you. Be Visible with Information. Get out front. Wave and/or flash lights when you see them.

What information should you give them about the person?

Medications — Gather any medications. Bag them if you can.
Allergies — Are there any? Ask. Write them down.

So, Hazards and Holler, a little PLT, and flash the paramedics. Remember that, and you know how to React when you see an emergency develop.

Now let's move on to Resuscitation...

HOLD IT! Stop everything! Did they really just say you were supposed to "flash the paramedics"?

NO! NO! They meant to say "flash the lights"! ...the porch lights ...the house lights ...any lights.

MODULE 5a

IV. Resuscitate (CPR)

CPR: Simple as CAB-D

Compressions
Airway
Breathing
Defibrillation

If a person has stopped breathing with no circulation needs CPR until either the person is breathing and circulation returns, or until medical help takes over ... and how do you do that?

CPR is as simple as CAB-D!

C — **Compressions.** Start chest compressions to help blood circulate.

A — **Airway.** Something in the mouth blocking air from getting in? Get it out of there.

B — **Breathing.** Not breathing? Do mouth-to-mouth. Breathe for this person.

D — **Defibrillation.** If you started CPR, make sure help is coming, especially someone with a defibrillator.

Well, you **remember your CAB-D**, and just do what you are trained to do on the next pages!!!

The High School CPR & AED program offers two options for teaching adult/teen CPR.

1. The 'Heartsaver Level CPR' course in which the CPR technique includes giving breaths.

2. The 'Compression-Only CPR' course in which the CPR technique does not include giving breaths.

"I've been trained. I can do this."™

Often people stand around in an emergency waiting for someone else to do something, hopefully someone trained and capable. Hey! ... If that is you, Focus! Act now!! "I've been trained. I can do this."™ Say something. Do something. Act now! Others will help.

Ask permission to help...

Before touching a person who needs help but who is still conscious, you must ask for and get permission to help. Say you have had CPR training. Ask, "May I help you?"

Go ahead and help if the person is unconscious or is a young child who is alone. The law assumes the person wants help. Provide care just as you would want someone to care for you. Do what you are trained to do. Do your best.

ONE RESCUER CPR — ADULT

If someone collapses...

Remember say to yourself: "I've been trained. I can do this."™

1 **Check for hazards.**

Make sure there is nothing around that can hurt you (e.g. electric wires, traffic, fire, glass, gas).

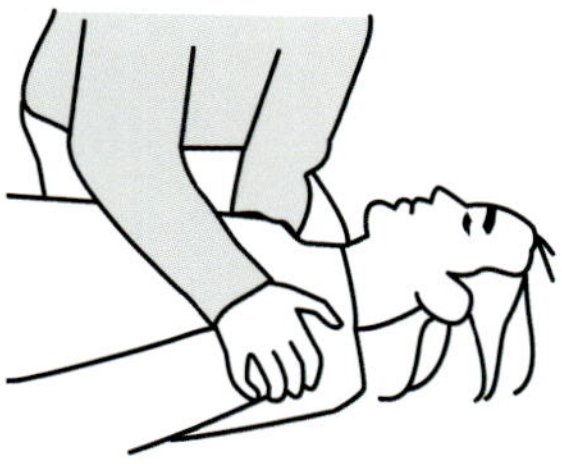

2 **Assess responsiveness and check for breathing.**

Tap shoulders, call out to the person. Look at the face and chest for signs of breathing.

> Note: You are checking an unconscious person for breathing and suddenly the person takes a breath or two - a sort of gasp or sigh. Sometimes this happens, especially if a person's heart has just stopped. It will not look like normal breathing. The person is in cardiac arrest.

3 **Call 911.**

Or your local EMS, or have someone call for you, if the person is not moving, is not responsive and is not breathing (or there is only an occasional gasp of air). Send someone for an AED.

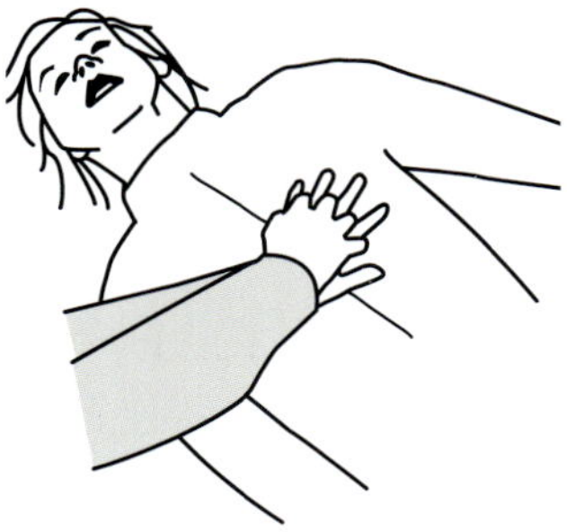

4 **Landmark for chest compressions.**

Compress the lower half of the person's breastbone in the centre of the chest, between the nipples.

Place the heel of your hand on the breastbone in the centre of the chest between the nipples. Place the heel of your second hand on top of the first so that your hands are overlapping and parallel.

Interlock your fingers off the chest. Position your shoulders directly above the heels of your hands. Keep your arms straight, with your elbows locked in position. Your instructor will show you how.

5 **Give chest compressions.**

Compress straight down on the breastbone. Compress at least 5 cm (2 inches) at a rate of 100-120 compressions per minute.

Push hard, push fast.

It helps if you count aloud (e.g. 1 and 2 and 3 and 4 and 5 and 1 and 2 and 3 and 4 and 10 and 1 and 2 and 3 and 4 and 15 and etc. on up to 30).

Without losing contact with the chest, allow the chest to return to its normal position between compressions. Find your landmark with each new cycle of compressions.

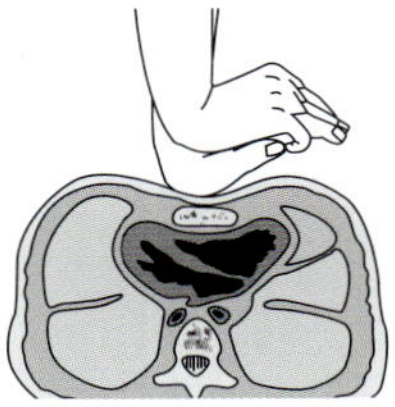

Note: Push hard! Push fast! Chest compressions squeeze the heart and all the big blood vessels in the chest. That is how CPR circulates blood. It only provides about 30% of normal circulation but studies show early CPR is the most important thing to save someone whose heart has stopped.

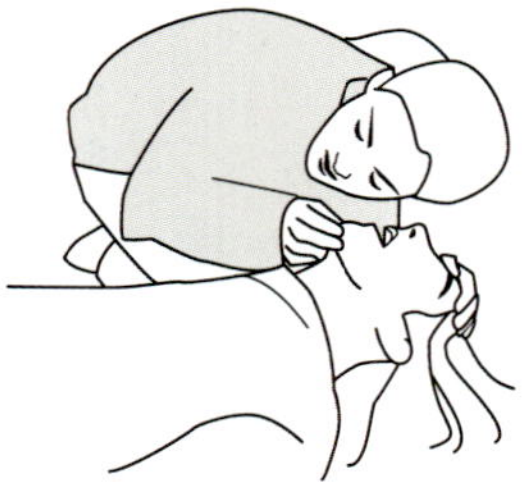

Note: If your teacher is teaching you the 'Compression-Only CPR' course (CPR technique without giving breaths), proceed from Step 5 directly to Step 8. If your teacher is teaching you the 'HeartSaver CPR' course, continue with Steps 6, 7 and 8.

6 After 30 chest compressions, **open the airway** using the head-tilt chin-lift method.

Head-tilt Chin-lift:

Place one of your hands on the person's forehead and the fingers of your other hand under the bony part of the lower jaw near the chin. Tilt the person's head back by pushing down on the forehead. At the same time, gently lift the chin up to open the airway.

7 **Give 2 breaths** (if the person is not breathing).

Maintain the head-tilt chin-lift. Pinch the person's nose, take a normal breath and cover their mouth with your mouth (assuring a good seal at the nose and mouth).

Give 2 breaths, 1 second for each breath. Watch the person's chest to make sure it rises and falls with each of your breaths.

If your breaths do not go in, reposition the head to open the airway, check your seals at the mouth and nose, and try again.

Continue CPR at a rate of 30 compressions to 2 breaths.

*Note: You are learning how to do mouth-to-mouth breathing, but some people may be nervous to do it as part of CPR. That is OK, but it is important to do something! If you are reluctant to perform mouth-to-mouth, just do the chest compressions ***(Compressions-Only CPR)***. It's better to do something than nothing!

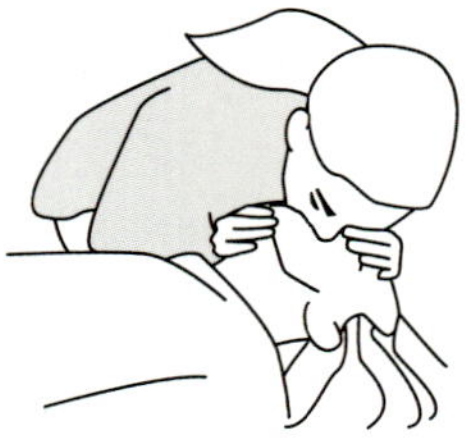

8 **Continue CPR** even when someone brings an AED. Stop when the AED is ready to use or when you see signs of life, breathing, movement or Emergency Medical Service (EMS) personnel take over.

Getting Tired?

If you get tired while doing CPR and there are others around who know how to do it, ask for someone to take over. Do your best until help arrives.

MODULE 5b

DEFIBRILLATION

"PAD"
Public Access Defibrillation

An AED placed where everyone can see and use it.

Look for them in airports, health clubs, arenas, city swimming pools … and in your school.

Remember: The most common kind of cardiac arrest is due to ventricular fibrillation. The heart's main muscles, the ones around the ventricles, lose their rhythmic pumping action. They fibrillate - a squirmy kind of muscle contraction that doesn't pump blood.

Work quickly and you may be able to fix this. Do CPR and use an AED.

What is an AED?

It is a device that automatically analyzes heart rhythm and, if necessary, gives an electric shock to return a heart to its normal rhythm.

Sticky pads are placed on the chest to allow the AED computer chip to see if the heart's electrical rhythm is in ventricular fibrillation. If it is, the computer tells you to stand back. Then it sends a type of electrical shock through the pads to the heart, trying to reset the heart. If the person's heart starts to beat normally again - if it is no longer fibrillating - you have defibrillated someone … and saved a life.

How do I use an AED?

If you find someone in cardiac arrest, this is what you do...

Remember, say to yourself, "I've been trained. I can do this."™

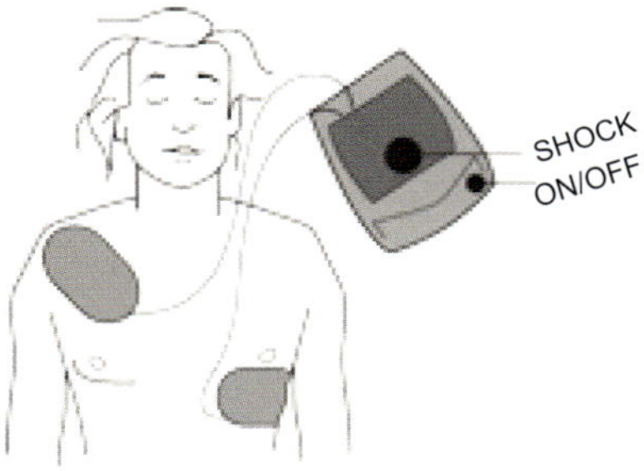

1 **Call 911** or your local EMS, or have someone call for you, if the person is not moving, is not responsive and is not breathing. Send someone for an AED

2 **Start CPR.**

3 **If there is an AED…**

- Turn it on and follow the voice prompts.
- Continue CPR while setting up the AED.
- Expose the chest, dry skin, and remove excess hair or medical patches from the person's chest prior to applying the pads.
- Apply the electrode pads to the person's bare chest.
- Stop CPR when the AED tells you and DON'T LET ANYONE TOUCH THE PERSON. If the AED prompts you to press the shock button, do it. (Some AEDs shock automatically, but most will tell you to press a button to shock the person.)
- Start CPR again when the AED tells you. Follow the voice prompts. If you see signs of life, breathing, and/or movement, place the person in the Recovery Position.

"All Clear!"

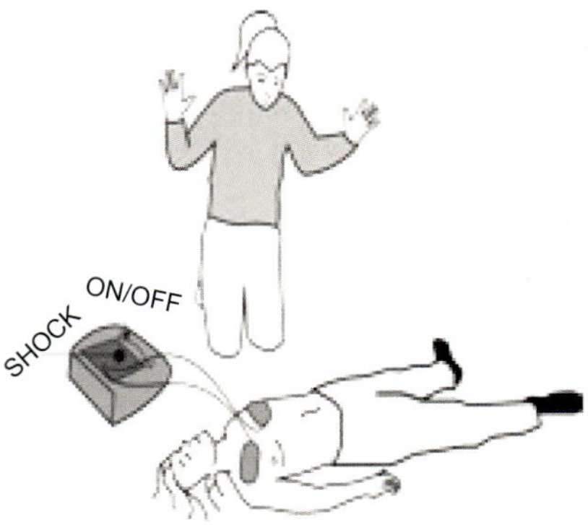

MODULE 5c

CHOKING

When a person chokes on food or a small object that is lodged in the throat, air cannot reach the lungs. The person may die if help is not given immediately. Recognize that a person is choking by the universal distress sign of choking — hands to the throat.

When a person chokes, the throat or airway can be either mildly or severely blocked.

A **mildly blocked airway** allows some air to get in. If a choking person can still speak, cough or breathe, you know the blockage is not complete. Encourage the person to cough to try to clear the obstruction themselves.

With a **severely blocked airway**, there is no air getting in. If that person can't speak, cough or breathe, you have to **React** quickly. This is a serious emergency.

Adult Conscious

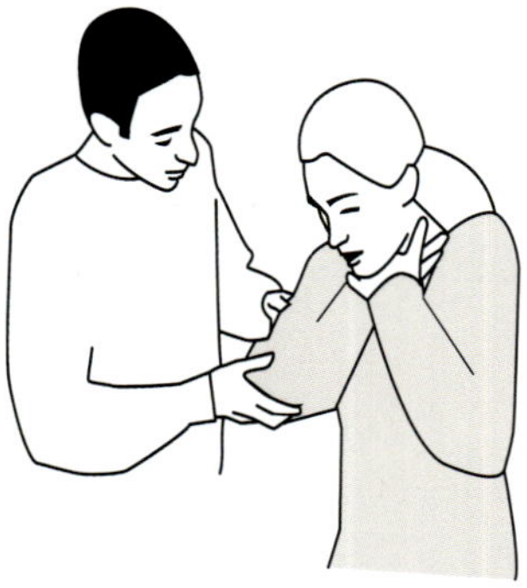

1 **Assess the airway blockage**. Remember, say to yourself, "I've been trained. I can do this."™ Ask, "Are you choking?" "Can I help you?"

2 **Holler for help**. Reassure the person and explain what you are going to do. Call 911 or your local Emergency Medical Service (EMS), or have someone call for you if the person is having difficulty breathing.

"Are You Choking?"

3 **Give abdominal thrusts** (sometimes called the Obstructed Airway Manoeuvre) if the choking person cannot speak, cough or breathe. Stand behind the person and wrap your arms around his/her waist. Make a fist with one of your hands and place the thumb side of that fist in the belly button area, slightly above the belly button and well below where the ribs meet. Grasp your fist with your other hand and press inward and upward with a sudden forceful thrust.

4 **Repeat abdominal thrusts** in rapid sequence until either the obstruction is removed or the person becomes unconscious. When the obstruction is removed, the person should see a doctor to rule out complications from the obstruction or the abdominal thrusts.

If the Choking Person Becomes Unconscious

(Carefully support the person to the ground. You have already activated EMS. Begin CPR.)

1 You have already **called 911** or your local Emergency Medical Service (EMS), or had someone call for you. You have already sent someone for an AED.

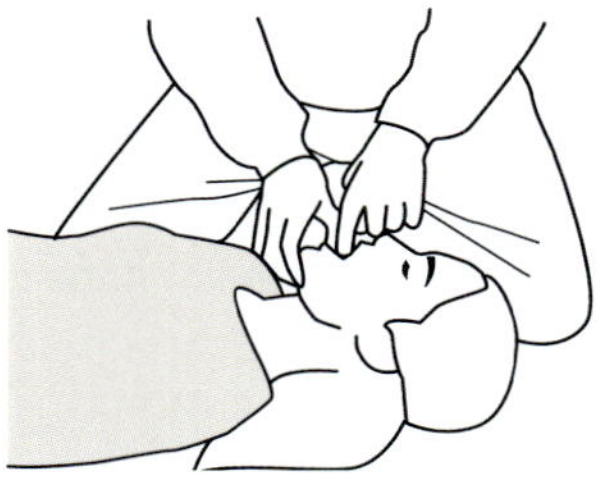

2 **Landmark and give 30 chest compressions.** This may remove the obstruction.

3 **Open the mouth and look for the obstruction**. If you can see the obstruction, try to remove it with a hooked finger.

4 **Open the airway** using the head-tilt chin-lift. Even though you may not be able to see the obstruction, it may have loosened enough to let some air pass by it and enter the lungs.

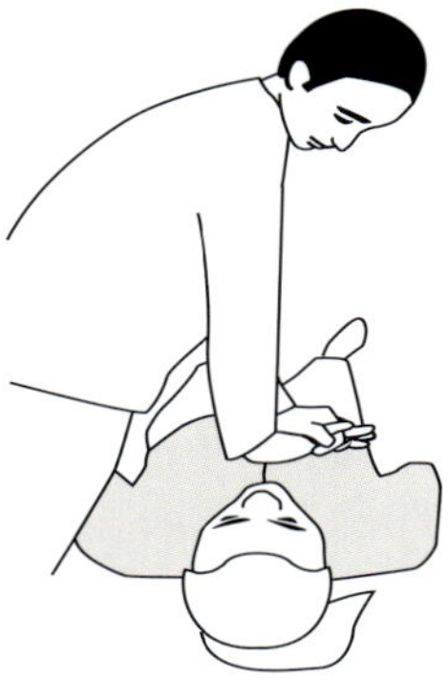

5 **Try to give a breath**. If air won't go in, reposition the head, check your seals at the mouth and nose and try to give another breath.

6 **Repeat sequence of chest compressions**, looking in the mouth, opening the airway and attempting to ventilate until you are successful, or until medical help takes over.

Adult Found Unconscious

Remember, say to yourself, "I've been trained. I can do this."™

1 **Check for hazards**. Make sure there is nothing around that can hurt you (e.g. electric wires, traffic, fire, glass, gas).

2 **Assess responsiveness and check for breathing**. Tap shoulders, call out to the person. Look at the face and chest for signs of breathing.

3 **Call 911** or your local EMS, or have someone call for you if the person is not moving, is not responsive and is not breathing. Send someone for an AED.

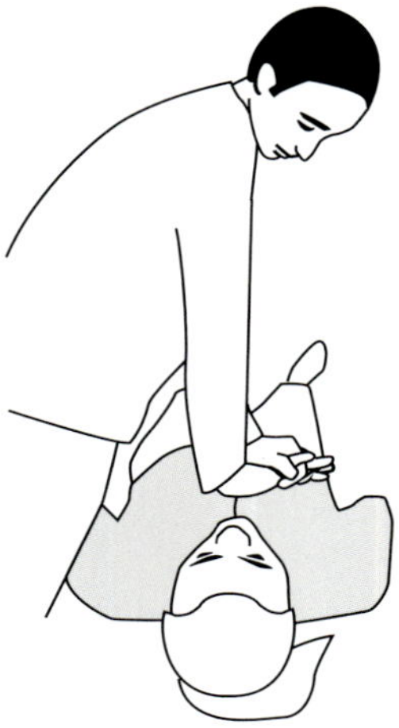

4 **Landmark and give 30 chest compressions.**

5 **Open the airway** using the head-tilt chin-lift method.

6 **Try to give a breath** if the person is not breathing. If air won't go in, reposition the head, check your seals at the mouth and nose and try to give another breath. If the chest still does not rise, conclude that the airway is blocked by something.

7 **Open the mouth and look for the obstruction**. If you can see the obstruction, try to remove it with a hooked finger. Open the airway and attempt to ventilate again. If air still won't go in...

8 **Repeat sequence of chest compressions**, looking in the mouth, opening the airway and attempting to ventilate until you are successful, or until medical help takes over.

Follow-Up Care *(Your Teacher will show you how)*

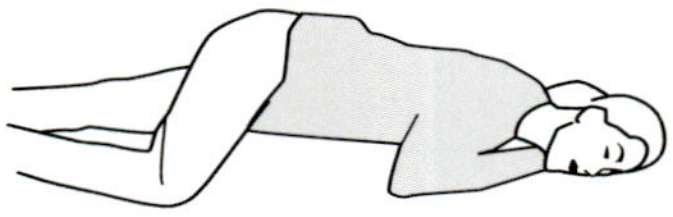

Recovery Position

When the person starts to breathe, place him/her into the **recovery position** if injuries permit. The person may gag or vomit, and the recovery position will help keep the airway open and allow fluids to drain from the mouth. Monitor the breathing carefully. The person may stop breathing again. Stay with the person until medical help takes over.

For information on different rescue scenarios you may encounter, as well as new information relating to the world of CPR (including guideline updates), check out ACT's website!

MODULE 6

It's not just about CPR!! It's about

CP-R-R-R-R...

So you thought this CPR course was all about learning CPR. Well OK, that is understandable. But wait! Think of what you have learned. Think about the **4 "Rs"**.

You now know about **Risk** factors, that a life of burgers and fries and stinky cigarette breath can be a short one. Lots of overweight adults and parents who struggle to quit smoking would have loved to know what you know when they started out.

Maybe you will never see anyone collapse. Maybe you won't ever have to do CPR. But chances are greater that you will be around someone who falls ill. You have learned to **Recognize** if that person might be having a heart attack or stroke.

Seeing someone in your family having chest pain, looking pale and sweaty (remember your Ps) should push you to help them get to the hospital. If your dad has chest pain, he may not know about clot busters. But you do. You were not trained to be shy. Step up! **React!**

The "CPR thing" is only part of this course. **Resuscitate** is only one of the **4 "Rs"**. Not everyone who falls sick has a cardiac arrest, but you can still help them. The sequences of CPR are important to remember. However, it is more likely you will need to remember the **"5 Ps of chest pain"** than how to do CPR. You need to remember **"Hazards and Holler and a Little PLT."** You need to be **Visible with Information** for the paramedics.

Be a champion! You have the knowledge. You know **"Risks"**. Help others avoid trouble.
But if there is trouble, you know **"Recognize"**. You know **"React"**.
And yes, sometimes you will need to **"Resuscitate"** and do CPR.

SO, LET'S TEST YOUR 4 "Rs" IQ...

True Scene From Life

Seventeen-year-old Kasia Smetny-Sowa was vacationing in Halifax when she saw a man collapse at a local tennis club. The Ottawa student rushed to his side, where a crowd was already forming. The man had no pulse and an ambulance had been called. It had been two years since Kasia had learned CPR at her high school, but she remembered what to do. She began CPR and, with help from another bystander, continued until the ambulance arrived.

Success!

Thanks to Kasia, 60-year-old Nick Weatherston is alive and well. And for that, his wife Pat is eternally grateful. "I feel we were truly blessed by a guardian angel."

SCENES FROM LIFE

1 You are on a field trip to a local museum. You notice that Mrs. Jones, one of your teachers, is standing very quietly. She does not look well. Speaking with Mrs. Jones you **Recognize** her pain might be cardiac.

(The 5 Ps of Chest Pain)

You **React**, getting someone to look for another teacher. If there is none, you get someone to call 911. You sit Mrs. Jones down and open a window so she can get some air.

(Hazards and Holler and a little PLT)

Now that the paramedics are coming, ask Mrs. Jones about medications, allergies, etc... While you are doing that, ask someone else to go to the front door of the museum to guide the paramedics to where you are.

(Visible with Information)

2 Your allergic brother comes home from a friend's house wheezing badly. He played with a dog there and his asthma is severe. He is using his inhaler too often and not getting better. You holler for your mom, who calls 911. You reassure him help is coming. You stay right with him. You tell your mom to bag his inhalers and go to the front to wave at the paramedics as they come down the street.

(Hazards and Holler and a little PLT)
(Visible with Information)

Your brother gets sicker and suddenly you realize he is very quiet. He is unresponsive and is not breathing. You are scared, but you start CPR.

(Resuscitate)

3 You are hanging out with your friends at the mall when you hear a man yell that a woman has collasped. Bystanders are already performing CPR and you know where the AED is located.

(CAB-D)

4 You are on the sidelines of a school basketball game when you see a player suddenly collapse on the court. Another player yells that he/she is not breathing.

(CAB-D)

True Scene From Life

Mark was watching television in his basement when his mother called him to hurry upstairs to help his 46-year-old father Joe, who was choking. He rushed upstairs to find his father standing in the kitchen, his face red and his hands at his throat. No sound was coming from his mouth. He couldn't breathe.

Despite his shock, Mark sprung into action, performing the Obstructed Airway Manoeuvre, which he had learned in school. A piece of his father's chicken dinner shot across the room.

MORE SCENES FROM LIFE

5 At a family dinner, you notice your grandmother is suddenly having trouble speaking. She drops a fork and can't pick it up. She looks ill. You **Recognize** she might be showing signs of a stroke.

(The "P" Sign of a Brain Attack — Paralysis)

You **React**, pointing out to everyone that Granny is sick. You note this could be a stroke. Your mom calls 911 as you help Granny into the recovery position.

(Hazards and Holler and a little PLT)

While your dad checks Granny's purse looking for medications, you ask your mom questions. You write the answers down for the paramedics. Your brother moves the car out of the driveway so the ambulance can get close to the house.

(Visible with Information)

6 You and your dad are alone watching TV. You suddenly notice he doesn't look comfortable. He says he has pain, which you **Recognize** might be a heart problem.

(The 5 Ps of Chest Pain)

You **React,** urging him to call 911. You tell him you are afraid for him and you let him know about clot-busters. He says it is nothing, probably indigestion. He is sweaty and vomits. You decide to act on your own. You call 911. You help dad lie down.

(Hazards and Holler and a little PLT)

You leave him for a second to turn the porch light on so the paramedics can see the address number. You ask your dad where his medications are. When the paramedics arrive, you tell them dad's medications are in the bathroom.

(Visible with Information)

7 At a party, a girl is found unconscious in the backyard pool. Someone has lifted her to the poolside. You step up and say, "I know CPR." (It scares you a little that people are suddenly listening to you and doing what you say). You **Recognize** that this person is in cardiac arrest.

(CAB-D)

You **React**, yelling for someone to call 911.

(Hazards and Holler and a little PLT)

And you **Resuscitate**, starting CPR. Be careful to support her neck, because you don't know how she fell into that pool! You tell someone to get any information about this girl. Who is she? Does she have a wallet? Does it have any medical information in it? You send someone to the street to flag down the paramedics and guide them through the house to the backyard.

(Visible with Information)
(Resuscitate)

There is No "S rvival" Without "u"

I Know CPR

I know Risks
I know Recognize
I know React
I know Resuscitate

I know CPR!
I know how to use an AED
"I've been trained. I can do this."™

LAST WORDS...
WE WANT YOU TO RATTLE THE CHAIN

Lots of people die. They die from drowning, from heart attacks, from all kinds of things. They are someone's mom or dad, someone's brother or sister, someone's child, someone's friend... you get the picture. Maybe someone in your family died of a heart attack — someone close to you? Was everything done that could have been done? The thing is, some of them didn't have to die. If only someone had known how to help, how to rattle the **Chain of Survival**.

A person collapsing in cardiac arrest will have a much better chance of survival if someone calls 911 fast and starts CPR fast, if someone defibrillates the person fast, and if paramedics arrive fast... all those things, FAST! These are links in the **"Chain of Survival."** The missing link? It's you! That is going to change now that you know CPR and how to use an AED. You are never going to be helpless if someone collapses in front of you.

Not everyone is going to live just because you start CPR. But **no cardiac arrest patient lives if you don't start CPR**. The 911 system, defibrillators, paramedics... forget it all if you don't do CPR until more help arrives. You know how to **"RATTLE THE CHAIN."** You are the key link!

If you feel good about learning this new skill, tell your teacher. But also tell your family and friends. Show them what you have learned. Bug them to take a course as well.

You should refresh your CPR and AED skills over time. There will be changes in the course and you will want to stay on top of things. Flashing a current CPR and AED card might look good when you apply for a job, even babysitting.

Congratulations! Stand up and say, "I've been trained. I can do this."™ No, shout it. Remember, you are CPR trained in your house. You are the one to make a difference, perhaps a difference between life and death for someone because of what you know. Be proud! When someone needs you, step up!

Finally, have you **"RATTLED THE CHAIN"** already? If so, turn to the end of this manual to learn how to tell a **"Rattle Tale."**

GOT SOME QUESTIONS? GET SOME ANSWERS...

1 If I just don't want to do CPR on someone, do I have to?

Some people are nervous about infection if they have to do mouth-to-mouth breathing. Resuscitation emergencies usually happen at home, most often involving people close to you. Hopefully, you will react and help. If a stranger collapses in a public place, you will be equipped to make a difference, to start CPR if necessary. But, it is your decision. If you are hesitant to do mouth-to-mouth, Recognize what is happening, React by calling for help (911) and Resuscitate, performing chest compressions.

2 What do I do if I am reluctant to do mouth-to-mouth?

If you are reluctant to do mouth-to-mouth breathing (e.g. fear of infectious disease, drug overdose, vomit on the mouth, etc.), just performing chest compressions is still valuable. Just making the 911 call can still save a life!

3 Can I get AIDS (HIV) or other infectious diseases from doing CPR?

You may risk infection if you come in contact with someone's saliva, whether it is kissing or performing mouth-to-mouth CPR. The risk is low and saliva has not been known to spread HIV. The real danger from HIV is from intimate sexual contact or sharing needles with an HIV-infected person.

Most people who suffer a cardiac arrest do so at home. We are talking about family. You will usually know if the person has some serious infection.

4 Can I be sued for doing CPR?

Some provinces have a "Good Samaritan Act" or a law like it that protects people who just try to help (visit the ACT Foundation's website for information on your province). Lawsuits just haven't happened if people meant well and tried their best to do CPR the way they were trained. Again, remember most people who suffer a cardiac arrest do so at home.

5 Does everyone whose heart stops need CPR?

It may be no surprise when a person suffering from a serious terminal illness, or extreme old age, has a cardiac arrest. Technically, everyone dies that way. The heart stops. Life ends. CPR is not usually meant for people whose death was anticipated and perhaps quite natural. CPR is meant for those people who have a sudden cardiac arrest — for whatever reason — when it wasn't expected.

6 Should people with a possible heart attack or stroke take Aspirin (ASA)?

If a person's chest pain might be cardiac, doctors often try to give the patient an Aspirin (ASA) pill. It works as a blood thinner, it may limit the damage done by a heart attack. Tylenol or Advil don't work for this. Some patients are allergic to ASA but if the person with pain says, "ASA, no problem. I take it all the time," then OK. Just one is all that's needed. When the paramedics arrive, tell them ASA was given.

If you suspect a person might be suffering a possible stroke, no Aspirin. Let the paramedics decide that one.

7 If someone has chest pain that might be a heart pain, (remember the 5 Ps?) should they take Nitroglycerin?

Many patients take a medication called **Nitroglycerin** that helps open up those clogged blood vessels and relieves the pain of **angina**. If a person with a possible heart pain wants to take Nitroglycerin, help out. Check their pockets or purse. "Nitro" is usually in a little spray bottle. It is squirted under the person's tongue. If you see it, help the person use it.

8 When people fall down unconscious, do I have to worry about their neck?

Sometimes when people collapse, they hurt their neck. Suspect a neck injury when the collapsed person has:

A head injury; Fallen from a height or down stairs; Been in a motor vehicle collision; Bleeding from the mouth, ears, nose; Swelling along the neck or spine.

You have learned how to assess responsiveness, the airway, breathing and how to do mouth-to-mouth breathing. If you suspect either a head or neck injury, you must protect the head and neck from movement when you are doing these things to prevent further injury to the neck.

9 What if it is not a heart attack? Will I look foolish if it is a false alarm?

At the emergency department of the hospital, doctors will examine the person. They may do special tests. If there is an important problem the person may stay in the hospital. But often the problem is not caused by a heart problem and the person may get sent home. Did you make a mistake? No! It is OK to be wrong like this. Even doctors can't tell without tests. Doctors will say you did the right thing. No one should make you feel stupid. Do it again next time.

10 What if the emergency is not caused by a heart problem?

People who drown or choke on something have cardiac arrests, but for different reasons. They can't breathe. Oxygen can't get to their lungs and into their bloodstream. The brain stops working. Soon, they are unconscious. Other organs like the heart start to fail.

People who are badly injured and bleeding may "bleed to death". When they lose too much blood, there is no way oxygen can be delivered to various organs, which soon start to die.

CPR helps maintain the circulation and oxygen delivery for any of these people. By breathing for those people and pumping their hearts, the person doing CPR tries to keep them going until paramedics arrive. Hearts stop for many reasons, not just because of heart problems. CPR can help in any of these cases.

11 What do I do if I suspect an unconscious person may have suffered a drug overdose?

There is an increase in overdoses in many communities, especially due to narcotics (also called opiates) like morphine, heroin or fentanyl. Know the Risk that an unconscious person may have suffered an overdose of narcotics. Recognize whether the person is in cardiac arrest. React by calling for help (911) and for someone who can administer a Naloxone kit. Resuscitate: if the person is not responsive but is breathing, place the person into the recovery position. If the person is not responsive and not breathing, start CPR.

FREQUENTLY ASKED QUESTIONS ABOUT AEDS...

1 What if the person is in water, is all wet or has vomited?

Move the person away from the water. Dry the chest before applying the pads. Yes, even wipe away the vomit if you have to. It is OK to use the AED if the floor is just a little wet or if the person is lying on snow. Just make sure you dry off the chest before trying to stick the pads on.

2 What if the person might be pregnant?

Use the AED as you would for anyone.

3 What if the person is young?

Current CPR and AED guidelines allow you to use an AED on any size of person, including children (considered between 1 and 8 years old) and babies (considered as 1 year old or less). If child or baby pads or a child key or switch are available, use them. If not, use the adult pads. When you put the pads on the chest, make sure the pads don't touch each other. If there is less than 2.5 cm (1 inch) between the pads when they are placed on the chest, place one on the chest (anterior) and one on the back (posterior).

4 What if a person has a medication skin patch?

Don't stick the electrode pads over the patch. Either place the pads to one side or remove the patch and wipe the skin clean before applying the electrode pads.

5 What if the person has a pacemaker?

When you expose the chest, you might see a scar and lump, usually on the left side of the chest. Place electrode pads 2-3 cm away from that.

6 What if the AED says "Check pads"?

Press firmly on the pads to make sure they are stuck on properly. If you had previously dried the chest because it was wet, dry it and try again. If the chest is hairy, is there a way to quickly shave the hair or move the pads a bit to a better area? Is there a second set of pads with the AED? If there is any delay, keep doing CPR.

7 What if another person wants to take over?

Ask if that person has been trained. If not, you are the best one to continue CPR and guide them on how to use the AED.

8 What if a player at a hockey game collapses near where you sit? What if you see people running around, but not doing what you know needs to be done?

Like anywhere else, stand up and say "I know CPR. Call 911 and get the defibrillator!" Do it!

Rescued Someone? Tell Us! Tell Your Teacher. Tell Your Parents To Tell Us.

Or... Tell Us Yourself!

RESCUED SOMEONE? KNOW SOMEONE WHO HAS? TELL US A "RATTLE TALE"!

Rattled the Chain? Someday you may use some of the skills and knowledge you have just learned.

Someone in your family quit smoking because you spoke up? You helped someone recognize they might be suffering from a heart attack or stroke? You had to call for an ambulance for someone? You helped the situation by being Visible with Information? You helped someone who was choking on food? You provided CPR and/or used an AED for someone? Something else?

LET US KNOW! Phone (it's free!):1-800-465-9111

CLOSING NOTES...

Your teacher will give you the ACT High School CPR & AED Program Student Course Completion Card at the end of this program. Wondering what to do with it? Present this card when applying for a job or put it in your portfolio! You've done a great thing by learning CPR and AED, so don't hesitate to let others know you have the skills to save a life! Think about taking more advanced training in CPR and First Aid, and remember to take a refresher course over time!

Saving people Touching lives

The ACT Foundation is a national, award-winning charitable organization that works alongside health professionals, governments and community groups in promoting health and empowering Canadians to save lives. ACT is working with partners to establish CPR and defibrillator training programs in high schools across Canada.

ACT's health partners are:

AstraZeneca Canada
Sanofi Canada
Amgen Canada

Source: "ACT High School CPR & AED Student Manual" reproduced courtesy of the ACT Foundation, 2017

A Call to Action

Truth and Reconciliation Commission of Canada Report

(Truth and Reconciliation Commission of Canada: Calls to Action, p. 10)

1. We call upon all levels of government, in collaboration with Aboriginal peoples, sports halls of fame, and other relevant organizations, to provide public education that tells the national story of Aboriginal athletes in history.

2. We call upon all levels of government to take action to ensure long-term Aboriginal athlete development and growth, and continued support for the North American Indigenous Games, including funding to host the games and for provincial and territorial team preparation and travel.

3. We call upon the federal government to amend the Physical Activity and Sport Act to support reconciliation by ensuring that policies to promote physical activity as a fundamental element of health and well-being, reduce barriers to sports participation, increase the pursuit of excellence in sport, and build capacity in the Canadian sport system, are inclusive of Aboriginal peoples.

4. We call upon the federal government to ensure that national sports policies, programs, and initiatives are inclusive of Aboriginal peoples, including, but not limited to, establishing:

i. In collaboration with provincial and territorial governments, stable funding for, and access to, community sports programs that reflect the diverse cultures and traditional sporting activities of Aboriginal peoples.
ii. An elite athlete development program for Aboriginal athletes.
iii. Programs for coaches, trainers, and sports officials that are culturally relevant for Aboriginal peoples.
iv. Anti-racism awareness and training programs.

5. We call upon the officials and host countries of international sporting events such as the Olympics, Pan Am, and Commonwealth games to ensure that Indigenous peoples' territorial protocols are respected, and local Indigenous communities are engaged in all aspects of planning and participating in such events.

Source: Reproduced from "Truth and Reconciliation Commission of Canada: Calls to Action," 2015

Glossary

% Daily Value—The column in the Nutrition Facts table on a food label that tells you how much, or how little, of a nutrient the serving size contains in relation to what a person needs every day. The recommended daily values are based on two sets of standards: (1) reference standards for fat, saturated and trans fats, cholesterol, carbohydrate, fibre, potassium, and sodium; and (2) recommended daily intakes (RDIs) for vitamins and minerals. Daily values for carbohydrates, total fat, and saturated and trans fat are based on a 2,000-calorie diet since this calorie intake meets the average needs of adults.

Aboriginal Long Term Participant Development Pathway—Recognizing that mainstream models do not necessarily align with Indigenous needs or experiences, Indigenous educators and Sport for Life developed the Aboriginal Long-Term Participant Development Pathway. The stages of the pathway provide programs for all ages with the aim of increasing participation and optimizing performance in a wide range of culturally appropriate activities.

abstinence—A conscious decision to refrain from a behaviour of activity. This resource uses the term in reference to abstinence from all forms of sexual intercourse and other sexual activities.

action plan—A plan that, if well designed and implemented, can help you achieve your health and fitness goals. It can also help you achieve any other changes you would like to make as well—from getting good grades to developing successful relationships. An action plan involves four stages: setting SMART goals, developing action steps, identifying barriers and solutions, and identifying a final "success reward" for yourself.

aerobic fitness—The overall efficiency of the heart, lungs, blood vessels, and muscles used when you exercise. It is a measure of a person's ability to perform sustained physical activity requiring considerable use of the circulatory and respiratory systems. Aerobic fitness results in an increase in the amount of oxygen that is delivered to your muscles, which, in turn, allows them to work harder and longer.

alcohol—A mood-altering substance produced by fermenting or distilling various fruits, vegetables, or grains. Aside from caffeine, alcohol is the most widely used substance in Canada and around the world.

anabolic steroids—Synthetic substances related to male sex hormones (such as testosterone). These synthetic substances promote the growth of skeletal muscle as well as the development of male sexual characteristics in both males and females.

anger management strategies—How well you channel your own anger and other people's affects how well you can resolve a conflict. Anger management strategies such as the following can help: determine the cause; use relaxation techniques; avoid triggers; walk away; think before you react.

biphobia—Aversion toward bisexual people as a group or toward them as individuals. This aversion can be a denial that bisexuality is a genuine sexual orientation or it can be based on negative stereotypes about people who are bisexual. Biphobia is considered a hate crime in Canada.

blood-alcohol concentration (BAC)—The amount of alcohol in a person's bloodstream. BAC is a good measure of how much a person will be affected by the alcohol they have consumed. The drinker's BAC depends mostly on the amount consumed in a given time, but also on factors such as the person's size, gender, and metabolism.

body composition—The relative distribution of fat throughout the body in relation to bone, muscle, and other tissue.

body image—The mental picture each of us has of our own body. Body image includes how you feel and what you believe about your body, how you see yourself, and how you think you look to others.

Body Mass Index (BMI)—An indication as to whether your body weight (mass) is appropriate for your height. BMI is calculated by dividing your weight (kg) by your height squared (m^2).

bullying—Aggressive and typically repeated behaviour that is intended to cause harm, fear, or distress to another individual, including physical, psychological, or social harm, harm to the individual's reputation, or harm to the individual's property; also, creating a negative environment for another individual.

Calls to Action—The Truth and Reconciliation Commission of Canada was one of the results of the Indian Residential Schools Settlement Agreement, the largest class-action settlement in Canadian history. In June 2015, the TRC held its Closing Event in Ottawa and presented the Executive Summary of the findings in its multi-volume Final Report, including 94 "Calls to Action" to further reconciliation between Indigenous and non-Indigenous peoples in Canada.

calorie—A calorie is a measure of heat—technically, it is the amount of energy needed to raise the temperature of 1 gram of pure water by 1 degree Celsius. In a dietary context, what we call a calorie is in fact a kilocalorie (1,000 calories). Calories are a measure of the amount of energy that food will produce as it is processed by the body. This energy can also be measured in metric units—one food calorie equals 4,186 joules.

Canada's Food Guide—A resource developed by the Canadian government to help people plan their food choices on a daily basis. It translates Recommended Dietary Allowances (RDAs) of nutrients into practical advice that people can use to change or monitor their eating habits.

Canada's Physical Activity Guide to Healthy Active Living—A resource developed by the Canadian government that sets out guidelines regarding how much physical activity we should integrate into our lives every day.

Canadian 24-Hour Movement Guidelines for Children and Youth—These guidelines were developed by the Canadian Society for Exercise Physiology (CSEP), the Conference Board of Canada, ParticipACTION, and the Public Health Agency of Canada and are aimed at reducing sedentary behaviours among Canadian children and youth. The guidelines make recommendations, based on sound research evidence, as to how much young people should ideally "sweat, step, sleep, and sit" each day.

carbohydrates—The body's preferred source of food energy. The body converts carbohydrates into a sugar called glucose, which it can use to fuel physical activity and burn fat. The two types of carbohydrates are simple and complex.

cardiorespiratory appraisals—Appraisals that measure the efficiency of your heart and lungs; sometimes regarded as the most important of all fitness appraisals.

concussion—A traumatic brain injury that causes changes in how the brain functions, leading to signs and symptoms that can emerge immediately or over the course of 24 to 48 or 72 hours. A concussion may be caused either by a direct blow to the head, face, neck, or elsewhere on the body, with an impulsive force transmitted to the head that causes the brain to move rapidly and hit the walls of the skull.

conflict resolution strategies—Skills and abilities (such as empathy, clear and direct verbal communication, assertiveness, active listening, patience, tolerance, and creative and critical thinking) that can help you deal with, manage, or resolve stressful or difficult situations involving some kind of conflict.

consent—Consent, in the context of sexual activity, means clearly saying "yes." It is (1) freely given; (2) informed; and (3) something you can take back. Consent means that it is okay to stop sexual activity at any time, and saying "yes" once does not mean saying "yes" forever or "yes" to other sexual activities.

continuum of gambling risk—The degree to which gambling is a problem can be described as a continuum—ranging from the non-gambler, to the casual gambler, the serious gambler, the problem gambler, and, finally, the chronic gambler. Gambling can affect not only our finances and family relationships but also our mental and physical health and future opportunities.

CSEP-PATH—The Canadian Society for Exercise Physiology (CSEP) has developed evidence-based fitness appraisals known as CSEP–Physical Activity Training for Health (or CSEP-PATH). The CSEP-PATH appraisals and training guidelines allow exercise professionals trained through CSEP to design a personalized exercise program to suit each and every individual, including persons with disabilities, children and youth, pregnant women, older adults, and persons with chronic illnesses.

cyberbullying—The use of information and communication technologies to bully others. Cyberbullies use websites, e-mail, and phone or text messages to threaten, intimidate, humiliate, antagonize, embarrass, or socially exclude others or to damage reputations and friendships.

dating violence—Any sexual, physical, or psychological attack on one partner by the other in a dating relationship. Dating violence is often motivated by sexist stereotyping, a lack of respect for a partner, jealousy, insecurity, or an imbalance of power between the dating partners. It can happen in heterosexual and same-sex relationships.

delayed onset muscle soreness (DOMS)—Discomfort that is thought to be a result of microscopic tearing deep within the muscle fibres. The amount of soreness depends on the activity performed and the intensity of the activity. It can occur during any type of physical activity and at any time. DOMS can be minimized by performing proper movement preparation and cool-down exercises.

deliberate practice—An approach to practice that is purposeful and systematic. It involves focused attention and having a specific goal related to improvement in mind. Deliberate practice involves constant feedback, observations, and reflection about how we can improve our performance.

demands capacity framework—To perform at our best and maintain good health both today and in the future, we must build the capacity to handle the demands imposed on us. How we move is central to the daily balancing act of adjusting our capacity to meet our demands. This perspective is known as a demands capacity framework.

depressants—Substances that slow down the body's central nervous system (CNS) and reduce inhibitions. Examples of typical depressants are alcohol, solvents (e.g., glue or gasoline), opiates such as heroin, painkillers, tranquilizers, and sleeping pills.

dietary supplements—Products taken by mouth that contain a "dietary ingredient" and that are intended to add to, or supplement, the foods that you eat. The "dietary ingredients" in these products may include: vitamins, minerals, herbs, or other substances.

dislocation—An injury that occurs when a bone is displaced from its joint. Dislocations are often caused by collisions or falls and are common in finger and shoulder joints. Do not attempt to put the bone back into place yourself as this could cause more damage.

drug dependence—A physical condition in which the body has adapted to the presence of an addictive drug such that if an individual suddenly stops taking that drug, the person will experience predictable and measurable symptoms (known as "withdrawal syndrome"). A person who cannot stop using a substance compulsively despite growing problems in areas such as health, school, family, relationships, or finances has a drug dependence problem.

e-cigarette—An electronic cigarette (e-cigarette) is a handheld device that operates by heating a liquid to produce an aerosol (called a "vapour") that is inhaled (hence the term "vaping" used for inhaling vapour from an e-cigarette). The composition of the liquid varies but it is typically comprised of nicotine, propylene glycol, glycerine, and flavourings, but not all liquids contain nicotine.

eating disorders—Unhealthy eating habits that become so serious that they affect both physical and mental health. They are the outcome of manipulation of food and weight in an attempt by an individual to attain a sense of self-control, achievement, and mood regulation. Eating disorders negatively impact every aspect of the individual's life, and are life-threatening illnesses.

energy balance equation—A model to help you maintain a healthy body weight. The equation requires you to balance your "energy in" (caloric intake) with your "energy expenditure" (the calories you burn in a day).

energy nutrients—Three macronutrients—carbohydrates, proteins, and fats—provide our bodies with energy. These three energy nutrients supply energy (calories) in different amounts: 1 gram of carbohydrate provides 4 calories; 1 gram of protein provides 4 calories; 1 gram of fat provides 9 calories.

ethnic violence—Violence that occurs when people become violent toward other groups based on differences of religion or culture.

fats—A concentrated source of energy that is especially useful during prolonged physical activity. Fats help in the absorption of the fat-soluble vitamins that your body needs.

fetal alcohol spectrum disorder (FASD)—A range of disabilities that may affect people whose mothers drank alcohol while they were pregnant. FASD can cause children to have reduced growth, mental disabilities, and a different facial makeup.

FITT principle—A method that can help you design a fitness training program. FITT stands for the four elements of any good training plan: Frequency, Intensity, Time, and Type of activity.

flexibility—A health-related component of physical fitness; flexibility is the capacity of muscles to stretch.

fracture—The medical term for a broken bone. The three types of fractures are simple, compound, and comminuted.

functional fitness training—An approach to training that focuses on training muscles for daily tasks by simulating common movements that you might perform at home, at work, or during sports or physical activities.

fundamental movement patterns—The fundamental movement patterns (push, pull, squat, lunge, hinge) are basic movements that can prepare us to perform other activities that involve these patterns. Learning these basic patterns is especially important in our younger years but they can be learned at any stage of life. More advanced skills are acquired more easily if these fundamental movement patterns are developed early.

fundamental sports skills—Sport for Life has identified a series of fundamental sports skills that are important to learn, especially in the early years. Once a certain level of competence has been established, these fundamental skills become transferable across various sport activities (throwing, catching, striking, running, jumping, kicking, and agility, balance, and coordination—the "ABCs" of movement).

gender identity—The manner in which an individual experiences their own gender. Gender identity can align with assigned sex at birth or it can differ from it completely. Many people describe themselves as either male or female, but some people experience gender identity differently and identify themselves in another way.

hallucinogens—Substances that alter individuals' perceptions of the world around them, causing distortions in the way they sense their surroundings. While overdoses are rare, these drugs can pose a risk of harm and injuries because they distort sensory experiences. LSD, psilocybin (magic mushrooms), mescaline, ecstasy, and peyote are examples of hallucinogens.

harassment—A form of discrimination involving any unwanted physical or verbal behaviour that offends or humiliates another person. It occurs when someone makes unwelcome remarks about another person's race, religion, sex, age, appearance, or disability; when they threaten or intimidate another person; or when they make unwelcome and harmful physical contact, such as touching, patting, pinching, or punching.

harm reduction—A humane approach to substance use and dependence, and other high-risk health behaviours. Harm reduction strategies recognize that abstaining from substances may not be realistic or even desirable for everyone. Harm reduction strategies tend to be community-based, client-driven, and non-judgemental and they address systems that isolate and marginalize individuals.

Harris-Benedict formula—A widely established way to estimate total daily caloric need. You can use this equation to calculate the amount of energy your body uses when it is at rest (Resting Metabolic Rate), and then multiply that amount by an activity factor (how much activity you do).

hate crime—A crime that is committed against a person or group of people because they are members of an "identifiable group," meaning any segment of the public who can be distinguished by colour, race, religion, ethnic origin, or sexual orientation.

hazard—Any source of potential damage, harm, or adverse health effects on someone or something.

health—The World Health Organization (WHO) defines health as "a state of complete physical, mental and social well-being and not merely the absence of disease or infirmity." Today's concept of what it means to be "healthy" extends beyond disease reduction and injury prevention to include gaining greater control over the factors that enable us to lead healthy and meaningful lives.

health literacy—Health literacy refers to how well a person can access, understand, and use the health information needed to make good health decisions for themselves. People who are not health literate have difficulty using the everyday health information that is available in health care facilities, pharmacies, retail outlets, schools, media channels, and community centres.

health-related fitness—The components of physical fitness that contribute to optimal health: cardiorespiratory fitness, muscular strength, muscular endurance, flexibility, and body composition.

healthy active living—A state in which you are not merely thinking about your health from time to time, but actively doing things to enhance your health all the time. It involves learning how to develop healthy relationships, dealing with stress and difficult situations, and helping to improve not only yourself but also your community.

healthy relationships—Relationships in which people feel good about themselves. In healthy relationships, partners respect themselves and one another. They consider and show concern for each other's needs and feelings.

heterosexism—Heterosexism refers to the misconception that everyone is or should be heterosexual.

holistic health—Traditional Indigenous approaches to medicine and healing as well as approaches typically associated with Eastern philosophical traditions embrace a concept of holistic health. These approaches consider the mind, body, and spirit as one and focus their attention on the well-being of the whole person.

homophobia—A disparaging or hostile attitude or a negative bias, whether overt or unspoken, toward people who are lesbian, gay, bisexual, transgender, queer, or other (LGBTQ+); may exist at an individual and/or a systemic level.

human rights codes—Federal and provincial legislation that gives everyone equal rights and opportunities without discrimination or harassment on the basis of sexual orientation.

IDEAL method (of decision-making)—IDEAL is an acronym that summarizes an approach to making decisions, helping you sort through your options, prioritize them, and then make the best possible decision. The key components of this approach are: Identify the problem, Discuss your options, Evaluate your options and prioritize your concerns; Act on the best choice, and Learn from the experience.

individual activities—A category of games and activities within the Teaching Games for Understanding (TGfU) model; activities that are not structured as games, e.g., running, walking, jogging, wheeling, swimming, power walking, gymnastics, canoeing, and dance.

individuality principle—An underlying principle that acknowledges the importance of developing a fitness training plan with the needs of the individual in mind. Every person (and every body) is unique, so to optimize performance, training plans should take into account the individual's personal preferences, social environment, and physical environment.

intergroup conflict—Conflict that occurs when two groups (or teams) find themselves in opposition to one another. In sports, as in life, healthy competition is acceptable, but if intergroup conflict is not handled properly, a dispute can have serious consequences.

internal conflict—The opposing emotions you often feel within yourself. Sometimes, it is hard to decide what to believe, especially when you can see both sides of an issue and you must choose which path to take, whom to support, or where to draw the line.

interpersonal conflict—A dispute you have with someone else. You may have a completely different point of view about a certain current event than someone else, for example, but it is important to try to understand what the person thinks about it, and why.

intersex—A term used to describe a person whose sex chromosomes, genitalia, and/or secondary sex characteristics (e.g., facial hair, breasts) are determined to be neither exclusively male nor exclusively female. An intersex person may have biological characteristics of both the male and female sexes.

intragroup conflict—Conflict among members of a group or team. Group members may take positions on either side of an argument. They may choose their position based on loyalty to the people voicing an opinion, or they may choose their position because of strong personal feelings.

joint range of motion—The most commonly occurring joint in the body is the synovial joint. This is the joint that allows the most movement (e.g., knee, shoulder, and ankle). Each specific joint has a normal range of motion. If the muscles and tendons around the joint are injured (e.g., by inflammation) or if the joint is injured (e.g., by cartilage damage), the range of motion permitted at that joint is impaired and full movement cannot occur.

key movement features—Important movement behaviours that you, your friends, and your family can use to improve your movement. Besides enhancing your performance, adhering to these seven key features will help make you more durable and less prone to injury.

Kids Help Phone—A Canadian charitable organization that provides free online and telephone counselling to children and youth across Canada. In addition to its counselling services, Kids Help Phone also provides information on how to access support services for children and youth

ligaments—Connective tissues that attach bone to bone.

list of ingredients—The labelling on food packages that will undergo changes over the next few years, with major improvements to the Nutrition Facts Table that will make it easier to find, read, and understand what is in a food product.

Long-Term Athlete Development Framework (LTAD)—Sport for Life's Long Term Athlete Development (LTAD) model is a framework for an optimal training, competition, and recovery schedule for each stage of development, for both athletes and non-athletes. Coaches who engage in the model and its practices are more likely to produce athletes who reach their full athletic potential.

long-term goals—Goals that specify what you want to achieve over a comparatively long period of time, for example, over a month, a semester, or even a few years.

macronutrients—The nutrients that we need in relatively large amounts every day. In addition to water, the macronutrients are carbohydrates, proteins, and fats (these three are also known as the "energy nutrients" because they provide us with energy or calories).

marijuana (cannabis)—The most popular form of cannabis. It acts mostly as a hallucinogen, but it also has depressant effects (it slows response time and affects memory) and a stimulant effect (it raises the heart rate).

maximum effort—In the context of physical activity or sport, maximum effort requires that all the joints that can be engaged in a movement are used in performing that movement, and that they are used in order from largest to smallest. If a joint's range of motion is impaired or if the movement of the joints is not sequenced properly, then the full execution of the movement will be restricted and maximum effort will not be achieved.

medicine wheel—For many indigenous peoples, the medicine wheel symbolizes the interconnection of all life, the various cycles of nature, and how life represents a circular journey. Traditional depictions of the medicine wheel typically show four quadrants with their associated colours and meanings: physical, spiritual, mental, and emotional. The medicine wheel symbolizes health and healing, as well as harmony and connections.

mental health—Mental health refers to a person's psychological and emotional well-being. The best way to understand mental health is to view it as a continuum ranging from mental wellness to mental illness. According to the World Health Organization, positive mental health is "a state of well-being in which the individual realizes his or her own abilities, can cope with the normal stresses of life, can work productively and fruitfully, and is able to make a contribution to his or her community....There is emerging evidence that positive mental health is associated with improved health outcomes."

methods of contraception—Methods designed to impede fertilization and prevent pregnancy during sexual intercourse.

micronutrients—Essential nutrients needed by our bodies only in small amounts. We need less of each micronutrient compared to macronutrients, but these nutrients still play an important role in the way our bodies function. These "non-energy nutrients" help the body use the energy provided by carbohydrates, proteins, and fats.

minerals—Minerals are inorganic substances that help make bones, proteins, and blood. For example, calcium, which the body gets from dairy products, is important to the structure of bones and teeth. Iron, found in some meat and some dark-green vegetables, helps carry oxygen to body tissues.

movement competence — Movement competence refers to how someone is moving—when we demonstrate movement competence, we move in a safe or effective manner, or both, in order to achieve the objective of the activity that we are performing. Movement competence is an important component of physical literacy.

movement principles—Understanding and applying movement principles can help you build movement competence in daily life, school, sports, or work. Three principles discussed in this resource relate to whole-body stability, joint range of motion, and joint sequencing.

multiple-repetition maximum—A method used to predict how much weight you can maximally lift at once.

muscular endurance—A muscle's ability to perform an action repeatedly without fatigue.

muscular strength—The maximum force a muscle can exert in a single contraction.

musculoskeletal fitness—A term referring to muscular strength and endurance, as well to as the mobility of your joints.

net/wall activities—A category of games and activities within the Teaching Games for Understanding (TGfU) model; activities in which players send an object toward a court or target area that their opponent(s) are defending; examples include badminton, sepak takraw, squash, table tennis, tennis, volleyball, and wheelchair tennis.

nutrient content claims—Claims printed on food packaging to highlight a positive feature of the product (e.g., "high fibre," "light," or "low in fat"). Manufacturers are permitted to use nutrient content claims on food labels to attract attention to their products as long as their products meet specific rules and standards.

nutrition—The science underlying how your body uses the components of food to grow, maintain, and repair itself.

Nutrition Facts table—A table, printed by law on most food packaging, that gives nutritional information about which nutrients you are getting from your food and in which proportions. It appears in a standard format so that it looks the same from one product to another, making it easier to find and use.

online communication technologies—Online communication technologies allow you to connect through the internet with more people, more rapidly and more widely. Online communication also poses privacy risks that we need to be aware of—every time we send a text or go online.

outdoor activities—A category of games and activities within the Teaching Games for Understanding (TGfU) model. Outdoor activities include cycling, rowing, hiking, downhill and cross-country skiing, triathlon, mountain biking, skating, kayaking, canoeing, and sledding.

overload principle—A fitness training principle based on the concept that to improve fitness, the body must do more work than it is accustomed to doing. Overload can be achieved by adjusting the frequency, intensity, time, and/or type of activity.

performance-level appraisals—The group of fitness appraisals that focus on specific movement skills such as speed, agility, and coordination. They are referred to as "performance-level appraisals" because they are intended to measure and improve particular aspects of performance (as opposed to overall health).

personal flotation device (PFD)—A life jacket, life preserver, life belt, buoyancy aid, or similar piece of equipment designed to assist a wearer to keep afloat in water. PFDs are available in different sizes to accommodate different ages and body weights.

personal safety plan—A set of proactive strategies aimed at minimizing your risk of experiencing harassment or violence and serving as a guide if you are in an unsafe situation.

phases of a movement skill—A movement skill can be broken down into its various phases of execution: preparation; force production; critical instant; and recovery and follow-through.

physical dependence—The condition experienced by people who use drugs once their bodies become accustomed to a drug. They experience unpleasant and even painful physical symptoms of withdrawal if they try to go without the drug.

physical literacy—Physical literacy is the motivation and confidence, physical competence, and knowledge and understanding to value and take responsibility for engagement in physical activities for life (Canada's physical literacy consensus statement, June 2015).

PIER—An acronym to help you remember the steps to take when treating an injury: *Pressure* should be administered at the same time that ice is applied to the affected area; *Ice* should be placed on the affected area; *Elevate* the injured area while it's being iced to help reduce the swelling; *Restrict* and *Rest* the affected area with the use of tensors or slings.

problem gambling—Risky and recurring gambling behaviours with potentially negative consequences. Gambling becomes a problem when it (1) interferes with school, work, and other aspects of life; (2) affects family and personal relationships, creating marital problems, family violence, or the loss of friendships; and (3) causes wasteful spending, reckless use of family resources, increasing debt, or loss of home, job, or savings.

progression principle—A fitness training principle whereby fitness improvements occur gradually by progressively adding to the overload. If you are just starting fitness training, you may experience fairly rapid improvement (and probably soreness), but over time the rate of improvement will gradually slow down and the gains will be more evenly paced.

protective factors (related to mental health)—Resilience is an important aspect of mental, emotional, and spiritual well-being. It gives us the strength to deal with difficult situations and to rebound from challenges and setbacks. Things that promote resilience, such as strong family ties and close relationships, are known as "protective factors." Things that reduce resilience, such as a family history of substance abuse or difficult relationships, are known as "risk factors."

proteins—Macronutrients that can be found in all the cells in our bodies. Proteins also play a role in sight, hearing, taste, and smell. Proteins are the building blocks of enzymes that help digest food, fight infection, and build blood. If your body is short of carbohydrates, protein can also act as an energy source.

psychoactive drugs—Mood-altering drugs that affect our mental and emotional state.

psychological dependence—The condition experienced by people who habitually use drugs even in the absence of physical cravings. Users may find that drug use begins to play a predominant part in their lives, and that they cannot find an easy way to quit. Psychological dependence is a serious form of addiction.

Quality Physical Education (QPE)—Progressive and inclusive physical education as a regular part of the school curriculum. In addition to promoting healthy living, UNESCO, the United Nations agency responsible for coordinating international cooperation in education, science, culture, and communication, released a major policy document urging all UN member states to facilitate participation in daily quality physical education.

racism—The belief in the superiority of a particular race and the prejudice, antagonism, or violence shown toward other races as a result of this harmful attitude.

repetitions—The number of times you continuously perform an exercise. If you lift a barbell once, that is one rep. If you lift it 25 times consecutively, that amounts to 25 reps.

resilience—The ability to recover or "bounce back" from disruptive change, illness, or misfortune. Resilience is an important aspect of mental, emotional, and spiritual well-being.

resistance training—Exercising a particular muscle or muscle group by subjecting it to additional weight stress. The weight may be an external object, such as a dumbbell, or it can involve using your body weight as a form of resistance, such as when performing a push-up. The objective of resistance training is to develop the targeted muscle or muscle group and to make it stronger.

Resting Heart Rate (RHR)—The number of times your heart beats per minute when at rest. The average Resting Heart Rate is between 70 and 80 beats per minute (bpm).

Resting Metabolic Rate (RMR)—An estimate of the amount of energy your body uses when it is completely at rest. It varies between individuals of different heights, weights, and ages, and can be accurately estimated using the Harris-Benedict formula.

reversibility principle—A fitness training principle that states that if you stop training for a while, you will start to lose or reverse the gains you have made.

risk—The effect of uncertainty on our objectives; this effect can deviate either positively or negatively from what we expected.

risk factors (related to mental health)—Traits, characteristics, or environmental contexts that research has shown can predict mental health problems or illnesses in childhood or adolescence. Examples include poverty or having parents with limited parenting skills.

sedentary behaviour—Activities that need very little physical movement and that do not use much energy, for example, sitting or lying down for long periods of time.

self-esteem—A feeling of pride in yourself and a sense of self-worth. When people respect themselves and act according to their beliefs and values, they feel positive about themselves and have high self-esteem.

separation—An injury that occurs when bones separate. For example, your collar bone (clavicle) is attached to your shoulder blade (scapula) by strong ligaments. When these ligaments are torn, as a result of a collision or an awkward fall, the bones may separate. This is the most common type of separation.

sets—The number of times you perform a certain number of repetitions. If you lift a barbell for 25 reps, then rest, then perform another 25 reps, you will have done 2 sets of 25 reps.

Seven Sacred Truths—Seven Sacred Teachings (Truth, Humility, Honesty, Wisdom, Respect, Courage, and Love) are lessons that have been passed down from Indigenous Elders and Traditional Knowledge Keepers. These sacred teachings align with the core values of Health and Physical Education programs in schools.

sexual decision making—A process that entails making conscious and thoughtful choices about your sexual activity.

sexual harassment—Unwanted sexual behaviour of any kind. It is serious and illegal and, in some cases, can escalate to the level of physical violence, leading to sexual abuse and assault.

sexual intimacy—An aspect of intimacy that can include how much personal information we share with our partner, how we communicate, and to what extent we want to be physically close to one another.

sexual orientation—An individual's sense of sexual attraction to people of the same sex, the opposite sex, or both sexes.

sexuality—A term that encompasses sex, gender identities and roles, sexual orientation, pleasure, intimacy, and reproduction. Sexuality is experienced and expressed in thoughts, desires, beliefs, values, practices, behaviours, and relationships, and is influenced by the interaction of biological, psychological, social, economic, political, cultural, ethical, legal, historical, religious, and spiritual factors.

sexually transmitted infections (STIs)—Infections caused by bacteria, viruses, or parasites that are transmitted through semen, vaginal fluid, blood, or other bodily fluids during sexual activity.

SHARE qualities—Every relationship is unique, but healthy relationships have some things in common. These are sometimes referred to as the SHARE qualities: Safety, Honesty, Acceptance, Respect, and Enjoyment.

SHARP—An acronym to help you remember the signs of an injury: Swelling of affected area, instantly or over time; Heat or increased temperature of the area; Altered joint or area that will not function properly; Redness; Pain when you move or touch the affected area.

shin splint—Painful tearing of the connective tissue between the tibia and the fibula along the front shaft of the shinbone.

short-term goals—Goals that are specific and can be completed in a few hours, days, or weeks. Short-term fitness goals may involve measuring your progress in a single workout, or completing an exercise session more successfully than you did previously.

skill — The ability we have developed to perform an activity well, especially because we have practised it.

skill-related fitness—Physical fitness that is related to the following six components: agility, balance, coordination, power, reaction time, and speed.

skill transferability—Skill transferability can occur when activities involve similar fundamental movement patterns and key features. For example, the pushing, pulling, and lunging movement patterns used in snowshoeing and cross-country skiing are quite similar to each other. Thus, the skills involved in these two activities are likely to be transferable.

SMART goal setting—A strategy to help motivate you when setting goals for yourself. SMART stands for Specific, Meaningful and Measurable, Action-oriented, Realistic, and Time.

specificity principle—A fitness training principle based on the concept that improvements in fitness are directly related to the type of fitness training program an individual is following. For example, flexibility can be improved by doing certain stretching exercises.

sprain—An injury that occurs when a ligament is stretched or torn. Similar to strains, which occur in muscles and tendons, sprains are classified according to the severity of the injury.

stability—Stability skills involve the ability to balance the body in one place (static) or keep the body balanced while moving (dynamic) by sensing a shift in the relationship of the parts of the body and altering body position to maintain balance.

stimulants—Substances that speed up body systems, such as the central nervous system (CNS) and cardiorespiratory system, delay fatigue, and often produce hyperactivity. Stimulants include nicotine, caffeine, diet pills, Ritalin®, cocaine, crack, speed, methamphetamine, and other drugs.

strain—An injury that is caused by twisting or pulling a muscle or tendon. Depending on the severity of the injury, a strain may be the result of a muscle or a tendon being overstretched. If strains remain untreated, tears in the muscle or tendon fibres may worsen. Strains can be either acute or chronic.

stress—Stress is a physiological and emotional response to a perceived stimulus, including a danger or a threat. When we are under negative stress, we may feel tense, nervous, or on edge. Stress triggers a surge of a hormone called adrenaline that temporarily affects the nervous system.

stress fracture—Tiny cracks along the bone that are almost undetectable by an X-ray. They are very painful and can take a long time to heal.

striking/fielding activities—A category of games and activities within the Teaching Games for Understanding (TGfU) model. Striking/fielding activities include baseball, beep baseball, cricket, kick-ball, rounders, softball, and t-ball.

substance abuse—Excessive use of a substance, e.g., alcohol, despite the physical, cognitive, emotional, social, legal, spiritual, or economic harm that occur to oneself, family, and friends.

substance misuse—Use of a substance in ways that are illegal or not recommended medically as being the intended and proper use of that substance.

target activities—A category of games and activities within the Teaching Games for Understanding (TGfU) model. In activities such as bocce, bowling, curling, disc golf, lawn bowling, shuffleboard, and wheelchair bocce, players score by avoiding obstacles to get an object closer to a target more often than their opponents.

Target Heart Rate Zone—The range within which you should aim to exercise your heart. It is normally calculated using the Heart Rate Reserve method.

Teaching Games for Understanding (TGfU)—An approach to teaching activities and games based on actually playing games. Instead of learning sport-specific technical skills, TGfU helps you gain skills and knowledge that you can apply to different activities and sports by playing a variety of games associated with six game categories.

tendonitis—Inflammation of a tendon caused by irritation due to prolonged or abnormal use.

territory activities—A category of games and activities within the Teaching Games for Understanding (TGfU) model; players control an object, keeping it away from opponents, and move it into position to score. The same playing area is shared by both offensive and defensive players as they try to prevent the other team from scoring. Territory activities include basketball, football, goal ball, European handball, hockey, lacrosse, rugby, sledge hockey, soccer, tchoukball, Ultimate, water polo, and wheelchair basketball.

tobacco—The shredded, dried leaf of the tobacco plant, which can be smoked in cigarettes, e-cigarettes, cigars, or pipes, or chewed. Tobacco is the only natural source of nicotine, one of the most addictive substances.

total daily caloric need—The recommended amount of calories you need each day, calculated by multiplying your RMR (Resting Metabolic Rate) by an appropriate activity factor (*see* Harris-Benedict formula).

transphobia—A fear of or contempt for others on the basis of their identification as transgender. The terms *homophobia* and *biphobia* refer to fear of or contempt for other people on the basis of their sexual orientation. Like racism, these forms of prejudice are considered hate crimes in Canada.

Truth and Reconciliation Commission of Canada (TRC)—The Truth and Reconciliation Commission of Canada was one of the results of the Indian Residential Schools Settlement Agreement, the largest class-action settlement in Canadian history. The TRC was part of a holistic and comprehensive response to the abuse inflicted on Indigenous peoples through the Indian residential school system and the harmful legacy of those institutions. The Commission was established on June 2, 2008. In June 2015, the TRC held its Closing Event in Ottawa and presented the Executive Summary of its multi-volume Final Report, including 94 "Calls to Action."

ultraviolet radiation (UVR)—Sunlight is the main source of UV rays. Tanning lamps and beds are also sources of UV rays. Exposure to ultraviolet radiation is a major risk factor for most skin cancers.

UV Index—The ultraviolet index (UV Index) is a standard measure of the strength of sunburn-producing effects of ultraviolet radiation. The scale was developed by Canadian scientists in 1992, and then adopted and standardized by the UN's World Health Organization in 1994. It is used in forecasts provided to the general public to alert them to the risks of UV radiation.

vaping—The term used for inhaling vapour from an e-cigarette. An e-cigarette is a handheld device that works by heating a liquid to produce an aerosol (called a "vapour") that a person inhales.

vegetarianism—A term that describes many different types of eating styles that emphasize fruits, vegetables, nuts, grains, and seeds. Most vegetarians eliminate meat, fish, and poultry from their diets, but many do not exclude all animal foods, and some vegetarians eliminate red meat only.

vitamins—Chemicals that the body needs to build and maintain cells and to release energy from macronutrients. Vitamins are either water soluble or fat soluble, meaning that they are absorbed by being dissolved, or broken down, in water or in fat.

VO_2 max—The amount of oxygen consumed during intense (maximal) effort, commonly used as an indicator of aerobic fitness. A high VO_2 max score indicates that you have a strong cardiorespiratory system and that your working muscles are able to receive and use a great deal of oxygen.

Credits

All anatomical illustrations (pages **24, 25, 26, 27, 143, 145, 147, 152, 156, 158, 160, 162, 164, 166, 168, 170, 172, 261, 264**) by Bart Vallecoccia for Thompson Educational Publishing

Cover

Main: stock_colors/Getty Images; centre circle: Alexander Raths/Shutterstock; small circles (from left to right): Ted Temertzoglou; Matthew Maaskant; Gary Blakeley

Chapter 1

Page **2**, Matthew Maaskant; **4**, Gary Blakeley; **6**, Matthew Maaskant; **9**, Ovchinnikova Irina/Shutterstock; **12**, Rawpixel/Shutterstock; **13**, Matthew Maaskant (left); Gary Blakeley (centre); Ted Temertzoglou (right); **15**, The Benefits of Investing infographic reproduced from "Quality Physical Education Policy" courtesy of the United Nations Educational, Scientific and Cultural Organization (UNESCO), 2013; **16**, Cheapbooks/Shutterstock; **17**, Matthew Maaskant; **18**, Matthew Maaskant; **19**, Muzsy/Shutterstock (left); Peter Istvan/Shutterstock (centre); Yury Birukov/Shutterstock (right); **20**, Matthew Maaskant; **21**, Ted Temertzoglou; **22**, Gary Blakeley

Chapter 2

Page **28**, Conrado/Shutterstock; **30**, Matthew Maaskant; **32**, Ververidis Vasilis/Shutterstock; **33**, Eduard Goricev/Shutterstock; **35**, Mooremedia/Shutterstock; **36**, Catalin Petolea/Shutterstock; **37**, Maathew Maaskant; **38**, Matthew Maaskant; **40**, Kovalevaolga/Shutterstock (inlay); **41**, Szymon Mucha/Shutterstock (inlay); **42**, iStockphoto/yanik88; **43**, Ted Temertzoglou; **44**, Ted Temertzoglou; **45**, Matthew Maaskant; **46**, CHEN WS/Shutterstock; **47**, Ted Temertzoglou; **48**, Ted Temertzoglou; **49**, Rawpixel/Shutterstock; **50**, Microgen/Shutterstock; **51**, (left to right) Monkey Business Images/Shutterstock; nd3000/Shutterstock; Vitalii Nesterchu/Shutterstock; GROGL/Shutterstock; **52**, (top to bottom) Ted Temertzoglou; Ted Temertzoglou; Lightpoet/Shutterstock; DayOwl/Shutterstock; **53**, Matthew Maaskant; **54**, Ted Temertzoglou; **55**, Ted Temertzoglou; **56**, Ted Temertzoglou; **57**, Ohrim/Shutterstock; **58**, RZ Images/Shutterstock; **59**, Tanya Winter; **60**, Jamie Roach/Shutterstock; **61**, Tanya Winter; **62**, Tanya Winter; **65**, Gary Blakeley; **67**, Stuart Monk; **69**, Aspen Photo/Shutterstock; **71**, Wavebreakmedia/Shutterstock; **73**, Gary Blakeley; **75**, 2shrimpS/Shutterstock; **77**, Santypan/Shutterstock; **78**, Matthew Maaskant

Chapter 3

Page **80**, Gary Blakeley; **82**, Matthew Maaskant; **84**, Thompson Educational Publishing; **85**, Gary Blakeley; **86**, "Canadian 24-Hour Movement Guidelines for Children and Youth" reproduced with permission of the Canadian Society for Exercise Physiology (CSEP); **88**, Nalaphotos/Shutterstock; **90**, Matthew Maaskant; **91**, Matthew Maaskant; **93**, Tanya Winter; **94**, Tanya Winter; **96**, YanLev/Shutterstock; **98**, Matthew Maaskant; **99**, Matthew Maaskant; **100**, Ted Temertzoglou; **103**, Matthew Maaskant (TDSB) (left); Tanya Winter (right); **104**, Matthew Maaskant (inlay); Tanya Winter (bottom); **105**, Matthew Maaskant (inlay); Tanya Winter (bottom); **107**, Tanya Winter; **108**, Tanya Winter; **109**, Matthew Maaskant; **111**, Gary Blakeley (inlay); Tanya Winter (centre); **112**, Ted Temertzoglou; **114**, Tanya Winter; **115**, Ksanawo/Shutterstock (shoeprint graphic); **116**, Tanya Winter; **117**, Tanya Winter; **118**, Tanya Winter; **119**, Michelle Prata; **120**, Matthew Maaskant; **121**, Matthew Maaskant; **123**, VGstockstudio/Shutterstock; **124**, Ted Temertzoglou; **126**, Matthew Maaskant

Chapter 4

Page **128**, Lzf/Shutterstock; **130**, Courtesy of Angel Blainey; **132**, Matthew Maaskant; **133**, Matthew Maaskant; **134**, Thompson Educational Publishing; **135**, Ted Temertzoglou; **136**, Gary Blakeley; **137**, Matthew Maaskant (left); Gary Blakeley (right); **138**, Gary Blakeley; **139**, FITT Principle table adapted with permission from "Ontario Health and Physical Education Curriculum Support: Grades K–10," Ontario Physical Health Education Association (OPHEA), Toronto; photo courtesy of Ted Temertzoglou; **140**, Sorin Alb/Shutterstock; **141**, Gary Blakeley (left); Matthew Maaskant (right); **142**, Maridav/Shutterstock; **144**, Cunaplus/Shutterstock; **146**, Ammit Jack/Shutterstock; **148**, Margaret Kite/Shutterstock; **149**, Ted Temertzoglou; **150**, Wavebreakmedia/Shutterstock (left); Gary Blakeley (right); **153**, **156**, **157**, **158**, **159**, **160**, **161**, **162**, **163**, **164**, **165**, **166**, **167**, **168**, **169**, **170**, **171**, **172**, & **173**, Tanya Winter; **174**, Gary Blakeley

Chapter 5

Page **176**, Roman Stetsyk/Shutterstock; **178**, Matthew Maaskant; **180**, Bitt24/Shutterstock; **181**, Alexander Raths/Shutterstock; **182**, Gary Blakeley; **183**, Bart Vallecoccia; **184**, Elenadesign/Shutterstock; **185**, Gary Blakeley; **186**, Alex Staroseltsev/Shutterstock; **187**, Antony McAulay/Shutterstuck; **188**, LADO/Shutterstock; **190**, SageElyse/Shutterstock; **192**, Andrey Kuzmin/Shutterstock; **193**, Moibalkon/Shutterstock; **194**, Gary Blakeley (top); Matthew Maaskant (centre); ESUN7756/Shutterstock (bottom-right); **195**, Gary Blakeley; **196**, Kwangmoozaa/Shutterstock; **197**, Pete Saloutos/Shutterstock; **198**, Kati Molin/Shutterstock; **199**, Songquan Deng/Shutterstock; **200**, Monkey Business Images/Shutterstock; **202**, Photosync/Shutterstock; **203**, Dori Dumrong/Shutterstock; **204**, Trong Nguyen/Shutterstock; **205**, Image Point Fr/Shutterstock; **206**, Elisanth/Shutterstock; **207**, Marina_Art/Shutterstock; **208**, ChameleonsEye/Shutterstock; **209**, Rasulov/Shutterstock; **210**, ViChizh/Shutterstock; **211**, Stockforlife/Shutterstock; Gary Blakeley; **212**, Matthew Maaskant

Chapter 6

Page **214**, Beatriz Vera/Shutterstock; **216**, Gary Blakeley; **218**, Mike Flippo/Shutterstock; **219**, Threerocksimages/Shutterstock; **222**, Sergei Bachlakov/Shutterstock; **224**, Matthew Maaskant; **225**, LightField Studios/Shutterstock (bottom); WAYHOME studio/Shutterstock (top); **227**, Andrei

Korzhyts/Shutterstock (left); N.Melanjina/Shutterstock (right); **228**, Leszek Glasner/Shutterstock; **229**, Look Studio/ Shutterstock (left); DGLimages/Shutterstock (right); **230**, Golden Pixels LLC/Shutterstock; **231**, Peter Hermes Furia/ Shutterstock (left); Dragon Images/Shutterstock (right); **232**, Antonio Guillem/Shutterstock (left); Agnieszka Marcinska/ Shutterstock (right); **234**, Dean Drobot/Shutterstock; **235**, Stokkete/Shutterstock (top); AnemStyle/Shutterstock (centre); Phovoir/Shutterstock (bottom); **236**, iStockphoto/ kali9; **237**, Twinsterphoto/Shutterstock (left); Lopolo/ Shutterstock (right); iStockphoto/Ahmadmahmood (right); **239**, Cloki/Shutterstock (left); Blend Images/Shutterstock (right); **240**, Image Point Fr/Shutterstock (top); Image Point Fr/Shutterstock (centre); Thalerngsak Mongkolsin/ Shutterstock (right); **241**, Kzenon/Shutterstock (left); Puhhha/ Shutterstock (right); **242**, By Chinnapong/Shuttterstock (left); Microgen/Shutterstock (right); **243**, Leah-Anne Tompson/ Shutterstock; **246**, XiXinXing/Shutterstock; **247**, Mooshny/ Shutterstock; **248**, Matthew Maaskant

Chapter 7

Page **250**, Warpboyz/Shutterstock; **252**, Gary Blakeley; **254**, Premkh/Shutterstock; **255**, Monkey Business Images/ Shutterstock; **257**, iStockphoto/Chris Schmidt; **258**, Voronina Svetlana/Shutterstock; **259**, Hazem.m.kamal/Shutterstock; **260**, iStockphoto; **263**, Leungchopan/Shutterstock (left); Thompson Educational Publishing (right); **265**, Africa Studio/ Shutterstock; **266**, OpenRangeStock/Shutterstock; **267**, Ted Temertzoglou; **268**, Jochen Schoenfeld/Shutterstock; **269**, Shidlovski/Shutterstock; **271**, Imageman/Shutterstock; **272**, Alexander Raths/Shutterstock; **273**, Syda Productions/ Shutterstock; **274**, MsYihra/Shutterstock; **275**, Monkey Business Images/Shutterstock; **276**, Andrewvect/ Shutterstock; **277**, Georgejmclittle/Shutterstock (top); iStockphoto/Nishan Sothilingam (gambling icons, bottom); **278**, Matthew Maaskant; **279**, Antoniodiaz/Shutterstock; **280**, ALDECAstock/Shutterstock; **281**, ALL best fitness is HERE/Shutterstock; **282**, Syda Productions/Shutterstock; **284**, iStockphoto; **285**, iStockphoto/Nuno Silva (top); VGstockstudio/Shutterstock (bottom); **286**, iStockphoto/ track5; **288**, Gary Blakeley

Chapter 8

Page **290**, Rawpixel/Shutterstock; **292**, Matthew Maaskant; **294**, Shutterstock/Stas11; **295**, Matthew Maaskant; **296**, Sean Locke Photography/Shutterstock; **297**, Jingjits Photography/Shutterstock; **298**, Olga Danylenko/ Shuttterstock; **299**, Julie Keen/Shutterstock; **300**, BlurryMe/ Shutterstock; **301**, Matthew Maaskant; **302**, Matthew Maaskant; **303**, GuruXOX/Shutterstock; **304**, Chinnapong/ Shutterstock; **305**, Rawpixel/Shutterstock; **306**, Stokkete/ Shutterstock (top); Vasileios Karafillidis/Shutterstock (bottom); **307**, Tommaso79/Shutterstock; **308**, Tanya Winter; **309**, Lucky Business/Shutterstock; **310**, Bfk/Shutterstock; **311**, Monkey Business Images/Shutterstock; **312**, George Rudy/Shutterstock; **314**, Rawpixel/Shutterstock; **315**, Antonio Guillem/Shutterstock; **316**, Pixelheadphoto Digitalskillet/Shutterstock; **318**, Matthew Maaskant

Appendices

Pages **323–47**, "ACT High School CPR & AED Student Manual" courtesy of the ACT Foundation, 2017; **348–9**, reproduced from "Truth and Reconciliation Commission of Canada: Calls to Action," 2015

Index